Tell It Again! 2

Easy-to-Tell Stories with Activities for Young Children

Rebecca Isbell
Shirley C. Raines

Cover art and illustrations by Joan C. Waites

gryphon house
Beltsville, Maryland

Copyright © 2000 Rebecca Isbell and Shirley Raines
Published by Gryphon House, Inc.
10726 Tucker Street, Beltsville MD 20705

Visit us on the web at www.gryphonhouse.com

Text and cover illustrations by Joan Waites

Library of Congress Cataloging-in-Publication Data

Isbell, Rebecca T.
    Tell it again! 2 : easy-to-tell stories with activities for young children / Rebecca Isbell, Shirley C. Raines ; illustrations by Joan Waites.
        p. cm.
    Includes bibliographical references and index.
    ISBN 0-87659-208-6
    1. Storytelling. 2. Children's literature—Study and teaching. 3. Early childhood education—Activity programs. I. Title: Tell it again! two. II. Title: Tell it again!. III. Raines, Shirley C. IV. Title.

LB1042.I79 2000
372.67'7--dc21   00-020783

To

Teachers and Librarians,
Mamas and Papas,
Grandfathers and Grandmothers,
Great Aunts and Great Uncles,
And Elders far and wide.
To storytellers everywhere
Who invite children
To sit by their sides.

To Lazy Jack
And Knee-High Man,
To Johnny-Cake
And Pancakes in a Pan,
To Kings and Queens
And Princesses and Such,
To goodness over wickedness,
To truth over liars.

To storytellers everywhere
Enjoy a page or two.
Then pass it on.
As Tellers of the Story,
Enjoy the magic, the tricksters, and the dreams. . .
The lessons and the schemes.
We have but one request,

Tell it again!
And tell it to the young.

Shirley Raines

Table of Contents

Introduction

The beautiful swan was once an ugly duckling. The boy who cried wolf had no help when the real wolf came. The modest turtle won the race while the boastful rabbit bragged about his speed. Some of life's greatest lessons are remembered best through the recollection of stories heard in childhood.

Storytelling involves three essential elements: the story, the teller, and the listener. A well-selected story told by an effective storyteller captivates young listeners' attention and the three elements work in harmony. The gifts of storytelling are many, including moments filled with the wonder and excitement of stories, universal truths and morals to remember and use throughout life, and the special bond that connects the storyteller and the listener.

The Power of Storytelling

Storytelling is a powerful medium. A well-told story can inspire action, foster cultural appreciation, expand children's knowledge, or provide sheer enjoyment. Listening to stories helps children understand their world and how people relate to each other in it.

When children listen to stories, they use their imaginations. They picture the "talking pot" or the "curious Elephant's Child" from the teller's vivid descriptions. This creativity is dependent upon the storyteller's lively telling of the story and the listener's active interpretation of what is heard. The more delightful the story and the storyteller, the more the children get out of the whole experience.

The storytelling experience also helps young children develop an appreciation of the story form. Because children are more involved in creating the pictures of the story, they are more likely to remember the characters, the sequence, and the moral of the story. Storytelling can motivate young children to explore various types of literature and become a storyteller, story reader, and story writer.

How to Select Stories to Tell Young Listeners

We wrote this book because we found few books devoted to story-telling for young children. Storytellers often have a difficult time finding the right stories for young children. We selected the stories for this book because they are excellent tales for telling that fit the developmental needs of young children.

Excellent stories for young listeners often have one or more of the following characteristics:

 Easy-to-follow sequence;

 Repetitive words and phrases;

 Predictable and cumulative events;

 Action-packed adventure;

 Humorous twists and turns;

 Interesting and entertaining happenings;

 Exciting ending with an appropriate conclusion; and

 Clear message or moral.

General Storytelling Tips

The following storytelling tips apply to the telling of most stories to young children:

 Observe the young children during the telling. Adjust and make clarifications as needed.

 Encourage interaction and participation.

 Modify the pace and length to match the experiential and developmental level of the children in the audience.

 Use voice variations, facial expressions, gestures, and repetitive phrases to draw the young listener into the story.

◉ Use appropriate words and descriptions that help young children imagine the happenings in their mind's eye.

◉ Retell the same story many times, since young children are building their understanding of the story.

Storytelling to young children provides special possibilities as well as unique challenges. Young children enjoy predictability, repetition, humor, and active participation in the story presentation. When stories are too complicated or the storyteller is too dramatic, the child will "turn off" or simply move away from the experience.

Design of the Book

The 16 multicultural stories in this book are grouped by common themes: Rich and Poor, One Good Turn Deserves Another, Learning from Mistakes, and How the Animals Came To Be As They Are. Each section contains from three to five stories and at least one of them is a well-known tale. These familiar stories are good choices for the beginning storyteller.

Each story was written to touch the hearts of young children and engage their lively minds and undivided attention. The entertainment value, the structure, and the sequence of the tales make them easy to tell. While written to be told, all the stories are strong enough to be read to children.

The layout of each story is easy to follow. Each story begins with a short introduction followed by the complete story, and ends with a simple statement of the message or moral. Storytelling tips and questions to ask children come next. Because young children learn best by doing, we included activities that enhance and enrich the experience of the story. A unique feature of the book is a collection of story cards, one for each story in the book, beginning on page 162. The card for each story includes the characters in the order they appear and an outline of the story.

Message of the Story

The message or moral of the story is included so that the storyteller can focus on the inherent value or "truth" of a story. Often the stories contain lessons that are different depending on the age of the listener. For example, when hearing "The Fisherman and His Wife," the young listener will enjoy the action of the story, the slightly older child will think more about the excitement of getting one's wishes granted, and the adult will recognize that this is a story about the danger of greed.

Storytelling Tips

We have included storytelling tips at the end of each story. These suggestions have grown from our experience telling stories to young children. The storytelling tips will help the teller identify specific aspects of the story that can be expanded and adjusted to meet the needs of the young listeners. Of course, each storyteller will make the story his or her own by selecting or modifying the suggestions so the story will relate to the specific audience.

Questions

At the end of the story, there are several questions for the storyteller to use. It is not always necessary to ask questions after the story. Good storytellers can sense the mood of the listeners and decide whether or not to ask these thought-provoking questions. Higher-level thinking and creativity are required to answer many of the questions.

Story Activities

These activities connect to the story or to the main idea of the story. The activities are open-ended to encourage young children's creativity. Many of the activities reinforce early literacy and help the child remember the main idea of the story.

Story Cards

The story cards, found at the back of the book beginning on page 162, help the storyteller to remember the order of the main characters, the sequence of events, the recurring phrases, and even the punch line. The cards will help both beginning and experienced storytellers. Use these story cards to practice telling the story until you are more comfortable with a new story, to build a collection of stories to tell, or to review stories for retelling at another time.

The Pleasure of Storytelling

What were your favorite stories as a child? Do you recall listening to "Goldilocks and the Three Bears," or "The Gingerbread Man," or "Jack and the Beanstalk?" A friend remembered her mother telling her these three classic stories. After hearing her mother tell the stories, she was startled when she went to school and the teacher read them from a book. Assuming her mother had made them up, she was surprised that teachers and parents knew the same stories.

One way to appreciate the power of the told story is to recall enjoyable stories from your childhood. Reflect on your feelings, the strength of each character, and the ways the storyteller involved you in the story. Remember being scared for Goldilocks who was lost in the forest, relieved when she spotted a charming little cottage, and anxious for her not to be caught when the bear family returned. Feel the hard, not-so-hard, and just-right bed. Taste the hot, too-cool, and the just-right porridge.

Our own delight when remembering stories and the experiences of listening should encourage us to become storytellers. Clearly the told story has found a place in literary history. How does one begin? How does one become a storyteller? Remember the stories from your past, select an appropriate story, and tell it to a child or a small group of children. Practice the tips we mention. Keep a story card handy for a quick peek, then let yourself go and enjoy the flow of the story. Observe the positive reactions of the young listeners and you will forever be a storyteller.

Whether you are a beginning teacher or an experienced librarian, a parent with a first child or a grandparent of five, the message is the same. Stories told by you are gifts that will last a lifetime. Enjoy the storytelling experience and savor the children's request when they plead,

"Tell it again!"

Rich and Poor

The
Thrifty Tailor

IN THIS RETOLD STORY, A BUSY TAILOR FINALLY
MAKES HIMSELF A WINTER COAT. WHEN IT
WEARS OUT, HE FINDS THAT SOME OF ITS FABRIC
CAN STILL BE USED FOR OTHER THINGS: FIRST A
JACKET, THEN A VEST, THEN A CAP, AND
FINALLY A BUTTON.

Once there was a tailor. He lived in

a village and worked very hard making clothes. He made coats and jackets and hats for the people in the village. Because he spent all of his time making clothes for other people, he never had time to make anything for himself.

The tailor really needed a heavy coat to keep him warm in the winter, but he didn't have the money to buy the cloth or the time to make the coat. He decided to save a little money each time he sold clothes to the people in the village. He could use the money to buy fabric for a heavy winter coat.

Use a sad voice.

He sewed many clothes and saved for a very long time. Little by little he saved enough money to buy the cloth he needed for his coat. Then he made himself a big heavy coat. It was a very warm coat. He was very proud of the warm coat he had made for himself. He wore it anytime that it was cold. He even wore it when it was just a little chilly.

Sit tall and look proud.

He wore his warm coat until it was worn out, but he loved his coat so much that he didn't want to throw it away.

Hug yourself as if you love your coat.

So, he took a closer look at his warm coat. He found that some of the cloth in the coat was not worn out. He looked at the size of the cloth that was still good and decided that it was just enough to make a jacket. He took the good piece of cloth from the coat and made himself a beautiful jacket.

Pretend to inspect fabric.

He was very proud of the beautiful jacket that he had made for himself. He wore it often. He wore it when it was cold and when it was chilly. He wore it when it was

Look happy.

cloudy. He wore it almost every day. He wore the beautiful jacket until it was worn out. It was his favorite jacket and he really hated to throw it away.

So, he took a closer look at his beautiful jacket and found that there was a piece of cloth that was still good. The piece of cloth was just enough to make a fancy vest. So he took the cloth from the jacket and made himself a fancy vest. He was very proud of the fancy vest. He wore it often. He wore it when it was cold. He wore it when it was cloudy and he even wore it on warm days. He wore it almost every day until the vest was worn out. The tailor was very sad that his fancy vest was worn out.

So, he took a closer look at his fancy vest and found some cloth that was not worn out. There were still some pieces of cloth that were good. The pieces of cloth were just enough to make a small cap. He took the good pieces from the vest and sewed them together. He made himself a small cap.

When he tried on his small cap, it fit perfectly. He was very proud of how it looked. He wore his cap often. He wore his cap when it was cold and when it was warm.

He wore his cap outside and he wore his cap inside. He wore his small cap everywhere until it was all worn out. He was very upset that his cap was worn out. He didn't want to throw his cap away.

Pretend to inspect fabric.

Sit tall and look proud.

Sigh loudly.

Make a sewing motion.

Pretend to put on a cap.

Look delighted.

So, he took a closer look at his small cap and he found a tiny piece of cloth that was not worn out. He cut up his cap and he made himself a very special button. It was a very lovely button and he was very proud of it. He wore it when it was cold, and when it was warm. He wore it outside and inside. He wore it every day. The tailor wore the button until it was worn out. At least he thought it was worn out.

Touch a button on your shirt.

So, he took a closer look at his lovely button and realized that there was just enough left to make a story. So, the tailor told his story to the people of the village just as I am telling his story to you.

There are many ways to recycle old items instead of throwing them away.

Storytelling Tips

◉ This tale would be a great flannel board story. A jacket, coat, vest, cap, and button are the only flannel pieces you will need. The same fabric (felt, flannel, plaid, wool) should be used for each of the items of clothing. After you tell the story, the children can retell it using the flannel board props.

◉ Because most children today have little experience with a tailor, you might discuss what a tailor does before telling the story.

◉ "Worn out" is a key phrase used throughout the story. If the listeners don't understand the meaning of this phrase, you should expand by explaining that it means torn, threadbare, ragged, used, rumpled, etc.

◉ When repeating the phrase, "So, he took a closer look at the___," draw out the words to demonstrate how carefully the tailor looked at the cloth. When telling how he found good fabric left to use, speed up your words and use an excited voice to show that he was happy.

Questions

◉ How did the tailor get the cloth to make himself a coat?

◉ What other pieces of clothing could the tailor have made out of the fabric he bought?

◉ If you had only a tiny piece of cloth, what would you make?

DRESS-UP PLAY

Materials

Box or suitcase

Hats, gloves, vests, jackets,
    scarves, earmuffs, pants,
    shirts, and other items of
    clothing that fit the
    children

Full-length mirror
    (optional)

Steps

◉ Present the box or suitcase filled with clothing to the listeners.

◉ Encourage them to explore the items, try them on, pretend, and
    role play.

◉ Ask the listeners if any of the clothes are worn out. If so, which
    ones? How can they tell? Can any of them be used again?

◉ Sort the clothes into groups. Possible groupings could be *new*,
    worn out, and *recycle*.

SEWING LIKE A TAILOR

Materials

Loosely woven pieces of fabric (burlap, netting, linen)

Scissors

Brightly colored pieces
  of yarn

Plastic needles with large eye

Steps

◉ Cut the fabric into pieces that will be easy for the listeners to manipulate.

◉ Invite the children to choose a piece of fabric and some yarn. They can help thread the yarn into the needle. Be sure to tie a large knot in the end of the yarn.

◉ Have the children sew designs on their pieces of fabric. Younger children will simply go in and out of the fabric with their needle and yarn. Older children may choose to sew pieces together or create an item mentioned in the story.

◉ Display the creations for all to enjoy.

Lazy Jack

IN THIS ENGLISH TALE, A LAZY BOY TRIES
TO EARN A LIVING BUT IN THE PROCESS
MAKES MANY FOOLISH MISTAKES. ONE
OF THESE MISTAKES MAKES A SICK GIRL
LAUGH, AND FOR THIS HE IS GREATLY
REWARDED.

Once upon a time there was a very poor old woman. She lived in a little cottage. She had very little money. What money she had, she earned by knitting. She knitted all day long and into the night. She worked very hard but she still had very little money.

Pretend to knit.

The poor woman had a son name Jack. He lived with her in her house. Jack was so lazy he just sat by the fire from morning to night. He never did any work. He didn't have a job. All the people called him "Lazy Jack."

Stretch, yawn, and then close your eyes.

The old woman became very irritated with Jack. He was always sitting by the fire, never working, never helping buy the food, never doing anything useful.

One day, when she could not stand Jack's laziness any longer, she said, "Jack you must go to work. You have to help pay for the food. If you don't go to work you will have to move out of our home and find your own food."

Shake your finger as if scolding.

The next day, Jack went out and found a job working for a farmer. Jack earned one penny for the day's work. He had never had any money of his own before. He had never worked before. He didn't know what to do with the penny.

On his way home he had to cross a bridge. On the bridge he slipped and fell. He dropped his penny. The penny rolled into the river and was lost forever. When he got home and told his mother what happened, his mother said, "You silly boy. You should have put your penny in your pocket."

Look upset.

"I'll do that next time," said Jack.

The next day Jack went out and found another job. This time he worked for a dairy farmer. At the end of the day the dairy farmer gave Jack a jug of milk for his day's work. Jack remembered what his mother said and he put the neck of the jug of milk in his pocket. By the time Jack arrived at his home, all the milk had spilled out of the jug.

Look down in disgust.

"You silly boy," said his mother. "You should have carried the jug of milk on your head."

"I'll do that next time," said Jack.

The next day Jack found a job at a cheese shop. At the end of the day the woman who owned the shop paid Jack with a big wheel of cheese. Jack remembered what his mother had told him. He put the big wheel of cheese on his head. It was a hot day so by the time he got home, all the cheese had melted and was running down over his face.

Wipe your face.

When Jack's mother saw him she said, "You silly boy, you should have carried the cheese in your hands."

Jack said, "I'll do that next time."

The next day Jack worked all day for a baker. At the end of the day all the baker gave Jack was an old cat. Jack remembered what his mother had said. Jack tried to carry the cat carefully in his hands. It wasn't long before the old cat scratched him, and he let the cat go. When he got home, he told his mother about the cat.

Pretend to drop a cat.

She said, "You silly boy, you should have tied a rope around the cat's neck and pulled it home."

Jack said, "I'll do that the next time."

The next day Jack found work at a butcher shop. All day long he cut and packaged meat. At the end of the day the butcher gave Jack a ham for his day's work. Jack took the ham, tied a rope around it, and pulled it home. By the time Jack got home, the ham was covered with dirt and spoiled.

Pretend to pull a ham.

No one could eat the ham that had been pulled through the dirt. His mother shouted, "You silly boy. You should have carried it on your shoulder!"

Jack said, "I'll do that the next time."

On the next day, which was a Saturday, Lazy Jack worked at the stables with the horses and donkeys. He worked so hard that day that he was given a donkey for his work. Jack remembered what his mother had said. He remembered that she had told him to carry the next thing on his shoulders. He tried to lift the donkey up on his shoulders. The donkey was very heavy. He tried and tried to lift the heavy donkey. At last he succeeded in getting the donkey on his shoulders. Slowly he began walking home with the donkey on his shoulders.

Pretend to hoist a donkey.

As Jack was walking home he passed a very fine house. In the house lived a rich man and his daughter who had been very sick. She had never laughed in all of her life. The doctors had told the father that she could get well if she would only laugh. Many people had tried, but no one had been able to make her laugh or smile.

Make a sad face.

RICH AND POOR

The young girl was looking out her window as Jack went by. She saw Lazy Jack struggling to hold the donkey on his shoulders. The donkey was very upset about being carried upside down. He was kicking his four legs in the air and braying, "Hee-haw, hee-haw," as loud as he could.

Look amazed.

It was the funniest thing the young girl had ever seen. She burst out laughing, and she laughed and laughed and laughed. The laughter cured her immediately.

Point and shake with laughter.

Her father was so overjoyed that he gave Jack much money and a big house. Now Jack lives with his happy mother in the big house, and he makes the beautiful young girl laugh all the time.

No matter how many mistakes you make, sometimes things work out.

Storytelling Tips

◉ Lazy Jack's mother becomes more irritated with him each time he returns home. When telling the story, let your voice communicate her building frustration and anger as she gives him instructions for what to do the next time.

◉ When Jack responds to his mother's irritation by saying, "I'll do that the next time," make your voice sound resigned and a little discouraged.

◉ To emphasize the humor of Jack carrying the donkey on his shoulders, use your arms to show how the donkey was kicking and include several "hee-haws" to add to the ridiculous event.

Questions

◉ Why did the people call the young man, "Lazy Jack"?

◉ What were some of the jobs that Jack tried? What was he paid for his work?

◉ Why do you think the young girl laughed so hard at Jack and the donkey?

JOBS FOR JACK

Materials

Pictures that show people working (including farmer, butcher, baker, shop owner, and others mentioned in the story as well as other occupations the listeners may be familiar with)

Paper and pen or tape recorder and cassette

Steps

◉ Talk about the work that Lazy Jack did in the story.

◉ Discuss the pictures in the collection with the listeners.

◉ Invite the children to create another story about Lazy Jack using different occupations. As the story develops, the children can decide what Jack will be paid for his day of work.

◉ Write down the story as it is created or record it on a tape player.

STORY ROLL

Materials

Drawing paper

Markers and crayons

Scissors

Glue

Roll of butcher paper
   or wrapping paper

Steps

- ❂ Review the sequence of events in the story with the listeners.

- ❂ Invite each child to draw a picture of a specific happening.

- ❂ Encourage the children to cut out their pictures.

- ❂ When all the drawings are complete, let the children decide the order in which they occurred in the story.

- ❂ Have them glue their pictures on the long roll of paper in that order.

- ❂ Invite the listeners to "read" the story by rolling out the paper and seeing the pictures.

The Talking Pot

THIS RETOLD
VERSION OF A
DANISH FOLKTALE IS
ABOUT A POOR MAN WHO
TRADES HIS COW FOR A MAGIC
COOKING POT THAT BRINGS HIM
AND HIS WIFE GREAT FORTUNE.

Once upon a time, there was a poor couple who had no food and only a thin cow as a possession. They were so hungry that they decided to sell the cow to buy some food. The poor man placed a rope around the cow's neck and started along the road to the market.

Use a bright, friendly voice.

Soon the poor man met a stranger on the road. The stranger inquired, "Good man, are you off to market to sell your fine cow?"

"Yes," the poor man replied, although he did not think his thin cow was very fine.

"Do you want to buy my cow?" he asked, thinking he would save himself the long walk to the market in town.

"I have no money, but I would like to make a trade," said the stranger. "I have this wonderful pot. Would you trade your cow for this pot?"

Look uncertain.

The poor man looked at the pot, which was rather ordinary. It was a big, iron, cooking pot just like many others he had seen. The poor man said, "No, I must sell my cow for money so that I can buy some food. I must have at least twenty dollars for my cow."

"Take me, take me, and you shall never regret it," said the pot.

Look amazed.

The poor man was stunned to hear a talking pot. What a surprise! Perhaps what made the pot wonderful was that it could talk. So the poor man traded his cow for the pot. He walked the miles back to his cottage and placed the pot in the barn where the cow had been kept.

When he went into the cottage, the poor woman asked, "How much money did you get for the cow? Did you buy food for us to eat?"

"No, but I do have something wonderful," he said and took his wife to the barn to see the pot.

Use an excited voice.

"A pot, a plain iron cooking pot is all you have to show for our fine cow!" she shouted.

Just as the poor man was about to explain, the pot said, "Take me and clean me, polish me, and hang me by the fire."

The poor woman was stunned. She thought that a talking pot was something of value after all. So the poor woman cleaned the pot, polished it, and hung it by the warm fire.

Pretend to polish a pot.

The next morning, the pot said, "I skip, I skip," and the pot skipped out the front door of the poor couple's cottage. It skipped over dale and hill, hill and dale and up to the rich man's house. The pot skipped into the rich man's kitchen where his wife was making her favorite pudding. The pot jumped up on the table.

The rich wife, seeing the pot in the middle of the table, said, "This pot is just the right size for my favorite pudding." She chopped some nuts and raisins and added them to the pudding.

Pretend to chop.

After the pudding was cooked, the pot said, "I skip, I skip," and started out the door.

The rich wife said, "Where are you skipping with my favorite pudding?"

Look angry.

"I skip over dale and hill, hill and dale to the cottage of

the poor man and the poor woman who live up the road." And away the pot skipped.

When the pot arrived at the poor man's and the poor woman's house, they ate their fill of delicious pudding and thanked the pot. Then the poor woman cleaned the pot, polished it, and hung it by the warm fire.

Smile and rub your tummy.

The next morning, the pot said, "I skip, I skip," and the pot skipped out the front door of the poor couple's cottage. It skipped over dale and hill, hill and dale and up to the rich man's barn. The pot skipped into the rich man's barn where the workers were storing the wheat for the winter. The pot jumped in the middle of the barn floor. It looked just the right size for the workers to store the wheat. They shoveled wheat over and over again into the pot, which never seemed to fill until almost all of the wheat was gone from the barn.

Pretend to shovel.

After the pot was filled with wheat, the pot said, "I skip, I skip," and started out the barn door.

The workers said, "Where are you skipping with almost all of the rich man's wheat?"

"I skip over dale and hill, hill and dale to the barn of the poor man and the poor woman who live up the road." And away the pot skipped.

When the pot arrived at the poor man's barn, it dumped so much wheat that it completely filled the barn. There was enough wheat to last over two years. The poor man and the poor woman were very grateful. The poor woman cleaned the pot, polished it, and hung it by the warm fire.

Nod and smile.

The next morning, the pot said, "I skip, I skip," and the pot skipped out the front door of the poor couple's cottage. It skipped over dale and hill, hill and dale and up to the rich man's counting room, where the rich man was counting his money.

The pot jumped up on the table in the middle of the room. The rich man said, "This pot is just the right size for some of my gold coins." He placed handful after handful of gold coins into the pot. Soon it held all of the rich man's gold coins.

Pretend to scoop up coins.

After the pot was filled with the gold, the pot said, "I skip, I skip," and started out of the counting room.

The rich man jumped up and shouted, "Stop, stop, where are you skipping with my gold coins?"

Shake both fists.

"I skip over dale and hill, hill and dale to the cottage of the poor man and the poor woman who live up the road." And away the pot skipped.

When the pot arrived at the poor man's and the poor woman's cottage, it dumped all the gold coins out on the table. There was so much gold that the poor man and the poor woman would never be poor again. The poor man and the poor woman were very grateful. The poor woman cleaned the pot, polished it, and hung it by the warm fire.

The next morning, the pot said, "I skip, I skip," and the pot skipped out the front door of the poor couple's cottage. It skipped over dale and hill, hill and dale and up to the once-rich man's house. When the man saw the pot, he screamed, "You wicked pot! You thief! You took my

Shake both fists.

wife's favorite pudding! You took the wheat from my barn, and you took the gold I was counting!"

"I skip, I skip," said the pot.

"Skip to the North Pole for all I care," said the once-rich man. And with those words, the pot stuck to the man's arm and started skipping down the road toward the North Pole.

And to this day, if you ever see a skipping pot, it is probably on its way to the North Pole. And the man with the pot—he was once a rich man.

Share what you have with those less fortunate.

Storytelling Tips

◉ Sound very sad at the beginning of the story, when the poor man has to sell his last possession, the thin cow.

◉ Use a musical voice for the pot. Sing or say rhythmically, "I skip, I skip."

◉ Teach children a gesture, such as two fingers skipping along, to use whenever they hear the word *skip*.

◉ Practice an angry voice for the poor wife and an angry voice for the rich man.

◉ At the end of the story, lean close to the listeners and say, "And to this day. . ."

Questions

◉ Why do you think the man traded his cow for the pot?

◉ Do you think the rich man would have helped the poor man and his wife if they had asked him to?

◉ Have you ever helped someone who needed assistance?

MAKING A TRADE

Materials

Household items or office supplies

Toys

Steps

◉ Offer to trade something that the listeners enjoy playing with for something from the home or office.

◉ Trade throughout the day. Offer to trade half of a sandwich for an apple, etc.

◉ Trade chores.

PUDDING IN A POT

Materials

Pudding mix

Raisins

Nuts

Pot for use as
   mixing bowl

Measuring cup and spoons

Bowls and spoons

Steps

◉ With the listeners, read the directions on the package of pudding mix.

◉ Invite the children to help mix the pudding in the pot.

◉ Have the children add some raisins and chopped nuts like in the story.

◉ Serve and enjoy.

The Fisherman and His Wife

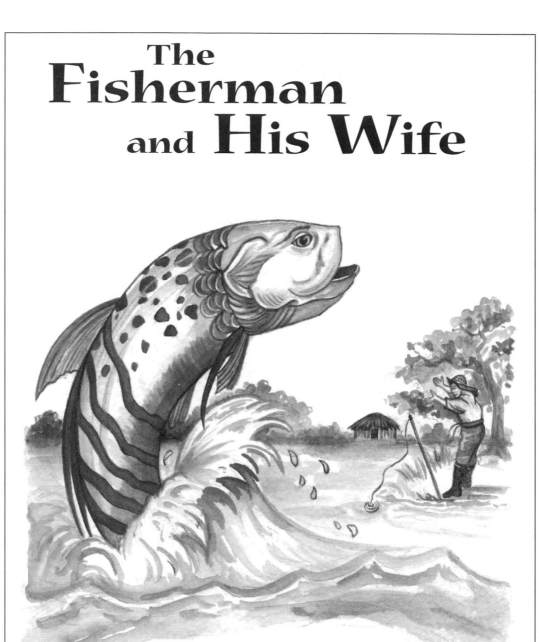

THIS STORY, ADAPTED FROM THE
WORK OF JACOB AND WILHELM
GRIMM, TELLS OF A MAGIC FISH THAT
GRANTS A FISHERMAN AND HIS WIFE
MANY WISHES UNTIL THEY ASK FOR
TOO MUCH.

Once upon a time there was a fisherman and his wife. They lived together in a hut on the top of a high hill. Every day the fisherman went to the ocean and fished all day long. Some days he caught many fish, and other days he didn't catch any fish at all.

Pretend to throw out a fishing line.

One day, after fishing for many hours without catching anything, he suddenly felt a powerful tug on the end of his line. After much pulling and tugging, he reeled in an enormous fish. The fisherman was delighted at his catch. To his surprise the big fish began to talk.

Pretend to reel in a large fish.

Gasp in surprise.

The fish pleaded, "Please don't keep me. I won't taste very good because I am a magic fish. Please throw me back into the water so I can swim away."

Use a pleading voice.

The man said, "You are indeed a very special fish because you can talk. I will throw you back into the water and you can swim away."

Pretend to throw the fish back in.

The man returned home to his wife in the hut at the top of the hill. He told her about his day fishing. He explained that all he had caught was a magic fish that could talk. Because the magic fish was so special, he had thrown him back into the water.

His wife was very angry with him. She said, "A magic fish that could talk? Didn't you ask the fish for a magic wish?"

Put your hands on your hips and use a stern voice.

The man shrugged. "I didn't ask for anything. There is nothing that I really want," he said.

Shrug your shoulders.

The wife said sharply, "We live in a shabby hut and you can't think of anything to wish for? Go back to the ocean and tell the magic talking fish that you want a house to live in."

Cup your hands
around your
mouth each
time you call
the fish.

So the man went back to the ocean. He called, "Magic fish, magic fish, we have a wish."

The magic fish swam up to the top of the water and asked, "What is your wish?"

Use a deep voice
whenever the
fish speaks.

"My wife doesn't want to live in a shabby hut any more. She would like to live in a house."

The magic fish said, "Go back and see what you find."

Look surprised
and pleased.

When the fisherman returned home, he found a lovely cottage with a living room, bedroom, and a kitchen. Behind the house was a little garden with ducks and chickens. He and his wife were very pleased. They agreed that this was a very nice house and garden. Yet, after a week had passed, the wife became very discontent. She told her husband, "This house is much too small. We don't have enough room. It is too crowded. The garden is too small. The magic fish could give us a much larger house. Go back and ask the magic fish for a castle."

Speak in a stern
voice.

The man didn't want to go back, but his wife insisted. When he got to the ocean he called, "Magic fish, magic fish, we have a wish."

The fish came swimming up out of the water. He asked, "What do you want?"

Speak in an
embarrassed
way.

The man said, "My wife thinks the house is too small and wants a castle instead."

"Go home and see what you find," said the magic fish.

When the fisherman returned home, he saw a huge castle sitting on the top of the hill. His wife invited him inside to see the magnificent castle. Inside were many rooms: living rooms, dining rooms, kitchens, and fifteen bedrooms with baths. Each room was filled with fancy furniture that was finished in gold. Behind the castle was a big pasture with horses and cows. In front of the castle was a beautiful garden.

The man said, "This is wonderful! Let's live in this beautiful castle and be happy."

Use an excited voice and open your arms.

The very next day the wife woke up early. She looked at the beautiful castle and the wonderful land. She woke her husband up and said, "You should be King of this country." The fisherman explained that he didn't want to be King.

She said, "If you don't want to be King, then I will be Queen. Go tell the fish that I want to be Queen of the castle."

Use a demanding voice.

The man slowly walked to the ocean. He didn't want to ask the fish to make his wife the Queen of the castle, but he called, "Magic fish, magic fish, we have a wish."

Lower your head and look sad.

The fish slowly came swimming out of the water and asked, "What do you want?"

The man hesitated and then said, "My wife wants to be Queen."

Speak in an embarrassed way.

The fish replied, "Go home and see what you find."

When the man returned home he was amazed at what he saw. The castle was bigger and much grander than before. It was behind golden gates with fancy ironwork. Soldiers in bright red uniforms were outside the gate and castle. Inside the castle were marble floors and walls cov-

Look amazed.

ered in gold. In one of the enormous rooms, his wife was sitting on a golden throne. She wore a diamond and ruby crown on her head and a velvet cape trimmed in white fur around her shoulders.

The man said, "Now you are Queen. You have a fine castle, gardens, horses, and soldiers. You have all you have ever wished for."

The wife thought a moment and then quickly demanded, "Well there is one more thing I would like. I would like to be ruler of the universe." The man felt very sad. He could not believe that his wife still wanted more. He did not want to ask the magic fish for anything else, but his wife insisted.

Use a demanding voice.

So, he slowly walked back to the ocean. This time the water was not clear and blue, as it had been before. The ocean water was black and rough with many waves. The wind was blowing and the trees were shaking.

The man called, "Magic fish, magic fish, we have a wish."

Sound nervous.

The magic fish did not come, so he called again, "Magic fish, magic fish, we have a wish."

Use a louder voice.

The magic fish still did not appear, so he called again, "Magic fish, magic fish, we have a wish."

Use an even louder voice.

Slowly the magic fish came out of the water and asked, "What do you want now?"

Use an angry voice.

RICH AND POOR

"My wife wants to be ruler of the entire universe," the man said.

The fish replied, "Go home and see what you find."

When the man returned home, there were no soldiers, no horses, no cows, no garden, and no castle. Nothing was left but a shabby hut. And to this day, the man and his wife live in that same shabby hut, on the top of the hill.

Shake your head.

Make the most of what you have.

Storytelling Tips

- Sing or chant the following phrase each time the magic fish is called from the water: "Magic fish, magic fish, we have a wish." If chanted, use a rhythmic pattern. On repeated tellings, invite the children to join in the musical phrase, demonstrating their understanding of the sequence of the story.

- Each time the wife makes new demands, show that the fisherman is not happy about asking the fish for another favor by changing your voice to reflect these unhappy feelings.

- Use a twirling hand motion to show the magic fish rising up out of the water. This helps the children "see" the magic fish. This gesture also invites active participation of the children.

- Encourage the listeners to help call the fish from the ocean. Call a little louder each time.

- Add drama to the end of the story by pausing before saying, "Nothing was left but the shabby hut."

Questions

- What were some of the things that the fisherman's wife wanted the magic fish to give them?

- Why do you think she asked for so many things?

- What would you ask the magic fish to give you?

MAKING A MAGIC FISH

Materials

Construction paper

Cellophane, foil, gift wrap, tissue paper

Fabric scraps

Scissors

Markers or crayons

Glitter

Glue

Steps

◉ Talk with the children about how a magic fish might look.

◉ Invite the children to cut out a fish shape from one of the materials and decorate it.

◉ Display the finished magic fish so that everyone can enjoy them.

MUSICAL CHANT

Materials

Paper

Markers

Simple musical instruments or items that make noise

Steps

◉ Print the phrase "Magic fish, magic fish, we have a wish" on paper.

◉ Sing or chant the musical phrase.

◉ Invite the children to sing the chant with you as you move your hand along the written words.

◉ Ask the children to choose another way to add sounds to the chant such as hand clapping, rhythm sticks, drums, spoon tapping, and bells.

One Good Turn Deserves Another

The
Great Lion and the
Tiny Mouse

WHEN A GREAT LION DOES NOT HARM A TINY
MOUSE, THE TINY MOUSE RETURNS THE FAVOR
IN THIS STORY INSPIRED BY AESOP'S FABLE.

ONE GOOD TURN DESERVES ANOTHER

Once upon a time, a Great Lion was king of the jungle. He ran where he wanted to run. He ate what he wanted to eat. And he slept where he wanted to sleep.

Look proud.

No one bothered Great Lion. The monkeys did not bother him. The zebras did not bother him. The water buffaloes did not bother him. The giraffes did not bother him. Even the elephants did not bother Great Lion.

One day, Tiny Mouse was hurrying home to his tiny burrow. Because he was in a hurry, he was not looking where he was going. He ran over the paw of Great Lion while he was sleeping. Tiny Mouse tickled Great Lion's paw as he ran over it, and Great Lion awoke. He slapped his huge paw down and caught Tiny Mouse by the tail.

Slap one hand.

"Well, what do we have here?" Great Lion said in a huge booming voice.

"Oh, please, Great Lion, please let me go. Do not hurt me. I am just a tiny little mouse."

Use a high voice when the mouse speaks.

"Just a nice little afternoon snack for me, I should think," boomed Great Lion.

"Oh, please, Great Lion, please let me go. If you let me go, some day I will do a favor for you," squeaked Tiny Mouse.

Clasp hands as if pleading.

"A favor, a favor for me? You will do something good for me some day?" laughed Great Lion. "Well, I don't think a great strong lion like me will ever need a little mouse like you to do me a favor, but I'm not very hungry, so I'll let you go." And Great Lion lifted his great paw.

Pretend a hearty laugh.

Tiny Mouse ran away as fast as he could, but he yelled back to the lion. "I always keep my promises. Some day, I will do something good for you. I will do you a favor."

Pretend to sleep.

But Great Lion was already sleeping, making great snoring sounds. He didn't even hear Tiny Mouse. From that day on, Tiny Mouse was careful to stay away from sleeping lions.

Not long after Great Lion spared Tiny Mouse's life, Tiny Mouse thought he heard something in the far distance. It sounded like Great Lion's roar. Sure enough, Great Lion was roaring. He was roaring and clawing, stretching and straining, trying to get loose. Great Lion had been caught in a trap. Some trappers had rigged a net to fall on Great Lion. The more Great Lion stretched and strained, rolled and tumbled, the more he became entangled in the ropes of the net.

Cup hand over ear.

Make clawing movements.

Great Lion roared and roared, calling for the other animals to help him. The monkeys came to see what all the commotion was about. But they just stared at Great Lion, laughed at him caught in the ropes, and swung back into the trees, chattering all the while.

Pretend to laugh.

Great Lion roared and roared, calling for the other animals to help him. The zebras came to see what all the commotion was about. But they just stared at Great Lion, laughed at him caught in the ropes, and trotted on back to their grazing.

Pretend to laugh.

Great Lion roared and roared, calling for the other animals to help him. The water buffaloes came to see what all the commotion was about. But they just stared at

Great Lion, laughed at him caught in the ropes, and went on down to the watering hole to drink.

Pretend to laugh.

Great Lion roared and roared, calling for the other animals to help him. The giraffes came to see what all the commotion was about. But they just stared at Great Lion, laughed at him caught in the ropes, and went back to nibbling leaves from the treetops.

Pretend to laugh.

Great Lion roared and roared, calling for the other animals to help him. The elephants came to see what all the commotion was about. But they just stared at Great Lion, laughed at him caught in the ropes, and went back to swinging their trunks and herding their babies along the path.

Pretend to laugh.

Tiny Mouse was rushing as fast as he could in the direction of the roaring lion. He passed the monkeys swinging in the trees. He passed the zebras grazing on the grass. He passed the water buffaloes by the watering hole. He passed the giraffes nibbling leaves from the treetops. He passed the elephants herding their babies along the path.

Finally, Tiny Mouse reached Great Lion. He saw him caught in the ropes, but Tiny Mouse did not laugh at Great Lion.

Look concerned.

He told him to be still and rest. Then Tiny Mouse gnawed and chewed, chewed and gnawed, until he gnawed right through one rope. Then he gnawed right through another rope. Finally, he had gnawed a hole in the ropes big enough for Great Lion to escape.

Pretend to gnaw.

Tiny Mouse said, "I always keep my promises. I promised you that one day I would do something good for you. I promised you that if you let me go, I would do you a favor."

Great Lion lay his great paw down on the ground gently. Tiny Mouse stepped on it. Great Lion lifted Tiny Mouse up to his great strong back and they walked away.

And, to this day, if you ever see a great sleeping lion, look for a tiny mouse. He is sure to be close by.

Even the smallest creature has something important to offer.

ONE GOOD TURN DESERVES ANOTHER

Storytelling Tips

◉ Use a huge, blustery voice for Great Lion and a squeaky, timid voice for Tiny Mouse.

◉ Roar loudly and call for help when Great Lion is caught in the ropes.

◉ For very young children, shorten the story by having fewer animals come by to see Great Lion in the trap.

Questions

◉ Do you think Tiny Mouse was brave? Why?

◉ Why do you think the other animals didn't help Great Lion?

◉ What would you have done if you came across Great Lion trapped in a net?

REPAYING A FAVOR

Materials

None needed

Steps

◉ Ask the listeners to recall when someone did a favor for them. For example, a brother or sister might have helped pick up toys or hang up clothes.

◉ Discuss how people help us without expecting to be repaid.

◉ Mention that sometimes we need to repay favors.

◉ Invite the listeners to think of ways they can return a favor.

ONE GOOD TURN DESERVES ANOTHER

RETELLING THE STORY

Materials

Index cards

Markers or
    crayons

Steps

 Write the
name of the story, "The Great Lion and the Tiny Mouse," on the
top card of the stack.

🌀 Help the listeners recall all the animals in the story—the lion, the
mouse, the monkeys, the zebras, the water buffaloes, the giraffes,
and the elephants.

🌀 Write each on a card. If possible, draw the animal on the card, or
ask a child to draw one animal from the story on a card.

🌀 Shuffle the cards with the names of those animals that did not help
Great Lion—the monkeys, the zebras, the water buffaloes, the
giraffes, and the elephants.

🌀 Pick up the cards and retell the story with the animals appearing in
the order that the shuffled cards dictate.

MOVE LIKE THE ANIMALS

Materials

Marching music

Tape recorder

Steps

🌀 Remind the children of all the animals in the story: Tiny Mouse, Great Lion, monkeys, zebras, water buffaloes, giraffes, and elephants.

🌀 Divide the children into animal groups by their choice.

🌀 Ask individual children to mimic how these animals move, then let others join them.

🌀 Begin the marching music and encourage the children to move like the animals.

🌀 Stop the music and let the children select a new animal to imitate.

The Great Gigantic Turnip

IN THIS STORY ADAPTED FROM A RUSSIAN FOLK-
TALE, EVERYONE TRIES TO PULL A GIGANTIC
TURNIP FROM THE GARDEN, BUT IT STAYS PUT
UNTIL A TINY MOUSE JOINS THE TUGGING.

Each spring Grandfather planted

a garden beside his house. One spring he decided to plant a turnip seed.

Each day Grandfather would work in his garden and check on his turnip to see how it was growing. He watered the turnip when it was dry and pulled up the weeds that grew around it. The turnip grew and grew and grew. Grandfather watched the turnip and took care of it every day.

Grunt and pretend to pull.

Finally, Grandfather decided it was time to pull up the turnip. It had grown into a gigantic turnip. Grandfather took hold of the stem of the turnip and he pulled and he pulled and he pulled, but the turnip was so gigantic that he could not pull it up.

He called to his wife, "Grandmother, come and help me pull up this gigantic turnip." Grandmother ran to help her husband. She put her arms around his waist, and he held on to the stem of the turnip. Grandfather and Grandmother pulled and they pulled and they pulled, but the gigantic turnip did not move.

Grunt and pretend to pull.

Grandmother called to her daughter, "Come help us pull up the turnip."

Pretend to wipe your brow.

Her daughter ran to help. She put her arms around Grandmother, who had her arms around the waist of Grandfather, who was holding on to the stem of the gigantic turnip. They pulled and they pulled and they pulled together, but the gigantic turnip did not budge. Grandmother's daughter called her daughter, "Come help us pull up the turnip."

ONE GOOD TURN DESERVES ANOTHER

The little girl hurried to help. She pulled on her Mother, while Mother pulled on Grandmother, while Grandmother pulled on Grandfather, while he held on to the stem of the turnip. They pulled and they pulled and they pulled together, but the gigantic turnip did not move.

Look discouraged and shake your head.

The little girl called to her puppy, "Come help us pull up the big turnip." The puppy barked excitedly and came running to help.

The puppy caught hold of the little girl's dress and pulled. The little girl pulled on her Mother, who pulled on Grandmother, while she pulled on Grandfather, while he held on to the stem of the turnip. They pulled and they pulled and they pulled together, but the gigantic turnip did not come up. It did not move.

Make pulling motions with your arms.

Then the puppy called to the cat who came running to help pull up the turnip. The cat pulled on the dog. The dog pulled on the little girl. The little girl pulled on Mother. Mother pulled on Grandmother and Grandmother pulled on Grandfather, who pulled on the stem. They pulled and they pulled and they pulled together, but nothing happened. The turnip did not come up.

Pretend to be out of breath.

A tiny mouse heard all the noise and came to see what was happening. The mouse said, "I will help you."

Sound confident.

The mouse pulled on the cat, who pulled on the dog, who pulled on the little girl, who pulled on Mother, who pulled on Grandmother, who pulled on Grandfather, who held onto the stem of the turnip. Together they pulled and they pulled and they pulled. Out popped the great gigantic turnip!

Clap with joy.

That night everyone—Grandfather, Grandmother, Mother, the little girl, the puppy, the cat, and the tiny mouse—had a big dinner made from the great gigantic turnip.

When there is a difficult job, even the smallest person can make a big difference.

ONE GOOD TURN DESERVES ANOTHER

Storytelling Tips

◉ Some listeners may not be familiar with a turnip, so you might want to show them one. Talking about other vegetables that grow in the ground might be a good expansion.

◉ This story is especially good for telling because it is a cumulative tale. Practice repeating the characters in the order they are added to help pull the turnip.

◉ Emphasize how hard they must pull to get the gigantic turnip out of the ground. "They pu-l-l-ed and they pu-l-l-ed and they pu-l-l-ed."

◉ After each segment of pulling, pause to see if the turnip has moved. These pauses will help build anticipation for the story climax.

Questions

◉ How many different people and animals were needed to pull the great gigantic turnip out of the ground?

◉ Why did the tiny mouse make the gigantic turnip finally come out of the ground?

◉ Who would you ask to help pull up the big turnip? Why?

TASTING PARTY

Materials

Vegetables that are familiar and unfamiliar (include a turnip
if possible)

Tray

Cutting board and
knife

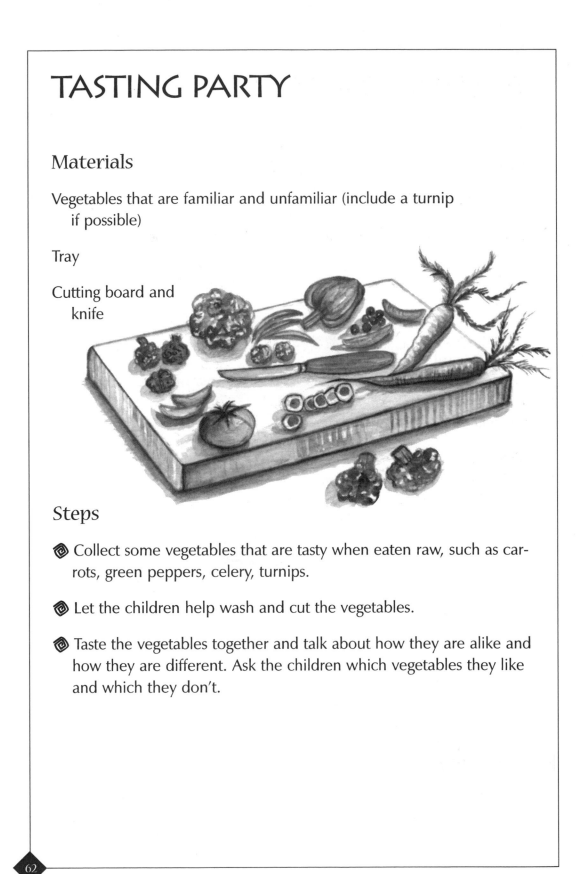

Steps

◉ Collect some vegetables that are tasty when eaten raw, such as carrots, green peppers, celery, turnips.

◉ Let the children help wash and cut the vegetables.

◉ Taste the vegetables together and talk about how they are alike and
how they are different. Ask the children which vegetables they like
and which they don't.

PULLING TOGETHER

Materials

A jump rope or thick rope

Household items that the child could pull with the rope

Steps

◉ Help the listeners tie the rope around a toy chest, small garbage can, or old chair. (Choose an item that would be difficult for one child to pull.)

◉ Invite each child to try pulling the item without help.

◉ Suggest that two people pull the item together. Talk about how much easier it is when the two of you pull together. If other adults or children are around, ask them to help pull too.

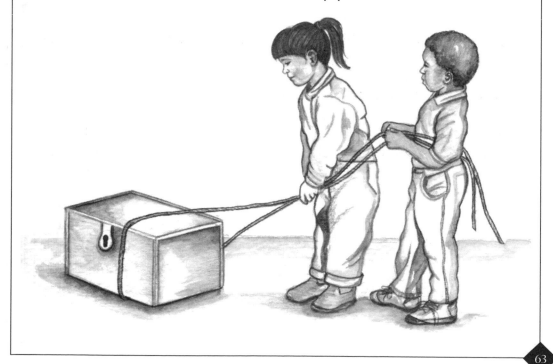

The Little Red Hen

IN THIS VERSION OF A FAMOUS ENGLISH TALE, A
LITTLE RED HEN ASKS HER THREE LAZY COM-
PANIONS FOR HELP, BUT THEY REFUSE AND SHE
MUST DO ALL THE WORK HERSELF.

Once upon a time, right here in this county, there lived a Little Red Hen who shared her home with three friends—a dog, a cat, and a mouse. Little Red Hen enjoyed working. She kept a neat little house at the edge of a farmer's lush green field. She also had a garden plot beside her house.

One day, when Little Red Hen was planting her garden, she found some grains of wheat left from the farmer's harvest. Little Red Hen was very excited to find the grains of wheat. She ran inside to tell her friends.

At the doorway to her house, Little Red Hen found Beagle, a plump dog.

Beagle was stretched across the entrance. He spent most of the day sleeping and dreaming of chasing rabbits through the woods. He never actually chased them, he just slept and dreamed, dreamed and slept, right there in the doorway. He never moved from his favorite spot.

Pretend to sleep.

Inside, stretched across the windowsill, was Calico, a big, fat cat. She spent most of her day in that position, snoozing and stretching in the warm sun.

She dreamed of chasing mice in the barn. She never actually chased them, she just snoozed and stretched, stretched and snoozed, right there on the windowsill. She never moved from her favorite spot.

Pretend to snooze and stretch.

Inside the kitchen, stretched across the entrance to a mouse hole, was Brown Mouse. He spent most of his day napping and nibbling, nibbling and napping. He dreamed of finding a large chunk of cheese. He never actually searched for any, he just napped and nibbled, nibbled and napped, right across the entrance to the mouse hole. He never moved from his favorite spot.

Pretend to nibble and nap.

Little Red Hen was so excited about finding the grains of wheat, she rushed inside the house, hopped over Beagle in the front door, and said in her loudest cluck, "Look at the grains of wheat I found! The garden plot is ready for planting. Who will help me plant this wheat?"

Use a sleepy voice.

"Not I," said Beagle, as he rolled over and went back to sleeping.

Pretend to yawn.

"Not I," said Calico, as she yawned and went back to snoozing.

Close your eyes.

"Not I," said Brown Mouse, as he wiggled his whiskers and went back to napping.

"Then I will," said Little Red Hen, as she rushed outside with the hoe under her wing and planted the seeds.

After many days, there was a fine stand of wheat. Little Red Hen watered the wheat, pulled the weeds, and watched her crop grow in the garden plot beside the little house. One day, when the wheat was ready, Little Red Hen rushed excitedly into the little house to tell her friends that the wheat was ready to be cut. "Who will help me cut the wheat?" she asked.

66

ONE GOOD TURN DESERVES ANOTHER

"Not I," said Beagle, as he rolled over and went back to sleeping.

Use a sleepy voice.

"Not I," said Calico, as she yawned and went back to snoozing.

Pretend to yawn.

"Not I," said Brown Mouse, as he wiggled his whiskers and went back to napping.

Close your eyes.

"Then I will," said Little Red Hen. And, she rushed outside to harvest the wheat.

She gathered the stalks of wheat. Then, Little Red Hen rushed excitedly into the little house to tell her friends that the wheat was ready to take to the mill to be ground into flour. "Who will help me take the wheat to the mill?" she asked.

"Not I," said Beagle, as he rolled over and went back to sleeping.

Use a sleepy voice.

"Not I," said Calico, as she yawned and went back to snoozing.

Pretend to yawn.

"Not I," said Brown Mouse, as he wiggled his whiskers and went back to napping.

Close your eyes.

"Then I will," said Little Red Hen, as she rushed outside to take the wheat to the mill to be ground into flour. When Little Red Hen returned from the mill, she rushed into the house to tell her friends that the wheat was now flour. "Who will help me bake the flour into bread?" she asked.

Use a sleepy voice.	"Not I," said Beagle, as he rolled over and went back to sleeping.
Pretend to yawn.	"Not I," said Calico, as she yawned and went back to snoozing.
Close your eyes.	"Not I," said Brown Mouse, as he wiggled his whiskers and went back to napping.

"Then I will," said Little Red Hen, as she rushed into the kitchen and began to bake the bread.

Pretend to sniff the air.	While the bread was baking, Beagle smelled the delicious aroma of baking bread and awoke from his sleeping and dreaming, dreaming and sleeping. He got up from the doorway and came to sit by the stove and wait for the bread.
Pretend to sniff the air.	Calico smelled the wonderful smell and stopped her snoozing and stretching, stretching and snoozing. She got up from the windowsill and came to sit by the stove and wait for the bread.
Pretend to sniff the air.	Brown Mouse smelled the heavenly scent of bread baking and stopped his napping and nibbling, nibbling and napping. He got up from the mouse hole and came to sit by the stove and wait for the bread.
Pretend to slice and butter bread.	Little Red Hen took the warm bread from the oven, sliced it, spread butter over each warm slice and watched it melt. "Who will help me eat this bread?" asked Little Red Hen.

"I will," said Beagle.

"I will," said Calico.

"I will," said Brown Mouse.

ONE GOOD TURN DESERVES ANOTHER

"No," said Little Red Hen. "You did not help me plant the grains of wheat.

You did not help me water and weed the wheat. You did not help me cut the wheat. You did not help me take the wheat to be milled into flour. You did not help me bake the bread. Now, you will not help me eat it." And, she ate the whole loaf of freshly baked bread all by herself.

But the next time Little Red Hen asked for help, Beagle awoke from his sleeping and dreaming, and dreaming and sleeping, and he helped. And the next time Little Red Hen asked for help, Calico awoke from her snoozing and stretching, stretching and snoozing, and she helped. And the next time Little Red Hen asked for help, Brown Mouse awoke from his napping and nibbling, nibbling and napping, and he helped.

Now, Little Red Hen loves to tend her garden with her friends, and she loves to bake bread with her friends.

To share the rewards, do your share of the work.

Storytelling Tips

◉ Use motions to create the illusion of the sleeping dog; the stretching, snoozing cat; and the nibbling, napping mouse.

◉ Use your voice to sound happy and enthusiastic as you describe Little Red Hen enjoying her work.

◉ Speak slowly to emphasize the lazy replies from Beagle, Calico, and Brown Mouse. When the Little Red Hen says, "Then, I will," make the phrase hurried and excited.

◉ Encourage the children to join you in the recurring phrases, "Not I," said the Beagle and the Little Red Hen's words, "Then I will."

◉ Speak like the animals. For example, "Woof, woof, not I," said Beagle. "Meow, meow, not I," said Calico. "Squeak, squeak, not I," said Brown Mouse. "Cluck, cluck, then I will," said Little Red Hen. Try to use a very different voice for each character.

Questions

◉ Do you ever feel lazy? What do you do when you feel like that?

◉ Do you think Little Red Hen should share the bread with Beagle, Calico, and Brown Mouse even though they didn't help her?

◉ Tell us about a time when you helped cook something.

WHAT IS WHEAT?

Materials

Wheat on the stalk (from a farmer, health food store, or bakery)

Metal bowl

Large metal mixing spoon

Steps

◉ If you live in a farming area, ask a farmer for wheat from the fields, or purchase wheat on the stalk from a health food store or bakery.

◉ Show the wheat to the children in its rawest form.

◉ Put the grains of wheat in the metal bowl and crush them with the back of the metal spoon. Show the children how wheat can be ground up to make flour.

◉ Give each child a chance to crush some wheat.

TRY TO REMEMBER

Materials

Paper

Markers

Steps

● Let the children help you recall the story. Remember that younger listeners will probably recall fewer events of the story.

● Encourage the children to draw a sketch of each character (Little Red Hen, Beagle, Calico, and Brown Mouse) or write their names on a sheet of paper.

● Retell the story and help the children arrange the pictures of the characters in the order in which they appeared.

LITTLE RED HEN'S BREAD

Materials

Sheet of paper	Mixer
Marker	Spatula
Box of bread mix	Measuring cup
Water	Measuring spoons
Vegetable oil	Bread pan
Bowl	Breadboard
Oven	

Steps

◉ On the sheet of paper, print the simple instructions for baking bread from the mix.

◉ Read the instructions aloud.

◉ Invite the listeners to participate by saying, "Who will help me measure the flour?" The children can reply, "I will."

◉ Continue with each step of measuring the ingredients and mixing the bread dough with your helpers.

◉ Bake the bread.

◉ Turn the baked bread out onto a breadboard for the children to smell and ask, "Who will help me eat this bread?"

The Elves and the Shoemaker

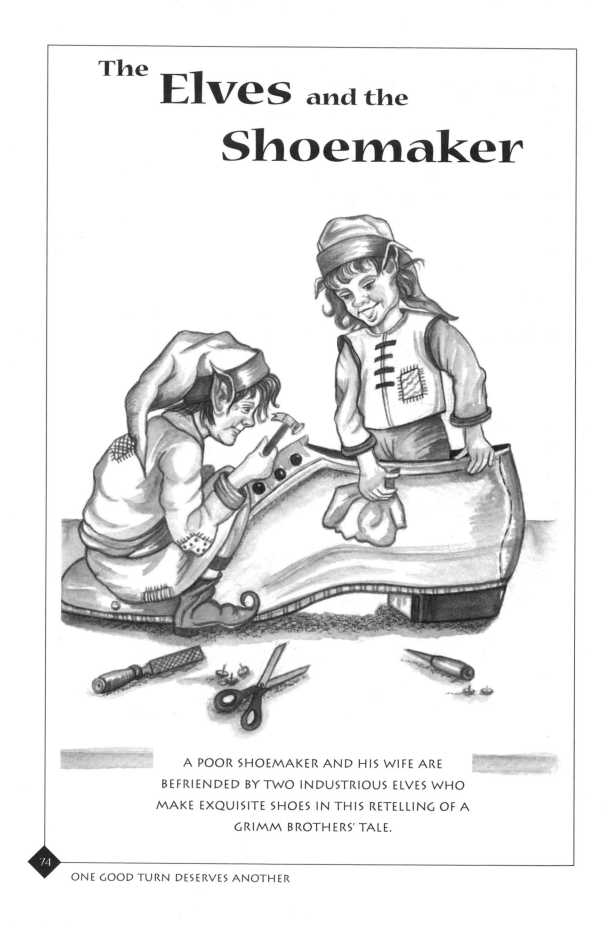

A POOR SHOEMAKER AND HIS WIFE ARE
BEFRIENDED BY TWO INDUSTRIOUS ELVES WHO
MAKE EXQUISITE SHOES IN THIS RETELLING OF A
GRIMM BROTHERS' TALE.

ONE GOOD TURN DESERVES ANOTHER

Once upon a time, a poor shoemaker had a shop on a busy street where many rich people shopped. The shoemaker, his wife, and his children lived above the little store. Rich ladies and gentlemen passed by, but they did not stop because the poor cobbler did not have enough money to buy the leather to make many different pairs of shoes.

The poor shoemaker was very sad. He had just enough leather left in his shop to make one more pair of shoes. He smoothed the leather, found the pattern he wanted to use, and threaded the sharp needle with strong thread. He laid everything out on his workbench—the leather, the pattern, and the sharp needles with strong thread. The clock struck, and he knew it was time to go upstairs for supper. So the poor cobbler left his work on the workbench. He said, "It will be easier to sew tomorrow in the bright morning sunlight."

Make a sad face.

Pretend to thread a needle.

The shoemaker went upstairs. His wife had cooked soup with the last bit of meat and vegetables in the cupboard.

> The poor shoemaker knew that unless he sold the pair of shoes he was going to make tomorrow, his family would have nothing to eat.

After supper, the shoemaker and his wife tucked their two small children into bed. That night, all the shoemaker could dream about was the pair of shoes he would make tomorrow and hope that someone would see them and buy them.

Yawn and use slow, sleepy voice.

Meanwhile, down in the shoemaker's workshop, there were two little visitors.

> Two little elves had sneaked into the shoemaker's shop. They were busy making shoes. They loved their work. They whistled and hummed, sang and laughed as they worked.

Make sewing motions.

They took the shoemaker's leather and cut a new pattern of stylish shoes. They shaped the leather and stitched it together with tiny little stitches. They made delicate designs on the toes and heels. Satisfied with their work, the two little visitors left just before dawn.

Rub eyes in amazement.

The next morning, the shoemaker awoke early and went down to his shop just as the bright sunlight was beaming in the window. The shoemaker rubbed his eyes. He could not believe what he was seeing. There on the workbench was the finest pair of shoes, with the best workmanship he had ever seen. He could not imagine who had made them. The poor shoemaker, desperate for help, placed the shoes in his shop window. Just as he turned to go back to clear his workbench, he heard the bell over his door jingle. A fine gentleman walked into his shop.

The gentleman admired the shoes and tried them on. They were just the right size. The gentleman paid the poor shoemaker much more money than the cobbler usually got for his shoes. With the money, the poor shoemaker bought enough leather for another pair of shoes and enough food to feed his family for a week.

That night, the grateful cobbler carefully laid the leather on his workbench, put the pattern beside the leather, and threaded the sharp needles with the strong thread. He said, "It will be easier to sew tomorrow in the bright morning sunlight." Then, the poor shoemaker went upstairs to enjoy the good supper his wife had cooked for the family. That night he dreamed of making beautiful shoes.

Pretend to sleep.

Meanwhile, down in the shoemaker's workshop, there were two little visitors. Two little elves had sneaked into the shoemaker's shop. They were busy making shoes. They enjoyed their work, so they whistled and hummed, sang and laughed. They took the shoemaker's leather and cut a new pattern of stylish shoes. They shaped the leather and stitched it together with tiny little stitches. They made delicate designs on the toes and heels. Satisfied with their work, the two little elves left just before dawn.

Make sewing motions.

The next morning, the poor shoe-maker went down to his shop. The sunlight was streaming across his workbench. Much to his surprise, there was another beautiful pair of shoes.

Open mouth in amazement.

This time the shoes were for a lady. The leather was stitched with tiny stitches, the soles were soft and smooth, and a beautiful design was stitched on the toes and heels.

The poor shoemaker could barely believe his good fortune. He rushed over to the shop window and placed the beautiful shoes in the window for all the people to see.

THE ELVES AND THE SHOEMAKER

Look pleased.

Everyone stopped to admire them. As the cobbler was clearing off his workbench, he heard the bell over his door jingle. In walked a lovely lady who asked to try on the shoes. They were just the right size for her. She was delighted and paid the poor cobbler twice as much money as he usually received for shoes. After the lady left, the cobbler went and bought enough leather for two pairs of shoes.

That night, the grateful cobbler carefully laid the leather on his workbench, put the pattern beside the leather, and threaded the sharp needles with the strong thread. He said, "It will be easier to sew tomorrow in the bright morning sunlight." Then, the poor shoemaker went upstairs to enjoy the good supper his wife had cooked for the family. That night the shoemaker dreamed of making beautiful shoes.

Pretend to sleep.

Meanwhile, down in the shoemaker's workshop, the two little elves were singing a cheerful song. They whistled and hummed, sang and laughed as they worked twice as fast to make two pairs of shoes. They cut two new patterns for stylish shoes, shaped the leather, and stitched it together with tiny little stitches.

Make sewing motions.

They made delicate designs on the toes and heels. Satisfied with their work, the two little elves left just before dawn.

The poor shoemaker awoke early the next morning to get down to his workbench and begin his long day. He wanted to try to make two pairs of shoes in one day. As he approached his workbench, the sunlight streamed across it. The poor shoemaker rubbed his eyes. He could not

Rub your eyes.

ONE GOOD TURN DESERVES ANOTHER

believe what he was seeing. There on his workbench were two pairs of shoes—two pairs of shoes for two little children. One pair of shoes had laces and the other pair of shoes had straps. The poor shoemaker held them up and admired the tiny stitches, the lovely patterns, and the delicate designs stitched on the toes and heels.

The poor shoemaker placed the two pairs of children's shoes in his store window and turned to go back and clear his workbench. Just then, he heard the jingle of the bell over his shop door. There, standing in the doorway, was a mother with a little boy and girl. She had the children try on the shoes. They fit perfectly.

The mother paid the poor shoemaker much more than the amount of money he was usually paid for shoes.

Look pleased.

The shoemaker hurried to the leather shop and bought enough leather for four pairs of shoes. That night, the grateful cobbler carefully laid the leather on his workbench, put the patterns beside the leather, and threaded the sharp needles with the strong thread. He said, "It will be easier to sew tomorrow in the bright morning sunlight." Then, the poor shoemaker went upstairs to enjoy the good supper his wife had cooked for the family. The shoemaker went to bed and dreamed of making beautiful shoes.

Pretend to sleep.

That night, the shoemaker thought he heard a commotion downstairs in his shop, but he turned over and went back to sleep in his warm bed by the nice fire. In the morning, the shoemaker hurried downstairs to begin his work. After all, he had enough leather for four pairs of shoes so he must hurry and get started. Just as the shoemaker came into the shop, the sunlight streamed across

THE ELVES AND THE SHOEMAKER

Gasp in amazement.

his workbench. There, sitting on the workbench, were four pairs of shoes. One pair for a gentleman, one pair for a lady, and two pairs for children—one with laces and one with straps. The shoemaker could not believe his eyes.

The shoemaker went upstairs to tell his wife about the shoes that seemed to appear like magic. They could scarcely believe their good fortune.

As soon as the shoemaker placed the shoes in his window, a rich family passing by saw the shoes and came in the shop. The shoemaker's wife helped the children try on their shoes while the shoemaker helped the gentleman and the lady. And what do you know? Those shoes fit. The family was so pleased with their beautiful new shoes that they paid the shoemaker much more than the amount of money he was usually paid for shoes.

Look pleased.

After months and months of buying leather, leaving it on the workbench, and finding beautiful shoes, the shoemaker became so curious that he could stand it no longer. So one night, after eating a delicious dinner with his family, and after the children were all tucked in their warm beds, the shoemaker and his wife crept downstairs and hid in a closet in the shoemaker's shop.

When it became pitch dark, they saw a little light begin to shine around the workbench. Then they saw two little men, small as elves, begin to cut and hammer, stitch and sew.

Make sewing motions.

ONE GOOD TURN DESERVES ANOTHER

They cut four new patterns for stylish shoes, shaped the leather, and stitched it together with tiny little stitches. They made delicate designs on the toes and heels. They worked until dawn, then satisfied with their work, the two little elves left.

The shoemaker and his wife were delighted to know who had been making the beautiful shoes. But they were also embarrassed. Here they were dressed so nicely in their new clothes, and the little elves were shivering from the cold with no shoes and jackets to keep them warm.

Pretend to shiver.

The shoemaker and his wife decided to make the elves some clothes and shoes. They stitched little green jackets and made pants and shirts. The wife embroidered the shirts with the tiniest delicate stitches. The shoemaker made teeny, tiny shoes from scraps of leather. When the clothes and shoes were finished, they placed the small jackets and pants, the little embroidered shirts, and the teeny, tiny shoes on the workbench.

Make sewing motions.

That night, the shoemaker and his wife again hid in the closet. The elves arrived when it was pitch dark, and a light shone on the workbench.

Instead of the leather, which they expected to find, the elves saw the small green jackets and pants, the little embroidered shirts, and the teeny, tiny shoes. Surprised, they tried on the clothes, and the clothes fit. They tried on the shoes, and the shoes fit.

Use an excited voice.

The little elves sang and whistled, hummed and laughed. Seeing no more leather on the workbench, they danced out of the shoemaker's shop, making the bell over the door jingle. That jingle was the last the shoemaker and his wife ever heard of the two little elves. But the shoemaker did not mind. He was busy making shoes using the beautiful patterns the elves had left behind. The shoemaker's wife did not mind. She was busy helping all the ladies, gentlemen, and children find the shoes they wanted in the lovely shop on the busy street.

Always repay kindness by being kind.

ONE GOOD TURN DESERVES ANOTHER

Storytelling Tips

- Add drama by speaking slowly and using a sad tone to describe how poor the family was. Speak in a lively way when describing how happy the elves were as they sang and worked.

- Emphasize the size of the elves. Play on the words of the little tiny jackets, small little pants, and t-e-e-e-n-y, t-i-i-i-n-y shoes.

- For younger children, shorten the story by having fewer repetitions of the scenes.

Questions

- How did the elves help the poor shoemaker and his wife?

- Why do you think the elves did not come back after they received their tiny clothes and shoes?

- Have you ever been to a shoemaker's shop? What did you see?

SHOE COLLAGE

Materials

Pictures of shoes cut out from magazines or advertisements

Poster board

Scissors

Glue

Steps

◉ Show the listeners the pictures of different kinds of shoes. Talk about how different shoes are worn for different occasions. Try to include pictures of sneakers, dress shoes, slippers, baby shoes, sandals, boots, and dance shoes.

◉ Tape a large piece of poster board to the wall and invite the children to take turns pasting a shoe picture on it. Encourage the children to overlap the pictures a little to create a collage.

OUR OWN SHOE SHOP

Materials

Pairs of shoes

Measuring device (optional)

Steps

◉ With the children, collect several pairs of family members' shoes.

◉ Arrange them as if they were for sale.

◉ Pretend to be a customer wanting shoes.

◉ Interact with the children by taking the lead in pretending the different roles of shop owner, salesperson, cashier, and customer.

The
White Crane

A POOR FISHERMAN WHO HELPS A WHITE
CRANE ESCAPE FROM A NET IS REPAID BY AN
ORPHAN GIRL WHO WEAVES BEAUTIFUL CLOTH
IN THIS VARIATION OF A TRADITIONAL
JAPANESE FOLKTALE.

ONE GOOD TURN DESERVES ANOTHER

Long ago, there lived a fisherman and his wife who were very poor. Each day, the poor fisherman went to fish on the beautiful lake, so early that the mist from the lake was still rising. Each day, he barely caught enough fish for a meal for himself and his wife.

One day as the poor fisherman was about to pull up anchor and return home, he spotted a beautiful white crane at the edge of the marsh, wildly flapping its wings. **Flap your arms like wings.** The poor fisherman paddled his boat over to the white crane and saw that it was caught in an old net left by a careless fisherman.

The poor fisherman comforted the beautiful white crane, "You are such a beautiful white crane, you should be flying free. Just hold still for a moment while I cut the net so you will be free."

Speak in a gentle voice.

The beautiful white crane stopped flapping its wings and allowed the fisherman to cut the net away.

When the beautiful white crane was free, it flapped its large wings, circled the lovely lake with the mist still rising, and flew right over the small boat of the poor fisherman, as if to say, "Thank you for setting me free!"

That night, the poor fisherman took the day's catch of fish to his wife, who cooked a dish of fish and rice. After the meal, the couple sat by the fire. They were content, except that they wished for a son or daughter for company and to take care of them in their old age, but they had none. They were startled when they heard a knock on the door. When they opened the door, there stood a

Pretend to open the door.

beautiful girl, with long black hair. She was dressed in a lovely white kimono. The old couple invited her in to warm herself by the fire. When she said that she was an orphan, the old couple invited her to stay the night.

Look very happy.

The next morning when the old couple awoke, they found that the young girl had cooked their breakfast, made their tea, straightened all the mats in the house, and cleaned up all the pots that needed scouring. The old couple was delighted. They said, "If we had a daughter, we would want her to be just like you." The young girl said that since she had no parents, she would be their daughter and take care of them in their old age.

Use a serious voice.

For weeks and months, the old couple and the young girl were happy as a family. Every day, the old man went to the lake to fish for their supper. Every day, the old woman went to the fields to work. And, every day while they were gone, the young girl went to the loom and spent the day weaving. She told the old couple that they must never look at her while she was weaving, that what she was weaving was to be a surprise. The old couple remembered the rule and never watched the young girl weaving.

When market day was almost there, the young girl brought out the beautiful cloth she had been weaving. It was the most beautiful fabric the old couple had ever seen.

It was long and flowing, made of beautiful silk with lovely white threads running throughout. When it was held up to the light, it glistened like the mist on the lake at sunrise.

The young girl said to the old couple, "You must take the cloth to the market and sell it so that you will have money for food during the harsh winter."

As the old man was traveling to the village market, each neighbor who saw him asked about the cloth, admired it, and told him how much he should charge. One said, "Oh, you must charge ten gold coins for a cloth as silky as this." Another said, "No, you must charge fifty gold coins for a cloth with these lovely white threads running the length of it."

Pretend to examine the cloth.

Another man said, "No, no, poor fisherman, a cloth as beautiful as the mist on the lake will surely bring you 100 gold coins, enough to last for many harsh winters."

And so it was, the beautiful cloth was sold for 100 gold coins. The old couple could not believe their good fortune. They had enough money for food for many winters, but more importantly, they were blessed with a beautiful daughter to comfort them in their old age.

Look happy.

Each day, the beautiful young girl went into the weaving room to work, and each day she reminded the old couple that no one should look inside the room while she was weaving. The old couple did as she instructed them.

But one day, a curious neighbor came to visit. She had seen the old couple's good fortune, knew they had enough to eat, and admired their beautiful young daughter. The old couple shared their food with their neighbor and recalled all the blessings they had received since their beautiful young daughter came to live with them. They talked about how wonderful it would be to have a daughter to take care of them in their old age.

The neighbor was curious. She wanted to meet the beautiful young daughter. The old couple told the neighbor that the daughter was in the weaving room, weaving cloth so that they could sell it and have enough coins for their old age. But the rule was that no one was to see her while she was working away at the loom. The curious neighbor said, "Oh, I'll just take a peek," and opened the door slightly.

Look amazed.

There she saw a white crane, plucking out beautiful white feathers and turning them into lovely white cloth, as delicate as the mist on the lake. Then, poof—the crane disappeared!

Later, the beautiful young daughter came out of the room with only a half-finished length of cloth with strands too loose to hold it together.

Look sad.

She said, "I'm sorry you did not remember the rule. Thank you for freeing me from the net. I wanted to stay on as your daughter to comfort you in your old age, but the spell is broken. I must return to live on the misty lake."

And before their eyes, their beautiful young daughter turned into the beautiful white crane and flew away.

Flap your arms like wings.

The old fisherman goes each day to fish on the lake. Just as the mist is rising, the beautiful white crane flies twice over the boat of the poor fisherman. The old couple scrape by, but every night they recall the beautiful girl who was almost their daughter.

Shade your eyes and look up.

You must follow the rules or risk losing everything.

Storytelling Tips

◉ Speak in a humble and appreciative voice to express the white crane's gratitude and the ways of the beautiful girl. Use an excited voice when the villagers talk about the beauty of the cloth.

◉ Speak in a serious voice and shake your head "no" each time the young girl reminds the old couple not to look at her while she is weaving.

◉ When the curious neighbor sneaks a peak, pause, let the excitement grow, then say, "Poof! The white crane disappeared!"

Questions

◉ Did the beautiful orphan girl remind you of a fairy godmother? Why or why not?

◉ Do you think the old couple was sad when their daughter turned back into a crane?

◉ Did you ever befriend an animal? What did you do?

STORY SCENES

Materials

Crayons, markers, or
    paint and paint-
    brushes

Paper

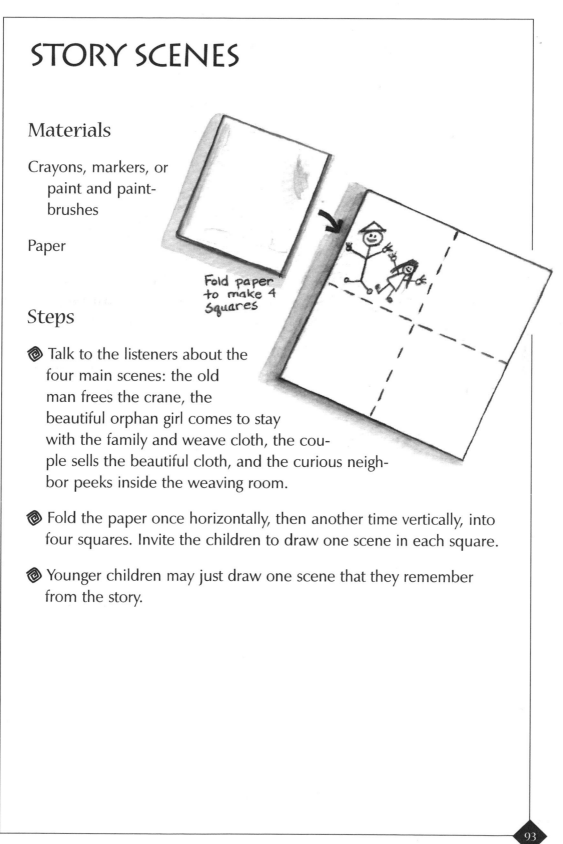

Fold paper
to make 4
Squares

Steps

◉ Talk to the listeners about the
four main scenes: the old
man frees the crane, the
beautiful orphan girl comes to stay
with the family and weave cloth, the couple sells the beautiful cloth, and the curious neighbor peeks inside the weaving room.

◉ Fold the paper once horizontally, then another time vertically, into
four squares. Invite the children to draw one scene in each square.

◉ Younger children may just draw one scene that they remember
from the story.

HELPING THE BIRDS

Materials

Bag of birdseed

Shallow pan for holding birdseed

Toilet paper tubes

Peanut butter

Butter knives

Yarn

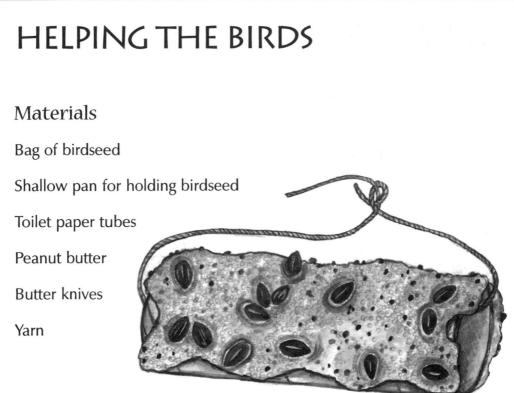

Steps

◉ Pour birdseed into the shallow pan.

◉ Invite the listeners to spread peanut butter on their tubes, then roll them in the birdseed.

◉ Help the children thread a length of yarn through their tubes. Tie ends together to create a loop for hanging.

◉ Take the children outside to hang their birdfeeders. Watch for a while to see if any birds come to feed.

KIMONO MATCH-UP

Materials

Wallpaper samples with delicate floral designs

Scissors

Paper, glue, markers (optional)

Steps

◉ Ahead of time, cut two kimono shapes from each wallpaper design.

◉ Spread out the kimono shapes on a flat surface and invite the children to find the matching pairs.

◉ When they are tired of the matching game, they might paste a kimono shape on a piece of paper and draw the girl from the story wearing it.

Learning From Mistakes

Henny-Penny and Four Fine-Feathered Friends

IN THIS VARIATION OF A POPULAR TALE, HENNY-
PENNY THINKS THE SKY IS FALLING WHEN AN
ACORN HITS HER ON THE HEAD, AND SHE SETS
OFF WITH HER FRIENDS TO WARN THE KING.

Once upon a time, there was a pretty little red hen named Henny-Penny. She lived in a barnyard with other fine-feathered friends. The farmer's wife scattered lots of good corn around the barnyard. The barnyard was circled with big oak trees where the fine-feathered friends could rest in the shade.

One day, Henny-Penny was peck, peck, pecking along, eating the corn the farmer's wife had scattered in the barnyard when suddenly something hit her right on top of her head. Plunk! Henny-Penny raised up from her peck, peck, pecking, and said, "What was that?"

Wince and touch your head.

She looked up into the sky and said at the top of her clucking voice,

"Something just hit me on the head. The sky must be falling. Goodness, gracious me! It must be that the sky is falling! I must go and tell the King so that he can warn all the animals and tell all the people in the land."

Look up in a puzzled way.

So, she set off on the path walking as fast as she could to find the King to tell him that the sky was falling.

Soon, Henny-Penny met Cocky-Locky. Cocky-Locky said, "Where are you going in such a hurry, Henny-Penny?"

Rushing along, Henny-Penny said, "I am off to see the King."

"Why are you going to see the King?" asked Cocky-Locky.

"The sky is falling!" said Henny-Penny. "I am going to tell

the King so that he can warn all the animals and tell all the people."

Look up in a puzzled way.

Looking up at the sky, Cocky-Locky said, "I see the sky. It is not falling."

"Yes, it is," said Henny-Penny. "A piece of it hit me on the head."

With that explanation, Cocky-Locky said, "I will go with you." And he strutted along behind Henny-Penny, who rushed along as fast as her little legs would carry her.

Soon they met Ducky-Lucky, who asked, "Where are you going in such a hurry?"

"The sky is falling!" said Cocky-Locky. "We are going to tell the King so that he can warn all the animals and tell all the people."

Look up in a puzzled way.

Looking up at the sky, Ducky-Lucky said, "I see the sky. It is not falling."

"Yes, it is," said Cocky-Locky. "A piece of it hit Henny-Penny on the head."

With that explanation, Ducky-Lucky said, "I will go with you." And he waddled along behind Cocky-Locky, who strutted along after Henny-Penny, who rushed along as fast as her little legs would carry her.

Soon they met Turkey-Lurkey, who asked, "Where are you going in such a hurry?"

"We are going to see the King," said Ducky-Lucky.

"Why are you going to see the King?" asked Turkey-Lurkey.

"The sky is falling!" said Ducky-Lucky. "We are going to tell the King so that he can warn all the animals and tell all of the people."

Looking up at the sky, Turkey-Lurkey said, "I see the sky. It is not falling."

Look up in a puzzled way.

"Yes it is," said Ducky-Lucky. "A piece of it hit Henny-Penny on the head."

With that explanation, Turkey-Lurkey strolled behind Ducky-Lucky, who waddled behind Cocky-Locky, who strutted behind Henny-Penny, who rushed along as fast as her little legs would carry her.

Soon they met Goosey-Loosey, who asked, "Where are you going in such a hurry?"

"We are going to see the King," said Turkey-Lurkey.

"Why are you going to see the King?" asked Goosey-Loosey.

"The sky is falling!" said Turkey-Lurkey. "We are going to tell the King so that he can warn all the animals and tell all the people."

Looking up at the sky, Goosey-Loosey said, "I see the sky. It is not falling."

Look up in a puzzled way.

"Yes, it is," said Turkey-Lurkey. "A piece of it hit Henny-Penny on the head."

With that explanation, Goosey-Loosey said, "Then, I will go with you." And Goosey-Loosey waddled behind Turkey-Lurkey, who strode behind Ducky-Lucky, who waddled behind Cocky-Locky, who strutted behind Henny-Penny, who rushed along as fast as her little legs would carry her.

Use a sly, calm voice.

Soon the five friends met Foxy-Loxy. "Where are you five feathered friends going in such a hurry?" asked Foxy-Loxy.

"We are going to see the King," they all said in unison.

"Why are you going to see the King?" asked Foxy-Loxy.

"The sky is falling!" said the five feathered friends in one voice. "We are going to tell the King so that he can warn all the animals and tell all the people."

"Do you know the way to the King's castle?" asked Foxy-Loxy.

Point to your right.

The five feathered friends looked at each other and said in unison, "No, but we think that it is this way."

Foxy-Loxy said, "Well, let me lead you. I know the way."

Point to your left.

So, Foxy-Loxy pointed his nose in a new direction and Goosey-Loosey, Turkey-Lurkey, Ducky-Lucky, Cocky-Locky, and Henny-Penny followed him.

They walked over hill and valley, up and down, until they came to a cave. Foxy-Loxy said, "Through this cave on the other side is the castle where the King lives."

The five feathered friends thanked Foxy-Loxy for pointing the way. But, they never found the King. And they never got to tell him that the sky was falling. Henny-Penny, Cocky-Locky, Ducky-Lucky, Turkey-Lurkey, and Goosey-Loosey were never seen again. But, five different kinds of feathers were spotted all around Foxy-Loxy's cave.

Do not believe everything you hear.

Storytelling Tips

● Speak Henny-Penny's words in an excited, frightened voice.

● Add animal sounds by saying, "Cluck, cluck, the sky is falling!" "Cock-a-doodle-doo, the sky is falling!" "Quack, quack, the sky is falling!" "Gobble-gobble, the sky is falling!" "Honk, honk, the sky is falling!"

● Simplify the story for younger listeners by using fewer feathered friends.

● Ask the children to say the names of Henny-Penny's friends as they form a line to follow Henny-Penny.

● Use a hand motion to signal to the children to repeat phrases with you. For example, every time you point to the sky the children say, "The sky is falling."

Questions

● Why do you think all of Henny-Penny's friends believed her when she said the sky was falling?

● If the five feathered friends had reached the King, do you think he would have believed them?

● Have you ever been alarmed by something that later turned out to have a simple explanation?

LEARNING FROM MISTAKES

BARNYARD ANIMALS

Materials

None needed

Steps

 After telling the story several times, ask the listeners if they remember all of the characters.

 Invite them to think of some other barnyard animals that Henny-Penny could have met in addition to Cocky-Locky, Ducky-Lucky, Turkey-Lurkey, and Goosey-Loosey. You might add Piggy-Wiggy, or Kitty-Katty, or Sheepy-Sleepy.

 Retell the story, adding the children's new characters.

 Let younger children retell the story by changing the characters' names—for example, by reversing the words in a name (Lucky-Ducky), by simplifying the names (Duck), or by making up new names (Quacky).

GOSSIP GAME

Materials

Sheet of paper and pencil

Steps

🌀 Write down a phrase such as, "Henny-Penny got so excited and scared all the other fine-feathered friends." Make the phrase long enough that it is hard to remember. Fold the paper and put it away. Do not show it to the children.

🌀 Invite the children to sit in a circle. Whisper the phrase in the first child's ear and ask her to "pass it on" by whispering it to the next child and so forth until everyone has both heard and repeated the phrase.

🌀 When the last child whispers it to you, say it aloud just the way you heard it from him. Unfold the paper, read the phrase that you started with, and compare the two versions.

The Boy Who Cried Wolf

IN THIS VERSION OF THE AESOP FABLE, A YOUNG BOY LEARNS THAT IF HE CALLS "WOLF" WHEN THERE IS NO WOLF, PEOPLE WILL NOT TRUST HIM WHEN HE TELLS THE TRUTH.

Once there was a young boy

who lived with his family in a valley surrounded by high mountains. It was the tradition in his village that young boys go to the mountains and watch over the sheep herds owned by the village people.

One day the young boy's father came to him and said, "The time has come for you to go to the mountains and watch the sheep. It is a job with great responsibility, but you are now old enough and capable of assuming this important work."

Speak in a serious tone.

The father explained to his son that he would be alone on the mountain with the sheep for long periods of time. The father warned the boy that he must constantly watch the sheep because wolves and bears lived on the mountain, too.

> If the boy ever felt that the sheep were in danger, he was to call "Wolf! Wolf!" The villagers would come and help.

The young boy was pleased that his father felt he had reached an age where he was capable of such great responsibility. He packed his backpack with food, warm clothing, and a flute. Then he herded the sheep to the mountains so they could graze on the grass.

Speak in an excited tone.

During the first weeks on the mountain, the young boy was very happy. He watched the sheep as they ate and walked around the mountain ridges. He threw stones. He watched the clouds. He played his flute. He felt very proud that he was able to take care of the sheep.

Pretend to play a flute.

After many weeks alone on the mountain, the young boy became very lonely. He missed his family and friends. He grew tired of watching the sheep. He was even tired of playing his flute. The young boy thought of a way he could get some of the villagers to come to the mountain. If his plan worked, he would no longer be lonely.

Look sad.

He ran to the top of the mountain ridge and called loudly, "Wolf! Wolf! Wolf!"

The villagers heard his cry. They were afraid that the young boy was in trouble and that a wolf was attacking the sheep. They rushed to the mountains to help the boy. When they arrived, they found no wolf. Because they had been so concerned about the safety of the young boy and his sheep, they stayed and talked to him. They admired his sheep. Later in the evening, they returned to their homes in the valley.

Sound concerned.

The young boy was happy that the villagers had come. He missed them and was lonely again. So, he went to the top of the mountain and he called, "Wolf! Wolf! Wolf!"

The villagers heard his cry. They were concerned for the safety of the young boy and the sheep. So they walked the long road up the mountain to help the boy again. When they reached the top of the mountain, they did not find a wolf. Since there was no danger for the boy and the sheep, they walked the long way back down the mountain and returned to their homes.

Look concerned.

Sound very
alarmed.

Shortly after the villagers had returned home, a real wolf came to the mountain. As the young boy was watching the sheep, he saw the wolf creep from behind the trees and slowly move toward the sheep. The young boy was frightened. He ran to the top of the mountain and called, "Wolf! Wolf! Wolf!"

Sound even
more alarmed.

But no one came. He called louder, "Wolf! Wolf! Wolf!"

The villagers heard the cry of the young boy. They remembered that they had walked the long road up the mountain and had found no wolf. They thought the boy was playing another trick on them. So no one went to the mountain to help the young boy.

The young boy was very afraid. He threw rocks at the wolf, then yelled and screamed. All of the sheep ran away. He climbed across the mountain ridges and looked and looked for the sheep. He searched for days but he never found the villagers' sheep. Finally, the boy had to return to the village.

Look ashamed.

His father saw him coming down the steep mountain trail. He ran to meet his son and asked, "Where are the sheep?"

The boy told his father, "A wolf came and I threw stones at him to scare him away. Then all the sheep ran away. I have looked and looked for the sheep, but I cannot find them."

His father asked, "Why didn't you call 'Wolf! Wolf! Wolf'?"

The boy answered sadly, "I called 'Wolf! Wolf! Wolf!' but no one came to help me."

The young boy always remembered the day the wolf came. He promised himself that never again would he call "Wolf!" when there was no wolf.

Always tell the truth or no one will believe what you say.

Storytelling Tips

- When telling this story, describe the boy as being about the same age and size as the listeners.

- Cup your hands around your mouth each time the boy calls "Wolf."

- When the boy calls "Wolf, wolf, wolf" the very last time (when the wolf is really there), make your voice sound louder and more alarmed than when he calls "Wolf! Wolf! Wolf!" to get the villagers to come.

- You can vary the length of this story and still maintain the essential elements. Shorten or lengthen the story depending on the needs, interests, and abilities of the specific audience.

Questions

- Why was the young boy proud to be selected to take care of the sheep on the mountain?

- Why did the villagers refuse to help the boy when the wolf came to the mountain?

- What would you have done if you were lonely on the mountain?

LEARNING FROM MISTAKES

SHEEP AND WOOL

Materials

Pictures of sheep and lambs

Collection of wool clothing or fabric

Steps

◉ Share the pictures of sheep and lambs with the listeners.

◉ Discuss how they look, what they eat, and the wool they produce.

◉ Collect clothing and fabric made of wool.

◉ Compare and feel the different textures of the materials.

HELPING OUT

Materials

Paper

Marker

Steps

◉ Discuss some of the
responsibilities of individual
family members. For exam-
ple, mother takes out
garbage, sister takes
dog for walks, brother
brings in the paper.

◉ Encourage the children to suggest new
responsibilities they can assume to help the family. Examples might
be to feed a pet, water a growing plant, or put dirty clothes in a
hamper.

◉ Write down the task on the paper. Let the children record (on the
chart paper or on a calendar) each time the "new responsibility" is
accomplished.

LEARNING FROM MISTAKES

How the Animals Came to Be as They Are

Why the Possum Has a Skinny Tail

THIS ADAPTATION OF A CHEROKEE TALE TELLS
HOW POSSUM, WHO ONCE HAD A LONG, BEAU-
TIFUL, BUSHY TAIL LIKE THAT OF THE SQUIRREL,
CAME TO HAVE A LONG, SKINNY TAIL
WITH NO FUR.

HOW THE ANIMALS GOT TO BE AS THEY ARE

Long ago, Possum used to stay awake in the daytime and sleep at night. And, long ago, Possum had a long, beautiful bushy tail, not a long skinny tail. Possum used to prance around the woods, showing her long, beautiful bushy tail to all the other animals.

Whenever Possum saw Squirrel scampering up a tree, she would call out, "Why Squirrel, I do admire your bushy tail, but it isn't nearly as long and bushy as my tail is."

Use a bragging voice.

Whenever Possum met Rabbit scurrying through the underbrush, she said, "Rabbit, I do admire your soft cottony tail, but my tail is so long and bushy, not a short little tail like yours."

Whenever Possum met Deer crossing one of the trails through the woods, she said, "Deer, I do admire your white tail and the way it points up to the sky, but my tail is so long and bushy that I can wrap it around my shoulders."

Pretend to throw tail over shoulder.

Soon, all the animals grew tired of hearing about Possum's long, beautiful bushy tail. They began to avoid Possum. Whenever they saw her coming, they ran in the opposite direction.

Every year in the fall, when the leaves turned lovely colors, the animals of the woods had a stomp dance. All the animals came to say good-bye to each other before they hibernated or migrated, or had to wander far to graze for food. Every year they looked forward to the pow-wow and the stomp dancing and the time they would spend together. At the pow-wow, Bear beat a big hollow log and

Stomp feet.

all the animals danced. The squirrels did the stomp dance. The rabbit and all the other animals of the forest joined in and danced around in a circle.

Possum always looked forward to the fall pow-wow and stomp dance. She got to show off her long, beautiful, bushy tail. Possum arrived late to the stomp dance. She pranced into the line of dancers with her long, beautiful bushy tail draped around her shoulders. Bear beat the log drum for an extremely long dance. Possum moved back and forth, swaying and parading her beautiful tail, but she became so tired that she let her tail drag on the ground. Someone stepped on the end of her tail. She shouted for them to move, but Bear was beating the drum so loud that no one could hear her.

Use tired voice.

The animals kept on dancing around in the circle, taking more and more steps on Possum's tail.

Make pulling motion.

So Possum began to pull. She pulled and tugged on her tail trying to get it out from under the feet of the dancers. She pulled harder, and harder, and harder. Finally, she pulled her tail free. There was nothing left but a long, skinny tail with not a single hair or tuft of fur. Possum ran away and hid. She vowed never to come out in the day-light and let the other animals see that she no longer had a long, beautiful bushy tail. She had a long, skinny, hair-less tail instead.

And, to this day, all possums have skinny tails. And, to this day, the possum sleeps all day and only comes out at night.

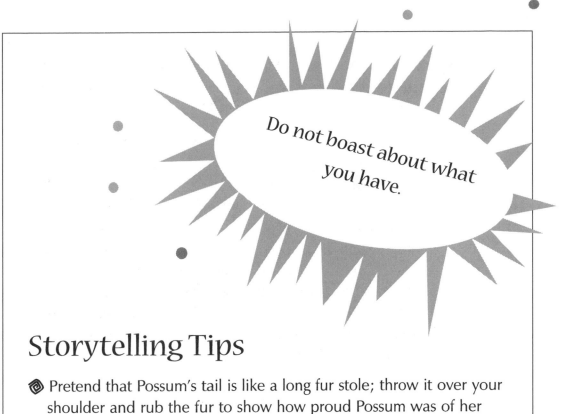

Do not boast about what you have.

Storytelling Tips

◉ Pretend that Possum's tail is like a long fur stole; throw it over your shoulder and rub the fur to show how proud Possum was of her beautiful tail.

◉ When telling about the animals at the stomp dance, tap on your legs to imitate the sound of a drum.

◉ Young listeners might not be familiar with the stomp dance. Show them how stomp dancers move their feet but keep their upper body rigid. Pretend to stomp to the beat of a drum.

Questions

◉ Do you think that this is a true story? Why or why not?

◉ Why did the other animals avoid Possum?

◉ Have you ever felt really proud of something? How did you act?

DANCE TO THE DRUM

Materials

Drum

Drumstick or mallet

Steps

◉ Beat a drum slowly and steadily.

◉ Invite the children to move around in a circle, dancing with feet and legs but little upper body movement.

◉ Change the beat of the drum and let the children improvise movements to different tempos.

PLAYING OPOSSUM

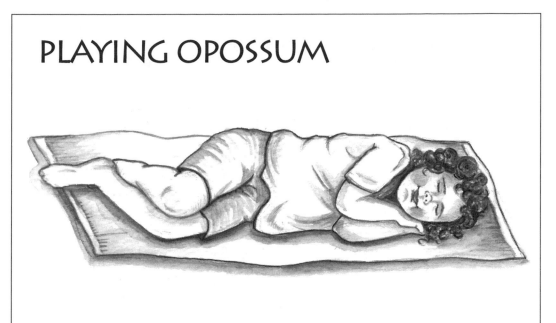

Materials

None needed

Steps

◉ Explain to the listeners that an opossum can escape its enemies by laying very still and not attracting their attention.

◉ Invite the children to play Opossum. One at a time they lie on the floor in the middle of a circle of children. They should try for one minute not to move or giggle. Let each child have a turn.

Why Crocodile Does Not Eat Hen

IN THIS SHORT BANTU TALE, HEN CONVINCES
CROCODILE THAT THEY ARE BROTHER AND SIS-
TER, AND FOR THIS REASON HE SHOULD NOT
EAT HER.

Hen was out for a stroll one day

when she decided to walk along the bank of the river. She enjoyed the river walk because she could always find good food to eat.

As Hen strolled and pecked, and pecked and strolled, Crocodile saw her coming and thought, "Yum, yum, yum, that little hen would make a tasty morsel." He raised his huge head out of the water, opened his powerful jaws, and almost chomped down on Hen, who was chasing a dragonfly and not paying attention to where she was going. She almost walked into Crocodile's open jaws.

Use a sly voice.

Put palms together and open hands like jaws.

Hen jumped back and said, "Brother Crocodile, do not eat me. Did you not recognize me? I am your sister, Hen." She showed no fear.

Use a brave voice.

Crocodile was so surprised that he shut his huge open jaws with a loud SNAP. He thought, "Why did that little morsel of a hen call me her brother? I am not a brother to a hen. I am a crocodile. Crocodiles don't have sisters who are hens. She has tricked me."

Snap hands shut.

But it was too late to catch Hen now. She had gone on strolling and pecking, pecking and strolling along the riverbank. And Crocodile slid back into the water and swam away.

The next day, Hen came strolling and pecking, pecking and strolling along the bank of the river. She was chasing a water bug. Just then, up from the edge of the river, appeared a large head, with huge jaws that were open wide. As they were about to close around her, Hen said,

Open hands like jaws.

"Brother Crocodile, do not eat me. Did you not recognize me? I am your sister, Hen." And showing no fear, she stood her ground.

Snap hands shut.

SNAP! Crocodile shut his huge jaws, empty. Before he could ask Hen what she meant, she had hurried along the riverbank. So again, Crocodile thought, "Hen has tricked me a second time. My brothers and sisters are crocodiles, not hens."

He vowed to catch her the next day. As he swam off he thought, "Hens cannot be related to crocodiles. Hens live on the land. Crocodiles live in the water. I am going to eat that hen for my lunch tomorrow."

Open hands and snap them shut.

Crocodile was so angry with himself for missing Hen for lunch that he slapped his tail on the water and snapped his jaws open and shut. He made such a commotion that Lizard, who had been sunning himself on a nearby rock said, "Why are you so angry? What's bothering you?"

"It's Hen, that one who strolls and pecks, pecks and strolls by the river bank. She said that I am her brother. She even calls me Brother Crocodile. She says that she is my sister. How can that be?" asked Crocodile.

Lizard, who was the wise one, said, "It is true, Crocodile. You and Hen are members of the same family."

Speak with disbelief.

"It can't be," said Crocodile. "I live in the water. She lives on the land."

Lizard repeated, "I tell you it is true. Turtles lay eggs, ducks lay eggs, birds lay eggs. Crocodiles and lizards lay eggs. And, you know, Hen lays eggs. So, all who lay eggs are brothers and sisters."

"All? Even Hen?" asked Crocodile for one last time.

"Even Hen," Lizard reassured him.

"Hen is my sister. What a lunch that little morsel of chicken would have made. What a shame to have such a delicious sister and not be able to have her for lunch," Crocodile thought as he slid back into the water.

The next day, Hen came strolling and pecking, pecking and strolling along the bank of the river. Up from the water came the huge head of the Crocodile. "Why aren't you afraid of me?" said Crocodile. "I could SNAP my jaws shut and you would be my lunch."

Open hands like jaws.

"I'm not afraid of you because you are my brother," clucked the confident little Hen. And, she stood her ground. She stared right straight into those big Crocodile eyes and clucked, "I am your sister. You would not eat your sister." And Crocodile got a big Crocodile tear in his eyes, and slid back into the water.

To this day, when Hen goes strolling and pecking, pecking and strolling, Crocodile thinks, "There goes my sister." And Hen just waves and says, "There goes my big brother."

Snap hands shut.

We are not as different from others as we might think.

Storytelling Tips

◉ Whenever Crocodile rises from and slides into the water, raise and lower your hands with palms together like jaws.

◉ Say "Cluck, cluck" before Hen speaks.

◉ Show the listeners how to make the sound of snapping Crocodile jaws. Put one hand on top of the other and open and shut them to create a snapping sound.

◉ Even though Hen is little, you should speak her lines in a strong, confident voice.

Questions

◉ What other animals lay eggs?

◉ Do you think Crocodile and Hen are alike in any other ways?

◉ Do you think Hen is brave? Why or why not?

I'M A BIG HUGE CROC

Materials

Large piece of paper and pencil or poster board and markers

Steps

◉ Write the following words on the paper or poster board. Chant them or sing them to the tune of "I'm a Little White Duck Swimming in the Water."

I'm a big huge croc,
Swimming in the water.
A big huge croc,
Doing what I oughter.
Snap! Snap! Snap!

I'm a little red hen,
Strolling and pecking,
I'm a little red hen,
Strolling and pecking,
Cluck! Cluck! Cluck!

I'm a big huge croc,
Looking for my lunch.
I'm a big huge croc,
Looking for my lunch.
Snap! Snap! Snap!

Brother Croc,
Swimming in the water,
Sister Hen,
Strolling and pecking,
Snap! Cluck! Snap! Cluck!
Fam-i-ly.

◉ Sing or chant the words more than once and leave the printed page or poster out for the children to read or "pretend" to read when singing along.

ANIMAL FAMILIES

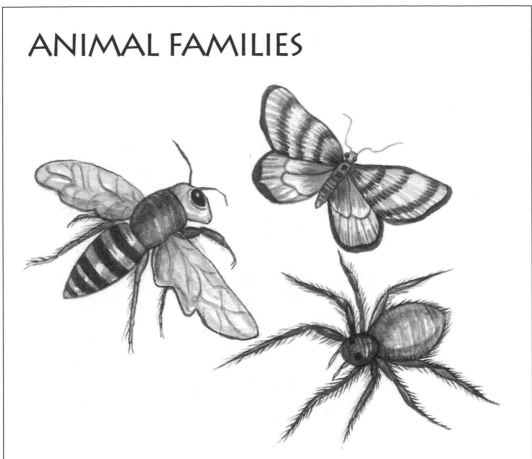

Materials

Pictures cut from magazines of different kinds of animals, or plastic
animals including mammals, fish, birds, and insects

Steps

◉ Show the listeners the animal pictures or plastic figures and talk
about how the animals are alike and how they are different.

◉ Invite the children to sort the pictures or plastic figures according
to their own criteria for how they are alike.

◉ Ask the children to explain how they sorted the pictures or plastic
animals.

HOW THE ANIMALS GOT TO BE AS THEY ARE

How the Camel Got His Humph

IN THIS VERSION OF A RUDYARD KIPLING STORY,
A LAZY CAMEL IS GIVEN A "HUMPH" BY THE
DJINN, A MAGIC MAN, WHEN HE REFUSES TO
HELP THE OTHER ANIMALS WITH THEIR WORK.

When the world was new there

was a lot of work to do, and all the animals had to work very hard. Camel lived in the middle of the Howling Desert because he did not want to work. He ate sticks and thorns and milkweed and prickles. He never worked and he didn't talk. If anyone spoke to Camel all he would say was "Humph!"

Move your jaws slowly as if chewing.

Horse came by the desert one day and he saw Camel. Horse had a saddle on his back and a bit in his mouth. "O Camel, O Camel," he said. "Come and work with us. There is much work to do."

Use a pleading voice.

Camel looked at the Horse working. All he said was "Humph!" Horse went away and told the man that Camel would not work and that all he said was "Humph!"

Soon Dog came to the Camel. Dog had a stick in his mouth. He looked at Camel and said, "O Camel, O Camel, come and work with us. There is much to do."

Use a pleading voice.

Camel looked at the dog and all he said was "Humph!"

Dog went to tell the man that Camel was not working. All he would say was "Humph!"

Use a pleading voice.

Later, Ox came to Camel, who was standing in the desert. Ox had a yoke on his neck. "Camel, O Camel, come plow and work with us. There is much work to do," said Ox.

"Humph!" said Camel.

HOW THE ANIMALS GOT TO BE AS THEY ARE

Ox went to the man and told him that Camel would not work. All he would say was "Humph!"

At the end of the day the man called Horse, Dog, and Ox together. He said, "The world is so new and there is so much to do. Because Camel in the desert will not work, you three must work twice as hard. You have to do more work to make up for Camel not working."

Use a deep strong voice.

This made the three—Horse, Dog, and Ox—very angry. They held a big meeting at the edge of the desert to talk about their problem. Camel walked over to where they were meeting. All he said was "Humph!" and walked away.

Hold up three fingers.

Now the Djinn, the magic man in charge of the deserts, came rolling along in a cloud of dust. He stopped at the meeting of the three: Horse, Dog, and Ox.

"Djinn of all the Deserts, is it right for anyone not to work when the world is so new and there is so much to do?" they asked.

Speak in a desperate voice.

"Certainly not," said the Djinn. "Who is not working?"

Horse said, "In the middle of the Howling Desert is a thing, he has a long neck and long legs. He has never worked. All he says is Humph!"

Nod your head knowingly.

"Ooh, that must be Camel," said the Djinn.

"He won't carry," said Dog.

"He won't plow," said Ox.

"Does he do anything?" asked the Djinn.

Spin hands around.

"He only says Humph!" said the three.

The Djinn rolled himself up and flew across the desert. When he found Camel standing next to a pool of water looking at himself, he asked, "What is this I hear? You are not doing any work? When the world is so new and there is so much to do?"

"Humph!" said Camel as he continued to admire his reflection in the pool.

> "Because you are not working, the Horse, Dog, and Ox must work extra hard. They must do all of the work," said the Djinn.

Use an angry voice.

"Humph!" said Camel.

"You shouldn't say that word again. You might say it once too often," said the Djinn.

Look amazed and speak slow- ly.

Camel said, "Humph!"

Suddenly, Camel's back began to puff up. It puffed and puffed into a great big humph.

Sound confused.

"Do you see that great big humph on your back? That's your humph, which you brought upon yourself for not working. Now you are going to work," said the Djinn.

"How can I?" asked Camel.

"You missed three days of work, so now you can go three days without eating. You will work for three days without stopping because you can live off your humph. You will not have to have any food or drink. You will work very hard."

Camel joined the other three working: Horse, Dog, and Ox.

Hold up three fingers.

Since that time Camel has always had a humph on his back, so he can work three days without eating or resting. And from that day to this one, Camel has always worn a "Humph."

When there is much work to do, everyone needs to help.

HOW THE CAMEL GOT HIS HUMPH

Storytelling Tips

- ◉ Try different ways of saying "Humph" that will match Camel and his attitude about working. Once you select an intonation, use it consistently.

- ◉ Repeat the sentence, "Why are you not working when the world is so new and there is so much to do?" in the same rhythm and phrasing each time even when said by different characters. Repeated phrases help young children follow the story line and join in the telling.

- ◉ The Djinn is a magic man, so his voice should have a very mysterious quality. Using a soft voice will sometimes communicate a character's unique qualities.

- ◉ Make sure the children have time to visualize the transformation of the Camel's back. Speak slowly when you say, "Camel's back began to puff up. It puffed and puffed and puffed…"

Questions

- ◉ What kind of work did Horse, Dog, and Ox do?

- ◉ Have you ever felt angry when someone didn't help you do some work?

- ◉ Why was it possible for Camel to work three days without eating after he got his "humph?"

THE MYSTERIOUS CAMEL

Materials

Children's book, magazine article, or encyclopedia entry about camels

Paper

Markers or crayons

Steps

◉ Show the listeners an informational book or article with pictures telling about camels.

◉ Read some of the information to them, especially about the camel's hump and what's inside it.

◉ Invite the children to draw a camel with one or more humps.

SANDY FUN

Materials

Baby bathtub or large plastic bowl

White sand

Household items to use in the sand, such as measuring cups, spoons/forks, sifter, small cups, empty clear plastic bottles, strainer

Steps

◉ Put about three inches (eight centimeters) of sand in the plastic tub.

◉ Place the sand-filled tub where the children can explore it.

◉ Add a few household items to extend the possibilities.

◉ Ask the children about the sand. How does it feel? How does it move? Can it be measured? Can you build with it?

◉ Add a small amount of water to the sand so the children can mold it.

Why the Burro Lives with the Man

THIS STORY, BASED ON A MEXICAN FOLKTALE,
TELLS WHY BENITO THE BURRO CHOSE TO GIVE
UP HIS FREEDOM ON THE MESA TO LIVE ON THE
MAN'S LAND, WHERE HE WOULD ALWAYS HAVE
TO WORK FOR THE GREEN GRASS AND COOL
WATER.

Once there was a burro named

Benito, who lived in a place where he felt very safe. Benito was happy there, but sometimes Benito complained, "Hee-haw, hee-haw, I have only sagebrush and cactus to eat. It is so sandy here. I wish I could live where there is green grass to graze and cool water to drink."

Sigh
unhappily.

But Benito stayed where he was because there on the mesa he was safe from Mountain Lion. Mountain Lion did not come to the areas where there was so little water to drink.

One day, tired of eating only cactus and sagebrush and being afraid of Mountain Lion, Benito pranced around the mesa and said, "If I ever meet Mountain Lion again, I will not be afraid of him. I will turn my backside toward him and, with my hind legs, I will kick Mountain Lion all over this mesa." And with those courageous words, Benito galloped around and kicked and kicked every sagebrush bush in sight.

Pretend to kick.

Just as Benito finished a very big kick, he thought he heard a sound behind him. As he turned he saw Don Coyote.

"Buenos dias, Senor Benito," said Don Coyote. "I am very pleased to see you enjoying your new home on the mesa."

Use a sly, coy
voice when Don
Coyote speaks.

"Why do you sneak up behind me?" asked Benito. "I thought you were Mountain Lion. Have you no respect for others, that you sneak up behind them and frighten them?"

HOW THE ANIMALS GOT TO BE AS THEY ARE

"Oh, amigo!" said Don Coyote. "Are you not glad to see your dear friend? Yes, no?"

Smile insincerely.

"I know you too well, Don Coyote. What is it you want from me?" asked Benito.

"Well, Amigo Benito, just this morning, I was speaking of you when I met Mountain Lion. He said, 'Do you know where Benito has gone? I am looking for him.' In my mind I thought, there are only two places where Benito can be, *here* or *there*. Since he is not *here*, Benito must be *there*. Now where could *there* be but over on the mesa. So I decided to pay you a visit and see if you were there. And you are. You are here on the mesa."

Point in different directions.

"Did you tell Mountain Lion where you were going to look for me?" asked Benito.

"No," said Coyote, "but he wants me to tell him where you are."

"You mean varmint, Don Coyote. You would tell the lion where to find me? You deserve to be kicked!"

Benito turned to kick Coyote with his hind legs, when Coyote said, "Oh, amigo, you are wrong. I did not tell Mountain Lion where to find you. I came here to tell you that Mountain Lion was looking for you, not to show Mountain Lion where to find you."

"I don't know whether to believe you or not, Don Coyote. You are a sly one," said Benito.

"How would you like to live where it is safe from Mountain Lion?" asked Don Coyote. "In a place that is lush with green pastures and much cool water to drink?"

Change tone to
sound interest-
ed.
"Where is that?" asked Benito.

"At the foot of those hills below the mesa," he answered, pointing over the cliff to the green pastures below. "It is where the man lives. The man is the only creature Mountain Lion fears. You will be safe there," said Coyote coyly.

Point into
distance.

"I know about the man," said Benito. "The animals that live behind his fence must work for him. He gives them green pastures and much cool water to drink, but they are not free. The fence keeps them from going where they want to go."

"The fence keeps Mountain Lion from eating the animals," said Don Coyote.

"Why do you care what happens to me, if I am safe?" asked Benito.

"Amigo, amigo," said Don Coyote, "when I think of vicious Mountain Lion and the harmless animals he attacks, I am always concerned for the safety of one as good as you."

"Is that all that concerns you?" asked Benito.

"Well, amigo, there is just one other little thing. I hear the chickens that are kept behind the man's fence. I hear them clucking and squawking and crowing, saying that they want to be free. They even scratch along the fence trying to dig a way to get out. I would just like to set the chickens and the roosters free from behind the fence. I have tried to set them free many times, but the man will not let them go," said Don Coyote, almost crying.

Sound sad.

"Benito, amigo, Benito, I could lead you to the man's land—to a place where you will always be safe from Mountain Lion. A place where the grass is always green and the water is always cool. When we get there, you could jump the fence and kick a hole in it with your strong hind legs. Through the hole, you could pass the chickens out to me, so that I can set them free. I will help you, and you will help me free those nice, plump...I mean those poor chickens wanting to be free."

Smile slyly.

Benito looked at Don Coyote. Don Coyote looked at Benito with a pleading look in his eye. "Don Coyote, I am an honest burro. You just want me to help you steal those chickens from the man."

"This is how you repay me, by suspecting me of wanting to steal the chickens! You deserve to be eaten by Mountain Lion," replied Don Coyote.

"Get off my mesa, Don Coyote!" And with those words, Benito turned around and kicked Coyote with his strong hind legs. He kicked so hard that Don Coyote flew through the air, over the cliff, and landed below on a cactus bush. Don Coyote scrambled up and ran away as fast as his coyote legs could carry him. He yelled back to Benito, "Now, I will tell Mountain Lion where to find you."

Pretend to kick.

Cup hands over mouth as if shouting.

"Hee-haw, hee-haw," laughed Benito, as he set off in a trot to the man's green pasture. He jumped the fence and asked the man if he could stay behind the fence, where the grass was green, the water was cool, and Mountain Lion could not get in.

The man agreed but said that he would have to work for his keep. And, to this day, the burro works for the man in exchange for green grass and cool water. And, whenever a burro hears a coyote coming near the chickens, you can hear it, "Hee-hawing, hee-hawing," and kicking up its hind legs.

Look out for tricksters promising you an easy life.

HOW THE ANIMALS GOT TO BE AS THEY ARE

Storytelling Tips

◉ Before telling the story, practice braying or hee-hawing like a burro, donkey, or mule.

◉ Try out a few trickster sounding or sly voices. Be a bit boastful in tone when talking like Don Coyote.

◉ The first time that you say "Buenos dias" also say "good morning." The first time that you say "amigo" also say "friend."

Questions

◉ Do you think Benito was happy living on the mesa?

◉ Why do you think that Don Coyote wanted the chickens at the man's place to be set free?

◉ If you were Benito, would you choose to live on the mesa or on the man's land? Why?

ANIMAL SOUNDS

Materials

None needed

Steps

◉ Encourage the listeners to make the animal sounds of the "hee-hawing" burro, the clucking chickens, and even the imagined sound of the snarling mountain lion.

◉ Retell the story and let the children add the sound effects.

LIFE ON A MESA

Materials

Pictures of a mesa

Cactus plants (optional)

Paper

Markers or crayons

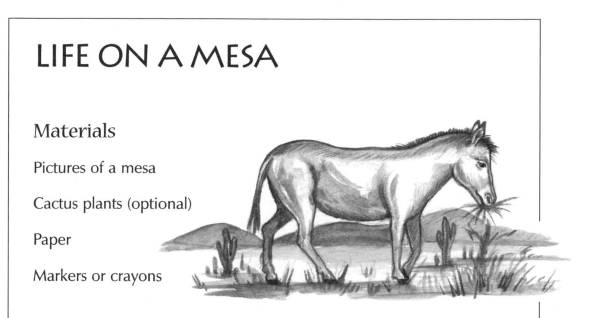

Steps

◉ Talk about where Benito lived—on a mesa. Explain that a mesa is a high area, and that the plants that grow there need less water. In the Southwest and in Mexico, these areas have sagebrush and cacti.

◉ If possible, let the children look at and touch (carefully) the cactus plants.

◉ If possible, show the listeners a picture of a mesa and talk about the differences between this type of land and the man's land, which had cool water and green grass.

◉ Invite the children to draw Benito on a mesa or Benito on the man's land. Have the children share their pictures and talk about the differences in their drawings.

SIMPLE SPANISH

Materials

Resource for simple Spanish words or
phrases, such as a foreign
language cassette or
book, or colleague
who speaks
Spanish

Steps

◉ If you do not already know
Spanish, learn a few words or
phrases in Spanish.

◉ With the listeners, talk about the Spanish words in the story,
"Buenos dias" and "amigo." Let the children rehearse saying
"Buenos dias" for good morning and "amigo" for friend.

◉ During the day, repeat the phrases when appropriate.

◉ On other days teach more Spanish phrases, such as "buenas
tardes" (good afternoon) and "buenas noches" (good night). If the
children are interested, teach them to count in Spanish.

The Curious Elephant's Child

THIS VERSION OF A RUDYARD KIPLING STORY
TELLS ABOUT A CURIOUS YOUNG ELEPHANT
WHO CAN'T STOP ASKING QUESTIONS OF
EVERYONE HE MEETS, INCLUDING A DANGEROUS
CROCODILE THAT TRIES TO EAT HIM
FOR DINNER.

Long ago and far away, the elephant

had no trunk. The elephant had only a small nose, about the size of a shoe. The elephant could move his short nose from side to side, but he could not pick anything up with it.

Indicate size with hands.

One elephant, a baby, was full of insatiable curiosity. Every day he asked many, many questions. He lived in Africa, and he filled Africa with all of his questions. He asked his tall aunt, the Ostrich, "Why do your tail-feathers grow so long?" He asked his tall uncle, the Giraffe, "What makes your skin so spotty?" He was so full of questions because he had an insatiable curiosity! He asked his aunt, the Hippopotamus, "Why are your eyes so red?" He asked his hairy uncle, the Baboon, "Why do melons taste so good?"

Use a childlike voice when the elephant speaks.

After all these questions he was still full of more questions. He had an insatiable curiosity! He asked questions about everything. He asked questions about what he saw, what he heard, what he smelled, what he felt, and what he touched. All of his aunts and uncles grew tired of all of his questions. They told him that he was full of insatiable curiosity!

Frown and look annoyed.

One morning the Elephant's Child thought of a fine question—one he had never asked before. He said, "What does the Crocodile have for dinner?"

Sound serious.

Everyone said, "Hush. Be quiet. No more questions."

As the Elephant's Child was walking away, he saw the Kolokolo Bird. He told the Kolokolo Bird, "Everyone is mad at me, and they tell me to be quiet. They say I have

HOW THE ANIMALS GOT TO BE AS THEY ARE

too many questions. But I still want to know what the Crocodile eats for dinner!"

The Kolokolo Bird told the Elephant's Child, "Go to the Limpopo River and sit on the bank. You will find out."

Flap you arms like wings.

The next day the Elephant's Child packed a basket with food: a hundred pounds of bananas, a hundred pounds of sugar cane, and seventeen melons. He said good-bye to all of his family. He told them, "I am going to the great gray-green, greasy Limpopo River. I will see what the Crocodile eats for dinner."

Wave your hand.

They all wished him luck and told him they hoped he found the answer to his question.

The Elephant's Child traveled east by north, eating bananas, sugar cane, and melons all the time. He dropped the rinds and peelings as he went. He had to leave them on the ground because he could not pick them up with his short nose. At last he came to the banks of the great gray-green, greasy Limpopo River. He sat on the bank by the fever-trees.

Sigh lazily.

Now it is important for you to know that the Elephant's Child had never seen a Crocodile. He didn't know what a Crocodile looked like. But he was still full of questions—he had an insatiable curiosity. The first thing that he saw was a Bi-Coloured-Python-Rock-Snake. It was curled around a rock.

"Excuse me," said the Elephant's Child, who was always polite, "have you seen a Crocodile in these parts?"

Use a distinguished voice.

"Have I seen a Crocodile?" said the Bi-Coloured-Python-Rock-Snake in a very irritated voice. "What question will you ask me next?"

"Excuse me," asked the Elephant's Child, "but what does the Crocodile eat for dinner?"

The Bi-Coloured-Python-Rock-Snake told the Elephant's Child, "Go right up to the edge of the great gray-green, greasy Limpopo River and sit by the trees. Watch for the Crocodile. You can see for yourself what he eats."

So the Elephant's Child thanked the Bi-Coloured-Python-Rock-Snake and walked down to the river. He sat on the bank and watched. The Elephant's Child saw a long green scaly thing, lying at the edge of the water.

"Excuse me," said the Elephant's Child very politely, "have you seen a Crocodile in these parts?"

Speak slowly and use a menacing voice.

The Crocodile winked one eye and lifted his tail out of the mud. "Come hither, little one," said the Crocodile. "Why do you ask me such a question?"

"Excuse me, I want to know what a Crocodile eats for dinner," replied the Elephant's Child.

"Come hither, little one. I am the Crocodile."

Sound happy.

The Elephant's Child got very excited. He kneeled down on the bank. "You are the Crocodile I have been looking for all these days. Will you please tell me what you eat for dinner?"

"Come hither, little one, I will whisper the answer to you," said the Crocodile.

The Elephant's Child put his head next to the Crocodile's large mouth. He wanted to hear the answer to his question.

"What do I have for dinner? Today I think I will have an Elephant's Child." And with that he grabbed hold of the Elephant's Child's short nose.

This annoyed the Elephant's Child. He said (speaking through his nose), "Let go, you are hurting me!"

The Bi-Coloured-Python-Rock-Snake scuffled down the bank and cried, "My young friend, pull as hard as you can. It is my opinion that the Crocodile will jerk you into the water if you don't."

The Elephant's Child sat back on his legs and pulled and pulled and pulled and pulled. His small nose began to stretch. The Crocodile flapped his tail and splashed the water. He pulled and pulled and pulled the Elephant's Child's nose.

The Elephant's Child's nose stretched longer and longer and longer. The Elephant's Child spread all his four legs out to get a firm footing on the ground. He pulled and pulled and pulled. His nose kept on stretching. It was getting longer and longer. The Crocodile pulled and pulled and pulled too. The Elephant's Child's nose grew longer and longer. Now his nose was nearly five feet long.

The Bi-Coloured-Python-Rock-Snake came down and knotted himself around the Elephant's Child. He and the Elephant's Child pulled and pulled and pulled. At last the Crocodile let go of the Elephant's Child's nose. It made a loud plop. The noise could be heard all up and down the great gray-green, greasy Limpopo River.

Tilt your head forward.

Speak while holding nose.

Slowly open arms to show stretching.

Open arms all the way.

Clap hands together.

The Elephant's Child was happy to be free from the Crocodile's mouth. But, his nose was so long and so out of shape. He wrapped it in cool banana leaves and put it in the water of the great gray-green, greasy Limpopo River to cool.

Pretend to examine a long nose.

"What are you doing?" asked the Bi-Coloured-Python-Rock-Snake.

"Excuse me," said the Elephant's Child, "but I am waiting for my nose to shrink."

"You are going to be waiting a very long time. Maybe you should think about how many good things this long trunk can do."

About that time a fly sat on the Elephant's Child's head. The Elephant's Child lifted up his long trunk and scared the fly away. He couldn't do that with his short nose. The Elephant's Child was getting hungry. He pulled up a bundle of grass with his trunk and stuffed it in his mouth. He couldn't do that with his short nose.

Pretend to pull up grass.

The sun was getting very hot. The Elephant's Child put his long trunk in the mud of the great gray-green, greasy Limpopo River and sprayed the cool mud on his head. The cool water and mud went all over his back. He was cool all over. He couldn't do that with his short nose.

Pretend to spray yourself with water.

The Elephant's Child decided to go home to show all his family his long trunk and all the wonderful things that he could do.

HOW THE ANIMALS GOT TO BE AS THEY ARE

As he walked home he ate all the fruit he wanted in the tall trees, he scratched his back with a branch, he put cool water on his back when the sun was hot. He even picked up the melon rinds that he had dropped on the way to the river. These were all things that he couldn't do with his short nose. He especially liked the way the long trunk made him sound when he sang. The trunk made his singing louder and more beautiful. It sounded like several brass trumpets.

Look happy.

When the Elephant's Child got home that evening, everyone was glad to see him.

He told them about his visit to the great gray-green, greasy Limpopo River.

"I asked the Crocodile what he ate for dinner, and he gave me this long trunk to keep," said the Elephant's Child.

Sound proud.

Some animals said that his trunk was ugly, but the Elephant's Child said, "It may be ugly but it is very useful." He showed them how he could get fruit from the tallest tree. How he could pull up clumps of grass and put them in his mouth. How he could spray water on his back when he was hot. He showed them how he could make a loud sound with his trunk that was like brass trumpets.

Make a horn sound.

His family was so excited. They thought his long trunk was very useful. One by one all the other the elephants went to the banks of the great gray-green, greasy Limpopo River to get long noses from the Crocodile.

THE CURIOUS ELEPHANT'S CHILD

Ever since that day, all the Elephants you'll ever see will have long and useful trunks exactly like the trunk of the insatiably curious Elephant's Child.

Asking questions can help you find the answers.

Storytelling Tips

● Before telling the story, discuss the word *insatiable*. Explain that it means a hunger for knowledge that is never satisfied.

● This story includes lyrical phrases that are very effective in story-telling. Use a special voice when you say *insatiable curiosity*; *great gray-green greasy, Limpopo River*; *excuse me*; and *Bi-Coloured-Python-Rock Snake*.

● Many young children ask a lot of questions, and they will identify with the curious Elephant's Child. Try to sound very young and curious when the Elephant's Child asks questions.

● To add humor to the tense moment when the Crocodile pulls on the Elephant's Child's nose, hold your nose when the Elephant's Child speaks. The voice that this produces will be funny.

● Take your time relating all the wonderful things that the Elephant's Child can do with his five-feet-long nose. This will help the child understand that change is positive and that asking questions is good.

Questions

● Why do you think the Elephant's Child asked so many questions?

● How did the Elephant's Child find out what the Crocodile ate for dinner?

● Have you ever been really curious about something? What did you do?

JUNGLE BOOK

Materials

Picture books or magazines that include pictures of animals in the jungle

Clear plastic bags

Small pieces of cardboard

Glue

Scissors

Tape

Steps

🌀 Look through a book or magazine with the listeners and find pictures of animals that might live in a jungle.

🌀 Talk about some of these animals.

🌀 If pictures are in an old magazine, let the children cut out the pictures and glue them on pieces of cardboard.

🌀 Put each cardboard piece inside a clear plastic bag. Tape a few bags together to create a jungle book that can be looked at and "read" over and over.

HOW THE ANIMALS GOT TO BE AS THEY ARE

STRETCHY STUFF

Materials

A collection of household objects and materials, some that stretch and some that don't. Suggestions of materials that stretch include elastic, stretchy fabrics, rubber bands, exhaust hose for dryer, socks, mittens, hair bands, and six-pack rings.

Steps

◉ Provide a collection of materials and objects for the listeners to examine.

◉ Ask the children which things will stretch and which things won't.

◉ Let the children explore, pull, and stretch the materials to find out.

◉ After the children have explored the objects and materials, encourage them to sort them into categories of *stretchy* and *not stretchy*.

IT HAPPENED TO ME

Materials

None needed

Steps

- After the story, talk about the curious Elephant's Child and ask the listeners if they have ever been told that they asked too many questions.

- If someone says yes, invite that child to tell about the experience. This is the beginning of storytelling.

- If the children are hesitant, tell them a personal experience you might have had involving asking questions and finding answers.

CURIOUS CHILDREN

Materials

Chart paper or large sheet of paper

Marker

Steps

◉ Ask the children if they have questions that they would like to know the answers to.

◉ Write their questions on the paper.

◉ When they run out of questions or the paper is filled up, select one or more questions to find the answers to.

◉ Help the children find the answers by looking at books, asking other people, and doing very simple research.

Story Cards

THE THRIFTY TAILOR

◉ A tailor who worked hard needed a warm winter coat.

◉ He sewed and saved to buy the cloth he needed.

◉ He made himself a very warm coat and felt proud.

◉ He wore it when it was cold and when it was chilly.

◉ He wore the warm coat until it was worn out.

◉ He didn't want to throw it away so he took a closer look.

◉ He found some cloth in the coat that was not worn out.

◉ It was just enough to make a beautiful jacket.

◉ He made himself a beautiful jacket and felt proud.

◉ He wore it when it was cold and when it was cloudy.

◉ He wore the beautiful jacket until it was worn out.

◉ He didn't want to throw it away so he took a closer look.

◉ He found some cloth in the jacket that was still good.

◉ It was just enough to make a fancy vest.

◉ He made himself a fancy vest and felt proud.

◉ He wore it on cold days, cloudy days, and warm days.

◉ He wore the fancy vest until it was worn out.

◉ He didn't want to throw it away, so he took a closer look.

◉ He found some cloth in the vest that was not worn out.

◉ It was just enough cloth to make a small cap.

🌀 He made himself a small cap and felt proud.

🌀 He wore his cap when it was cold or warm.

🌀 He wore his cap until it was all worn out.

🌀 He didn't want to throw it away so he took a closer look.

🌀 He found a tiny piece of cloth that was not worn out.

🌀 He cut up his cap and made a very special button.

🌀 He was proud of his lovely button and wore it often.

🌀 He wore the special button until it was all worn out.

🌀 He didn't want to throw it away so he took a closer look.

🌀 He realized there was just enough left to make a story.

LAZY JACK

CHARACTERS: MOTHER, JACK, FARMER, DIARY FARMER, CHEESE SHOP OWNER, BUTCHER, DONKEY, RICH MAN, YOUNG WOMAN

🌀 A hard-working mother had a lazy son who didn't work.

🌀 The old woman could not stand his laziness any longer.

🌀 She told him he must go to work to pay for his food.

🌀 Lazy Jack got a job on a farm and earned one penny.

🌀 He lost his penny crossing a bridge on the way home.

🌀 His mother said, "You should have put the penny in your pocket." And Jack said, "I'll do that next time."

🌀 Jack worked for a dairy farmer and earned a jug of milk.

🌀 Jack put the jug in his pocket and the milk spilled out.

🌀 His mother said, "You should have carried it on your head." And Jack said, "I'll do that next time."

🌀 Jack found a job in a cheese shop and earned cheese.

🌀 He put the cheese on his head and it melted on his face.

🌀 His mother said, "You should have carried the cheese in your hands." And Jack said, "I'll do that next time."

🌀 Jack worked for a baker and was given a cat.

🌀 He tried to carry it but it scratched him and he let it go.

🌀 His mother said, "You should have pulled it home with a rope." And Jack said, "I'll do that next time."

🌀 Jack worked for a butcher and earned a ham.

🌀 He pulled it home through the dirt with a rope.

◉ His mother said, "You should have put it on your shoulders." And Jack said, "I'll do that next time."

◉ Jack worked in the stables and earned a donkey.

◉ He hoisted the heavy donkey up onto his shoulders.

◉ As he walked home, the donkey kicked and brayed.

◉ On the way he passed the house of a rich man.

◉ The man's daughter was sick and had never laughed.

◉ When she saw Jack and the donkey she laughed.

◉ She laughed, and she laughed, and was soon cured.

◉ Her father was so happy he gave Jack many riches.

THE TALKING POT

CHARACTERS: POOR MAN AND WOMAN, STRANGER, TALKING POT,
RICH WIFE, GRAIN WORKERS, RICH MAN

- A poor man who had no food decided to sell his cow.

- On the way to market a stranger offered to buy it.

- He offered the poor man a pot instead of money.

- The pot said, "Take me and you shall never regret it."

- The man took the pot home and showed his wife.

- She was angry that he had traded the cow for a pot.

- The pot said, "Clean, polish, and hang me by the fire."

- The wife thought a talking pot was valuable so she did.

- The next morning the pot said, "I skip, I skip."

- It skipped over hill and dale to the rich man's house.

- The rich wife cooked some pudding in the pot.

- The pot skipped home to the cottage full of pudding.

- The poor man and his wife were very grateful.

- The wife cleaned, polished, and hung up the pot.

- The next morning, the pot said, "I skip, I skip."

- The pot skipped to the rich man's barn.

- Workers shoveled lots of wheat into the pot.

- The pot skipped home to the cottage with the wheat.

- The poor man and his wife were very grateful.

- The wife cleaned, polished, and hung up the pot.
- The next morning, the pot said, "I skip, I skip."
- The pot skipped to the rich man's counting room.
- The rich man placed handfuls of coins into the pot.
- The pot skipped home to the cottage with the coins.
- The poor man and his wife were very grateful.
- So much gold meant they would never be poor.
- The wife cleaned, polished, and hung up the pot.
- The next morning, the pot said, "I skip, I skip."
- The pot skipped to the once-rich man's house.
- The man saw the pot and began to scream.
- "I skip, I skip," said the pot.
- The once-rich man said, "Skip to the North Pole."
- With that, the pot stuck to the once-rich man's arm.
- It skipped down the road toward the North Pole.

THE FISHERMAN AND HIS WIFE

CHARACTERS: FISHERMAN, WIFE, MAGIC FISH

◉ A fisherman and his wife lived in a shabby hut on a hill.

◉ The fisherman went fishing every day in the ocean.

◉ One day he caught a magic fish that could talk.

◉ The fisherman set him free and he swam away.

◉ His wife was angry because he did not ask for a wish.

◉ She told him to go back and ask for a house.

◉ The fisherman returned to the ocean.

◉ He called, "Magic fish, magic fish, we have a wish."

◉ When the fish came, he asked for a house.

◉ The fish said, "Go back and see what you find."

◉ When he went home he found a lovely cottage.

◉ But the wife was not satisfied and wanted a castle.

◉ The fisherman returned to the ocean.

◉ He called, "Magic fish, magic fish, we have a wish."

◉ When the fish came, he asked for a castle.

◉ The fish said, "Go back and see what you find."

◉ When he went home he found a huge castle.

◉ The wife was not satisfied and wanted to be Queen.

◉ The fisherman returned to the ocean.

◉ He called, "Magic fish, magic fish, we have a wish."

◉ When the fish came, he asked that his wife be Queen.

◉ The fish said, "Go back and see what you find."

◉ When he went home he found his wife on a throne.

◉ His wife now wanted to be ruler of the universe.

◉ The fisherman returned to the ocean, black and rough.

◉ He called, "Magic fish, magic fish, we have a wish."

◉ The fish did not come, so he called again and again.

◉ Finally the fish said, "What do you want now?"

◉ The fisherman told him his wife's request.

◉ The fish said, "Go back and see what you find."

◉ When he went home he found only a shabby hut.

THE GREAT LION AND THE TINY MOUSE

CHARACTERS: GREAT LION, TINY MOUSE, MONKEYS, ZEBRAS, WATER BUFFALOES, GIRAFFES, ELEPHANTS

- Once upon a time, Great Lion was king of the jungle.
- He did as he pleased and no one bothered him.
- One day Tiny Mouse ran over Great Lion's paw.
- Great Lion woke up and caught him by the tail.
- Tiny Mouse pleaded with Great Lion not to hurt him.
- He promised he would do a favor for him some day.
- Great Lion laughed and laughed at Tiny Mouse.
- He didn't think a little mouse could do him a favor.
- But he wasn't hungry, so he let Tiny Mouse go.
- Not long after that, Great Lion was caught in a trap.
- He roared and struggled, but he could not get out.
- The monkeys came, but only stared and laughed.

*ONE AT A TIME, SUBSTITUTE ZEBRAS, WATER BUFFALOES, GIRAFFES AND ELEPHANTS FOR MONKEYS IN LINE ABOVE.

- Tiny Mouse also rushed to help the Great Lion.
- He gnawed and chewed right through the ropes.
- He gnawed a big hole so Great Lion could escape.
- Great Lion and Tiny Mouse become friends for life.

THE GREAT GIGANTIC TURNIP

CHARACTERS: GRANDFATHER, GRANDMOTHER, MOTHER, DAUGHTER, DOG, CAT, TINY MOUSE

- One spring, Grandfather planted a turnip seed.

- He watched the turnip and took care of it every day.

- The turnip grew and grew into a gigantic turnip.

- Grandfather decided it was time to pull up the turnip.

- He pulled and pulled and pulled but could not pull it up.

- He called Grandmother, who ran to help her husband.

- They pulled and pulled together, but could not pull it up.

- Grandmother called her daughter and she ran to help.

- They pulled and pulled together, but could not pull it up.

- The daughter called her little girl and she hurried to help.

- They pulled and pulled together, but could not pull it up.

- The little girl called her puppy and it barked excitedly.

- They pulled and pulled together, but could not pull it up.

- The puppy called the cat and it came running.

- They pulled and pulled together, but could not pull it up.

- A tiny mouse heard all the noise and offered to help.

- He joined the pulling and out popped the gigantic turnip!

- That night everyone ate the gigantic turnip for dinner.

THE LITTLE RED HEN

CHARACTERS: LITTLE RED HEN, BEAGLE, CALICO, AND BROWN MOUSE

- Little Red Hen lived in a neat house at the edge of a field.

- She shared her house with a dog, a cat, and a mouse.

- One day, Little Red Hen found some grains of wheat.

- She was very excited and ran home to tell her friends.

- Beagle, a plump dog, was asleep by the entrance.

- Calico, a fat cat, was asleep on the windowsill.

- Brown Mouse was asleep by the entrance to his hole.

- "Who will help me plant this wheat?" she asked.

- "Not I," said Beagle (repeat for Calico, Brown Mouse).

- "Then I will," said Little Red Hen, and she did.

- She watered the wheat and watched it grow.

- "Who will help me cut the wheat?" she asked.

- "Not I," said Beagle (repeat for Calico, Brown Mouse).

- "Then I will," said Little Red Hen, and she did.

- She gathered the stalks of wheat by herself.

- "Who will help me take the wheat to the mill?"

- "Not I," said Beagle (repeat for Calico, Brown Mouse).

- "Then I will," said Little Red Hen and she did.

- At the mill, the wheat was ground into flour.

- Little Red Hen rushed home with the flour.

- "Who will help me bake this bread?" she asked.

- "Not I," said Beagle (repeat for Calico, Brown Mouse).

- "Then I will," she said, and she began baking it.

- Soon a delicious warm smell filled the entire house.

- Beagle, Calico, and Brown Mouse all woke up.

- They came to sit by the stove in the kitchen.

- Little Red Hen took the warm bread from the oven.

- "Who will help me eat this bread?" she asked.

- "I will," said Beagle (repeat for Calico, Brown Mouse).

- Little Red Hen told them that no one had helped her.

- She said, "Now, you will not help me eat it."

- And she ate the whole loaf of bread all by herself.

- But the next time she asked for help, she got it.

THE ELVES AND THE SHOEMAKER

CHARACTERS: SHOEMAKER AND WIFE, TWO ELVES,
GENTLEMAN, LADY, CHILDREN

◉ A poor shoemaker had a shop on a busy street.

◉ He had only enough leather for one pair of shoes.

◉ He needed to sell the shoes to buy food for his family.

◉ He laid out his work on the workbench for the next day.

◉ As he slept, two little elves entered the workshop.

◉ They whistled and hummed happily as they worked.

◉ The made a pair of gentleman's shoes and left.

◉ The next morning, the shoemaker found the shoes.

◉ The shoemaker placed the shoes in his shop window.

◉ A fine gentleman bought them and paid more than usual.

◉ The shoemaker bought enough leather for another pair.

◉ He laid out his work on the workbench for the next day.

◉ As he slept, two little elves entered the workshop.

◉ The made a pair of ladies' shoes and left before dawn.

◉ The next morning, the shoemaker discovered the shoes.

◉ The shoemaker placed the shoes in his shop window.

◉ A fine lady bought them and paid more than usual.

◉ The shoemaker bought enough leather for two pairs.

◉ He laid out his work on the workbench for the next day.

- As he slept, two little elves entered the workshop.

- The made a two pairs of children's shoes.

- The next morning, the shoemaker discovered the shoes.

- The shoemaker placed the shoes in his shop window.

- A mother bought them for her little boy and girl.

- The shoemaker bought enough leather for four pairs.

- He laid out his work on the workbench for the next day.

- As he slept, two little elves entered the workshop.

- They made four pairs of shoes for a family.

- The next morning, a family paid well for the shoes.

- One night, the shoemaker and his wife hid in a closet.

- They watched the little elves cut, hammer, and sew.

- The noticed that the little elves had no shoes or jackets.

- The shoemaker and his wife made clothes for the elves.

- They left the tiny clothes and shoes on the workbench.

- That night the elves tried on the clothes and shoes.

- They were very happy and danced out of the shop.

- They never came back but the shoemaker didn't mind.

- He used their patterns to make many pairs of shoes.

THE WHITE CRANE

CHARACTERS: FISHERMAN, WHITE CRANE, FISHERMAN'S WIFE,
BEAUTIFUL GIRL, PEOPLE IN THE VILLAGE, CURIOUS NEIGHBOR

- A poor fisherman and his wife longed for a child.

- One day, a white crane got tangled in an old net.

- The fisherman spotted the crane and cut it free.

- That night, the fisherman and his wife heard a knock.

- When they opened the door, they found a young girl.

- She offered to take care of them in their old age.

- For a long time the old couple was very happy.

- The young girl spent her days weaving at the loom.

- She said never to look at her while she was weaving.

- The young girl gave them a beautiful flowing cloth.

- They sold it for enough money to buy lots of food.

- One day a curious neighbor came by to visit.

- She looked in the room where the girl was weaving.

- She saw a crane plucking out beautiful feathers.

- Later the girl brought out a half-finished piece of cloth.

- She said because they broke the rule she had to leave.

- Then before their eyes she turned into a crane.

- She flew away but the old couple never forgot her.

HENNY-PENNY AND FOUR FINE-FEATHERED FRIENDS

CHARACTERS: HENNY-PENNY, COCKY-LOCKY, DUCKY-LUCKY, TURKEY-LURKEY, GOOSEY-LOOSEY, FOXY-LOXY

- Henny-Penny was peck, peck, pecking in the barnyard.
- Suddenly something hit her on top of her head—plunk!
- Henny-Penny looked up and thought the sky was falling.
- She set off in a great hurry to warn the King.
- On the way, she met Cocky-Locky.
- Henny-Penny told Cocky-Locky the sky was falling.
- Cocky-Locky looked up and said the sky was not falling.
- Henny-Penny said a piece of it had hit her on the head.
- Cocky-Locky said he would go with her to tell the King.
- He strutted along behind Henny Penny.
- Repeat above six lines as they are joined "on the way" by Ducky-Lucky, Turkey-Lurkey, and Goosey-Loosey.
- Soon the five-feathered friends met Foxy-Loxy.
- They told him they were going to see the King.
- "Do you know the way to the King's castle?" he asked.
- The five-feathered friends said they did not.
- "Well, let me lead you," said Foxy-Loxy slyly.
- He pointed to a cave and said to go through it.
- They thanked him but they never found the King.
- And later, their feathers were spotted by the cave.

THE BOY WHO CRIED WOLF

CHARACTERS: FATHER, YOUNG BOY, SHEEP, VILLAGERS, WOLF

- A young boy was sent by his father to the mountains.
- His job was to watch over the sheep for many weeks.
- If the boy felt danger, he was to call "Wolf, Wolf, Wolf."
- Then the villagers would come to help him.
- At first the boy was happy on the mountain by himself.
- But after time had passed, he became very lonely.
- He decided to get the villagers to come and see him.
- He ran up the mountain and cried, "Wolf, Wolf! Wolf!"
- The villagers rushed to the mountains to help the boy.
- They were surprised when they found no wolf.
- They chatted with the boy, admired the sheep, and left.
- Soon the boy was lonely and cried, "Wolf, Wolf, Wolf!"
- Once again the villagers rushed to the mountains.
- Again they found no wolf and walked the long way home.
- One day, a real wolf came to the mountain.
- The boy was frightened and called "Wolf, Wolf, Wolf!"
- The villagers thought this was a trick and didn't come.
- The boy threw rocks at the wolf and the sheep ran away.
- The boy returned to the village to tell what happened.
- He always remembered the day when the wolf came.

WHY THE POSSUM HAS A SKINNY TAIL

CHARACTERS: POSSUM, SQUIRREL, RABBIT, DEER, BEAR,
ANIMALS OF THE WOODS

◉ Long ago, Possum had a long, beautiful bushy tail.

◉ Possum liked to brag and show off her beautiful tail.

◉ She bragged to Squirrel, to Rabbit, and to Deer.

◉ All the animals grew tired of Possum's bragging.

◉ Whenever they saw her coming, they ran away.

◉ Every fall, the animals had a stomp dance.

◉ Bear beat a hollow log and all the animals danced.

◉ Possum looked forward to the fall pow-wow and dance.

◉ She wanted to show off her long, beautiful, busy tail.

◉ Possum's tail got stomped on during the stomp dance.

◉ Possum shouted but no one could hear her.

◉ She tried to pull her tail out from under the dancers.

◉ She pulled and pulled until finally her tail was free.

◉ There was nothing left by a long, skinny tail with no fur.

◉ She was so embarrassed that she ran away and hid.

◉ She vowed never again to come out in the daylight.

WHY CROCODILE DOES NOT EAT HEN

CHARACTERS: HEN, CROCODILE, LIZARD

- One day, Hen strolled and pecked along the riverbank.
- Crocodile saw her and thought he would eat her.
- "Do not eat me," said Hen. "I am your sister."
- Crocodile was so surprised that he shut his jaws.
- He did not believe her, but it was too late to catch her.
- Hen went pecking and strolling down the riverbank.
- The next day, the same thing happened again.
- Crocodile thought, "Hen has tricked me a second time.
- My brothers and sisters are crocodiles, not hens."
- Lizard, sunning nearby, asked him what was wrong.
- Crocodile asked Lizard how Hen could be his sister.
- Lizard said hens and crocodiles both lay eggs.
- Lizard said all who lay eggs are brothers and sisters.
- Crocodile was sad that he couldn't eat Hen for lunch.
- The next day, Hen came strolling and pecking.
- Crocodile asked her why she was not afraid of him.
- She said, "Because you would not eat your sister."
- To this day, Crocodile thinks of Hen as his sister.

TELL IT AGAIN! 2

HOW THE CAMEL GOT HIS HUMPH

CHARACTERS: CAMEL, HORSE, DOG, OX, MAN, DJINN

◉ The world was new and there was a lot of work to do.

◉ Camel lived in the middle of the Howling Desert.

◉ He did not want to work, and he ate all day long.

◉ When spoken to he would only answer "Humph."

◉ Horse asked Camel to come and work like the others.

◉ Camel answered by saying "Humph."

◉ Horse told the man that Camel was not working.

◉ Dog asked Camel to come and work like the others.

◉ Camel answered by saying "Humph."

◉ Dog told the man that Camel was not working.

◉ Ox asked Camel to come and plow like the others.

◉ Camel answered by saying "Humph."

◉ Ox told the man that Camel was not working.

◉ At the end of the day, man called Horse, Dog and Ox.

◉ He said that they would have to work twice as hard.

◉ They had a meeting and decided this was very unfair.

◉ The Djinn was the magic man in charge of the deserts.

◉ He came rolling in a cloud of dust to the meeting.

- They told him that Camel in the desert would not work.

- The Djinn flew across the desert to talk to Camel.

- He asked Camel, "Why are you not doing any work?"

- Camel answered by saying "Humph."

- The Djinn told him not to say that word again.

- Came answered by saying "Humph."

- Suddenly Camel's back puffed into a great big humph.

- The Djinn said he could now work without stopping.

- He could live off his humph for three days without food.

- Since that time Camel has had a humph on his back.

- And he can work three days without eating or resting.

WHY THE BURRO LIVES WITH THE MAN

CHARACTERS: BENITO, DON COYOTE (MOUNTAIN LION, MAN, CHICKENS ARE MENTIONED IN THE STORY)

- A burro named Benito lived safely on the sandy mesa.
- He was sad that he had only sagebrush and cactus to eat.
- He longed for green grass to graze and cool water to drink.
- But on the mesa Benito was safe from Mountain Lion.
- One day Don Coyote sneaked up on Benito on the mesa.
- He told Benito that Mountain Lion was looking for him.
- He told Benito about a safe place where the man lived.
- There he would find green pastures and much cool water.
- And there he would also be safe from Mountain Lion.
- Don Coyote offered to lead Benito to the man's land.
- Benito was interested but did not trust Don Coyote.
- Don Coyote said the man kept chickens on his land.
- He asked Benito to free the sad, squawking chickens.
- Benito knew Don Coyote wanted to eat the chickens.
- He turned and kicked Don Coyote with his strong legs.
- Don Coyote ran away and Benito jumped the man's fence.
- The man said Benito could stay if he would work for him.
- To this day, the burro lives with man and earns his keep.

THE CURIOUS ELEPHANT'S CHILD

CHARACTERS: ELEPHANT'S CHILD, OSTRICH, GIRAFFE,
HIPPOPOTAMUS, BABOON, KOLOKOLO BIRD,
BI-COLOURED-PYTHON-ROCK-SNAKE, CROCODILE

- Long ago, the elephant did not have a trunk.
- The elephant's nose was too short to pick things up.
- One baby elephant was full of insatiable curiousity.
- This Elephant's Child asked many, many questions.
- He asked the Ostrich why her tail-feathers grew long.
- He asked the Giraffe what made his skin so spotty.
- He asked the Hippopotamus why his eyes were so red.
- He asked the Baboon why melons tasted so good.
- All of his aunts and uncles grew tired of his questions.
- They said he was full to insatiable curiosity!
- He asked Kolokolo Bird what Crocodile ate for dinner.
- The bird told him to go to Limpopo River and find out.
- The Elephant's Child packed some food and set off.
- He came to the great gray-green, greasy Limpopo River.
- There he met a Bi-Coloured-Python-Rock-Snake.
- He asked the snake what Crocodile ate for dinner.
- The snake told him to go the river and see for himself.
- The Elephant's Child walked down to the river.
- He asked a scaly thing if it had ever seen a Crocodile.

- The Crocodile said, "Why do you ask such a question?"
- "I want to know what the Crocodile eats for dinner."
- "Come hither, little one, for I am the Crocodile."
- The Elephant's Child was very happy and excited.
- He leaned close to Crocodile's large mouth to hear.
- The Crocodile grabbed Elephant's Child's nose.
- The snake told Elephant's Child to pull very hard.
- So he pulled and pulled, but his nose kept stretching.
- The Crocodile pulled and pulled and pulled, too.
- Soon the Elephant's Child's nose was five feet long.
- The snake helped him pull loose from Crocodile.
- Elephant's Child tried to shrink his stretched-out nose.
- The snake helped him realize that a long trunk is good.
- Elephant's Child could use his trunk to scare away flies.
- He could use his trunk to stuff grass into his mouth.
- He could use his trunk to get fruit from the tallest tree.
- He could use his trunk to spray cool mud on his head.
- Elephant's Child went home proud of his long trunk.
- All the elephants wanted new noses just like he had.

TELL IT AGAIN! 2

Story Sources

The multicultural stories in this book are retold, varied, or adapted for young children. Many of the sources for the stories are anthologies and collections, noted in the following list. Additional references cited in the anthologies and collections are included. We have told some of these stories to children and remember many from our own childhoods.

Any retelling is the storyteller's remembrance of a story heard or read in the past. For example, "The Boy Who Cried Wolf" is a retelling of a famous Aesop fable that we heard during childhood and that carries an important message about telling the truth. Our retelling stays true to the characters and the scenes.

A variation of a story is the storyteller's own flavoring with dialogue and interactions, which make the story come alive but remain true to the usual characters and the story actions. For example, the English version of "The Little Red Hen" has a pig, a duck, and a cat as Little Red Hen's friends. One of the most popular versions, by Paul Galdone, has a cat, a dog, and a mouse as Little Red Hen's friends. In our variation, the animals have names (Beagle the dog, Calico the cat, and Brown Mouse), and their characteristics are repeated throughout the telling.

Adaptations are more significant changes to the content of the story than simple variations in dialogue or narration. An adaptation of a story may include adding or deleting characters or scenes to make it more interesting to an audience or the readers. For example, in the Cherokee tale, "Why the Possum Has a Skinny Tale," we changed the animals and some of their actions.

"The Thrifty Tailor" is an easy-to-tell story that delights young children. It follows the transformation of the tailor's coat from warm coat, to short jacket, to fancy vest, to cap, to button, and finally to a story. Although there are many versions of "The Thrifty Tailor," the source and inspiration for our version is storyteller Nancy Schimmel. She first heard the story as a Yiddish folk song and uses it as a storytelling lesson by retelling the story with various endings. The song "I Had a Little Coat" is available on *Songs of the Holidays* and is sung by Gene Bluestein (Folkways FC 7554). Nancy Schimmel's version, "The Tailor," can be found in *Just Enough to Make a Story: A Sourcebook for Storytelling* (Berkeley, CA, 1992).

"Lazy Jack" is a charming story that brings out the giggles and builds to roaring laughter. Jack is found in many cultures and is always portrayed as someone who makes silly mistakes. His actions are so absurd and outlandish that they make everyone laugh. In spite of all the problems, good things sometimes happen to Jack as they do in this English tale. Read about Jack in Mariam Blanton Huber, *Story and Verse for Children* (New York, 1965); Joseph Jacobs, *English Fairy Tales* (New York, 1967); and Anne Tockwell, *The Three Bears and 15 Other Stories* (New York, 1975).

"The Talking Pot" is a Danish story, although there are stories of magic pots that feed the hungry in many cultures. This story includes another theme often found in folktales—taking from the rich to give to the poor. "The Talking Pot" was one of the tales collected by Jens Christian Bay and published in *Danish Fairy and Folk Tales* (New York, 1899). The version that we retold was found in Edna Johnson, Evelyn R. Sickels, Frances Clarke Sayers, and Carolyn Horovitz, *Anthology of Children's Literature* (Boston, 1977). The tale can also be found in Mary C. Hatch, *13 Danish Tales* (New York, 1947), and in Virginia Haviland, *Favorite Fairy Tales Told In Denmark* (Boston, 1971).

"The Fisherman and His Wife" is retold from a Grimm Fairy Tale. It was first published in 1819 in a collection of the brothers Grimm. Similar tales are found in cultures around the world. Other sources for this story are Hazel Gertrude Kinscella, *Folk Tales from Many Lands* (New York, 1939); Ralph Manheim's translation of *Grimms' Tales for Young and Old: The Complete Stories* (New York, 1983); and Elisabeth Shub's translation of "About the Fisherman and His Wife" in *About Wise Men and*

Simpletons (New York, 1971).

"The Great Lion and the Tiny Mouse" is an adaptation of the Aesop fable, "A Lion and the Mouse." In our adaptation, monkeys, giraffes, water buffaloes, and elephants are added with more dialogue and descriptions of animals' movements than in the Aesop fable. It is thought that Aesop was a sixth-century Greek storyteller, and he is credited with hundreds of short stories that were meant as lessons. Some scholars believe that Aesop was many people who told these simple tales to illustrate great truths, and anyone who told this type of story was said to be telling an Aesop fable. We also read the story in Edna Johnson, Evelyn R. Sickels, Frances Clarke Sayers, and Carolyn Horovitz, *Anthology of Children's Literature* (Boston, 1977).

"The Great Giant Turnip" is thought to be one of the peasant tales collected by Tolstoy. Our version of "The Great Giant Turnip" is retold from the Russian folktale. There are tales of giant vegetables and fruits from many cultures. We have heard tales about giant carrots, sweet potatoes, watermelons, and even rutabagas. In each story, it takes many people or animals to pull the giant plant from the ground. In the end, one tiny thing such as a mouse, a beetle, or a small child makes the difference. There were several sources for our retelling of "The Great Giant Turnip"—Kathy Parkinson, *The Enormous Turnip* (Morton Grove, IL, 1986); Pierr, Morgan (illustrator), *The Turnip: An Old Russian Folktale* (New York, 1990); and Katherine Milhouse and Alice Dalglish (collection), *Once On a Time* From an Old Russian Storyteller (New York, 1938).

"The Little Red Hen" is a well-known English tale frequently told by teachers in early childhood classrooms. Many teachers base their telling on Paul Galdone's version in which Little Red Hen shares her house with a pig, a duck, and a cat. Our variation keeps the same number of characters, but we have Beagle Dog, Calico Cat, and Brown Mouse, with appropriate descriptions of their laziness and the ways they move. As preparation for our telling of the tale, we read Paul Galdone, *The Little Red Hen* (New York, 1973) and Hilda Offen, "The Little Red Hen" in *A Treasury of Bedtime Stories* (New York, 1981).

"The Elves and the Shoemaker" is a Grimm brothers' tale. Jacob and Wilhelm Grimm collected German folk and fairy tales from the oral tradition and published them in the early 1800's. The story told here contains the essence of the original tale, but it is a retelling after reading numerous versions, including Hilda Offen, "The Elves and the Shoemaker" in *A Treasury of Bedtime Stories* (New York, 1981); John W. Griffith and Charles H. Frey, eds., "The Elves and the Shoemaker" in *Classics of Children's Literature* (New York, 1981); and Bill Alder, Jr., "The Elves and the Shoemaker" in *Tell Me A Fairy Tale: A Parent's Guide to Telling Magical and Mythical Stories* (New York, 1995).

"The White Crane" is a retelling of a Japanese folktale based on tales heard from a storyteller and our reading of similar stories. In our version, a poor fisherman helps a beautiful crane free herself when caught in an old fishing net. The crane later appears as an orphan, who lives with the childless couple to help them in their old age. She weaves a beautiful cloth but warns them never to watch her weave. They sell the cloth for much money and are never hungry again, but a nosey neighbor is too curious. During a visit, she opens the door on the weaver and the daughter turns back into a crane and flies away.

"Henny Penny and Four Fine-Feathered Friends" is a popular story with young children because of the rhyming names and the repeated characters. Henny Penny is also known by the name of Chicken Licken, Hen-Lenn, and Chicken Little. We read the story in a number of sources, including Edna Johnson, Evelyn R. Sickels, Frances Clarke Sayers, and Carolyn Horovitz, "Henny-Penny" in *Anthology of Children's Literature, 5th ed.* (Boston, 1977); Barbara Ker Wilson, "Henny-Penny" in *Animal Folk Tales* (New York, 1971); and Effie Power, "The Story of Chicken-Licken" in *Bag O'Tales* (New York, 1934).

"The Boy who Cried Wolf" is an Aesop fable. In addition to being remembered by one of the authors, we read it in Laura Rose, *Folktales: Teaching Reading through Visualization and Drawing* (Tucso, Arizona, 1992); Charles Sylvester, "The Shepard Boy and the Wolves" in *Journeys through Bookland, Vol. 1* (Chicago, 1922,1932); and Vernon Jones (translation), "The Shepherd's Boy and the Wolf" in *Aesop's*

Fables (New York: 1912,1967,1969). Stories remembered from childhood have a very special significance because they help us recall important lessons and a dear father who cared enough to tell the story. Rebecca Isbell says, "This retelling is dedicated to the memory of my first storyteller, my father."

"Why the Possum Has a Skinny Tale" is an extensive adaptation of a remembered story based on a Cherokee tale told by an unidentified teacher from Tahlequah, Oklahoma. The animals we use in the tale all have tails, to which the once beautiful tail of the possum can be compared. Several versions of this "pourquoi" tale (about how animals came to be as they are) are found in the Native American literature. The one we read was "Why the Possum's Tail is Bare," in a collection from James E. Connoly, *Why the Possum's Tail is Bare and other North American Indian Nature Tales* (Owings Mills, MD, 1985). Connoly acknowledges the Smithsonian Institution and *Myths of the Cherokee* by James Mooney (date unknown).

"Why Crocodile Does Not Eat Hen" is a Bantu tale. We first heard the story at the National Storytelling Festival in Jonesborough, Tennessee. Since that time, we have also read the tale in Martha Hamilton and Mitch Weiss, *Stories in My Pocket: Tales Kids Can Tell* (Golden, CO, 1996). The story can also be found in Joan M. Lexau, *Crocodile and Hen* (New York, 1969); Maria Leach, "Why Crocodile Does Not Eat Hen" in *How the People Sang the Mountains Up: How and Why Stories* (New York, 1967); and Marguerite P. Dolch, "The Crocodile and the Hen" in *Animal Stories from Africa* (Champaign, IL, 1975).

"How the Camel Got His Humph" was written by Rudyard Kipling and is included in his collection of *Just So Stories for Little Children*. The story, as many others in this collection, was designed to explain something in nature that seemed unexplainable. Throughout history many cultures have created stories to explain how things came to be. This story explains why the camel is equipped with a humph.

"Why the Burro Lives With the Man" is a retelling of a Mexican story that uses the terrain of Mexico and life of the desert as a backdrop. The tale has two features of folk tales—it is a trickster tale and a "pourquoi" tale, or an explanation of how an animal came to be as it is today. We read the story in Edna Johnson, Evelyn R. Sickels, Frances Clarke Sayers, and Carolyn Horovitz, *Anthology of Children's Literature*, 5th ed. (Boston, 1977). The authors of the anthology referenced Catherine Bryan and Mabra Madden, *The Cactus Fence* (New York, 1943).

"The Curious Elephant's Child" is from the works of Rudyard Kipling. It was written in 1900 and included in his collection of *Just So Stories*. It has been retold in many different ways and included in several picture books and story collections. The Elephant's Child is filled with questions about his world, just like young children. In the 1900's version the Elephant's Child was spanked for asking so many questions. This retelling values the importance of questions and deals with the "insatiable curiosity" as important in problem solving and a positive attribute for a child.

Storytelling References and Resources

The Thrifty Tailor

"I Had a Little Coat" on *Songs of the Holidays* (sung by Gene Bluestein on Folkways FC 7554).

Shimmel, Nancy. "The Tailor." *Just Enough to Make a Story*. Berkeley, CA: Sisters' Choice Press, 1992. Used by permission of the author.

Lazy Jack

Jacobs, Joseph. *English Fairy Tales*. New York: Dover, 1967.

Huber, Mariam Blanton. *Story and Verse for Children*. New York: Macmillan, 1965.

Rockwell, Anne. *The Three Bears and 15 other Stories*. New York: Thomas Y. Crowell, 1975.

The Talking Pot

Haviland, Virginia. *Favorite Fairy Tales Told in Denmark*. Illustrated by Margot Zemach. Boston: Little Brown, 1971.

Johnson, Edna, Evelyn R. Sickels, Frances Clarke Sayers, and Carolyn Horovitz. *Anthology of Children's Literature*. 5th ed. Boston: Houghton Mifflin, 1977. (Johnson et. al. reference Jens, Christian Bay. *Danish Fairy and Folk Tales*. New York: Harper, 1899 and Hatch, Mary C. *13 Danish Tales*. New York: Harcourt, 1947.

The Fisherman and His Wife

Grimm, Jacob, and Wilhelm K. Grimm. *Grimms' Tales for Young and Old: The Complete Stories*. Translated by Ralph Manheim. Garden City, NY: Doubleday, 1983.

Grimm, Jacob, and Wilhelm K. Grimm. *The Fisherman and His Wife*. Translated by Anthea Bell and illustrated by Alan Marks. Saxonville, MA: Picture Book Studio, 1989.

Kinscella, Hazel Gertrude. *Folk Tales from Many Lands*. Lincoln, Kansas City and New York: The University Publishing Co., 1939.

Shub, Elisabeth (translation). "About the Fisherman and His Wife." *About Wise Men and Simpletons*. New York: Macmillan, 1971.

The Great Lion and the Tiny Mouse

Johnson, Edna, Evelyn R. Sickels, Frances Clarke Sayers, and Carolyn Horovitz. "A Lion and a Mouse." *Anthology of Children's Literature*. 5th ed. Boston: Houghton Mifflin, 1977.

Kleven, Elisa. *The Lion and the Little Red Bird*. New York: Puffin, 192.

The Great Gigantic Turnip

Milhouse, Katherine, and Alic Dalglish (collection). *Once On a Time From an Old Russian Storyteller*. New York: Charles Scribner's Sons, 1938.

Morgan, Pierr (illustrator). *The Turnip: An old Russian Folktale*. New York: Philomel Books, 1990.

Parkinson, Kathy (retold and illustrated). *The Enormous Turnip*. Morton Grove, IL: Albert Whitman, 1986.

The Little Red Hen

Galdone, Paul. *The Little Red Hen*. New York: Clarion, 1973.

Offen, Hilda. "The Little Red Hen." *A Treasury of Bedtime Stories*. New York: Simon and Schuster Books for Young Readers, 1981.

The Elves and the Shoemaker

Alder, Bill, Jr. "The Elves and the Shoemaker." *Tell Me a Fairy Tale: A Parent's Guide to Telling Magical and Mythical Stories*. New York: Penguin, 1995.

Griffith, John W. and Charles H. Frey, eds. "The Elves and the Shoemaker." *Classics of Children's Literature*. New York: Macmillan, 1981.

Offen, Hilda. "The Elves and the Shoemaker." *A Treasury of Bedtime Stories*. New York: Simon and Schuster Books for Young Readers, 1981.

The White Crane

Bang, Molly. *Dawn*. New York: Mulberry Books, 1983.

Bodkin, Odds. *The Crane Wife*. New York: Harcourt, 1998.

Yaagawa, Sumiko. *The Crane Wife*. Translated by Katherine Paterson and Suekichi Akaba. New York: William Morrow, 1981.

Henny-Penny and Four Fine-Feathered Friends

Johnson, Edna, Evelyn R. Sickels, Frances Clarke Sayers, and Carolyn Horovitz. *Anthology of Children's Literature*. 5th ed. Boston: Houghton Mifflin, 1977. (Johnson et al. reference Jacobs, Joseph. *English Fairy Tales*. New York: Putnman, 1892).

Kellogg, Steven. *Chicken Little*. New York: Morrow, 1985.

Power, Effie. "The Story of Chicken-Licken." *Bag O'Tales*. New York: Dutton, 1934.

Wilson, Barbara Ker. "Henny-Penny." *Animal Folk Tales*. New York: Grosset and Dunlap, 1968, 1971.

The Boy Who Cried Wolf

Jones, Vernon (translation). "The Shepherd's Boy and the Wolf." *Aesop's Fables*. New York: Franklin Watts, 1912,1967,1969.

Rose, Laura. *Folktales: Teaching Reading through Visualization and Drawing*. Tucson, AZ: Zephyr Press, 1992.

Sylvester, Charles. "The Shepherd Boy and the Wolves" (collection). *Journeys Through Bookland*. Vol I. Chicago: Bellows-Reeve,1922,1932.

Why the Possum Has a Skinny Tail

Connolly, James E. "Why the Possum's Tail is Bare." *Why the Possum's Tail is Bare and other North American Indian Nature Tales*. Owings Mills, MD: Stemmer House, 1985. Connolly acknowledges the Smithsonian Institution and *Myths of the Cherokee* by James Mooney (date unknown).

Why Crocodile Does Not Eat Hen

Dolch, Marguerite P. "The Crocodile and the Hen." *Animal Stories from Africa*. Champaign, IL: Garrard, 1975.

Hamilton, Martha, and Mitch Weiss. "Why Crocodile Does Not Eat Hen." *Stories in My Pocket: Tales Kids Can Tell*. Golden, CO: Fulcrum Publishing, 1996. (Hamilton and Weiss reference Lexau, Joan M. *Crocodile and Hen*. New York: Harper Row, 1969.)

Leach, Marcia. "Why Crocodile Does Not Eat Hen." *How the People Sang the Mountains Up: How and Why Stories*. New York: Viking, 1967.

How the Camel Got His Humph

Kipling, Rudyard. *Just So Stories for Little Children*. Garden City, NY: Doubleday, Page and Co., 1925. This story was also copyrighted separately in 1897 by the Century Co.

Why the Burro Lives With the Man

Johnson, Edna, Evelyn R. Sickels, Frances Clarke Sayers, and Carolyn Horovitz. "Why the Burro Lives with the Man." *Anthology of Children's Literature*. 5th ed. Boston: Houghton Mifflin, 1977. (Johnson et al. reference Bryan, Catherine, and Mabra Madden. *The Cactus Fence*. New York: Macmillan, 1943.)

The Curious Elephant's Child

Kipling, Rudyard. *The Elephant's Child*. New York: Harcourt Brace, 1983.

Kipling, Rudyard. *Just So Stories for Little Children*. Garden City, NY: Doubleday, Page and Co., 1925. This story was also copyrighted separately in 1897 by the Century Co.

Index

Q ~ R

S

TELL IT AGAIN!

Tell It 2 Again!

Chess For Dummies™

BUSINESS AND
GENERAL
REFERENCE
BOOK SERIES
FROM IDG

Quick Reference Card

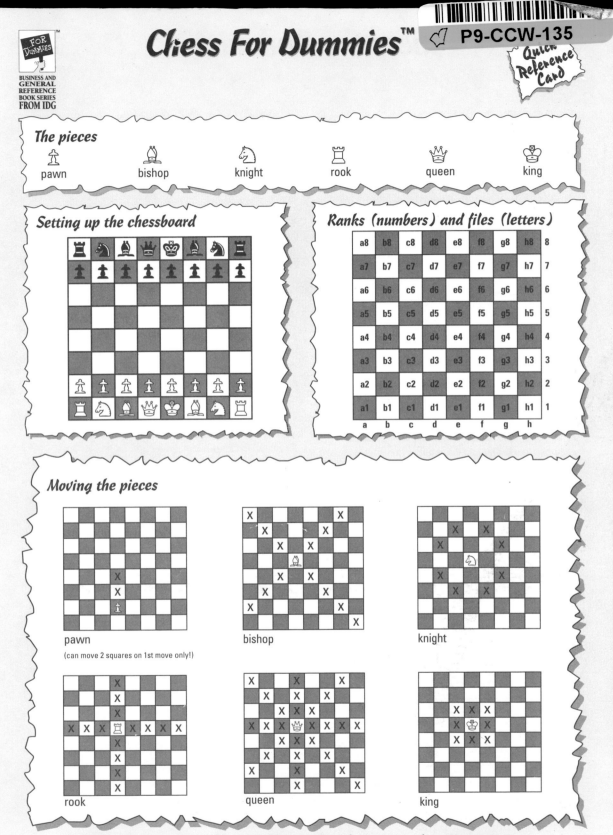

The pieces

pawn   bishop   knight   rook   queen   king

Setting up the chessboard

Ranks (numbers) and files (letters)

Moving the pieces

pawn
(can move 2 squares on 1st move only!)

bishop

knight

rook

queen

king

...For Dummies: Bestselling Book Series for Beginners

Chess For Dummies™

BUSINESS AND
GENERAL
REFERENCE
BOOK SERIES
FROM IDG

Quick Reference Card

Sound like a Grandmaster

Here are terms that have a *specialized* meaning in the world of chess. Use these to make yourself understood . . . or at least to impress your chess-playing friends!

active Description of a move that increases your mobility; a piece can also be *mobile*.

blunder A bad move that results in checkmate, the loss of material, or a seriously weakened position.

desperado A piece that is trapped or must inevitably be captured; this piece is moved in order to inflict the greatest possible damage to the opposing side.

development The movement of pieces from their starting squares.

duffer Disparaging term to describe a very poor player.

en prise French for "in a position to be taken." A chessman is *en prise* if it is left or moved to a square where it can be captured without loss to the capturing player.

fianchetto The placement of a bishop on b2 or g2 for white, b7 or g7 for black. The term is derived from the Italian *fiancata* (moves played on the flank).

fish Derogatory term for a chess player of little skill or experience.

fork An attack on two enemy chessmen at the same time.

hanging Slang term to describe a piece left *en prise*.

initiative Term to describe the advantage held by the player who has the ability to control the action and flow of the game — thus forcing the opponent to play defensively.

J'adoube French for "I adjust." Expression used by a player on the move before touching a chessman, generally to move it to the center of its square. A piece or pawn so adjusted does not have to be the man that will be the player's official move.

kibitz To comment during a game, or during analysis following a game, within the hearing of the players. The term is often used in a pejorative sense and is in many occasions applied to the comments of a spectator for whom the players have little respect.

mobility The ability to move one's pieces to important parts of the board quickly and easily.

passive Description of a move that contains no threats. Also a description of a piece with limited mobility. (That's to say, a piece that is not active.)

phalanx Pawn structure where two or more pawns of the same color are side-by-side (on the same rank and on adjacent files).

quiet move A move that contains no immediate threat, which does not make a capture, and which is not a check.

sacrifice To deliberately give up material to achieve an advantage. The advantage gained might be an attack, greater board control, and so on.

shot Colloquial term for a very strong and unexpected move.

simplify To exchange material in order to reduce the possibility of an opponent's attack. The player with the better position is more likely to simplify than the player with the worse position.

swindle A combination employed by a player with a losing position which converts his position into a win or draw. Such a combination is generally considered to be either avoidable by the opponent or the result of luck.

trap A move whose natural reply results in a disadvantage to the replying player.

...For Dummies: Bestselling Book Series for Beginners

Praise for Chess For Dummies

Everything you need to know about getting started, getting better, and even getting to play chess in cyberspace.

> — Grandmaster Larry Evans, five-time U.S. champion and syndicated chess columnist

Chess For Dummies has achieved a rarity: an entertaining and instructional book for everyone.

> — Grandmaster Yasser Seirawan, President, International Chess Enterprises, Inc., three-time U.S. champion

Jim Eade has written the best single-volume introduction to chess in the English language. The book enables anyone old enough to read to enjoy a complete game quickly and effortlessly. . . . Chess, like music, has the power to make men happy. Especially when it is so well presented.

> — Tom Dorsch, Chess Master, Treasurer, U.S. Chess Federation

I highly recommend *Chess For Dummies*. With his fine presentation of the fundamentals and amusing style, Jim Eade's work is perfect for budding chess players. His book is definitely the best of its kind.

> — Grandmaster John Fedorowicz

Not since the days of Fred Reinfeld has anyone produced a chess primer so logically presented, and so very entertaining. Reading *Chess For Dummies* from cover to cover, thanks to the icons, will elevate the new player well beyond the beginning level. And it is readable! Jim Eade is no dummy! And you won't be either. Your competition won't stand a chance!

> — Glenn Petersen, Editor, *Chess Life*

 ™

BUSINESS AND GENERAL REFERENCE BOOK SERIES FROM IDG

References for the Rest of Us!™

Do you find that traditional reference books are overloaded with technical details and advice you'll never use? Do you postpone important life decisions because you just don't want to deal with them? Then our *...For Dummies*™ business and general reference book series is for you.

...For Dummies business and general reference books are written for those frustrated and hard-working souls who know they aren't dumb, but find that the myriad of personal and business issues and the accompanying horror stories make them feel helpless. *...For Dummies* books use a lighthearted approach, a down-to-earth style, and even cartoons and humorous icons to diffuse fears and build confidence. Lighthearted but not lightweight, these books are perfect survival guides to solve your everyday personal and business problems.

> *"More than a publishing phenomenon, 'Dummies' is a sign of the times."*
> — The New York Times

> *"A world of detailed and authoritative information is packed into them..."*
> — U.S. News and World Report

> *"... you won't go wrong buying them."*
> — Walter Mossberg, Wall Street Journal, on IDG's ...For Dummies™ books

Already, hundreds of thousands of satisfied readers agree. They have made *...For Dummies* the #1 introductory level computer book series and a best-selling business book series. They have written asking for more. So, if you're looking for the best and easiest way to learn about business and other general reference topics, look to *...For Dummies* to give you a helping hand.

CHESS FOR DUMMIES™

by James Eade

IDG BOOKS WORLDWIDE™

IDG Books Worldwide, Inc.
An International Data Group Company

Foster City, CA ♦ Chicago, IL ♦ Indianapolis, IN ♦ Southlake, TX

Chess For Dummies™

Published by
IDG Books Worldwide, Inc.
An International Data Group Company
919 E. Hillsdale Blvd.
Suite 400
Foster City, CA 94404
http://www.idgbooks.com (IDG Books Worldwide Web site)
http://www.dummies.com (Dummies Press Web site)

Library of Congress Catalog Card No.: 96-78142

ISBN: 0-7645-5003-9

Printed in the United States of America

10 9 8 7 6 5 4 3

1B/QR/QU/ZX/IN

Distributed in the United States by IDG Books Worldwide, Inc.

Distributed by Macmillan Canada for Canada; by Transworld Publishers Limited in the United Kingdom and Europe; by WoodsLane Pty. Ltd. for Australia; by WoodsLane Enterprises Ltd. for New Zealand; by Longman Singapore Publishers Ltd. for Singapore, Malaysia, Thailand, and Indonesia; by Simron Pty. Ltd. for South Africa; by Toppan Company Ltd. for Japan; by Distribuidora Cuspide for Argentina; by Livraria Cultura for Brazil; by Ediciencia S.A. for Ecuador; by Addison-Wesley Publishing Company for Korea; by Ediciones ZETA S.C.R. Ltda. for Peru; by WS Computer Publishing Company, Inc., for the Philippines; by Unalis Corporation for Taiwan; by Contemporanea de Ediciones for Venezuela. Authorized Sales Agent: Anthony Rudkin Associates for the Middle East and North Africa.

For general information on IDG Books Worldwide's books in the U.S., please call our Consumer Customer Service department at 800-762-2974. For reseller information, including discounts and premium sales, please call our Reseller Customer Service department at 800-434-3422.

For information on where to purchase IDG Books Worldwide's books outside the U.S., please contact our International Sales department at 415-655-3023 or fax 415-655-3299.

For information on foreign language translations, please contact our Foreign & Subsidiary Rights department at 415-655-3021 or fax 415-655-3281.

For sales inquiries and special prices for bulk quantities, please contact our Sales department at 415-655-3200 or write to the address above.

For information on using IDG Books Worldwide's books in the classroom or for ordering examination copies, please contact our Educational Sales department at 800-434-2086 or fax 817-251-8174.

For press review copies, author interviews, or other publicity information, please contact our Public Relations department at 415-655-3000 or fax 415-655-3299.

For authorization to photocopy items for corporate, personal, or educational use, please contact Copyright Clearance Center, 222 Rosewood Drive, Danvers, MA 01923, or fax 508-750-4470.

is a trademark under exclusive license to IDG Books Worldwide, Inc., from International Data Group, Inc.

About the Author

James Eade began taking chess seriously in 1972 when Bobby Fischer was taking the chess world by storm. He competed on his high school and college teams and became a United States Chess Federation (USCF) chess master in 1981. In 1984 he became a USCF correspondence chess master as well. International organizations awarded him the master title in 1990 (for correspondence) and in 1993 (for regular tournament play), but his chess playing career has gradually given way to chess writing, organizing, and teaching.

James has written two previous books on chess: *Remember the MacCutcheon*, (Chess Enterprises) and *San Francisco, 1995* (Hypermodern Press). He has written numerous articles for a variety of magazines and has edited both the *Golden Gate Chess News* and the *California Chess Journal*.

He began taking an interest in chess political organizations in 1991 and was elected vice-president of CalChess, the Northern California Chess Association, later that year. In 1995 he became CalChess president and was also elected to be president of the Chess Journalists of America. In 1996 he was elected to the USCF's policy board, the executive committee charged with oversight of the multi-million-dollar corporation.

James holds a masters degree in organization development from the University of San Francisco and still bristles at being called a chess nerd.

ABOUT IDG BOOKS WORLDWIDE

Welcome to the world of IDG Books Worldwide.

IDG Books Worldwide, Inc., is a subsidiary of International Data Group, the world's largest publisher of computer-related information and the leading global provider of information services on information technology. IDG was founded more than 25 years ago and now employs more than 8,500 people worldwide. IDG publishes more than 275 computer publications in over 75 countries (see listing below). More than 60 million people read one or more IDG publications each month.

Launched in 1990, IDG Books Worldwide is today the #1 publisher of best-selling computer books in the United States. We are proud to have received eight awards from the Computer Press Association in recognition of editorial excellence and three from *Computer Currents'* First Annual Readers' Choice Awards. Our best-selling *...For Dummies*® series has more than 30 million copies in print with translations in 30 languages. IDG Books Worldwide, through a joint venture with IDG's Hi-Tech Beijing, became the first U.S. publisher to publish a computer book in the People's Republic of China. In record time, IDG Books Worldwide has become the first choice for millions of readers around the world who want to learn how to better manage their businesses.

Our mission is simple: Every one of our books is designed to bring extra value and skill-building instructions to the reader. Our books are written by experts who understand and care about our readers. The knowledge base of our editorial staff comes from years of experience in publishing, education, and journalism — experience we use to produce books for the '90s. In short, we care about books, so we attract the best people. We devote special attention to details such as audience, interior design, use of icons, and illustrations. And because we use an efficient process of authoring, editing, and desktop publishing our books electronically, we can spend more time ensuring superior content and spend less time on the technicalities of making books.

You can count on our commitment to deliver high-quality books at competitive prices on topics you want to read about. At IDG Books Worldwide, we continue in the IDG tradition of delivering quality for more than 25 years. You'll find no better book on a subject than one from IDG Books Worldwide.

John Kilcullen
CEO
IDG Books Worldwide, Inc.

**Eighth Annual
Computer Press
Awards ≥1992**

**Ninth Annual
Computer Press
Awards ≥1993**

**Tenth Annual
Computer Press
Awards ≥1994**

**Eleventh Annual
Computer Press
Awards ≥1995**

IDG Books Worldwide, Inc., is a subsidiary of International Data Group, the world's largest publisher of computer-related information and the leading global provider of information services on information technology. International Data Group publishes over 275 computer publications in over 75 countries. Sixty million people read one or more International Data Group publications each month. International Data Group's publications include: **ARGENTINA:** Buyer's Guide, Computerworld Argentina, PC World Argentina; **AUSTRALIA:** Australian Macworld, Australian PC World, Australian Reseller News, Computerworld, IT Casebook, Network World, Publish, Webmaster; **AUSTRIA:** Computerwelt Osterreich, Networks Austria, PC Tip Austria; **BANGLADESH:** PC World Bangladesh; **BELARUS:** PC World Belarus; **BELGIUM:** Data News; **BRAZIL:** Annuário de Informática, Computerworld, Connections, Macworld, PC Player, PC World, Publish, Reseller News, Supergamepower; **BULGARIA:** Computerworld Bulgaria, Network World Bulgaria, PC & MacWorld Bulgaria; **CANADA:** CIO Canada, Client/Server World, ComputerWorld Canada, InfoWorld Canada, NetworkWorld Canada, WebWorld; **CHILE:** Computerworld Chile, PC World Chile; **COLOMBIA:** Computerworld Colombia, PC World Colombia; **COSTA RICA:** PC World Centro America; **THE CZECH AND SLOVAK REPUBLICS:** Computerworld Czechoslovakia, Macworld Czech Republic, PC World Czechoslovakia; **DENMARK:** Communications World Danmark, Computerworld Danmark, Macworld Danmark, PC World Danmark, Techworld Denmark; **DOMINICAN REPUBLIC:** PC World Republica Dominicana; **ECUADOR:** PC World Ecuador; **EGYPT:** Computerworld Middle East, PC World Middle East; **EL SALVADOR:** PC World Centro America; **FINLAND:** MikroPC, Tietoverkko, Tietoviikko; **FRANCE:** Distributique, Hebdo, Info PC, Le Monde Informatique, Macworld, Reseaux & Telecoms, WebMaster France; **GERMANY:** Computer Partner, Computerwoche, Computerwoche Extra, Computerwoche FOCUS, Global Online, Macwelt, PC Welt; **GREECE:** Amiga Computing, GamePro Greece, Multimedia World; **GUATEMALA:** PC World Centro America; **HONDURAS:** PC World Centro America; **HONG KONG:** Computerworld Hong Kong, PC World Hong Kong, Publish in Asia; **HUNGARY:** ABCD CD-ROM, Computerworld Szamitastechnika, Internetto online Magazine, PC World Hungary, PC-X Magazin Hungary; **ICELAND:** Tolvuheimur PC World Island; **INDIA:** Information Communications World, Information Systems Computerworld, PC World India, Publish in Asia; **INDONESIA:** InfoKomputer PC World, Komputek Computerworld, Publish in Asia; **IRELAND:** ComputerScope, PC Live!; **ISRAEL:** Macworld Israel, People & Computers/Computerworld; **ITALY:** Computerworld Italia, Macworld Italia, Networking Italia, PC World Italia; **JAPAN:** DTP World, Macworld Japan, Nikkei Personal Computing, OS/2 World Japan, SunWorld Japan, Windows NT World, Windows World Japan; **KENYA:** PC World East African; **KOREA:** Hi-Tech Information, Macworld Korea, PC World Korea; **MACEDONIA:** PC World Macedonia; **MALAYSIA:** Computerworld Malaysia, PC World Malaysia, Publish in Asia; **MALTA:** PC World Malta; **MEXICO:** Computerworld Mexico, PC World Mexico; **MYANMAR:** PC World Myanmar; **NETHERLANDS:** Computer! Totaal, LAN Internetworking Magazine, LAN World Buyers Guide, Macworld Netherlands, Net, WebWereld; **NEW ZEALAND:** Absolute Beginners Guide and Plain & Simple Series, Computer Buyer, Computer Industry Directory, Computerworld New Zealand, MTB, Network World, PC World New Zealand; **NICARAGUA:** PC World Centro America; **NORWAY:** Computerworld Norge, CW Rapport, Datamagasinet, Financial Rapport, Kursguide Norge, Macworld Norge, Multimediaworld Norge, PC World Ekspress Norge, PC World Nettverk, PC World Norge, PC World ProduktGuide Norge; **PAKISTAN:** Computerworld Pakistan; **PANAMA:** PC World Panama; **PEOPLE'S REPUBLIC OF CHINA:** China Computer Users, China Computerworld, China InfoWorld, China Telecom World Weekly, Computer & Communication, Electronic Design China, Electronics Today, Electronics Weekly, Game Software, PC World China, Popular Computer Week, Software Weekly, Software World, Telecom World; **PERU:** Computerworld Peru, PC World Profesional Peru, PC World SoHo Peru; **PHILIPPINES:** Click!, Computerworld Philippines, PC World Philippines, Publish in Asia; **POLAND:** Computerworld Poland, Computerworld Special Report Poland, Cyber, Macworld Poland, Networld Poland, PC World Komputer; **PORTUGAL:** Cerebro/PC World, Computerworld/Correio Informático, Dealer World Portugal, Mac*In/PC*In Portugal, Multimedia World; **PUERTO RICO:** PC World Puerto Rico; **ROMANIA:** Computerworld Romania, PC World Romania, Telecom Romania; **RUSSIA:** Computerworld Russia, Mir PK, Publish, Seti; **SINGAPORE:** Computerworld Singapore, PC World Singapore, Publish in Asia; **SLOVENIA:** Monitor; **SOUTH AFRICA:** Computing SA, Network World SA, Software World SA; **SPAIN:** Communicaciones World España, Computerworld España, Dealer World España, Macworld España, PC World España; **SRI LANKA:** Infolink PC World; **SWEDEN:** CAP&Design, Computer Sweden, Corporate Computing Sweden, Internetworld Sweden, it.branschen, Macworld Sweden, MaxiData Sweden, MikroDatorn, Natverk & Kommunikation, PC World Sweden, PCaktiv, Windows World Sweden; **SWITZERLAND:** Computerworld Schweiz, Macworld Schweiz, PCtip; **TAIWAN:** Computerworld Taiwan, Macworld Taiwan, NEW ViSiON/Publish, PC World Taiwan, Windows World Taiwan; **THAILAND:** Publish in Asia, Thai Computerworld; **TURKEY:** Computerworld Turkiye, Macworld Turkiye, Network World Turkiye, PC World Turkiye; **UKRAINE:** Computerworld Kiev, Multimedia World Ukraine, PC World Ukraine; **UNITED KINGDOM:** Acorn User UK, Amiga Action UK, Amiga Computing UK, Apple Talk UK, Computing, Macworld, Parents and Computers UK, PC Advisor, PC Home, PSX Pro, The WEB; **UNITED STATES:** Cable in the Classroom, CIO Magazine, Computerworld, DOS World, Federal Computer Week, GamePro Magazine, InfoWorld, I-Way, Macworld, Network World, PC Games, PC World, Publish, Video Event, THE WEB Magazine, and WebMaster; online webzines: JavaWorld, NetscapeWorld, and SunWorld Online; **URUGUAY:** InfoWorld Uruguay; **VENEZUELA:** Computerworld Venezuela, PC World Venezuela; and **VIETNAM:** PC World Vietnam.
1/24/97

Dedication

To Sheri — for suffering chess fools gladly.

Author's Acknowledgments

The author would like to thank Sheri Anderson for all her encouragement and support throughout this writing project. Her brother, Bruce, also deserves my thanks for his wise and timely counsel.

My editors, Bill Helling and Bill Barton, deserve a special thanks from me for drilling it into my head that not everyone knows Ruy Lopez from Nancy Lopez, and for keeping me on the straight and narrow. My thanks also go to the technical editor, John Peterson, who is a better friend than chess player — and he happens to be a very good chess player.

Bob Burger, who helped with the section on chess problems and compositions, and Myron Lieberman, who I consulted for the chess online materials, were both kind and useful, and have my gratitude. M.L. Rantala was more than helpful with the glossary of terms, which I could not have done without her most able assistance. I wish to thank my father, Arthur Eade, for teaching me chess, and my mother, Marilyn, for her touching advance order for this book. Lastly, a special thank you to Lore McGovern, who was the wind at my back from start to finish.

Publisher's Acknowledgments

We're proud of this book; please send us your comments about it by using the Reader Response Card at the back of the book or by e-mailing us at feedback/dummies@idgbooks.com. Some of the people who helped bring this book to market include the following:

Acquisitions, Development, and Editorial

Project Editor: Bill Helling

Acquisitions Editor: Kathleen A. Welton,
Vice President and Publisher

Media Development Manager: Joyce Pepple

Copy Editors: William Barton,
Christine Meloy Beck, Michael Bolinger

Technical Editor: John Peterson

Editorial Manager: Mary C. Corder

Editorial Assistants: Chris H. Collins, Ann Miller

Production

Project Coordinator: Valery Bourke

Layout and Graphics: Elizabeth Cárdenas-Nelson, Dominique DeFelice, Todd Klemme, Mark C. Owens, Theresa Sánchez-Baker, Brent Savage

Special Art: Shelley Lea

Proofreaders: Joel K. Draper, Rachel Garvey, Dwight Ramsey, Robert Springer, Carrie Voorhis, Karen York

Indexer: Liz Cunningham

General and Administrative

IDG Books Worldwide, Inc.: John Kilcullen, CEO; Steven Berkowitz, President and Publisher

IDG Books Technology Publishing: Brenda McLaughlin, Senior Vice President and Group Publisher

Dummies Technology Press and Dummies Editorial: Diane Graves Steele, Vice President and Associate Publisher; Judith A. Taylor, Brand Manager; Kristin A. Cocks, Editorial Director

Dummies Trade Press: Kathleen A. Welton, Vice President and Publisher; Stacy S. Collins, Brand Manager

IDG Books Production for Dummies Press: Beth Jenkins, Production Director; Cindy L. Phipps, Supervisor of Project Coordination, Production Proofreading, and Indexing; Kathie S. Schutte, Supervisor of Page Layout; Shelley Lea, Supervisor of Graphics and Design; Debbie J. Gates, Production Systems Specialist; Tony Augsburger, Supervisor of Reprints and Bluelines; Leslie Popplewell, Media Archive Coordinator

Dummies Packaging and Book Design: Patti Sandez, Packaging Specialist; Lance Kayser, Packaging Assistant; Kavish + Kavish, Cover Design

♦

The publisher would like to give special thanks to Patrick J. McGovern,
without whom this book would not have been possible.

♦

Contents at a Glance

Cartoons at a Glance

By Rich Tennant • Fax: 508-546-7747 • E-mail: the5wave@tiac.net

page 217

page 7

page 265

page 153

page 39

Table of Contents

Introduction

• •

*S*ome chess players hate to hear someone call chess a *game*. They think that, by doing so, one trivializes what is actually a profound intellectual activity. Try as they may, however, chess enthusiasts seem incapable of convincingly placing chess solely in the context of art, science, or sport. Uncannily, chess contains elements of all three — and yet chess remains a game.

Actually, I prefer to think of chess as a game — the best game ever invented. Chess is a game loved by engineers and free-verse poets alike. Chess imposes a set of rules and has finite limits, but just as you start to think that you're finally solving its mysteries, chess thwarts you. Sometimes, therefore, the game is frustrating, but far more often, chess proves both surprising and delightful. The deeper you dig into chess, the more of its secrets you unearth — but the game has never been tapped out. Even today's monster computers are far from playing the theorized "perfect" chess game.

To master chess, you must combine a kind of discipline normally associated with the hard sciences and a creative freedom akin to the inspiration of artists. Few of us develop both aspects equally well, and few activities can help us do so. Chess, however, is one such activity. The plodding scientist is forced to tap into his creative energies to play well. The fanciful artist must, in turn, conform to certain specific principles or face the harsh reality of a lost game.

In study after study, chess has proven among the most effective educational training tools available. Children who are introduced to chess programs find that their standardized test scores increase in such critical abilities as reading comprehension and total memory recall. Control groups — and groups introduced to games other than chess — demonstrate no such increase. For a summary of these studies, write to the American Chess School, 140 School Street, Bradford, PA, 16701.

The point is that, not only is chess an excellent educational tool, chess is fun, too. Persuading kids to play a game of chess is far easier than enticing them to do math exercises, believe me! The great thing is that the kids are actually learning how to think while playing. They can't help it! Parents all across the nation are waking up to the fact that chess is an inexpensive and effective option for developing skills, such as the ability to sit still and concentrate, that are directly transferable back into the classroom.

Chess can also be an endless source of pleasure. The degree of fun derived from a game of chess is rarely a function of one's absolute playing strength, but rather of the relative strengths of you and your chess partner. If two players are horribly mismatched, neither is likely to have much fun. The best situation occurs if two players are evenly or closely matched. Some days you win in such matches and some days you lose — but the issue is always in doubt, often right down to the end of the game!

This book is designed to help the reader become a better chess player in several ways: First, the book contains a great deal of information and advice on how to play chess. You can also find in these pages information about how to talk about chess, which, to many players, is at least as important as knowing how to play. Part of the fun of chess is the social element involved in discussing other people's games (called *kibitzing*). Finally, the book offers numerous suggestions on how to find other players who are just about at your own level.

If you are a beginner, the great joys of chess await you. If you are an intermediate player, you can find in this book a wealth of material to help you improve your game and to enjoy chess even more.

Why a ...For Dummies Book about Chess?

After most people discover that I play chess, they usually say, "You must be very smart." They should instead say, "You must have a lot of spare time." Chess has been played throughout history by people with above-average leisure time, not necessarily by people with far-above-average intelligence.

Chess tutors can, in fact, teach preschoolers the rules of the game. (Can't get the tots to stop chewing on the pieces, maybe, but *can* teach them how to play.) In fact, anyone can learn how to play chess if you have a bit of spare time. And you don't even need too much of that.

This "smartness mystique" has grown up around chess partly because, historically, the ruling classes were the only ones with enough time to kill to play the game. And serfs could more easily rationalize this fact by saying, "Look, the Baron is playing chess; he must be smart." Saying, "Look the Baron is playing chess; he must be a lazy, shiftless bum," was far less conducive to maintaining good relations with the Baron (or the continued good health of the serf).

We chess players have ourselves carefully cultivated the smartness mystique surrounding chess — for what we consider a valid reason: We would greatly prefer that people think we spend our time in an intellectual pursuit than in the simple avoidance of work. We have thus carefully crafted our jargon to make the game seem far more complicated than it actually is. We make certain that foreign words are sprinkled liberally in our conversations, just to emphasize our worldliness. But don't let the terminology fool you; not everyone can *play* chess like a grandmaster, but everyone can *talk* like one!

Part of the chess club atmosphere is sitting around and talking about other people's games, or one's own game that should've been easily won. If you learn the terminology, you will be accepted into these circles more easily and will be more likely to make new friends.

All this "smartness mystique" does have a good side, however — one involving self-esteem. People *do* associate playing chess with being smart, and many people, after discovering that they, too, can really play the game, naturally conclude that they, too, must be smart. This confidence often carries over into other walks of life. Witnessing a child's self-assurance grow, simply from gaining skill in a *game,* is truly a wondrous thing.

Chess is an inexpensive and proven educational tool, and parents grasp this almost immediately. As a result, chess-in-the-schools programs are springing up all over America. But when I've asked a parent, who is coming by to pick up or drop off a child for a chess lesson, whether the parent plays chess, I'm met by a shocked expression and a wide-eyed, "Oh, no!" response. Sometimes, I think I see a little fear in the person's eyes as well. This is just silly. Parents can learn to play chess, too!

Well, enough of that! The time has come to demystify chess. And a ...*For Dummies* book is, as I see things, the best way to start! Those parents I just mentioned could pick up the game as easily as their children do, if they'd only give chess a chance. And in so doing, they'd open the door to an immense source of personal pleasure; they'd find, as I have — as I hope you do in reading this book — that chess truly is a deeply fascinating art, science, sport, and, above all, game.

How to Use This Book

Throughout this book, I use diagrams of actual chessboards to show the positions I discuss. This convention should sometimes eliminate the need for you to have a chessboard and set in order to use the book — but even so, it's better if you follow along with an actual chessboard and set. Just note that the white pieces always start at the bottom of the chessboards and the black pieces start at the top in these diagrams.

Sidebars are used throughout the book to introduce famous players or to add miscellaneous information that is not really necessary to know in order to play chess. This information is included to increase your enjoyment of the game.

If you have no knowledge of chess whatsoever, you need to start with Chapters 1 and 2. Otherwise, skipping around through the book to locate the chapters and sections of most interest or use to you is perfectly OK.

Part I: Laying the Groundwork

Chapter 1 assumes that you do have a chessboard and set. You may proceed in any case, because this chapter contains plenty of pictures, but your best course is to work through the chapter with a board and set of your own. Chapter 1 takes you through the basic setup of the chessboard and cues you in on some of the basic chess terminology used more extensively in later chapters.

Chapter 2 is an in-depth look at each piece in the chess set and its powers. In this chapter, you see how each piece moves on the chessboard and you learn the value of each piece, relative to one another. Each different chess piece has its own unique set of strengths and weaknesses, and you can read about these different powers here.

Part II: Getting Past the Rules

Chapter 3 introduces you to the basic elements of a game of chess. After reading this chapter, you can give a rough assessment of almost any chess position. Chapters 4, 5, and 6 deal with different types of tactical situations. Most games are lost by mistakes made in these areas, so pay careful attention to the lessons shared in these chapters if winning is your goal. Even if you are just playing for fun, these chapters will help you appreciate how combinations of chess moves can have a beauty all their own.

Chapter 7 and Chapter 8 deal with more general themes and look at chess from a slightly different, less hard-and-fast rule oriented perspective. (Chess players are not calculating machines but develop a feel for the game that helps them make sense out of what sometimes can look like chaos. Chapter 7 discusses this feel for positions in terms of pattern recognition, while Chapter 8 concentrates on the some of the guideposts we use to guide our play.)

Chapter 9 covers those rules of the game that are less commonly understood by most players. These rules start at least half the arguments that break out among beginning chess players, so learning them might save you some unpleasantness.

Part III: Let the Play Begin

Chapters 10, 11, and 12 break down the game of chess into three distinct units: the opening, the middlegame, and the endgame. These chapters provide rules of thumb for each phase of the game, as well as practical examples of play.

Chapter 13 covers chess etiquette. This chapter accounts for nearly all the remaining arguments you encounter in the game: Can you touch your opponent's pieces? Does a right way or a wrong way exist to offer a draw? And so on. This chapter offers a lot of tips for the beginner and for the intermediate player alike.

Part IV: Who to Play, When, Where, and How

Chapter 14 describes the various chess organizations you can contact, from your backyard to around the globe, and provides contact information for these groups. Chapter 15 deals with commercially available computer chess-playing games and gives advice on what to buy and why. Chapter 16 surfs the information superhighway for online chess opportunities and offers an account of what's out there now.

Chapter 17 explains the mysterious system of chess notation and walks you through the ways to record your games for posterity — or for anyone else you want to show the game to.

Part V: The Part of Tens

Chapters 18 through 21 are the Part of Tens, where I do a top ten countdown on various aspects of the game of chess. Specifically, in Chapter 18, I discuss the ten most famous chess games of all time; in Chapter 19, I list the ten best chess players of all time; Chapter 20 describes the most common chess openings; and Chapter 21 lists the ten best chess resources I know of.

Finally, I provide a glossary at the end of the book (Appendix A), in case some of these odd chess terms don't get past your short-term memory and you need to refer back to them at a later time. And if you really feel ambitious, check out Appendix B where I demonstrate the use of international chess notation.

Icons Used in This Book

The icons used in this book point you to important topics and help you pick out what you want to know.

This icon points to helpful hints — anything from playing better chess to where you find more chess stuff.

This icon warns you of impending danger that you just may be able to avoid.

I hope that I show you lots of good moves, but this icon points out moves that you should especially want to study — or admire.

Even a grandmaster can make a bad move! Learn from the mistakes of others.

Chess has a vocabulary all its own, but don't be intimidated. This icon alerts you to a special term or expression that you can add to your growing chess knowledge.

This icon wouldn't be necessary if chess didn't have so many good, general rules. Keep the rules of thumb in mind when you play. You'll be surprised how many you can retain — and how helpful they can be.

If you are interested in chess matters that just may take you beyond the introductory level, this icon points the way.

More books have been written about chess than all other games combined! This icon signals some of those books you may want to read — or even add to your chess library.

Part I
Laying the Groundwork

The 5th Wave · By Rich Tennant

Cowboy Chess

"...AND I'M SAYIN' NO ONE HAS THREE BISHOPS ON THE BOARD UNLESS HE'S A SLIMY, NO ACCOUNT CHESS CHEAT!!"

In this part . . .

Chess has a lot of rules! There is no getting around it. Sometimes people want to jump right in and start playing, even before they know the rules, but this behavior is not recommended. In this part, I start with the simplest rules of chess — the movements of the pieces on a chessboard. After you have worked through this part, you should know enough to actually play a game of chess!

Chapter 1

Setting Up the Board

● ●

In This Chapter

▶ Getting familiar with the chessboard

▶ Knowing your ranks, files, and diagonals

▶ Placing the pieces on the board

● ●

*1*f you're new to chess, don't despair. No chess gene decides who can and cannot play chess. Everyone can learn to play a passable game of chess, and — after you do — it's just a matter of time until you find someone you can play well against. If you're satisfied with participating in an endlessly fascinating and stimulating mental activity — an activity that sports a rich history and may provide you with countless hours of amusement — you're in luck. You can play chess, take my word for it.

The Chessboard

The first step is to purchase a chessboard and set. Note that I didn't say *checkerboard*. Chessboards and checkerboards may look the same, but you want a chessboard. This detail is important, especially if the pieces are included with the board. If you get a checkerboard, every piece will pretty much look like every other piece, and you'll have difficulty following the material in this book.

If you don't own a chessboard and chess set (a chess set is the collection of chess *pieces*), you can turn to the section on "Purchasing chess equipment" in Chapter 21 for mail-order information. It's extremely helpful to have a chessboard and chess set on hand when reading chess books. Some people can do without one — but some people can memorize the works of Milton, too. (And who wants to be like that?)

I include numerous diagrams in order to help you understand, but they don't take the place of a real set and board; these diagrams serve primarily as an error check.

Your first challenge is to sort through the many available types of pieces and boards. There is a tremendous range in terms of sizes, colors, and quality. The usual tournament set is made of plastic pieces in classic white and black, and the board is generally of a vinyl roll-up variety with white and green squares. Why not black squares, you might justifiably ask? Headaches, I would answer. I've learned that staring at a high contrast board is not to be recommended. The only exception is for the miniature traveling sets. These sets often have magnetic pieces that stick to the board, and it doesn't matter what color they are. It's assumed that you won't be staring at them too long (especially if you're driving!).

If price is no object, wood pieces and boards are the way to go. Wood boards provide the most soothing background possible, and the weight and feel of wood pieces are generally far more satisfying to the touch. There is a small cottage industry in collectible chess sets, and these sets vary in design as well as in quality. The standard design, however, is the Staunton (see Figure 1-1). If you play with strangers and bring anything other than a Staunton designed set, people may assume that you're trying to psych them out by using equipment that they aren't familiar with. You probably don't want to start off on the wrong foot.

Figure 1-1

(Photo courtesy U.S. Chess Federation. Photo of US1425s: Standard Tournament Chess Set.)

First things first, though, and I need to start by familiarizing you with the chessboard. Note again that I didn't say checkerboard. A checkerboard often comes with checkers — not chess pieces!

Figure 1-2 is that of a typical chessboard. Note the white square in the lower right-hand column as you face the board. The most common beginner mistake is to position the board incorrectly at the start of the game. As a matter of fact, this is a common mistake that Hollywood makes. Whenever you see a chess position in a movie, check to see whether the lower right-hand square is white. Chances are it won't be!

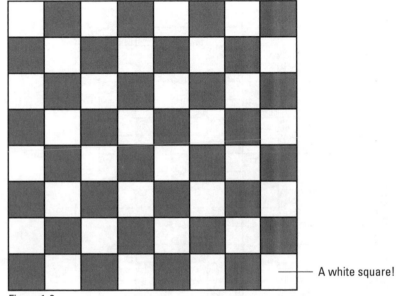

— A white square!

Figure 1-2

White on right. If you don't have a white square (or a very light color square) in the lower right-hand corner of the board, start over.

The first thing to notice about the chessboard is that all the squares are the same size but alternate between two colors (a light color — usually white — and a darker color). Colors are important in chess, and that is why chess players insist that a white square needs to be in the lower right-hand corner at the start of the game. Did I already mention that?

The chessboard is made up of 64 squares evenly divided between 32 white squares and 32 dark squares. The chessboard is symmetrical. It's square — in the geometric sense. The square is composed of eight ranks and eight files (and a bunch of diagonals), which you normally would call rows and columns (and diagonals!), but chess people shun such conventional language. We prefer our terminology because it makes us seem mysterious and smarter than we are! So if you want to avoid being intimidated by chess player terminology, read the following rank, file, and diagonal stuff . . . but don't worry too much about it yet.

Ranks

Ranks are rows that go from side to side along the chessboard and are referred to by numbers. There are eight ranks, so we have the first rank, the second rank, and so on. Figure 1-3 shows the ranks.

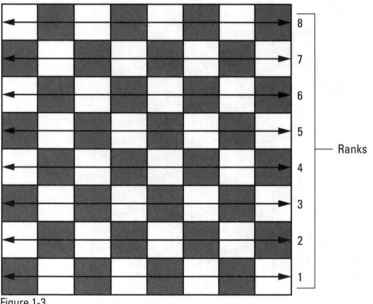

Ranks

Figure 1-3

Files

Files are columns that go up and down the chessboard. Because numbers indicate ranks, letters indicate files. Figure 1-4 shows the eight files. Remember that ranks and files are just like rows and columns, except that nobody in the chess world wants to call them that. (Using clear, easy-to-understand terms would be too easy, right?)

This naming convention of ranks and files allows you to give a unique identifier to every square using what is called the *file-first method.* For example, the lower right-hand square (which happens to be white!) is called h1. This name is shorthand for h file, 1st rank. In Figure 1-5, the squares are marked.

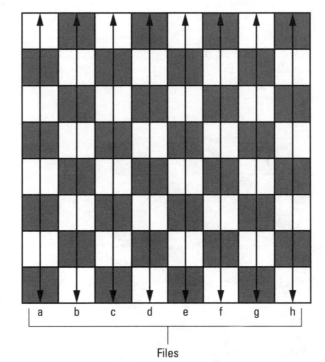

Figure 1-4

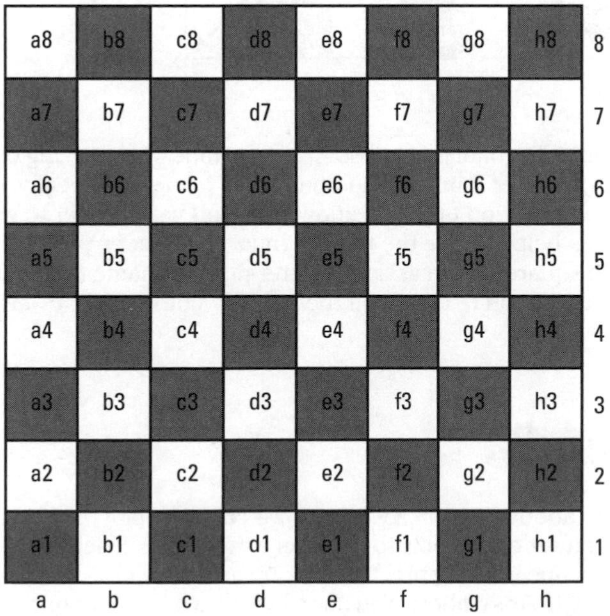

a b c d e f g h

Files

a8	b8	c8	d8	e8	f8	g8	h8	8
a7	b7	c7	d7	e7	f7	g7	h7	7
a6	b6	c6	d6	e6	f6	g6	h6	6
a5	b5	c5	d5	e5	f5	g5	h5	5
a4	b4	c4	d4	e4	f4	g4	h4	4
a3	b3	c3	d3	e3	f3	g3	h3	3
a2	b2	c2	d2	e2	f2	g2	h2	2
a1	b1	c1	d1	e1	f1	g1	h1	1

Figure 1-5

a b c d e f g h

Diagonals

Diagonals are defined by their starting and ending squares. For example, Figure 1-6 shows the h1-a8 diagonal. Diagonals are always composed of like-colored squares. You can have light-squared diagonals and dark-squared diagonals — but never two-toned ones.

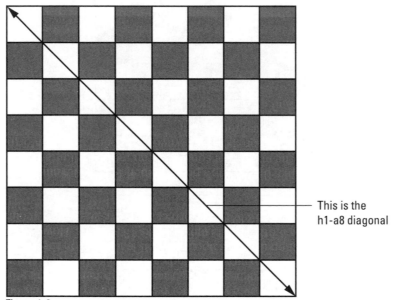

This is the h1-a8 diagonal

Figure 1-6

This rank, file, and diagonal information is important when talking or writing about chess, and I cover it in detail in Chapter 17 in case you really want to know more. You really don't need to know this stuff yet in order to enjoy playing chess, but it does help to have the basic terminology under your belt. Just don't forget that each square has an assigned letter-number name (which may be easier to figure out if you're sitting on the "white" side — or bottom — of the board).

Put the Pieces On

In order to write about chess in a way that we can all relate to, chess players have developed a set of symbols to represent the pieces. Each piece may be represented by a one-letter abbreviation or by an icon. See Table 1-1 for a list of all the pieces and their symbols. You may find it helpful to set up your own board piece by piece. Start with the corners. The rooks go on the corner squares, as in Figure 1-7.

Table 1-1	Chess Pieces and Their Symbols	
Piece	*Symbol*	
king	♚	♔
queen	♛	♕
knight	♞	♘
bishop	♝	♗
rook	♜	♖
pawn	♟	♙

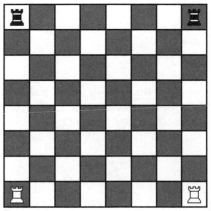
Figure 1-7

Next come the knights. The knights are placed next to the rooks (Figure 1-8).

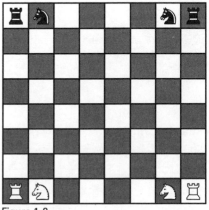
Figure 1-8

Then put the bishops on the board next to the knights (Figure 1-9).

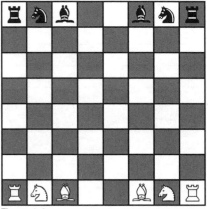

Figure 1-9

After the bishops come the queens. Note that the queens are always placed on the square of the same color. White queens go on white squares, dark-colored queens on dark-colored squares. Remember to make sure that a white square is in the right-hand corner. Your board should now look like the one in Figure 1-10.

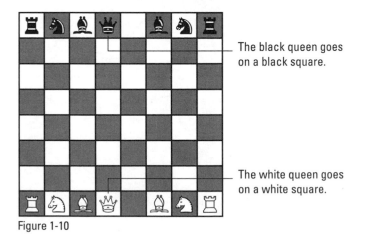

The black queen goes on a black square.

The white queen goes on a white square.

Figure 1-10

Next, place the kings next to the queens, which is only fitting (see Figure 1-11).

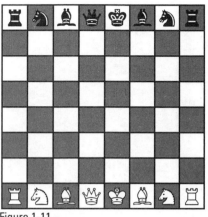
Figure 1-11

Lastly, add the pawns, as shown in Figure 1-12.

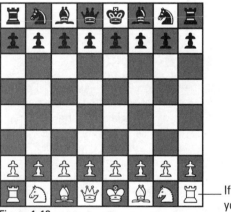
Figure 1-12

— If this square isn't white,
you have to start over! Sorry.

If you set up your chessboard by using the preceding directions and it looks like the one in Figure 1-13, pat yourself on the back! You're ready for a game.

Don't bother suggesting rule changes to chess. Everyone goes through this phase, but try to resist it. One of the greatest pleasures of chess is that you can replay games from long ago. And there is also the hope that today's games may live on indefinitely. If we were to change the rules, we would interfere with this sense of continuity. If you feel that you absolutely must share your brilliant new idea with the chess world, keep in mind that the last changes date from the end of the 15th century!

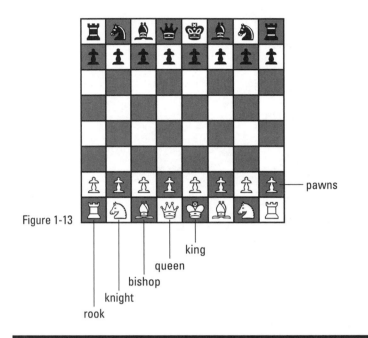

Figure 1-13

pawns

king

queen

bishop

knight

rook

The origins of chess

The true origins of chess are shrouded in the mists of pre-history. This is a good thing. It allows us to say just about anything we want about how the game started without fear of contradiction. Chess, or a game very much like chess, originated in Northern India sometime around 600 AD and eventually migrated to Europe through China and Persia (modern day Iran). The ancient Indian game was based on Indian armies and was undoubtedly a passtime for their rulers.

There is no doubt that this game, called *chaturanga,* was much like present-day chess. It was played on an eight by eight board and used six different kinds of pieces. Some people think that it may have originally involved the use of dice in order to determine which piece to move and so forth. This speculation seems to be based on little else other than the coincidence that there were six types of pieces and six different spots on the dice. It seems far more likely that the rulers playing the game preferred to exercise complete control over their armies, just as they would try to do in the battlefield.

The Indian Army was led by the rajah (king) and his chief advisor, the mantri, sometimes referred to as the vizier. The army was represented by foot soldiers, cavalry, chariots, and elephants. Of course, one can't spend all one's time waging war, and it must've been amusing for Indian royalty to *pretend* to wage war when they weren't engaged in actual battle.

By the time the game got to Europe, it had changed considerably and continued to change until about the end of the 15th century. The changes basically altered the game to make it more familiar to the Europeans who were then playing it. The rajah became the king, the mantri the queen, the foot soldiers the pawns, the cavalry the knights, the chariots the rooks, and the elephants the bishops. The game has been essentially stable since that time. Nowadays chess is played all over the world by the same rules under the control of the Fédération Internationale des Échecs (FIDE), which is French for the International Chess Federation.

Chapter 2
The Pieces and Their Powers

After years of teaching chess to elementary school children, I think I've found the easiest way to introduce the pieces to them. It seems to work. I start with the rook, because its simple up, down, side-to-side movement is easily grasped. I then move on to the bishop because it, too, moves in straight lines and goes where the rook cannot. Kids seem to pick this up right away. And what is good for kids is certainly good for older students of the game, right?

After you understand the moves of the rook and bishop, it's easy to understand the queen. The queen simply has the combined powers of the rook and bishop. After the queen comes the king. The king moves just like the queen, except only one square at a time. I leave the knight and pawn for last because they are the trickiest to explain.

Finally, when I teach the movements of the pawn, I explain that although we do sometimes refer to all the chess pieces collectively as pieces, we don't really consider a pawn to be a piece. If you lose a knight, you could either say, "I lost a knight" or "I lost a piece" (which is the same thing). But if you lose a pawn, you wouldn't say, "I lost a piece." You'd say, "I lost a pawn" instead. Pawns are only pawns, but there are a lot of them!

The Rook

Figure 2-1 shows where the rooks go on the chessboard.

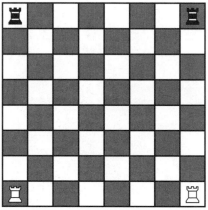

Figure 2-1

No, it isn't a tower, and it isn't a castle! The rook appears a bit shorter and squatter than the other pieces, which partly accounts for the perception of it as a heavy piece.

This heavy thing can be taken too far, of course. The rook is far from a plodding piece, and the player that gets his or her rooks into the game most effectively often turns out to be the winner. In the history of chess, the rook developed from the chariot: It is both fast and strong and therefore of considerable value. Unfortunately, it begins the game tucked into a corner and usually has to wait for the other pieces to settle into their preferred squares before receiving any attention.

The rook can move any number of squares — but only in straight lines, up and down, or side to side. Again, think of the chariot. After a chariot gets up a head of steam, turning corners isn't easy. Have you ever seen *Ben Hur*? It's just like that, but without the spikes.

Chess heavies

The rook and queen are sometimes referred to as heavy or *major pieces* because the rook and its own king, or the queen and its own king, can checkmate an enemy king by themselves (See Chapter 6 for a discussion of checkmate.)

Minor pieces — the knight and the bishop — cannot, by themselves, checkmate an enemy king with only their own king for assistance. The real heavies in chess are the rooks and queens.

The rook has the freedom to move any number of squares horizontally or vertically, as indicated in Figure 2-2. In Figure 2-3, you can see that the rook can't move to a square occupied by one of its own pieces — nor can it jump over the piece and move to any of the other squares along that rank.

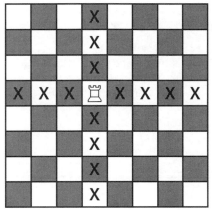

Figure 2-2

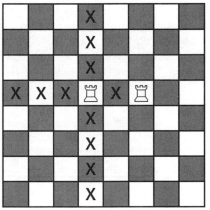

Figure 2-3

In Figure 2-4, a white rook and a black rook are ready for battle. The white rook cannot move beyond the black rook along that rank — but it can *capture* it. A rook thus captures by taking the place of an opponent's piece: The opponent's piece is removed and the attacking piece takes its square, as in Figure 2-5. This concept is the same for the other chessmen.

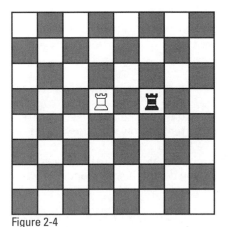

Figure 2-4

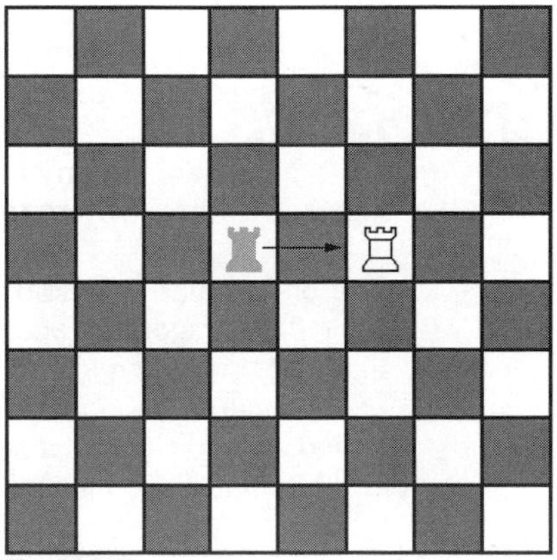

Figure 2-5

But don't think that you have to capture when given the opportunity. This isn't checkers!

Getting rooked in the end

Rook and pawn endings are the most frequently occurring of all chess endgames (the phase of the game where few pieces remain on the board) because the rooks are usually the last pieces developed and the last to be exchanged or captured. Rook endings are deceptively complicated, and even masters commit elementary mistakes.

Akiba Rubinstein (1882-1961), a grandmaster from Poland, is generally considered to have been the finest rook and pawn expert of his time. His handling of these positions has instructed entire generations who followed him, and this legacy now belongs to our common chess heritage.

Of course, few of us can play like a Rubinstein. A contemporary of his, Dr. Siegbert Tarrasch, summed up my feeling about rook and pawn endings when he said: "All Rook and Pawn endings are drawn (unwinnable)." That isn't true, of course, but it sure feels like it sometimes. My best advice would be to checkmate your opponent before you reach one of these endings!

When new players discover the power of the rook, they sometimes decide to move the pawns that are in front of the rooks forward (these pawns are known as the rook pawns). This action has the advantage of increasing the space available to the rook, but is usually a poor way to open the game. The rook must retreat when attacked by an enemy pawn, knight, or bishop because it is too valuable to be lost in exchange for one of them. Time is then lost shuffling the rook to and fro while the enemy pieces come out in force. The best strategy is to move a minimum number of pawns, get the minor pieces (knights and bishops) out, and only then move on to the rooks.

The Bishop

Figure 2-6 shows where the bishops start on the chessboard.

The bishop has a slender waist so that it can slide between squares along what are called diagonals (actually, I don't really know why the bishop was designed like that, but that's always how I've thought of it). The bishop is called a *minor piece* because you cannot deliver checkmate with just a king and bishop. Go ahead, set up a board and try it. If you can do it, you'll become world famous, and I'll include you in the next edition.

The bishop evolved from the elephant, which may be hard to imagine at first. Elephants don't have slender waists, at least not the ones I've seen. However, if you think about the ancient Indian soldier sitting *atop* an elephant tossing down spears at the enemy, or visualize the medieval archer in a castle tower firing

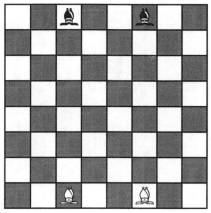

Figure 2-6

arrows down on a hapless foe, you can understand how this development came about. The bishop does not like hand-to-hand fighting and is at its best when attacking from long range.

It's easy to see how we went from the elephant to the archer (although the Russian word for bishop still means elephant to this day). It was just part of the Europizing of the Indian game. But why is the piece called a bishop and not an archer? Oddly enough, it's simply because the look of the carved piece resembled a bishop's miter (the pointed hat that bishops wear) to medieval Europeans. What probably started as an off-hand remark soon became our custom.

The bishop can move any number of squares, but only along the diagonals and until something gets in its way. If that "something" is an opponent's piece, the bishop can capture it, of course, by displacing it. Think of the archers firing their arrows around some kind of shield, which protects them from any frontal assault — but which also prevents them from firing straight ahead. They would've had to shoot along a diagonal in real life, too.

If you think about it, would you rather be shooting arrows safely out of harm's way or down in the trenches getting trampled? Archers weren't stupid. In Figure 2-7, the possible bishop moves are indicated. Unlike the rook, the attacking power of the bishop depends upon where it is located on the chessboard. You can see in Figure 2-7 that the bishop attacks 13 squares. How many squares does it attack in Figure 2-8? (The correct answer is 9 — I don't count the square that it occupies.)

Generally speaking, the bishop's power depends upon its mobility or *scope*, which is simply the number of squares it can move to. It attacks more squares in the center, so it is more powerful when positioned there. Unfortunately, it is also more easily attacked there.

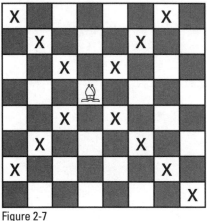

Figure 2-7

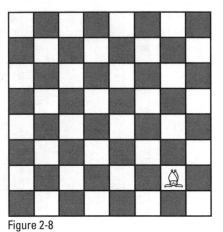

Figure 2-8

You can tell by looking at the board that some diagonals are longer than others. The diagonals that cross the board's center are longer than the ones that bisect the corners. Because the bishop does not like hand-to-hand combat, it is often positioned out of the way along a long diagonal, as in Figure 2-8.

The bishop, like the rook, can be blocked by its own army. In fact, the least desirable placement of the bishop is behind pawns of its own color: Pawns are the least mobile of the chessmen and can render the bishop nearly powerless, as shown in Figure 2-9. Enemy pawns can also be used to restrict the bishop's mobility, as in Figure 2-10.

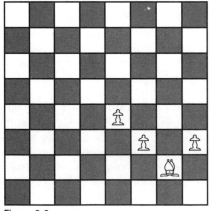

Figure 2-9

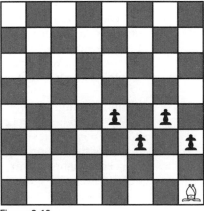

Figure 2-10

However, restricting a bishop with pawns is not always effective because it may be possible for the bishop to capture one of the enemy pawns. Just look at Figures 2-11 and 2-12 to see how.

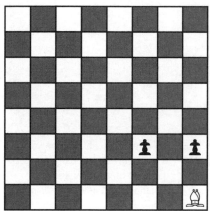

Figure 2-11   Figure 2-12

 If you plan on using your pawns to restrict a bishop's mobility — which is a good thing to do, as long as you aren't restricting your own bishops — you'd better make certain that the pawns are adequately defended!

There is also a unique natural restriction to the bishop's mobility: If it starts on a light square, it remains forever on the light squares, and if it begins the game on a dark square, it must always stay on dark squares. The bishop is color bound by birth! Fully half the board is forbidden territory! That is why chess people speak of having "the two bishops." In tandem, bishops can theoretically cover the entire board. However, they can never come to their comrade's aid directly and can never compensate for each other's loss.

 This quality is so unusual that there is even a special category of chess endings called the *opposite colored bishop ending.* This ending arises when each side remains with a bishop, but the bishops are sentenced to roaming their own mutually exclusive halves of the board. Figure 2-13 illustrates this type of ending. These bishops are close to one another — they can get close enough to blow each other kisses — but never close enough to *capture* one another.

 Bishop moves are relatively easy to master, but their long-range attacking ability is often surprising. Many is the time when I've been shocked to see my opponent's bishops spring from one corner of the board to the other. Just because your opponent's bishops aren't close to your pieces doesn't mean these bishops aren't attacking you!

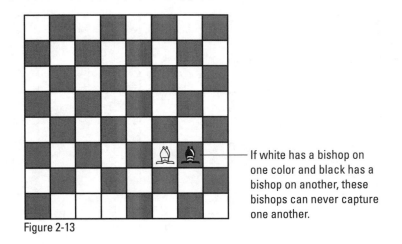

If white has a bishop on one color and black has a bishop on another, these bishops can never capture one another.

Figure 2-13

The Queen

Figure 2-14 indicates where the queens are placed at the start of the game.

Figure 2-14

The queen evolved from the Indian vizier who was the King's chief minister or advisor. Originally a weak piece, the queen was given its great powers towards the end of the 15th century. Whether this was an act of chivalry or just another attempt to speed up the game remains unclear. It seems certain, however, that medieval Europe was accustomed to powerful queens — and this reality can also explain the gender change.

If you understand the moves of the rook and the bishop, you will have no trouble understanding the moves of the queen. The queen's moves are simply the combination of the rook's up-down, side-to-side moves and the bishop's diagonal moves. The queen can move any number of squares in any direction. Its only restriction is that it cannot jump over pieces. The queen captures an opponent by taking the opponent's place on the board.

To get an idea of the queen's strength, just put one in the middle of an empty chessboard — which, by the way, is a situation that will never happen if you are playing chess by the rules! When placed in the center of the board, the queen can cover 27 squares and can move in 8 different directions. The queen's moves are shown in Figure 2-15.

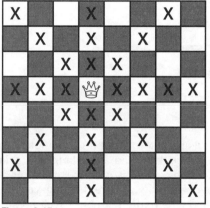

Figure 2-15

The queen covers fewer squares when placed on the side of the board, so its powers are slightly reduced in that case. However, it's far too dangerous to post the valuable queen in the center of the board too early in the game where it can be harassed by any of the opposing army. It's far more common to see masters post the queen in a more conservative position early and wait to centralize her later when pieces have been exchanged and the danger to her reduced.

The queen is not only the most powerful and dangerous chess piece, but also the most valuable! Moving her into positions where she can be easily attacked is generally frowned upon. Let your other pieces and pawns fight the early fight and bring the queen into the game after some of the dust settles. If your opponent moves the queen to your side of the board early on, take heart! It's probably a mistake. Look for ways to move your pieces so that they attack the exposed queen and force her to retreat.

The King

Figure 2-16 shows where the king resides on the chessboard at the start of the game.

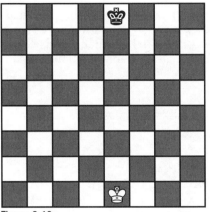

Figure 2-16

The king is not the most powerful chess piece, but it is the most important. When the king is attacked, he must be defended. If the king is attacked and can't be defended, it's checkmate . . . and the game is over (see Chapter 6 for information on checkmate). But you never actually capture the king; you simply force him to yield. Thousands may die on the battlefield, but royalty respects royalty. (Yet don't forget that the king can capture, just like the other pieces, by taking over an opponent's square!)

It's odd to think of the king as leading his troops into battle because the king usually hides away in a corner behind pawns until it's safe to come out. Generally, when the king becomes active, it's time for the endgame (when most pieces have been captured). During the endgame the king can become very powerful, but a king in the middle of the board during the middlegame is a recipe for disaster (so check out Chapters 11 and 12 for details on endgame and middlegame strategy).

The king is priceless because it doesn't matter how many pieces you have if the king is lost.

The king can move one square in any direction, except for the one time possibility of castling (see Chapter 9 for this special move). The kings may never get too close to one another, but must remain at arm's length (at least one square away) because one king may never put the other in check.

The king's possible moves are shown in Figure 2-17.

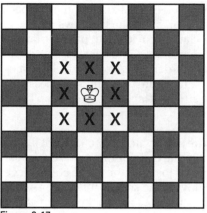

Figure 2-17

The Knight

Figure 2-18 indicates where the knights start out on the chessboard.

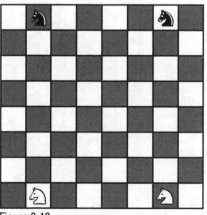

Figure 2-18

The knight is a tricky piece, and it usually takes a little practice in order to become comfortable with its movements. As its shape would suggest, the knight derives from the cavalry of the armies of old. Because it can't deliver checkmate against an opponent with only its own king to help, the knight is a minor piece, as is the bishop — but the knight's powers are very different. Unlike the long-range bishop, the knight loves combat in close quarters and is usually the first piece moved off the back rank in the opening and the first to come into contact with the opposing army. The knight is indeed hopping mad and ready to fight!

It helps me to think of the knight as a medieval knight on horseback with a lance. You can't throw a lance very far, but if the bad guys get too close they're liable to get run through. Oddly, if an enemy can get past the lance and closer still to the knight, the knight is defenseless. (The knight would need to dismount, drop its lance, and draw a sword in order to fight at very close range — but this is too time consuming, besides being against the rules of chess!) Strangely enough, although the knight is a strong attacking piece, it can't control the squares right next to it.

The easiest way to understand the knight move is to think of it as an L-shape in any direction. Two squares up and one over, or one square down and two over, or any such combination. It captures just like the other chess pieces, by replacing the piece or pawn occupying the square it lands on — and *not* the players it jumps over! Figure 2-19 illustrates where the knight can move from the center of the board. The knight controls 8 squares when positioned in the center of the board as opposed to 2 squares when it is in one of the corners, as seen in Figure 2-20.

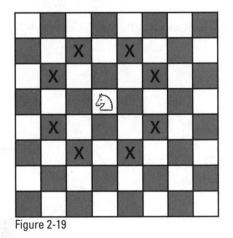

Figure 2-19

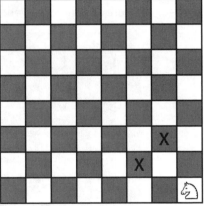

Figure 2-20

The knight must always move to a different colored square than the one it occupies. This alternation between colors is true of no other piece. If the knight is on a light square, it must move to a dark square, and vice versa.

The knight is much more effective when centralized — or positioned so that it occupies or attacks one of the four central squares. However, unlike the other pieces for which this general rule also holds true, the knight loves to be in the center of the action and is forced to retreat only when it is attacked by the lowly pawn. Otherwise, the knight just holds its ground and dares you to capture it. The knight considers it a question of honor to charge off into battle and hates to watch while others are left to carry the day.

CHESS MASTER

The knight's tour

The knight's tour is an interesting exercise where you position the knight anywhere on the chessboard and then move it to each square in turn without ever landing on the same square twice. Grandmaster George Koltanowski is famous for the knight's tour and can do it without sight of the board (calling out the name of the square where the knight is to move). In fact, he recently did it again in front of over 300 enthralled spectators on the occasion of his ninetieth birthday!

The knight's truly unique power is its ability to leap over pieces, either its own or those of the enemy. In fact, it's the only piece that can move off the back rank at the start of the game without a preliminary pawn move, as illustrated in Figure 2-21.

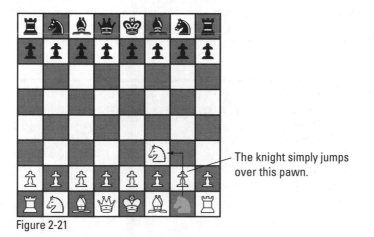

The knight simply jumps over this pawn.

Figure 2-21

The Pawn

The pawn is a piece that is not a piece! (Remember that the pawn is not really a piece, which makes it so difficult to talk about all the chess pieces — including the pawns — together!) Figure 2-22 shows how the pawns are set up at the start of the game.

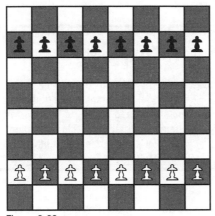

Figure 2-22

The pawns are the foot soldiers of chess, and you know how foot soldiers are treated. Their powers are very restricted. The pawn can move one square forward, except on its very first move, when it has the choice of moving one or two squares forward. A pawn cannot move backwards or sideways — *only forward*. The options for the white pawns are shown in Figure 2-23.

CHESS MASTER

Pawns: the soul of chess

Although the pawn is the lowliest of the chess pieces, so low in fact, that it isn't usually referred to as a piece, it has been called the "soul of chess." This honor is due to a number of factors.

✔ There are more pawns than anything else in a chess set.

✔ The pawns can dictate whether the other pieces have maneuvering room or not.

✔ Nobody wants to get exchanged for a poor pawn, so other pieces have to back down or move around them.

✔ Pawns can't move backwards, so each pawn move is a commitment and should be made only after due consideration.

This is what the great master François-André Danican Philidor (1726-95) meant when he said, "The pawns are the very life of the game."

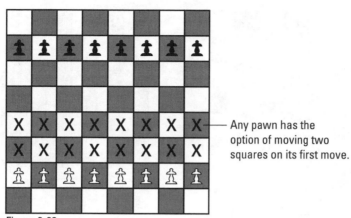

— Any pawn has the
option of moving two
squares on its first move.

Figure 2-23

The pawn, unlike the pieces, captures differently than it moves. It captures diagonally, one square forward to either side. But it still takes the opponent's place on a square when it captures, just like the other chessmen. Figure 2-24 illustrates the pawn's capturing ability.

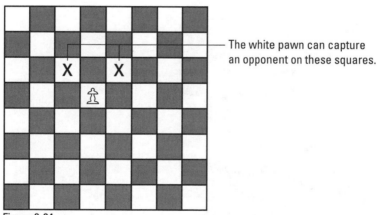

— The white pawn can capture
an opponent on these squares.

Figure 2-24

In Figure 2-25, an enemy pawn occupies one of the squares that the white pawn can attack. Figure 2-26 shows how the white pawn captures the black pawn (although the black pawn could have captured the white pawn if it were black's turn!).

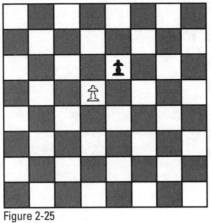

Figure 2-25

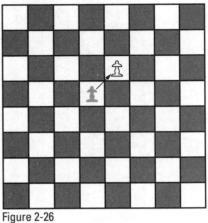

Figure 2-26

If no member of the opposing army occupies a square the pawn attacks, the pawn can move, but only forward. If a piece or another pawn is in front of it, but nothing is on the squares the pawn can capture, the pawn is stymied and cannot move. Figure 2-27 demonstrates locked pawns. Pawns that oppose one another like this can't move.

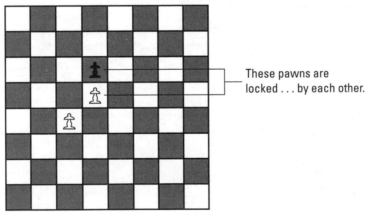

These pawns are locked . . . by each other.

Figure 2-27

It helps me to think of the foot soldier holding a spear and a giant shield. The shield is in front of the foot soldier so that the soldier can only thrust to the right or left side of the shield and can't thrust in front of it. The soldier needs a comrade in arms to come to his aid.

Because pawns can be stopped in their tracks so easily, chess players have learned that they are most powerful when they stay by each other's side. This way, both pawns — or *pawn-duos* — can guard the square in front of the other. By helping each other out, both pawns become more mobile and their influence on the game grows.

When two pawns are locked together as in Figure 2-27, you should try to bring another pawn alongside in order to help out. This strategy is so common that it is referred to as a *lever*. You can see where that term came from, as the second pawn attempts to pry the first one free. Figure 2-28 illustrates the use of the lever.

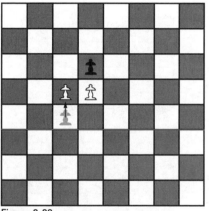

Figure 2-28

Now two of the pawns can capture each other. If the black pawn captures the white pawn, the remaining white pawn is free to move. Often the lever can be used to pry open an otherwise locked position, and it is seen over and over again in the games of the masters.

You need to know a few more things about pawns, but I don't discuss them in this chapter. Pawn promotion and something called *en passant* (or "in passing") are covered in Chapter 9, which deals with special moves. The pawn's placement collectively is referred to as the *pawn structure,* and I examine this concept in detail in Chapter 3.

Now you have been introduced to the pieces (including the pawns!) and you are at least passingly familiar with their powers. Chess is a science when pieces are considered in isolation from one another — but chess approaches an art when the pieces are combined in various ways. All pieces like company but they are fickle; sometimes a queen and knight are happy together and sometimes they are not. No easy rules explain this relationship. The chess genius seems to know how to make the pieces work together seamlessly, but the rest of us have to muddle along by trial and error. In Chapter 3, the elements of chess are considered in the same way — in isolation from one another — and then again in combination.

Beware the scholar's mate

Beginners are frequently seduced by the power of the queen and move her early and often. This tendency is unfortunately reinforced in their minds when they learn of the *scholar's mate*. The scholar's mate is one of the shortest mates possible, but it is easily defended against. Everyone who plays chess should know it, though, in order to avoid falling into it!

First, both players advance the pawns in front of their kings (1). Next, they both develop their bishops to a centralized square (2).

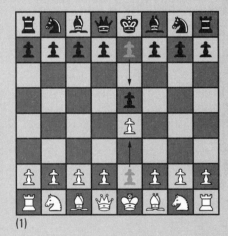

(1)

(2)

Third, white brings its queen out to attack several black pawns (3), and black's knight defends the pawn in the center of the board — which is the wrong pawn to defend(4)!

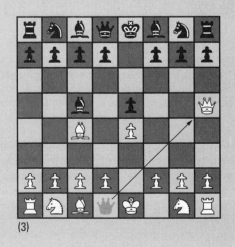

(3)

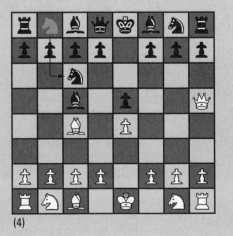

(4)

White delivers checkmate (5)! Flip ahead to Chapter 6 if you need an explanation of checkmate. But for now you should at least realize that black's king is trapped with nowhere to move and with no one to help him.

(5)

The black king can't simply capture the attacking white queen because this bishop supports her.

The scholar's mate is not a dangerous strategy. Here's just one idea that prevents white from executing its plan. By moving the knight out before the bishop, black not only takes away the queen move but also threatens the advanced white pawn (6). White would be frustrated on the second move!

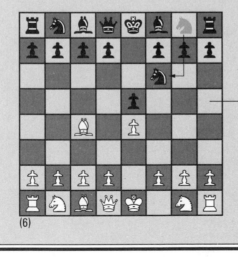

(6)

The white queen would be captured (by the black knight) if placed here.

Part II
Getting Past the Rules

The 5th Wave   By Rich Tennant

In this part . . .

1 often joke that after you know the rules of chess, you're at ground zero. Shuffling pieces back and forth around the board is not very interesting. The stuff that comes after learning the rules is what makes chess the fascinating game that it is. In this part, I look at the elements of the game and introduce the topics of tactics, mating patterns, and strategy. Finally, this part ends with a look at the special rules, the ones that I think start all the arguments.

Chapter 3

The Elements of Chess

*T*he elements of chess — space, material, development, king safety, and pawn structure — are the basic building blocks of the game. By understanding the individual elements, your knowledge of chess increases dramatically. Of course, understanding the elements in isolation from one another is far easier than understanding them in combination.

Unfortunately, the elements are always interacting with each other — as if they were volatile gases. Sometimes one element is far more important than all the others combined; other times, there is a dynamic balance between them all. When you come to understand each element's relationship to the others — in any given position — you will have approached chess mastery.

Space

Space may be the final frontier to some of you, but it's an essential element in the chess world. Chess really is a game of spatial conquest. All things being equal, the player who controls the most space controls the game: Maneuvering your pieces around is easier when you have space than when you don't. When you don't have space, you can't always get your pieces to the right place at the right time. Imagine trying to get from one side of the battlefield to the other when your own soldiers keep getting in your way.

Don't get cramped

If you're losing the space war, chess people say that your game is *cramped.* (So, for example, if your opponent maneuvers so that all your remaining pieces are stuck in a corner, you're definitely cramped.) A move that secures a spatial advantage for you by restricting your opponent's space is a *cramping move.* On the other hand, a *freeing move* is a move that gains back space.

Often the struggle in a chess game involves one player trying to play a freeing move while the other works just as hard to prevent it.

Gain control

Space is little more than the number of squares you control. *Control* refers to the number of squares attacked — not necessarily occupied — by your pieces and pawns. (Squares "attacked" are those squares that your pieces or pawns can go to on your next move.) If your opponent attacks the same squares, these squares are called *contested* and are not clearly controlled — and no one gets to claim them as space. This definition of control makes it a bit messy to calculate exactly who has how much space in some circumstances, but usually it's pretty easy to tell who is doing better space-wise.

Space strategies

Each side starts the game with the same amount of space. At this point neither side can control any squares on the opponent's half of the board (of course!). After the first move, white almost always secures a temporary spatial advantage by putting a pawn or piece on a square that allows it to attack and, at least temporarily, control squares on the other half of the board. The most common opening move is illustrated in Figure 3-1.

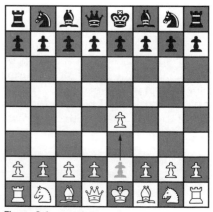

Figure 3-1

If you already know how pawns move, you can readily see that the pawn now attacks two squares in the opponent's side of the board. These squares are shown in Figure 3-2. (If you need a lesson or a refresher in how pawns move, see Chapter 2.)

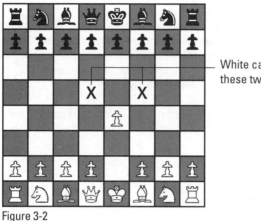

White can attack these two squares.

Figure 3-2

CHESS TALK

Typically, but not always, black opens with a move that evens up the space game. This action-reaction is sometimes referred to as the *dynamic equilibrium* of chess. That's just a fancy way of saying that one side can usually reestablish the initial equality when it's his or her turn to move. For example, black can reply on the next move with the same results (see Figure 3-3).

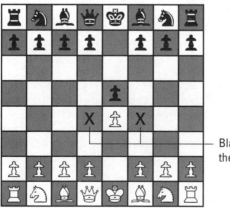

Black can attack these two squares.

Figure 3-3

Notice how white holds a spatial advantage after the first move, but black reestablishes spatial equality immediately. Because white moves first, the trick is to play in such a way that black cannot simply copy white's moves. In this way, white tries to force a concession from black and secure a lasting advantage. If black could always copy white's moves, the game would be a draw. (I provide an example of how to refute the "ape man" strategy in Chapter 10.)

Space is more important in the opening (Chapter 10) and middlegame (Chapter 11) phases of a chess game than it is in the endgame (Chapter 12). This is because, by definition, the endgame has the fewest pieces on the board. Getting cramped by a handful of pieces in the endgame is really hard, and you really have to be sort of clumsy to trip over your own pieces.

The key to controlling space in the opening is to control the *center*. In Figure 3-4, the key central squares are indicated. Taken together, these squares are called (appropriately!) the center.

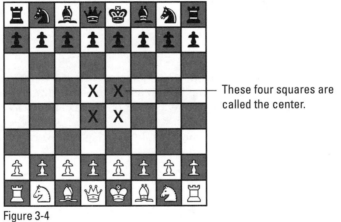

These four squares are called the center.

Figure 3-4

The most common opening strategy in chess is to try to maneuver your minor pieces (the bishops and the knights) and central pawns so that they control the four center squares and strike out into enemy territory. The minor pieces increase in power when mobilized towards the center. If you can post your pieces there and prevent your opponent from doing the same, you secure a spatial advantage and your pieces are stronger than your opponent's.

Remember that chess is not a static game — not only establishing a spatial superiority, but also maintaining it is important! Having one or two pieces cross over into enemy territory does little good if they are cut off from the rest of the troops. You must keep the supply lines open and invade only when you can adequately support the advanced pieces.

The laws of space

Don't try to memorize this list. No chessmaster ever does. Just becoming familiar with these concepts in a general way is important. Soon enough the laws of space will become second nature.

- Use your center pawns to gain space in the early phase of the game.
- Invade only if you can support your pieces.
- Don't lock in your bishops behind your own pawns.
- If you're cramped, look for a freeing move.
- If your opponent is cramped, try to prevent freeing moves.
- Exchange pieces to help relieve a cramped position.
- Control the center before attacking on the wings (sides of the board).
- If your opponent is attacking on a wing, strike back in the center!
- After you control a square in enemy territory, try to occupy the square with a knight.
- During the endgame, the king should generally be brought to the center of the board.

Central control makes use of the old adage "divide and conquer." If you split your opponent's army into two camps, you can bring a decisive amount of force into one arena before their reinforcements arrive.

Material (The Element That Really Matters)

Some pieces are more powerful than others. Some are stronger than others. The element of material is concerned with this relative strength of the pieces.

It is quite common to see advantages in other elements converted into an advantage in material, because an advantage in material is the easiest advantage to convert into a win.

Value your pawns and pieces

Each pawn or piece has a numerical value. The pawn is the basic unit of chess and is assigned a numerical value of one. The other pieces are evaluated in those same terms. Therefore, if a pawn is worth one point, a knight is worth more: three points. In other words, you lose two points in the element of material if you trade a knight for a pawn. You would need to capture three enemy pawns (or one knight) to compensate for the loss of your knight. The relative value of the pieces are shown in Table 3-1.

Table 3-1	The Relative Value of Chess Pieces (In Terms of the Pawn)
Piece	*Value*
pawn	1
knight	3
bishop	3
rook	5
queen	9

Note: Assigning a value to the king is not possible because its loss means the loss of the game!

Material superiority is decisive when all other things are equal. If you can win one pawn, winning another or forcing further concessions from your opponent is often possible. Things are rarely equal in chess, though, and it's sometimes impossible to correctly evaluate when an advantage in material matters more than an advantage in some other element. Is it worth a pawn to gain space? Usually, only experience can answer this kind of question.

Pieces themselves can gain or lose power depending upon their positioning. Having an advanced pawn deep in enemy territory may be far more important than having a measly knight tucked away in a corner. A bishop locked behind its own pawns may not be worth a fraction of a free roaming knight. These values are relative and can change many times over the course of the game. Nevertheless, remembering the piece's relative value when you consider trading it for another is a useful guide. If you give up your queen for a pawn, you'd better have a darned good reason!

A bishop and a knight are not created equal

Although the bishop and knight are considered to be of relative equal value, chess masters have learned over time to value the bishops slightly more. Some people assign the bishop a value of 3 $\frac{1}{4}$ points. Having the two bishops control both light and dark squares is especially important. In tandem they are usually considerably more powerful than two knights, or a knight and a bishop.

Material strategies

A good rule is to exchange pieces when you have an advantage in material. This strategy is referred to as *simplification*. For example, if you have an extra pawn, but both you and your opponent have a bishop, it's usually easier to win if you trade your bishop for your opponent's and play the rest of the game with just kings and pawns.

Material superiority takes on added importance the closer you come to an endgame. A single pawn advantage may mean little in the opening — but it may be decisive in the endgame. This strategy illustrates how you can force additional concessions from your opponents. If you keep offering to exchange pieces, and your opponents keep refusing, they will be forced to retreat. The result? You wind up with a spatial advantage, too!

Because exchanges are desired by the side with an edge in material, it's logical to avoid them if you are behind.

The intentional loss of material in return for an advantage in another element is referred to as a *sacrifice*. Sacrifices are near and dear to the heart of chess players who know that — should they not obtain an immediate advantage — time will work against them. The closer you get to an endgame, the more important the extra material becomes. This risky maneuver is considered courageous by some and foolhardy by others. You can often tell a lot about chess players by watching how they risk or conserve their material! Chapter 5 deals with the most common types of sacrifice in chess.

Material matters

These rules are meant to serve as guidelines and not as rigid rules. Every time chess players try to devise a rigid rule, some smart aleck comes along and breaks it! Nevertheless, it is useful to at least think about the concepts presented here.

- ✔ When ahead in material, force exchanges and steer towards the endgame. Simplify!

- ✔ Open files and diagonals when possible so that you may use them to engage the enemy and force further concessions. (See Chapter 1 for an introduction to files and diagonals.)

- ✔ If possible, win material without sacrificing in some other element.

- ✔ Material is usually more important than other elements, so take it if it is offered — unless you have a really good reason not to.

- ✔ If you are behind in material, avoid exchanging additional pieces, but do not become passive. You must attack!

Development

Development is the element of time. In chess, players take turns playing moves. There is no such thing as passing or giving up a turn, so you must make a move at every turn. Not all moves are equal, however, and only those moves that contribute to the increased mobility of your pieces are said to be *developing moves*. In practice, nearly every time a piece moves from its original square, it's a developing move.

Gain a tempo

If your opponent is playing developing moves and you are just marking time, you will soon lose the game. Every move is a precious resource, so don't waste any! Chess players call the move a *tempo*. For example, one often hears, "I just gained (or lost) a tempo." This means that you have gotten (or allowed your opponent to get) the chance to move what seems like twice in a row!

Sometimes this concept is very subtle. For example, you can develop a piece to a reasonable square but, as the course of events unfold, discover that your piece really belongs on another square. You may be forced to take a move to reposition the piece to where it really belongs. Such a move can be a loss of tempo.

White begins the game and has, by definition, a slight edge in time. White can squander this advantage easily or can make use of it. The advantage that comes with an edge in the element of time — or development — is often called the *initiative*. Thus, by virtue of the first move, white is given a slight initiative at the beginning of the game. This advantage is often compared to having the serve in tennis, and indeed in the hands of the grandmasters, the advantage of having white is quite significant.

Make a gambit (maybe)

Very often you can sacrifice a small amount of material for an advantage in development. Many openings sacrifice a pawn for this reason, and they are called *gambits*. A gambit is usually more effective for white than for black because white already has the initiative and can add to it at the small cost of a pawn. Gambits tried by black usually offer less chances for the initiative and often wind up as a simple loss of material.

The most common error beginners make is to lose a tempo by giving check (for more on check, see Chapter 6). These players give check at every opportunity, but this course of action is not always wise. Sometimes the checking piece is later forced to retreat, and a tempo is lost. If you plan on checking the king, make certain that you have a concrete reason for doing so. Chess players have a saying: "Monkey sees a check, monkey gives a check." Don't be a monkey! Check is not important by itself. Checkmate is!

King Safety

Of all the elements, king safety can be the most dramatic. If the king is in jeopardy, nothing else matters. It doesn't matter how many pieces you have in your pocket if your king is checkmated, because that's the end of the game. I explain checkmate in Chapter 6 — but even if you don't know what checkmate is now, you probably realize that you need to protect your king.

Many chess games begin with one or two pawn moves and the development of two or three of the minor pieces. The next step is usually to bring the king to safety by castling, a move that allows you to place your king closer to one of the corners (see Chapter 9 for this special move), which is usually farther from the action and behind other pawns and pieces.

This strategy is seen in countless openings that are otherwise completely different. The main idea is to engage the enemy only after the king is secure. Protecting the king with all your pieces is inefficient, so good chess players usually leave the guard duty to one or two of them and to the pawns. The knight is an excellent defender of the king and puts up fierce resistance in the face of an attack. With the help of a few pawns, the knight can usually hold down the fort.

Be careful about opening up lines of attack for your opponent against your king or moving the pawns away from your castled king who is now in a corner of the board. Check is not checkmate, but it does force your hand. Chess players, like anyone else, want to have things their own way, and postponing your plans in order to safeguard your king can be frustrating. History has taught us that by making a few early defensive moves to secure the king's position, we can go about our prime objective: attacking the opponent unhindered. You can't put a price on peace of mind.

Although you can find master games where the king is left in the center, this strategy is the exception. Until you get a great deal of experience in chess, you are better off following the tried-and-true method of protecting your king before launching an attack.

The center-counter: risky development

One opening that is seen occasionally in grandmaster play is the center-counter. The chief drawback to this opening is that the black queen is developed too early and comes under attack. When the queen is forced to retreat, white gains a tempo. Here are the usual opening moves of the center-counter. White moves out the king pawn two squares (1). Black makes a plausible reply to white's first move by advancing the pawn in front of its queen two squares (2). This move has the advantage of opening lines for the bishop and queen and of contesting white's control of the center. The drawback of this move will become clear in just a moment.

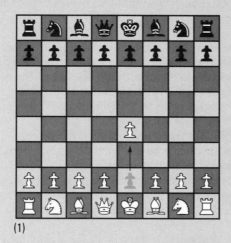

(1)

(2)

White captures the pawn and is temporarily ahead in material (3). Black now recaptures the pawn in order to reestablish the material balance (4).

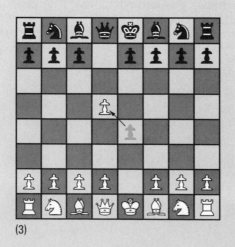

(3)

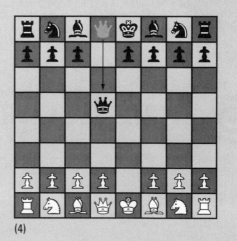

(4)

White can now develop a piece and simultaneously attack the black queen (5). Can you see how this is done?

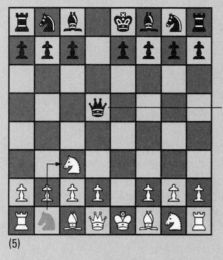

The black queen is now under attack from the white knight.

(5)

The knight develops with tempo, taking up its natural position and also attacking the black queen. Because the knight is worth three pawns and the queen worth nine, black cannot afford to ignore this threat and must move the queen again. White has won a tempo!

Pawn Structure

The pawns are called the soul of chess because, very often, the mobility of the pieces depends upon the positioning of the pawns. Also, as the endgame approaches, the pawns tend to become more valuable. The famous Australian chess player Cecil Purdy (1906-79) once wrote that "Pawn endings are to chess what putting is to golf." I couldn't have said it better myself.

A general rule is that mobility is the key to the power of any chess piece. This rule is true even of the lowly pawn. The pawn's mobility is clearly tied to its ability to advance. Pawns cannot attack the square directly ahead of them, so their mobility is often dependent upon help from another pawn. This limitation is why pawns are stronger together, or in pawn-duos, than they are alone. Figure 3-5 illustrates a pawn-duo. In a pawn-duo, the pawns can now guard the squares in front of each other and support one another should either of them advance. These are mobile pawns.

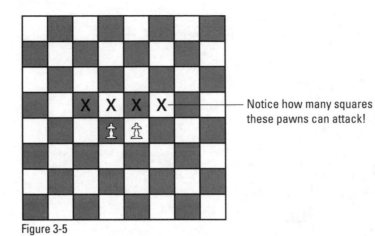

Notice how many squares these pawns can attack!

Figure 3-5

In Figure 3-6, the pawns are still mobile, but their potential to advance is restricted by the black pawns. You usually want to control a square prior to occupying it, but doing so is difficult in this case because the squares in front of the pawns are contested.

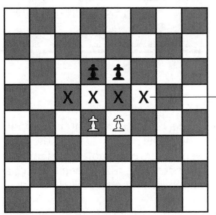

These squares are now contested — the white pawns and the black pawns can attack the same squares!

Figure 3-6

WARNING!

The quickest checkmate

If you need an example of how important the element of king safety is in chess, studying the quickest possible checkmate may help. With the first move, white advances the pawn in front of its kingside knight two squares (1). Black takes the opportunity to strike back in the center and to open lines for its bishop and queen (2). Remember, the best strategy for countering an advance on the wing is to advance in the center.

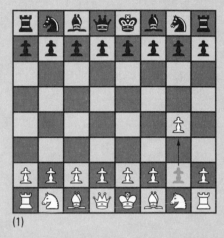

(1)

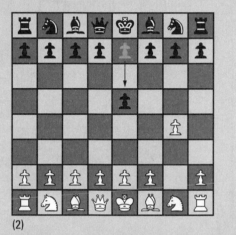

(2)

Now white really makes a huge mistake by advancing its king's bishop pawn to attack black's pawn (3). This opens a line against white's king. Does black have a piece that can make use of it? Indeed, black does, and white's disregard for king safety is quickly punished. Checkmate in two moves! The black queen attacks the white king along the diagonal and there is no defense (4). The king cannot move out of check, no defender can move in the way, and no piece or pawn can capture the black queen. This is an extreme example of the price you pay for ignoring the safety of your king, but believe me, you'll encounter others!

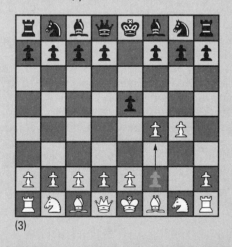

(3)

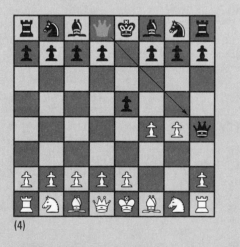

(4)

Figure 3-7 shows a position where the pawns are locked: Neither side can advance, and the pawns will require assistance before progress can be made. Locked pawns lead to what chess players call *closed positions,* which are characterized by slow maneuvering rather than by sharp hand-to-hand fighting. You can now see how the pawn structure dictates the further course of action, right?

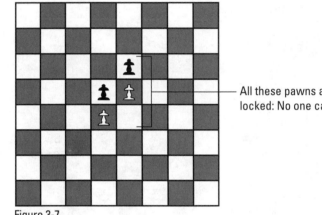

All these pawns are locked: No one can advance.

Figure 3-7

Passed pawns

Pawns play a critical role throughout the game of chess. During the endgame phase, they take on added significance because of the possibility of promotion (see Chapter 9 for the lowdown on pawn promotion). When pawns reach the eighth rank, they may be promoted to any piece other than the king. If pawns are locked or otherwise immobile, the chances of promoting them are remote.

However, if the pawn has a free path ahead of it — unobstructed by other pawns — the chances of promoting it are considerably greater. Such pawns are called *passed pawns.*

In Figure 3-8, the pawn on the far left for white is a passed pawn. No black pawn is between it and the eighth rank — and no black pawn can capture it.

Passed pawns must be pushed! A passed pawn becomes a tangible advantage whenever it is free to advance and is adequately supported. A passed pawn may force the opposing forces to assume a defensive posture in order to halt its advance, or it may deflect enemy pieces away from where the real action is. The late, great Latvian grandmaster Aaron Nimzovich (1886-1935) once wrote in his classic *My System* (1925) that a passed pawn "is a criminal, who must be kept under lock and key."

Nothing can stop this pawn from reaching the eighth rank and being promoted.

Figure 3-8

The best kind of passed pawn is the protected passed pawn. Such a pawn not only has an unobstructed path to the eighth rank, but also the support of one of its peer group as well. The protected passed pawn can be opposed only by pieces other than pawns and can often tip the scales in your favor all by itself.

Establish a protected passed pawn whenever you get the chance. A protected passed pawn is shown in Figure 3-9.

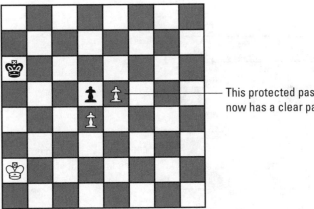

This protected passed pawn now has a clear path ahead.

Figure 3-9

Ideal pawn structure

The best pawn structure appears at the start of the game. All the pawns are mobile and their structure is unbroken. Figure 3-10 demonstrates this ideal pawn structure.

Unfortunately, in order to get the pieces out, the pawn formation must be altered.

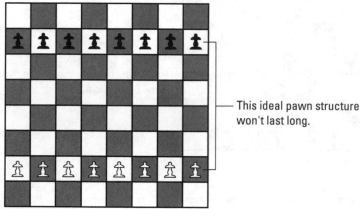

This ideal pawn structure won't last long.

Figure 3-10

Isolated pawns

CHESS TALK

Pawns are considered *isolated* when they do not have any pawns from their own team by their side. In Figure 3-11, the white pawn in the center of the board is isolated.

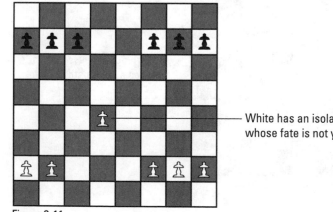

White has an isolated pawn whose fate is not yet decided.

Figure 3-11

Isolated pawns may or may not be passed pawns. If they are passed or mobile, pawns may become strong. If they are not passed or are immobile, they may become weak.

Because isolated pawns do not have any supporting pawns and cannot control the square directly in front of them, they may easily become blocked (blockaded).

Aaron Nimzovich, who wrote extensively on the subject of pawns, demonstrated that a mobile, isolated pawn may provide a sound basis for attack and that an immobile (blockaded), isolated pawn may, on the other hand, become subject to attack. The threatened pawn must then be defended by pieces, and pieces don't like to be on guard duty for pawns. Guarding pawns offends their lofty sense of self.

To keep a pawn isolated, you can blockade it. Nimzovich also taught that the knight was the ideal blockader. A knight camped in front of an isolated pawn cannot be driven off by pawns, and the knight just stands its ground in the face of attack by any other piece. The queen, in comparison, is a poor blockader because she must retreat in the face of attack by knights, bishops, or rooks and cannot maintain the blockade. After a blockade is broken, the isolated pawn becomes mobile and gains in strength.

Backwards pawns

The kissing cousin to the isolated pawn is the backwards pawn. A *backwards pawn* still has one or more pawns on adjacent files, but these pawns are more advanced. It may be difficult or even impossible for the backwards pawn to catch up with its sidekick(s), and in that case such a pawn is pretty much isolated. The backwards pawn (the pawn on the d-file in Figure 3-12) may come under pressure from the enemy's big guns because the file is open for the opponent's queen and rooks to use to attack it. You'll want to avoid this situation in most cases because you may end up using your pieces to guard the relatively insignificant pawn. The pieces then become listless and bored — and of no use to anybody.

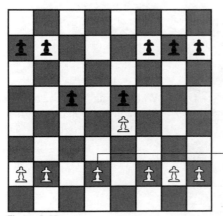

The open file in front of this pawn puts it at risk from a black queen or rook.

Figure 3-12

Hanging pawns

Hanging pawns are the second cousins once removed of the backwards pawn. The *hanging pawns* are in a pawn-duo, which we know to be strong, but they do not have any other supporting pawns around them. This means that should one or the other pawn advance, the remaining pawn may become a backwards pawn. In Figure 3-13, the advanced white pawns are hanging pawns.

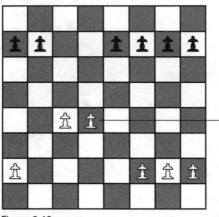

One of these hanging pawns risks becoming a backwards pawn.

Figure 3-13

Doubled pawns

Doubled pawns are produced when one pawn captures something and moves in front of another pawn of the same color. Figure 3-14 gives an example of doubled pawns. The black pawns in the upper-left corner of the board are now crowded together. Although four pawns occupy this corner, they really have the mobility of three.

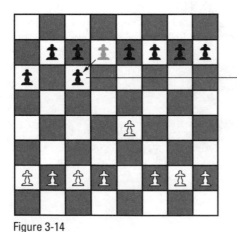

When this pawn moved to capture, it created doubled pawns. The trailing pawn now has limited mobility.

Figure 3-14

When such a situation happens, the pawns lose the ability to protect one another and reduce the chances of using each other for a lever (the act of dislodging an enemy pawn from blockading your own). Most importantly, the pawns' mobility — especially so for the trailing pawn — is significantly reduced.

Pawn chains

Pawn chains are pawns that are lined up along a diagonal, with each pawn supporting a more advanced one until the head of the chain is reached. These pawn chains represent a line drawn in the sand and make it difficult for the enemy to cross over. Figure 3-15 shows two pawn chains, one for white and one for black.

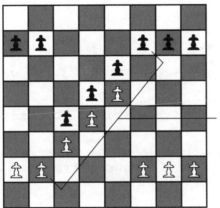

Both white and black have established a pawn chain.

Figure 3-15

It is difficult for the pieces to cross the pawn chain and come into contact with each other. This arrangement can make for a long game with few exchanges. A pawn chain also divides the board into two camps, one where the white pieces have more freedom to move about, and another where the black pieces can roam more freely. If you can crash through a pawn chain, however, you almost certainly can have the advantage.

Nimzovich taught us that the weakest link of the pawn chain is at the base. The base is the pawn that starts the chain. After the base is destroyed, the pawn chain is weakened. After you remove one base, another base is established, but each becomes easier and easier to attack and destroy. If you can't attack the base of the chain, attack at the head. This strategy isn't as effective an alternative — but it may create weaknesses in the chain that you can exploit later.

RULE OF THUMB

The pawn shop

These rules for pawns are not meant to be memorized. Give them a good once over and move on. But if you remember any of them, you'll be ahead of the game!

- Try to keep your pawn structure intact.

- Because some pawns must be advanced, try to keep them mobile or in pawn-duos.

- If some pawns become locked, use other pawns to pry them free.

- If you have an isolated pawn, keep it mobile; if your opponent has one, blockade it!

- Create a passed pawn and, when possible, a protected passed pawn.

- Push your passed pawns.

- Attack backwards pawns with the heavy pieces.

- Try to provoke a hanging pawn into an advance and then blockade.

- Avoid doubling your pawns, but if you can't, try to exchange one of the doubled pawns.

- Attack pawn chains at the base.

If you've managed to read chapter by chapter this far, give yourself a pat on the back. You probably don't yet realize just how much you've covered. Nothing about the rules of chess is very difficult — it's just that there are so many of them!

Chapter 4

Tactics: Hand-to-Hand Combat

. . . .

In This Chapter

▶ The fork (attacking two for the price of one)

▶ The pin (pinning down your opponent)

▶ The skewer (forcing your opponent to move or lose)

▶ Overloading (taking advantage of a workaholic)

▶ Zwischenzug (surprising your opponent with the "in-between" move)

. . . .

*N*ow *this* is mortal combat. When pieces engage one another, either at close quarters or from long range, tactics rule the day. Most chess games are decided by tactics, sometimes by elementary ones. It is critically important to become familiar with the most basic examples and to look for them throughout the game. You can make 40 great moves and still lose the game by overlooking your opponent's tricks on the 41st!

Tactics usually involve forcing your opponent into a sequence of moves that they don't want to make. If you initiate such a sequence, you are said to have made a *combination*. By combining threats, you force your opponent to choose among bad moves. You usually secure an advantage in one or more of the elements of chess as a result of tactics. (See Chapter 3 for a discussion of the elements of chess.)

The study of these basic types of tactics can lead to an immediate improvement in your results. There is no shortcut to chess mastery, but by becoming a strong tactician you can pocket many a point along the way.

The Fork

The *fork* is a simultaneous attack on two or more pieces by a single piece (and for the sake of brevity, I'll call the pawn a piece here). Forks are usually carried out by either knights or pawns, although any piece can fork. During a successful fork, your opponent can't protect all the threatened pieces at once and, as a result, must risk the loss of one.

A variation of the Vienna game (an opening sequence of moves that became popular after a tournament in Vienna) provides us with an example of both knight and pawn forks.

Chess players call an opening that has many tactical possibilities *sharp*. This Vienna game variation, featuring multiple forks, is one of the sharpest in all of chess.

The Vienna game begins with both sides advancing the pawns in front of their kings two squares (see Figure 4-1). On the next turn, both sides bring out one of their knights (see Figure 4-2).

Figure 4-1

Figure 4-2

Next, white develops the white-squared bishop (Figure 4-3). Black takes advantage of the *pawn fork* tactic in order to capture a pawn (Figure 4-4).

Figure 4-3

Figure 4-4

If white captures the knight with its own knight, the black pawn forks the bishop and knight (as seen in Figures 4-5 and 4-6). In this way, black regains the lost piece and has a free game. White can, of course, take the offending pawn with its bishop . . . but the black queen would then swoop down upon the white bishop. Notice how white can save one piece, but not both, from capture.

Figure 4-5

Figure 4-6

Usually, white avoids the pawn fork by making a counter threat instead, before the pawn fork can develop. Instead of capturing the knight, which captured the pawn, white brings its queen out with the immediate threat of checkmate (see Figure 4-7). If black does not respond well, white can capture the pawn in front of the black king's bishop with the queen and announce: "Checkmate!" (I explain check and checkmate in Chapter 6; you don't need to know this stuff now, but jump ahead if you want to.) However, because it is black's turn to move, black retreats the knight. The knight now guards against the threat of checkmate and simultaneously attacks white's bishop (Figure 4-8).

Figure 4-7

Figure 4-8

In one of the main variations of this opening, white chooses to retreat the bishop away from the attacking knight (see Figure 4-9). Black now chooses to develop the other knight and defend the king's pawn (see Figure 4-10).

Figure 4-9

Figure 4-10

White now takes advantage of the fact that one of black's knights is tied down to defend against the threatened checkmate, and white attacks the defender (see Figure 4-11)! "Removing the Defender" is a tactical theme that you see over and over again in chess.

Black can't capture the cheeky knight because of the threat of checkmate. Black also can't ignore the threat of its knight being taken by white's knight. This loss would put the black king in check and allow white to deliver checkmate in the next move. Instead, black moves a pawn up one square in order to defend the checkmate and to attack the white queen at the same time (Figure 4-12).

Figure 4-11

Figure 4-12

A move that defends and attacks simultaneously is almost always a good one!

Now it is white's turn to retreat, but white retreats to a square that keeps the threat to black alive (see Figure 4-13). Defense and attack at the same time! Black has the same problem as before and advances a pawn. This move once again blocks the threatened checkmate (see Figure 4-14).

Figure 4-13

Figure 4-14

Black once again threatens to simply take the advanced white knight that is left hanging (lacking protection) — or *en prise* in chess terms. So white finds still another way to renew the threat of checkmate by again moving the queen (see Figure 4-15). Black is out of defensive pawn moves and is forced to move the queen out to defend against the checkmate (see Figure 4-16).

Figure 4-15

Figure 4-16

Finally, it is time for the *knight fork!* The knight captures the pawn, gives check to the king, and simultaneously attacks the rook in the corner (see Figure 4-17). Black must move the king out of check and allow white to capture the rook. The fork is one of the most basic of chess tactics, and the knight is the ideal forking piece.

The black rook and king are victims of the knight fork.

Figure 4-17

This variation of the Vienna is sometimes called the "Frankenstein-Dracula" or "Monster" variation because the tactics are so scary. Almost every move in this opening contains a threat, which is the essence of chess tactics.

The Pin

The pin is the most frequently used chess tactic. If chess had not been developed before patent lawyers, somebody would've become a millionaire many times over by now by patenting this maneuver.

To achieve the *pin,* the pinning piece attacks one of two enemy pieces lined up along a rank, file, or diagonal (see Chapter 1 for information on ranks, files, and diagonals). The pinned piece is the one between the attacker and the remaining piece. Usually, the pinned piece is of lesser value than the other — so that if it were to move, the more important piece would be subject to capture.

Only queens, rooks, and bishops can pin an enemy piece because they are the pieces that can attack multiple squares along a rank, file, or diagonal. Of the three, the bishop is most commonly used to establish a pin because it is more likely to find pieces of greater value than itself to attack.

Pinned pieces can move (although you may not want them to!) except when they are pinned to the king. Exposing the king to capture is illegal, so pinned pieces in cases involving the king are *really* nailed down.

In Figure 4-18, the black knight is attacked by the white bishop but is not pinned. In Figure 4-19, however, the knight is pinned to the king and cannot move.

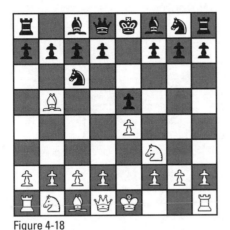

Figure 4-18

Figure 4-19

You can break a pin in four ways:

- Capture the pinning piece.

  It usually isn't much of a pin if you can take the pinning piece away, so capturing the pinning piece isn't often an option.

- Attack the pinning piece and force it to capture or retreat.

  This attack is called *putting the question to* the pinning piece.

- Place a less valuable piece or pawn in the path between the pinned piece and the more valuable one.

  This move is called *interposing.*

- Remove the more valuable piece from the pinning path.

  This strategy is appropriately called *running away.*

The Nimzo-Indian

One of the chess openings popularized by Aaron Nimzovich still bears a portion of his name. The Nimzo-Indian belongs to a class of openings that are referred to as *Indian defenses*. These openings are usually characterized by the development of a bishop on the flank, and this type of bishop deployment is called the *fianchetto*.

In the Nimzo-Indian, the queen's bishop is often fianchettoed. The king's bishop is used to establish an early pin. Here are the opening moves of the Nimzo-Indian.

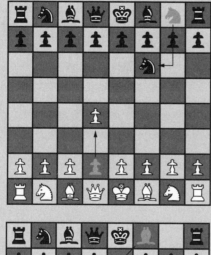
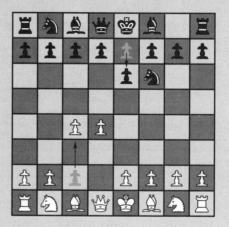

The white knight is pinned by the black bishop.

Black establishes a pin on the third move. The knight is pinned to the white king and cannot move. All sorts of strategies have been tried in this position, but it has proven to be one of the most effective defenses in all of chess. Black is ready to castle and can then safely counter-attack white's setup. (If you don't understand castling, see Chapter 9 for an explanation of this special move.) The pin proves to be more than just a minor annoyance for white. Sometimes the pin is mightier than the sword!

One very powerful type of pin can occur whenever the queen and king are lined up on a rank, file, or diagonal. When this positioning occurs, a bishop or rook may be able to pin the queen to the king. Be careful whenever your king and queen are on a line together, and be alert for the chance to pin when your opponent's are.

The Skewer

The pin's cousin is the skewer, because it also exploits the positioning of two enemy pieces along a rank, file, or diagonal. The *skewer* attacks a piece that must move or be lost. After the threatened piece moves, it exposes a second piece to capture. The bishop is the ideal skewer, and the king and queen are its frequent targets.

Can you find the skewer in Figure 4-20? It is white's move. (Black has an overwhelming material advantage, but white can even things up by making use of the skewer.)

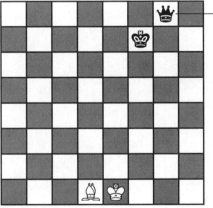

Black has a queen, and white has a lowly bishop. Black enjoys the material advantage.

Figure 4-20

The next figure shows the skewer in action. In Figure 4-21, white moves the bishop in order to put the black king in check. Figure 4-22 shows that the black king was forced to move out of check. And now the white bishop can simply capture the black queen!

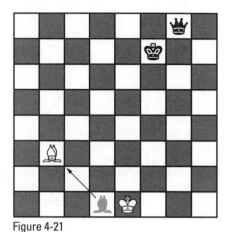

Figure 4-21

Figure 4-22

The skewer can also take place in another way, when the attacking piece is between the two defenders. This type of skewer is illustrated in Figure 4-23. In this case, the bishop attacks the two enemy pieces on either end of the diagonal. Think of a shish kebab! If black decides to move its king, the white bishop takes the queen. If black decides to take the white bishop with its queen, black loses its queen to the white king. In any case, black has let a chance to win slip away and now must accept a draw — no one can win!

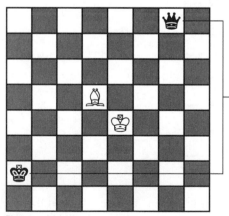

Figure 4-23

— The white bishop threatens both the black king and the black queen.

In practice, the skewer does not occur as often as the fork or pin, but it is so powerful that, when it does occur, it usually decides the game. So be alert for the possibility of a skewer at any time, especially when the king and queen are exposed along a rank, file, or diagonal.

Overloading

Sometimes a piece or pawn has too much on its hands to do everything asked of it. When this happens, the piece is said to be *overloaded*.

You can sometimes exploit an overloaded piece by removing it from its position. In Figure 4-24, the black rook is overloaded: It is charged with guarding the black queen (which is under attack from the white queen) and the black pawn (which is under attack from the white bishop and rook).

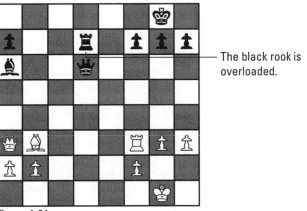

— The black rook is overloaded.

Figure 4-24

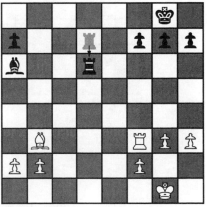

White can eventually win the pawn by taking the queen with its queen (see Figure 4-25). The white queen thus removes the black rook defender! The black rook must recapture the white queen in order to remain competitive (see Figure 4-26).

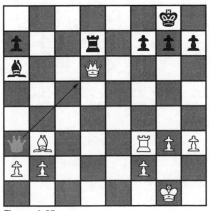

Figure 4-25

Figure 4-26

White can now take the defenseless pawn with either its bishop or its rook (see Figure 4-27).

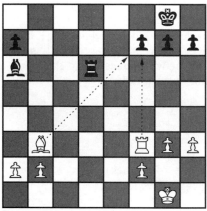

Figure 4-27

Or white can exploit the overloaded piece. The bishop simply captures the pawn and places the black king in check (see Figure 4-28). Notice that if the black rook captures the bishop, the white queen can take the black queen (see Figure 4-29). The overloaded rook could not guard both colleagues adequately.

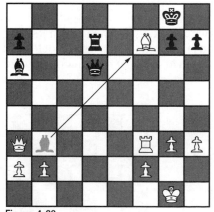

Figure 4-28

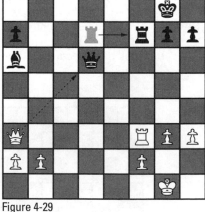

Figure 4-29

Zwischenzug

The Zwischenzug is my personal favorite, but I'm not sure I can pronounce it correctly. Remember, chess players love to use foreign words in order to emphasize their worldliness.

A *Zwischenzug* is the name of a common tactic that can catch even the best players in the world by surprise. It is an "in-between" move — which usually catches your opponent napping.

Chess players sometimes get lulled to sleep by *obvious* recaptures. "If I take your knight, you must take mine," they automatically assume. A Zwischenzug is like a cold slap in the face. Instead of the obvious move, you make a surprise move and then calmly go back to business as usual.

Here is an example of a Zwischenzug where Bobby Fischer, one of the best chess players in history, was caught unaware by *NY Times* columnist Robert Byrne.

Fischer, playing white, captures a black knight with his white knight (see Figure 4-30). Fischer assumes that black would have to recapture the knight with his pawn, but Byrne has a Zwischenzug surprise for him. Byrne plays his bishop to a different diagonal and threatens checkmate on his next move — with his queen capturing the pawn in front of it on the same file (see Figure 4-31).

Figure 4-30

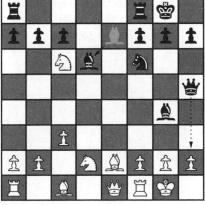

Figure 4-31

Fischer has to respond to that threat. Fischer moves his pawn up to stop the checkmate (see Figure 4-32), but Byrne has another surprise for him. Byrne lets the knight escape but captures the bishop instead (see Figure 4-33)! On the next move, Byrne captures the white rook and with it obtains a big advantage in material.

Figure 4-32

Figure 4-33

Fischer assumed that Byrne would recapture the white knight (after Fischer took one of Byrne's knights in the move shown in Figure 4-30) — but Byrne made no such assumption and found the winning move: a Zwischenzug. The advantage Byrne got from this tactic was enough to beat even Fischer!

Don't play a move in the hopes that your opponent will not see your threat. Instead, stick to the basic principles of play and you'll get your chance!

Many people believe that 90 percent of chess games are decided by tactics. There is no question that certain tactics recur continuously in chess games, sometimes many times in the same game. Thus, if you learn the basics, your playing strength will certainly increase.

Chapter 5

Sacrifices: When It's Better to Give than to Receive

If you were a single parent working two jobs just to send your little pawns to college, you'd undoubtedly consider yourself to be making a significant sacrifice. On the chessboard, however, a *sacrifice* (real or otherwise) is simply an intentional loss of something of value. (An *unintentional* loss of something of value is called, technically, a *blunder*.)

Many chess players occasionally refer to blunders as sacrifices, but try not to be fooled by this obvious ploy. (It's far too reminiscent of the kid who fell off his bike and then jumped up and said, "I meant to do that!")

One of the odd things about chess is that every move involves both advantage and disadvantage. You must give up something to get something. So, in the broadest terms, every move in a chess game involves some sacrifice. I try not to use broad terms, however, and so I intend in this book to confine myself to the more limited meaning of the word *sacrifice,* which is the intentional loss of a pawn or piece, either temporary or permanent, which a player performs in the hope of capitalizing on some other advantage.

Although speaking of a sacrifice in any one of the elements in chess (see Chapter 3) is technically correct, the most common sacrifice by far is that of material. Knights may impale themselves on spears so that other pieces can infiltrate behind enemy lines; pawns may throw themselves under the cavalry's hooves to slow an enemy advance; or the queen could take an arrow meant for the king — all so that other pieces on the board may some day be better off (that is, on the winning side).

Chess players, a bloodthirsty lot, love to sacrifice pieces. The greatest thrill is to sacrifice the queen, because she is the most powerful piece of all. We tend toward a flair for the dramatic, and if any chess player can give up a queen and still beat you, well, I'll just mention that no small amount of teasing may occur.

The Gambit

In trying to make chess seem difficult and mysterious, chess players have long called a common type of sacrifice by a different term entirely. We refer to these sacrifices, which occur early in the game, as *gambits*. Gambits almost always involve the sacrifice of material for time. In other words, you trade a pawn or a piece for development (an edge in the element of time; see Chapter 3 for details). The reasoning is simple. If you can get more pieces out into attacking formation much more quickly than your opponent can, you can conceivably win back the sacrificed material — and then some — while your opponent is scrambling to catch up.

One of the oldest gambits in chess is the *King's Gambit*. A player enters into this type of move by using the common double king's pawn opening, where both white and black advance the king's pawn two squares (see Figure 5-1).

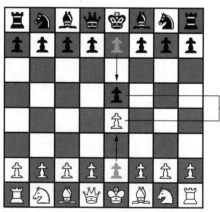

This is an example of the double king's pawn opening.

Figure 5-1

White's next move is to advance its king's bishop pawn by two squares, where the white pawn threatens and is itself threatened by the black pawn (as shown in Figure 5-2). Black takes the offered pawn and wins material (see Figure 5-3). White cannot immediately *recapture* the pawn. That's to say, white is unable to get even by capturing the black pawn that just took the white pawn.

Figure 5-2

Figure 5-3

Chess enthusiasts have written about and studied this particular opening gambit ad nauseam. The basic idea is that white goes about a normal development and recaptures the pawn later on with additional advantage. If black chooses to spend valuable time in defending the pawn, white builds up an attack by virtue of a rapid development.

Nowadays, players usually just give back the pawn — they let white recapture it — and complete their own development. But some of the more materialistic lines (where they try to hold on to the extra pawn) are still seen now and again, even at the higher levels of play. Gambits are very popular and can be very dangerous. I take a more detailed look at them in Chapter 10.

The Classic Bishop Sacrifice

A player from the so-called Italian school, Gioacchino Greco (1600-c.1634) made many contributions to chess. Primarily, Greco is remembered for his studies of chess openings, many of which still carry his name. The great thing about his analysis of the game was that much of it was recorded and preserved. He published numerous complete games, too. (I suspect, however, that Greco's published games were mostly made up. Recording games is now commonplace, but players today frown on publishing fictional ones.)

One of the earliest recorded sacrifices appears in Greco's chess handbook of 1619. This move, called a *classic bishop sacrifice,* has been used prominently ever since, wherever chess is played, and I advise the serious student of the game to become intimately aware of this type of sacrifice.

Is it gambling to gambit?

A certain amount of risk is involved in playing a gambit, but the term did not derive from the word gambling. It comes from the Italian word *gambetta*, which was a wrestling term for tripping up your opponent by the heels. It was first used in its chess sense by Ruy Lopez in 1561.

In the bishop sacrifice, one player sacrifices a bishop to expose the enemy king to a brutal attack by the queen and knight. The accompanying diagrams are based on Greco's analysis of this move. Figure 5-4 shows the basic pattern for the bishop sacrifice. The white bishop has access to the black king via the black pawn, and the queen and knight are prepared to quickly enter the fray.

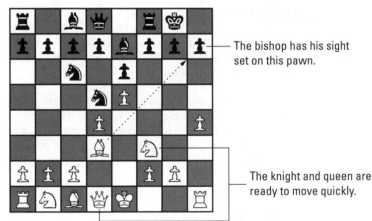

The bishop has his sight set on this pawn.

The knight and queen are ready to move quickly.

Figure 5-4

The white bishop captures a pawn, putting the king in check (see Figure 5-5). Black must then capture the bishop or lose a pawn for nothing (see Figure 5-6).

White is now behind in material, having traded a bishop for a pawn, or three points for one. (Consult Chapter 3 for the relative value of pieces.) Next, the knight jumps into the arena and gives check (see Figure 5-7). The black bishop can capture the marauding knight, but then white can capture the bishop by using the king's rook pawn (the pawn in front of the rook on the right side of the board). But the white rook would then check the black king. The white queen would then join the attack on the next move, and it's lights out for the black king. Black avoids this fate by moving its king to the back rank (see Figure 5-8).

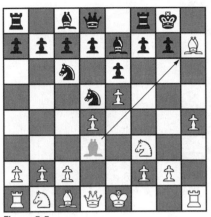

Figure 5-5

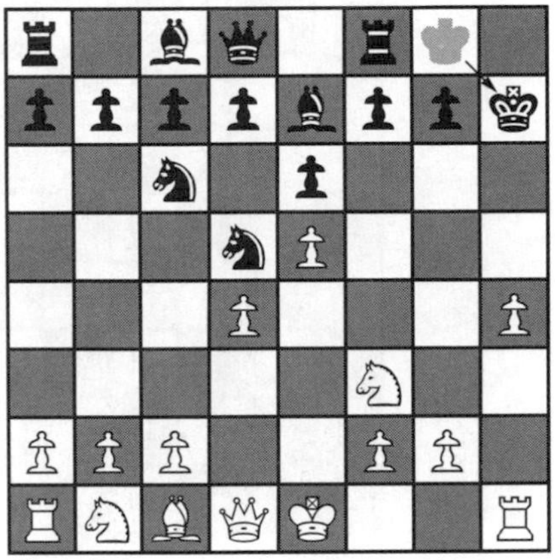

Figure 5-6

Figure 5-7

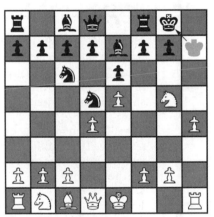

Figure 5-8

But black is still foiled once again by the relentless advance of the white queen, as shown in Figure 5-9. Checkmate is now unavoidable in the next few moves, no matter what black does. (If you need a lesson on checkmate, jump ahead to Chapter 6.)

The bishop sacrifice is especially powerful if a player uses the move to expose the enemy king to attack. Sometimes this sacrifice can lead directly to checkmate, as in the preceding example, but often the move just wins back the material — with interest.

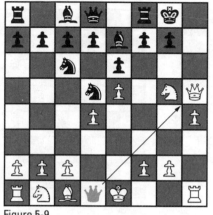

Figure 5-9

The Temporary Sacrifice

Chess players call sacrifices that lead directly to the win of more material pseudo-sacrifices or, more commonly, *temporary sacrifices.* Thinking in terms of "sacrifice" if you actually win your opponent's queen at the cost of a knight, however, is not quite correct. The knight feels like it is being sacrificed, but it is simply being traded for a piece of higher value.

The following example demonstrates this temporary (or pseudo-) sacrifice in practice. The position is pretty similar to the one in Figure 5-4, but in this case, white merely wins material and does not press on to checkmate (see Figure 5-10 for the setup).

As in the preceding example, white sacrifices the bishop by taking the pawn and putting the black king in check (see Figure 5-11). Black must capture the bishop or suffer the uncompensated loss of a pawn (Figure 5-12).

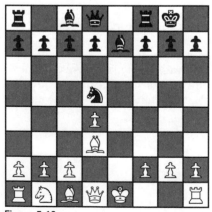

Figure 5-10

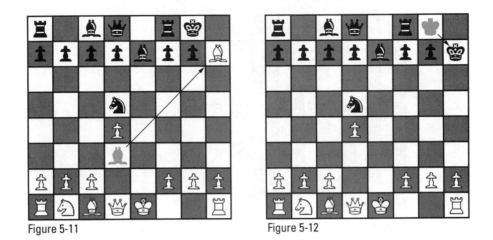

Figure 5-11   Figure 5-12

White brings the queen out to check the black king and simultaneously attacks the unprotected knight (see Figure 5-13). Black is forced to retreat (see Figure 5-14).

But black's retreat enables the white queen to capture the knight, as shown in Figure 5-15. White thus wins a knight and a pawn in exchange for the bishop by using a temporary sacrifice.

Figure 5-13

Figure 5-14

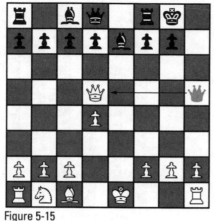

Figure 5-15

The Permanent Sacrifice

A *permanent sacrifice* is one where the material is not immediately recovered. Usually, the goal in making this type of sacrifice is a strategic one. One side gives up material in order to secure a lasting advantage in another area. These types of sacrifices can't be calculated but are a product of intuition and imagination — and are what elevate chess play to artistry.

In this classic example of a permanent sacrifice, white trades a pawn to disrupt black's development. In this case, you are not simply trading a pawn for a quick lead in development, as you do with a gambit, but rather for a lasting advantage based on black's difficulty in getting its pieces coordinated. The following example gives you an idea of how such a sacrifice may work. Our starting position is shown in Figure 5-16.

Figure 5-16

White advances its pawn and exposes it to capture (see Figure 5-17). Black takes the pawn (Figure 5-18).

But white does not try to regain the pawn. White simply continues to develop by moving out the knight (Figure 5-19). Black's position is disorganized as a result of white's sacrifice, and getting its pieces out to good squares is now going to be difficult. White may need to make many additional moves to take advantage of this fact, however, and that's why the sacrifice is called a permanent one.

Figure 5-17

Figure 5-18

Figure 5-19

Mikhail Tal (1936-1991)

A grandmaster from Riga, Latvia, Mikhail Tal became world champion in 1960 but lost the return match to Mikhail Botvinnik (1911-1995) the following year. Tal was widely popular for his brilliant sacrificial play. Poor health reduced his results, but he remained one of the most entertaining chess players right up until his death.

Tal was so taken with chess that he supposedly kept sneaking out of the hospital after undergoing surgery to remove a kidney, just to play in the local chess club. He was also famous for his intimidating stare. Combined with his ability to seemingly summon sacrifices out of the air, this stare gave Tal an almost mystical aura. One grandmaster even went so far as to wear sun glasses during a game to avoid Tal's "evil eye." (He lost anyway.)

No true chess aficionado can deny that sacrifices rank among the most dramatic events in a chess game. Sacrifices introduce an imbalance into positions and can often act as the proverbial bolt from the blue. If your opponent makes a sacrifice that you haven't considered, that move can be quite unnerving. The best thing to do in this situation is to take a few moments to compose yourself and then calmly figure out what's going on and how best to proceed. The rule of thumb here is that the only way to refute a sacrifice is to accept it! If you don't know what to do, take the material.

Chapter 6

Mating and Mating Patterns

. . . .

In This Chapter

▶ Getting the king's attention: check

▶ When no one can win: stalemate

▶ Winning the game: checkmate

▶ Mating patterns (chess is a sexy game after all)

. . . .

Dr. Ruth has never seriously studied mating patterns in chess, to my knowledge, but I think that everyone interested in the game should engage most seriously in such a study. One of the best ways to become familiar with the powers of each piece on the chessboard is to try to checkmate a lone king with each of them in turn. You quickly discover that, even with the help of the king, the knight and bishop can't accomplish checkmate by themselves, but the rook and the queen can (as long as the king helps them).

Ready to start your mating studies? Good. Your first task is to learn the differences between check and checkmate and between checkmate and stalemate.

Check

To *give check* simply means that you are attacking the enemy king. In Figure 6-1, white has a king and queen to black's lone king. The black king is currently in check because the white queen has moved and is now attacking it.

A check can't be ignored and must be responded to in one of three ways:

✔ The attacking piece may be captured.

✔ A piece may be moved between the checking piece and the king in order to block the attack.

✔ The king may be able simply to move out of check.

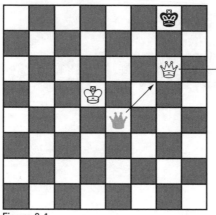

On white's turn, the queen moves into a position that places black's king under attack. Check!

Figure 6-1

In the example shown in Figure 6-1, the black king's only option is to move out of check.

You may actually say "check" when you attack your opponent's king, but it is not mandatory. If you do say "check," do so in a low voice so as not to disturb other players. It is considered bad taste to pump your fist in the air and yell, "Check . . . Yesssssss!" Under no circumstances is it correct to do a moonwalk or other dance step. Chess players try to keep their emotions under control at all times.

Stalemate: No Check, No Glory

Stalemate occurs when one side has no legal moves left to make but the king is not in check. In chess there is no such thing as *passing* a turn. You must make a move each and every time it is your turn. However, if your opponent puts you in a situation where you can't make a move (because you would be forced to move into check, for example, which would be illegal), the game is declared *drawn* due to stalemate.

King and queen versus king is the easiest two-piece combination for accomplishing checkmate, but you must make sure that you guard against delivering a stalemate. Because the queen can control so many squares, stalemating the opposing king by accident is actually quite easy! If, for example, it is black's move in Figure 6-2, the game is a stalemate.

It's black's move, but the king has nowhere to go: Every square it can occupy is under attack by the white king or queen. Stalemate!

Figure 6-2

Checkmate

Checkmate occurs when the king is in check and can't escape it. An example of checkmate is shown in Figure 6-3. The black king is now placed in check because the white queen has moved to attack it. But the black king has no legal moves:

> ✔ It can't capture the checking piece because the white queen is guarded by the white king.
>
> ✔ It has no other black piece that can block the check.
>
> ✔ It can't move out of check to a square that is not also under attack.

Black is therefore checkmated. Remember the old adage, "It is better to give checkmate than to receive it!"

White moves and places black's king in check. But black has no legal move. Checkmate!

Figure 6-3

Beginning chess players tend to fall in love with giving check, but remember that check is not checkmate. The key to delivering checkmate with the queen is to drive the enemy king to the edge of the board and to watch out for moves that could lead to stalemate.

This process is accomplished by *cutting off squares* (systematically reducing the number of squares the king has access to). Follow along with the next few figures and you see how easily you can set up a checkmate by cutting off squares.

Figure 6-4 shows the starting positions of the black king and the white king and queen.

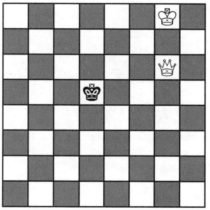

Figure 6-4

White cuts off squares by advancing the queen one square, as shown in Figure 6-5. (The squares that now are cut off from the black king are marked with *X*s.) Next, in Figure 6-6, the black king retreats to one of only three squares left open to it.

Figure 6-5   Figure 6-6

The white king advances diagonally to join the queen (see Figure 6-7). Even the mighty queen cannot deliver checkmate without the help of the king. The black king moves again (see Figure 6-8).

Figure 6-7

Figure 6-8

Remember that the best defense is to stay as far away from the edge of the board as possible. White can cut off more squares, as shown in Figure 6-9. (Figure 6-9 again uses *X*s to show how additional squares are cut off.)

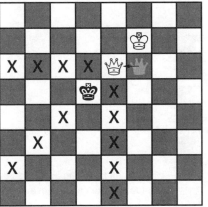

Figure 6-9

By comparing the setup shown in Figure 6-9 to the earlier one in Figure 6-5, you may see how white is shrinking the number of squares available to black's king. Chess players sometimes call this sequence *shrinking the square.*

White can continue to cut off squares in this manner until black's king is forced to the edge of the board, as shown in Figure 6-10.

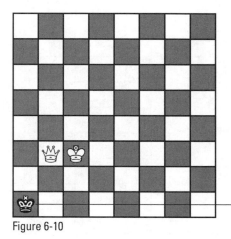

Figure 6-10

Black's king has eventually been forced into a corner as white continued to cut off squares.

Now white can force checkmate. Notice that the safest way to avoid stalemate is to force the opposing king to the edge of the board, use your queen to keep it trapped there, and then advance your king. If you cut off too many squares, you run the risk of giving stalemate, so be careful. Keep the queen at a safe distance, let your king stroll up to lend support, and then deliver checkmate as shown in Figure 6-11.

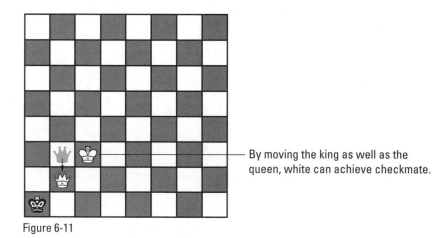

By moving the king as well as the queen, white can achieve checkmate.

Figure 6-11

CHESS TALK

Not all checks were created equal!

The nastiest check short of checkmate is the *discovered check*. This type of check occurs if you move a piece from a position between another of your pieces and the enemy king and your second piece then gives check. That is, its check is suddenly "discovered" because the intervening piece is now gone and the second piece now has line of sight — and movement — to the opposing king. The piece you move to reveal the check can thus move anywhere and capture anything in its power with immunity, because the other side must respond to the check. If the piece you move also gives check, this combination is called *double check*, and the enemy king is forced to move because there is no other way of warding off the two attacks.

When you can keep checking the enemy king on every turn but cannot checkmate it, you have *perpetual check*. Perpetual check results in a *draw*. If it is not checkmate (because the king can escape any individual check) and the king has no prospects of avoiding future, continuous checks, neither side can win. This type of check can be a handy strategy if you're losing. (Getting a draw isn't quite so much like kissing your sister if it takes the place of a loss!)

If your opponent is sure to lose but postpones defeat by giving a pointless check, the move is known as a *spite check*. Spite checks are considered an example of bad chess manners. Don't check out of spite!

Sometimes giving check can backfire. We have a saying in chess circles: "Monkey sees a check; monkey gives a check." Only a monkey would give check just because it could! We use the saying to remind ourselves not to give pointless checks. Make certain that when you give check, it somehow helps your cause. To give check and then be forced to retreat is simply a waste of time. If you play a check that ruins your position, you may say, quite correctly, that your check bounced!

Checkmating with king and rook

Achieving checkmate with the king and rook follows the same principle as that of using the king and queen but takes longer to achieve because the rook is not as powerful a piece as the queen. The next series of diagrams demonstrate how to force the king to the side of the board by using the rook and king.

Warning! The sequence that follows is long and tedious but is essential chess knowledge.

Step 1: The initial advance of the king

No single piece can deliver checkmate without the help of the king. A lone piece can't even force the enemy king to the edge of the board where the king is most easily checkmated. You must advance your own king into a position where it can help drive back the enemy.

The white rook cuts off squares from the black king (see Figure 6-12). The white king is supporting the rook so that black cannot capture it. The black king is forced to retreat (see Figure 6-13).

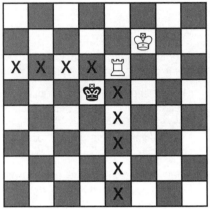

Figure 6-12

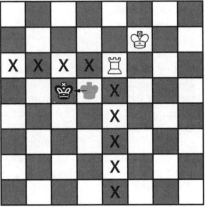

Figure 6-13

The white king advances in order to prepare to cut off more squares (see Figure 6-14). Black moves back to the center of the board, trying to stay as far away from the edge of the board as possible (see Figure 6-15).

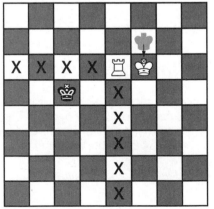

Figure 6-14

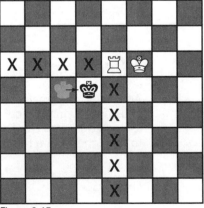

Figure 6-15

The white king advances again (Figure 6-16), and the black king is once again forced to retreat (Figure 6-17).

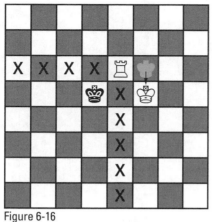

Figure 6-16

Figure 6-17

In Figure 6-18, notice how the white king is now also cutting off squares. An important part of this strategy is to advance the king, not in front of the enemy king, but off to its side. The reason for this course of action becomes clear in the next step. The black king again moves as far away from the edge of the board — as far as the white pieces will allow (see Figure 6-19). Now, however, the white king has advanced far enough to move onto phase two of the operation.

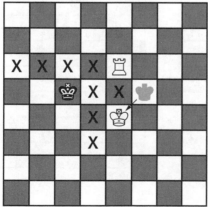

Figure 6-18

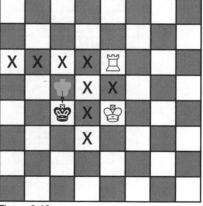

Figure 6-19

Step 2: Forcing the king toward the edge of the board

In this phase of the checkmating operation, the white rook and king combine forces to drive the black king closer to the edge of the board. The rook checks the black king and forces it to move closer to the edge of the board (see Figure 6-20). The black king moves to attack the undefended rook (see Figure 6-21).

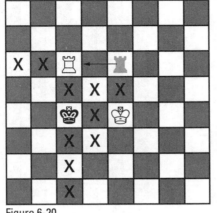

Figure 6-20

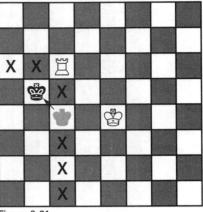

Figure 6-21

The white king advances in order to defend the attacked rook and continue to help cut off squares (see Figure 6-22). Finally, the black king is forced to once more give ground (see Figure 6-23).

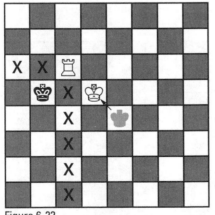

Figure 6-22

Figure 6-23

Step 3: Cutting off more squares

The preliminary objective of forcing the king to retreat has been accomplished. You must now return to the idea of cutting off squares in order to drive the king back still farther. In Figure 6-24 the rook is advanced in order to cut off more squares. Can you see why chess players sometimes call this "shrinking the box"? The method of achieving checkmate is to continue to cut off squares until the black king is finally forced to the edge of the board. In Figure 6-25, the black king retreats, but continues to stay away from the edge of the board.

Figure 6-24

Figure 6-25

Next, the rook is used once more to cut off additional squares (as shown in Figure 6-26). The black king again retreats (see Figure 6-27). Notice how the white rook is cutting off the black king's access to all the squares except for those in the lower-left corner.

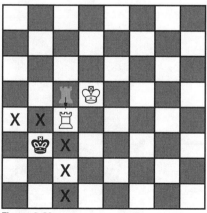

Figure 6-26

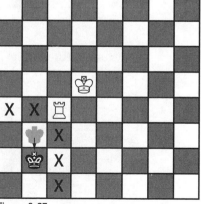

Figure 6-27

Step 4: Advance the king and cut off squares in combination

Now that additional squares are cut off, you return to the theme of advancing the king. You now alternate between the two themes. You cut off squares when you can and advance the king when you can't.

In Figure 6-28, the white king advances once more. This approach demonstrates why it takes so long to actually achieve the checkmate. The process itself is a fairly simple one; the same kind of moves are made over and over again for the same reason, but because the king is needed to force a checkmate, and the king moves only one square at a time, it takes quite a number of moves in order to execute the plan. In Figure 6-29, black moves the king to attack the rook. However, since the rook is protected by the white king, the attack is meaningless. Still, there is nothing better for black to do.

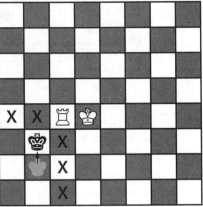

Figure 6-28   Figure 6-29

In Figure 6-30, the white king continues to advance and assist in the process of cutting off squares. In Figure 6-31, the black king once again is forced to retreat.

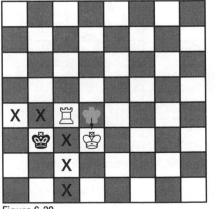

Figure 6-30   Figure 6-31

In Figure 6-32, white returns to the theme of using the rook to cut off squares. This finally forces the black king to the edge of the board (see Figure 6-33).

Figure 6-32

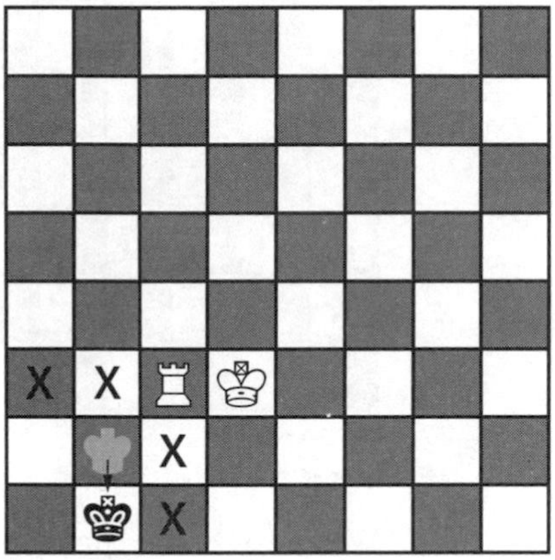

Figure 6-33

White can now trap the black king on the edge of the board (see Figure 6-34). The process of cutting off squares has been completed, and white can now take the final step towards delivering checkmate. Black can now only shuffle back and forth in the lower-left corner of the board (see Figure 6-35).

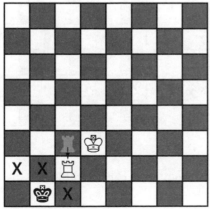

Figure 6-34

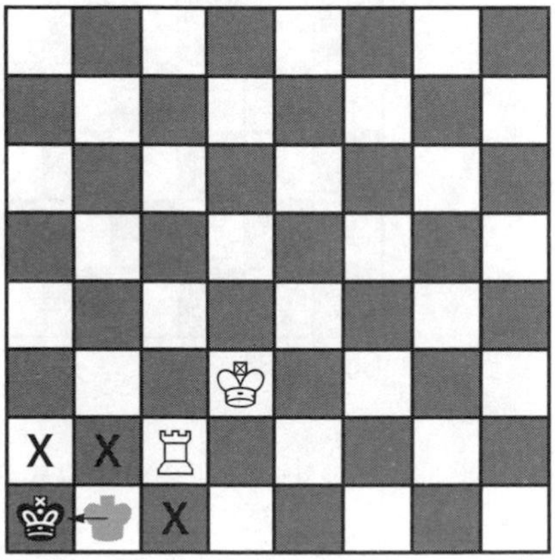

Figure 6-35

Step 5: Deliver checkmate!

Now white simply needs to move the king into the proper position (see Figure 6-36) to deliver checkmate. Black still has no choice but to shuffle back and forth (see Figure 6-37).

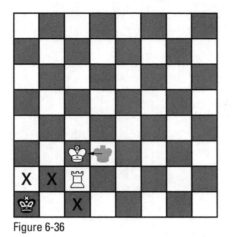

Figure 6-36

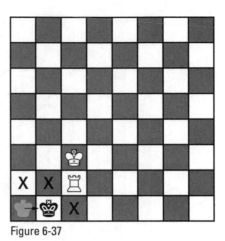

Figure 6-37

White continues the march of the king in Figure 6-38, but black can move only back into the corner (see Figure 6-39).

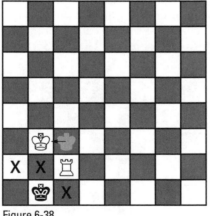

Figure 6-38

Figure 6-39

The time has come to deliver checkmate (see Figure 6-40).

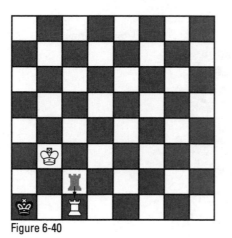

Figure 6-40

Checkmate! Finally! Don't worry, however: This series of moves is much easier to play than to explain. But you must practice this elementary checkmate until you understand it entirely. Learning this checkmate leads you to an appreciation of mating patterns.

Mating Patterns: Even Chess Players Have Them

Most strong players have committed a slew of mating patterns to memory. Memorizing such patterns makes calculating moves much easier, and so I highly recommend that every chess player become familiar with at least some of the patterns described in this section. These patterns occur again and again in chess, and nothing is quite like the feeling of seeing one pop up in one of your own games. You're either ecstatic to spot a way to checkmate your foe or downcast when you realize that you're the one caught in the net.

Back rank mates

The first and, by far, the most common mating pattern is the *back rank mate*. After the king castles, it is often protected by three pawns positioned directly in front of it. (See Chapter 9 if you need a lesson on castling.) Sometimes, however, these protectors become turncoats, as shown in Figure 6-41. The kings are protected by their pawns but are also trapped by them. The difference in the two sides' positions in Figure 6-41 is that the white rook protects the white back rank — while the black rook does not protect its back rank.

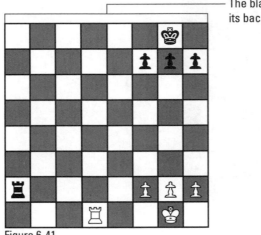

The black rook has left its back rank unprotected.

Figure 6-41

White takes advantage of this by checkmating the black king (see Figure 6-42.)

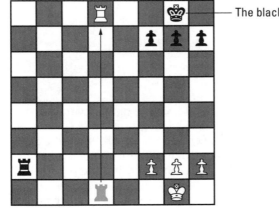

The black king is trapped!

Figure 6-42

If, instead, the turn to move had been black's, black could have avoided the checkmate by moving any of the pawns forward and giving its king some room to move.

Queen and pawn mates

The queen cannot deliver checkmate by itself but can do so with the aid of even a single pawn. Many chess games have been decided by a variation of this theme, which is set up for you in Figure 6-43.

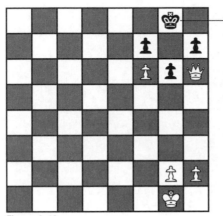

The black king has nowhere to flee.

Figure 6-43

Of course, white is a queen ahead in this position and should win in any case, but the point is to concentrate forces on the cluster around the black king. This position illustrates a typical mating pattern. The black king can't escape and can't avoid white's threat to deliver checkmate. The checkmate is shown in Figure 6-44.

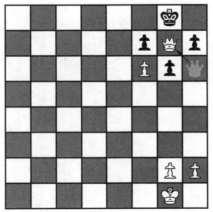

Figure 6-44

The pawn guards the queen, and so black is checkmated. This pattern also occurs where the advanced white pawn and queen exchange places.

A cute little study of the queen and pawn mating pattern was published in 1512 by a Portuguese apothecary named Damiano. White can force mate from the starting position shown in Figure 6-45.

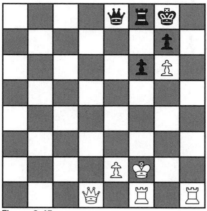

Figure 6-45

GOOD MOVE

The mating pattern is essentially the same as in the first example. The king is trapped behind a combination of white and black pawns. After white recognizes the mating pattern, finding the rather shocking rook sacrifice is easy (see Figure 6-46). Black is forced to capture the rook (see Figure 6-47) in order to escape the check.

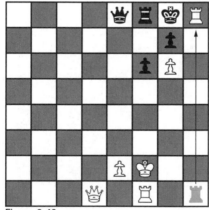

Figure 6-46

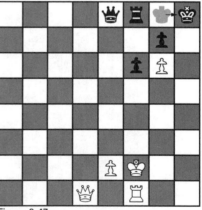

Figure 6-47

CHESS TALK

The idea behind this particular rook sacrifice is that the rooks cannot deliver checkmate in this position, but the queen can. This idea leads white to consider how best to get the queen into position without giving black any time to ready a counter move. The concept of clearing the rooks out of the way to enable the queen to deliver checkmate is now a standard one in chess. Chess players now call such moves *clearance sacrifices*. After this idea is understood, the rest of the moves in the following sequence make sense.

In Figure 6-48, white checks the king with the rook. Black has only one move in order escape the check and moves back to where it started from (see Figure 6-49).

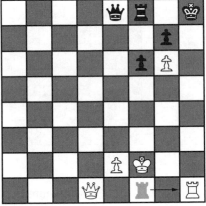

Figure 6-48
Figure 6-49 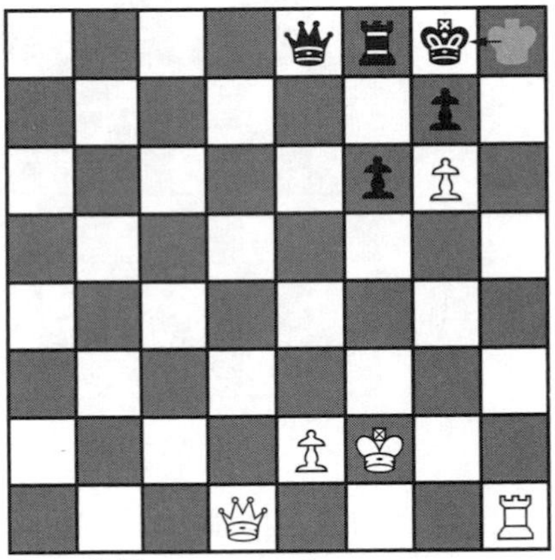

Now white repeats the same sacrifice as before (see Figure 6-50). Black must accept it, just as before (see Figure 6-51).

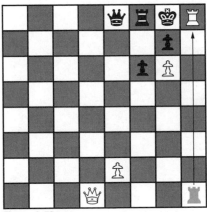

Figure 6-50
Figure 6-51

Now the difference is that it will be the white queen giving check (see Figure 6-52) rather than the rooks. Black must again move back to where it came from (see Figure 6-53).

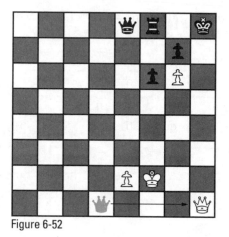

Figure 6-52

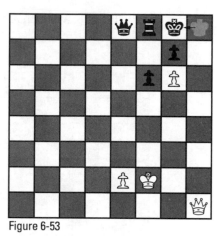

Figure 6-53

After all this, what has white accomplished? For starters, white has lost two full rooks! However, this is a case where material does not matter. White's next move is checkmate (see Figure 6-54).

Figure 6-54

The queen delivers mate, again protected by the pawn. These mates occur infrequently at the higher levels of chess competitions because both sides know them so well. At lower-level competitions, however, these mating patterns may not be well known at all. This type of queen and pawn mate, therefore, can be an important weapon to have in your arsenal as you begin your chess adventures!

Queen and knight mates

The queen and knight are especially powerful in mating combinations. This capability has something to do with the fact that the knight has powers that the queen does not, and the two pieces end up complementing one another. Figure 6-55 shows the beginning of a common mating pattern with queen and knight. The queen threatens checkmate on its next move. Notice that moving either pawn would not help black. The white queen still can deliver checkmate. Black's only chance is to move the suffocating rook away (see Figure 6-56).

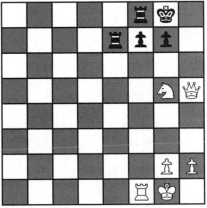

Figure 6-55

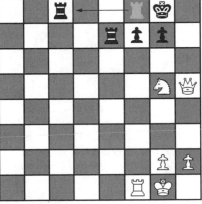

Figure 6-56

The rook retreat only prolongs the agony, however, as white still delivers check, as shown in Figure 6-57, forcing the king to move (see Figure 6-58). Note that the role of the knight is primarily to support the queen's incursion into the black king's position.

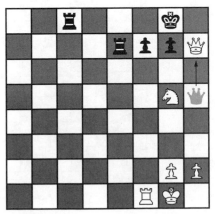

Figure 6-57

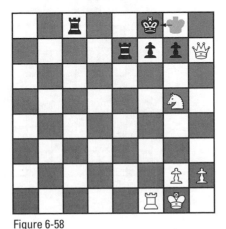

Figure 6-58

The white queen now delivers checkmate (see Figure 6-59).

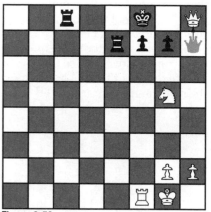

Figure 6-59

The queen and knight combine in several other ways to produce mating patterns. The next example is a bit rarer in practice but is still worth knowing. This pattern is called the *smothered mate*. If you get a chance to deliver mate in this way, consider yourself to be extremely cool.

In Figure 6-60, the black king is in check and must move. If the black king moves one square over, next to the rook, white's queen could deliver checkmate at once by moving the queen directly in front of the black king. Note how the queen would once again be supported by the knight in that event. So black tries to escape the threat by moving the king into the corner (see Figure 6-61).

Figure 6-60

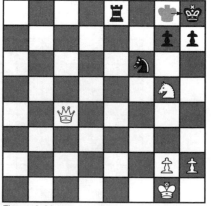

Figure 6-61

The knight jumps in (Figure 6-62), and forces the king back to where it started (Figure 6-63).

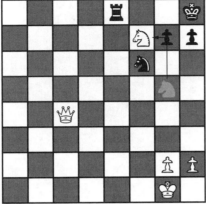

Figure 6-62

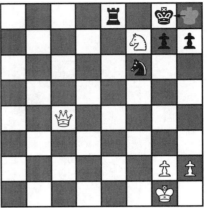

Figure 6-63

The knight then moves again, delivering *double check.* (Double check occurs if the king is attacked by two pieces at once, in this case, the white queen and knight (see Figure 6-64). This type of check is very powerful, because it forces the king to move. Black has no way to block both checks or capture both checking pieces. The king finds itself forced back into the corner (see Figure 6-65).

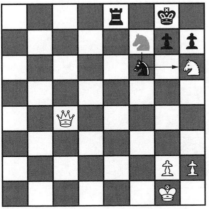

Figure 6-64

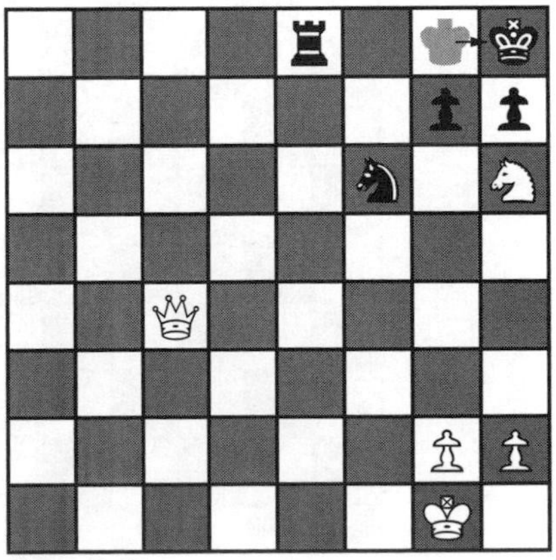

Figure 6-65

Now the next move on white's part, as shown in Figure 6-66, could seem quite bizarre, if you didn't know the smothered mate pattern! The white queen sacrifices itself so that the knight can deliver checkmate. The piece black uses to capture the queen — the knight or the rook — doesn't matter. (But notice that the white knight guards the queen so that the black king cannot capture her.) Black takes the queen with the rook (see Figure 6-67).

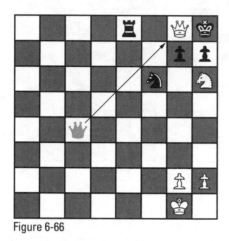

Figure 6-66

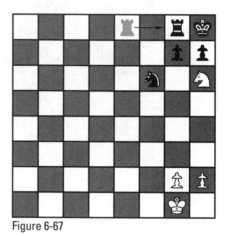

Figure 6-67

White then moves the knight, as shown in Figure 6-68.

Figure 6-68

Checkmate! You can understand why this type of mate is called the smothered mate, because you can clearly see that black's pieces are suffocating the black king.

Bishop and rook: Morphy's Mate

The final mating pattern presented here involves the rook and bishop. The two pieces compliment one another because the rook controls files and ranks while the bishop controls diagonals. It takes time for most of us to develop a sense for which pieces work well together and which ones don't (queen and knight do, bishop and knight don't, for example), but one of the keys to chess mastery is understanding this relationship between pieces. Morphy's mate is an example of the bishop and rook working well together.

Paul Morphy was one of the greatest attacking players of all time. He played some of the most beautiful games in chess history and introduced chess mavens to more than one mating pattern. This pattern has been named after him. The starting position for this mate is shown in Figure 6-69.

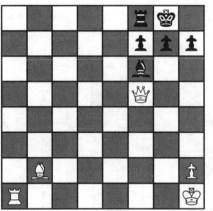

Figure 6-69

Again, don't worry about the piece count in this example; just concentrate on the mating pattern. Here, white makes a surprising move to produce the mate. By capturing the black bishop with the queen (Figure 6-70), white forces black to capture the queen (Figure 6-71). Otherwise white could take the pawn in front of the black king on the next move. (Note how the bishop is providing support along that long diagonal.)

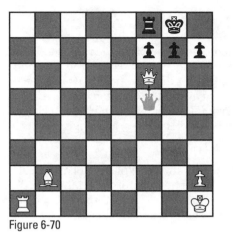

Figure 6-70

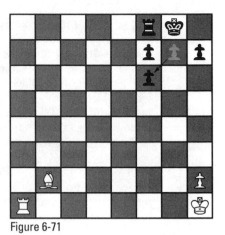

Figure 6-71

This move by black creates a line to the black king for the white rook along the now open g-file (see Figure 6-72). The rook's position forces the black king into the corner (see Figure 6-73).

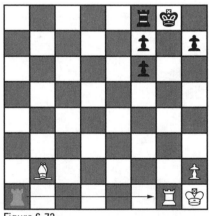

Figure 6-72

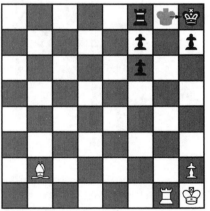

Figure 6-73

Next, white delivers checkmate by capturing the black pawn with the bishop (see Figure 6-74).

Mating patterns can surface multiple times in a single game. Often, players threaten to produce a mating pattern only to see the pattern successfully defended against by a wily opponent. Nevertheless, the players who firmly etch these mating patterns into their minds are sure to eventually get the chance to use them!

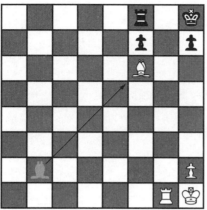

Figure 6-74

For more information on mating and mating patterns, I recommend *The Art of Attack* by Vladimir Vukovic. Most of what I know about the subject, I learned from that book.

Paul Morphy: the pride and sorrow of chess

Born in New Orleans, Paul Morphy (1837-84) had a truly meteoric chess career. He burst upon the international scene and defeated all comers. He did so in scintillating fashion. Morphy was gifted in other fields as well. He earned his law degree before the age of twenty-one but was too young to practice. His memory was such that he could recite much of the Civil Code of Louisiana verbatim. Morphy believed that he was simply marking time playing chess until he became old enough to practice law.

Morphy's descent from the top was as abrupt as his rise. At the height of his powers and fame, he abandoned the game and grew increasingly withdrawn. He was said to have suffered from a persecution complex and died a lonely death. Myths have been built up surrounding Morphy to account for his behavior, including unrequited love and bitterness at being snubbed by an elder champion. Unfortunately, the truth is more likely a prosaic, if sad, case of mental illness.

Chapter 7
Pattern Recognition

*O*ne of the great myths surrounding the game of chess is that you must be a human calculating machine — or (if you're a Star Trek fan) perhaps a Vulcan in order to play the game. A certain amount of calculation is involved in any chess game, of course, but chess players primarily rely on *pattern recognition* (the ability to spot similar configurations of pieces and pawns) and on *intuition* to choose their moves. They rarely tell you this fact because most of the time it is an unconscious process. If you ask them why they played this move instead of that, they often reply, "I just knew what the right move was" — or something equally unenlightening.

If you are unfamiliar with chess, all positions on the chessboard probably appear equally chaotic to you. If, however, you've seen scores and scores of games, the significance of many relative positions among chess pieces are understandable at a glance. Some chess aficionados have likened this building up of a store of recognizable patterns to a sort of chess vocabulary. The words of any non-native language seem unfamiliar to you at first exposure, but after you build your vocabulary, many words, terms, and concepts in the language can be understood without any conscious thought at all. The general idea here is pretty much the same in chess.

Analyzing Chess Positions on the Board

Researchers have conducted experiments to demonstrate this notion of chess as language, using a sampling of people of widely different chess strengths. The scientists involved in these experiments exposed players to several different chess setups consisting of both random positions and actual gamelike positions. Each exposure lasted for only a few seconds at a time. The researchers then asked the subjects to reconstruct the various positions as the players remembered them. The stronger players scored much better in reconstructing the actual gamelike positions than did the weaker players, but this advantage on the part of the better players virtually disappeared when they attempted to reconstruct the random positions. The conclusion? If you take away a player's knowledge base about chess, by removing any resemblance to actual game positions, you also take away that player's apparent superiority in recall.

Strong players can evaluate many types of positions quickly because they have seen something similar to them before. Of course, most positions in chess have their own quirks or involve other variables that require specific calculation to truly understand them, but chess players start from a base of common knowledge about the game and work out the variations from there. We can, therefore, zero in on a relatively few moves to study seriously, and being able to do so greatly reduces the amount of actual calculation involved. This mental process is unlike that of a computer, which treats all moves as equal and tries to process them all.

Processing and analyzing chess positions does seem to be one of those left brain-right brain things, though. People who are good at spatial relationships seem able to absorb the patterns in chess a bit easier than can those who are not so good in this area. Spatially oriented players build up their chess vocabularies more rapidly and become fluent in the language of chess much earlier than do their nonspatial brethren. True pattern recognition skills, however, come mostly from experience with the game. After you see enough different positions on the chessboard, you begin just to "know" what kinds of moves you should consider, almost without conscious thought, and you don't bother looking at all the alternatives.

Looking Ahead

Almost every chess master has heard this question: "How many moves can you see ahead?" One master answered, "Only one. The best one." This statement contains at least a kernel of truth. I always answer that "It depends." If you want to know whether I calculate all the possibilities in any given position, however, the answer is a definite no. If you want to know how many moves ahead I can see in any one particular sequence, the answer is that, in some cases, I can see quite far and, in other cases, I can see only a very few moves ahead. If the position is of a *forcing nature,* which means that my opponent's moves are highly predictable, and it is a position with which I'm familiar (that is, a pattern that I recognize), I can calculate about a dozen moves ahead, sometimes more. As you may deem reasonable, the more patterns that I recognize, the farther ahead I can calculate my moves.

The tree of analysis

Alexander Kotov (1913-81), a former Soviet champion, wrote a very famous book called *Think Like a Grandmaster*. (Well, at least the book's familiar to most chess players.) In the English translation, Kotov introduced players to the concepts of the *tree of analysis* and *candidate moves*.

You can't climb the tree of analysis, but you can understand its roots. You can meet each move made by your opponent in chess with one of several replies. Your opponent may respond to each reply with any of several other moves. The alternative moves available to you and your opponent "branch out" and quickly mask the forest for all the trees.

Kotov taught that, to reduce the bushiness of the tree and to better enable players to see farther ahead in their moves (as well as anticipate those

of their opponents), you first need to settle on which moves are the *candidate moves*. Candidate moves are those moves that you intend to examine closely based on your intuition. First you look around and figure out which moves are the important ones, again based on your intuition, and only then do you begin to calculate concrete variations. You must, according to Kotov, examine each candidate before making your final selection.

Candidate moves are chosen by a combination of intuition and judgment. The choices you make in determining candidate moves get better with experience. The calculation of concrete variations is more like work, but it, too, gets better with practice. The more you practice these aspects of your game (as well as all others), the better you get as a chess player.

If your goal is to improve your strength at chess, you must develop your ability to recognize patterns. If your goal is to just enjoy the game with a friend, you can skip this task. I know tons of players who play all the time and never get any better — and they enjoy themselves more than most masters I know. If you really want to "get good" at the game, however, you have no choice but to "do the pattern thing."

Mating patterns (see Chapter 6) are important to know and they come in very handy, but they may not be the most important patterns to recognize. The most important patterns, in fact, actually involve the lowly pawn.

Pawn Structures

The easiest patterns to recognize, besides mating patterns (described in Chapter 6), are the patterns of *pawn structures*. When I speak of pawn structures, I mean the positioning of the white pawns in relationship to the black pawns and vice versa. Most masters can come across a game in progress and make an educated guess as to how that game began simply by looking at the current pawn structure because pawns are relatively immobile, and it is difficult to radically alter their positioning from one phase of the game to the next.

The pawns tell you where to put your pieces, where to attack, and where to guard against attack by virtue of their relatively fixed nature. Because the pawns can't be as easily repositioned as the pieces, much of the middlegame's strategy revolves around pawn structures, and the many slightly differing endings that arise from these structures are tied together by common threads — so understanding pawn structures is pretty darned important to your game.

Because learning every opening in chess is impossible, most players concentrate on one or two openings to use if playing white and then a couple more when playing black. By understanding pawn structures, you can more easily understand the nuances of a certain opening; in turn, by limiting the numbers of openings you play, you cut down on the need to learn about all the different types of pawn structures. This strategy makes your goal of improving at chess a more manageable one.

The French Defense

The pawn structure that I understand best arises from what is called the *French Defense.* The French Defense, or simply *the French,* gained its modern name in 1834, when a Paris team used the opening to defeat a London team in a correspondence match. Figure 7-1 shows the starting position for the French Defense. White (the English) opens the game by moving out the king's pawn two squares. Black (the French) responds by moving out its king's pawn one square. (In the language of the time, black's first move was called *King's pawn one.*) The idea behind the French Defense is to strike back at white's center pawn. The first move provides support for the intended second move. After white advances the other center pawn two squares, black follows suit (see Figure 7-2).

Figure 7-1

Figure 7-2

Now many alternatives are available to white, but the advanced variation provides us with the best opportunity to discuss pawn structures. By advancing the pawn again, white fixes the position and creates what is called a *pawn chain,* as shown in Figure 7-3. Pawn chains, which is the way chess players refer to pawns that are linked together, occur in many games, and the ability to correctly manage such chains is one of the keys to playing chess well. Aaron Nimzovitch, a great expert in the French Defense, taught us to attack a pawn chain at its base. Armed with that knowledge, predicting the most usual response by black, an advance of a pawn to attack the base of the chain, is fairly simple (see Figure 7-4).

Figure 7-3

Figure 7-4

Attacking an advanced pawn chain aggressively is vital. If you don't attack the chain this way, your opponent gains an advantage in space and uses that advantage to mount an attack. You are then too cramped to meet the attack, unless you first go about chipping away at the chain. White's next move is also easy to understand if you think in terms of pawn chains (see Figure 7-5). Now white has established an even longer pawn chain, the base of which lies deep in white territory and thus is very difficult to attack. Black's strategy is to now move the knight to continue to attack the center pawn and to try to break the chain apart, as shown in Figure 7-6.

White knows exactly what black is trying to accomplish and brings up reinforcements, in the form of its own knight, to protect the threatened center pawn (see Figure 7-7). Black's next move may seem strange unless you understand the strategy involved. Once again, the goal is to attack a vulnerable point in the chain, the very same point that is attacked by the black pawn and the black knight and which is defended by the white pawn and white knight. The strategy in this opening revolves around the attack and defense of this single point. The queen moves, as shown in Figure 7-8, to a position that further supports the attack on this point. Do you see how the queen attacks this strategic point through the black pawn?

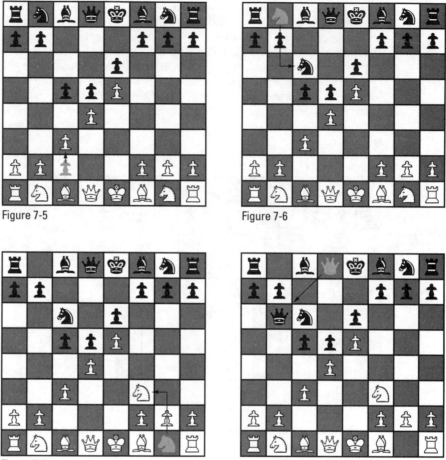

Figure 7-5

Figure 7-6

Figure 7-7

Figure 7-8

At this point, white's options are many, but they all revolve around the attack and defense of the pawn chain. If white secures the chain, this success will lead to a white advantage in space. This advantage in space can then be used to start an attack (see Chapter 3 for a discussion of space). White's pieces will have more options than black's because of this space advantage, and — unless black is very resourceful — white may be able to make threats that black will be unable to defend against.

Black, on the other hand, will continue to try to undermine the pawn chain. If the pawn chain becomes weak, white's pieces will be forced to defend it. These pieces may then become passive (doing little else but guard duty). Passive pieces generally become less powerful than active ones, and if black is successful in making white's pieces take up passive positions, it will soon be black's turn to become aggressive and launch an attack.

This back-and-forth tug-of-war over key points is what fills a chess game with tension. Whoever achieves the short-term goal of securing (or undermining) the pawn chain will then be able to turn their attention to a long-term goal, such as winning material.

It's time now to leave the examination of this one particular variation and turn to the types of structures that may result from different choices the players make along the way.

Typical French pawn structures, n'est-ce pas?

The first of the typical French pawn structures that I want you to consider in this section is the most basic one. I clear the board of pieces now, leaving only the pawns, to best draw attention to the structures themselves (see Figure 7-9). Of course, the pieces are still an important part of the strategy, but just pretend that they're invisible for now.

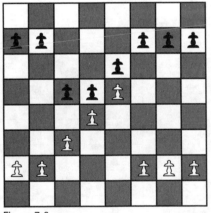

Figure 7-9

In this basic position, play revolves around the attack and defense of one of the links in the pawn chain I describe in the preceding section. Sometimes, white abandons the point by capturing the black pawn to whip up a speedy attack. Black would then capture the white pawn with a black piece (that is still invisible!). The resulting pawn structure is shown in Figure 7-10. Black could then begin an attack on the advanced pawn, which is suddenly shorn of its protector, forcing white to find a new way to defend it.

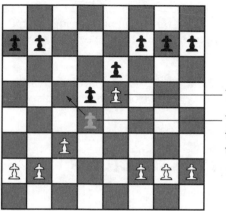

This pawn has lost its protector!

The white pawn that was here captured the black pawn . . . but was captured in turn by a black piece!

Figure 7-10

White will need to either use a piece to defend the advanced pawn (and pieces don't like guard duty) or bring up another pawn to serve as a defender. If white takes the latter course, the resulting structure may look like the one shown in Figure 7-11. Black may then strike at the head of the pawn chain, creating a structure that looks like that shown in Figure 7-12.

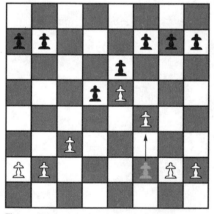

Figure 7-11

Figure 7-12

The pawns may or may not capture one another, but two different types of structures could result if they did. If the white pawn captures the black pawn, and a black piece captures the white pawn on black's next turn, the structure would look like the one in Figure 7-13 (but remember that the pieces on this series of boards are still invisible — so just trust me!).

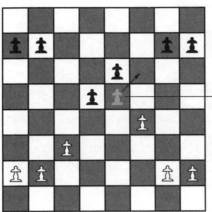

Figure 7-13

The white pawn moved to capture the black pawn and was captured by a black piece.

If, on the other hand, white does not choose to capture as shown in Figure 7-13 and makes some other move instead (not shown), another situation is possible. The black pawn can capture the white pawn and white can capture back (or as chess players say, *recapture*). The structure would look like the one in Figure 7-14.

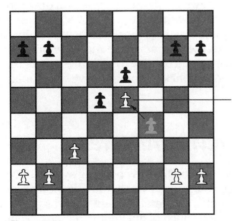

Figure 7-14

This white pawn has captured the black pawn that just captured the advanced white pawn.

Of course, there is a whole different strategy for white, going all the way back to Figure 7-9. White does not have to abandon the chain. If white plays in this manner, black may *exchange* pawns (black captures a pawn with a pawn, and white also captures a pawn with a pawn). The structure could then look like the one shown in Figure 7-15.

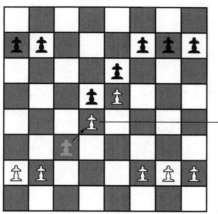

After the black pawn captures a white pawn, this white pawn captures it.

Figure 7-15

As you may observe, a wide variety of options are open to both players, especially when the pieces become visible again! Pawns may be exchanged or they may not, pawns may be attacked by pieces or by other pawns, and pawns may be protected by either pieces or other pawns.

Each side must make certain choices along the way. Regardless of these choices, however, the resulting pawn structures always boil down to a manageable size. After you become familiar with these structures, the best thing for you to do is to take a look at some master games that include them. You may begin to appreciate some moves the masters make that may previously have mystified you. Soon you have a handle on how to play these structures no matter what choices your opponent makes, and no move any opponent can make will ever freak you out!

Understanding pawn structures

Studying the pawn structures common to a few opening systems gives you the knowledge of a general strategy that guides you in the selection of specific moves at every turn. Understanding a general concept, such as pawn structures, is better than trying to memorize a bunch of different variations. Memorization does not always imply understanding. If you familiarize yourself with the structures, you can usually choose good moves — if not always the very best moves.

I learned about pawn structures from a book by the great American champion Ruben Fine (1914-1994) called *The Ideas Behind the Chess Openings*. A more modern book that deals with this topic is *Pawn Structure Chess* by Andy Soltis and is available through any of the mail-order houses listed in Chapter 21.

Endgame Patterns

The last type of pattern presented in this chapter is the *endgame pattern.* Certain types of endings (see Chapter 12 for endgame strategy) will be won, lost, stalemated, or drawn depending both on how they objectively should play out and on your ability to recognize certain patterns as they appear. You can try to figure out which endgame patterns work — and which don't — right at the chessboard as you play . . . or you can learn about these positions beforehand in the privacy of your own home. (I recommend the latter.) After you add a number of these patterns to your repertoire, expect to notice a big jump in your playing strength.

These patterns are also called *techniques,* a term chess players began to use because authors often abandon the analysis of a game with the phrase: "The rest is a matter of technique."

Sometimes you hear a player refer to a particular endgame pattern as a *book draw* (or something to that effect). This term means that the current endgame pattern is, theoretically, a well-known position and that the result of playing the pattern out has already been demonstrated in many past games. That's why you sometimes see players agree to a draw or see one of them resign at a point in the game where you may think the issue is still in doubt. Both of these experienced players, however, know these positions from past play or study and understand where the patterns lead. As a result, neither player wants to waste time and energy proving an already given point. Knowledge of such patterns also explains the following occasional reference in chess literature: "The rest is a matter of technique." In other words, players know that a certain position leads to a win because the winning process, based upon a recognized pattern, has already been well-established.

Endgame patterns are an important, but often neglected, area of chess — an area that all players need to understand. Inexperienced players, however, may simply think that they can worry about the end of the game when — and if — they get there. Such thinking is flawed for many reasons, primarily because of the enormous difficulty involved in inventing (or more precisely, re-inventing) the correct line of play as you reach that portion of the game — which you're likely to need to do if you've neglected to study your endgames. And, of course, most players find extremely helpful the ability to determine whether a certain endgame pattern is likely to end in a win, a draw, or a loss *before* going into it. Many of the decisions you make in your middlegame are likely to depend on your knowledge of these patterns. (For example, should I trade queens and go into the ending, or keep the queens on the board and go for an attack?)

Lucena the Lucid

The following endgame position was first recorded in the oldest surviving book on chess, written in 1497 by Luis Lucena. Chess enthusiasts know this pattern as *Lucena's position*. Figure 7-16 shows the starting lineup for this position.

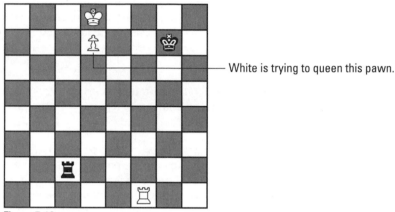

White is trying to queen this pawn.

Figure 7-16

White is trying to queen its pawn (which means advancing the pawn to the last rank and converting it to a new queen; see Chapter 9 for this special move), and black is trying to prevent that from happening. If black can keep the pawn from queening, the game ends in a draw. If white can force the black rook to sacrifice itself for the pawn, white can then use the king and rook to force checkmate, as described in Chapter 6 (on mating patterns).

Lucena demonstrated two methods of winning in this position. The first method is probably the easiest, but you really need to know both methods because a peculiar arrangement of pieces sometimes forces you to use one instead of the other. The first idea is for white to transfer the rook to the eighth rank, in two steps, in order to support the advance of the pawn. The first step in the transfer is shown in Figure 7-17. Black responds by bringing the king closer to the pawn (see Figure 7-18).

White now transfers the rook to the eighth rank (see Figure 7-19). Black marks time with the rook (see Figure 7-20). Notice that the black king should not be used to attack the pawn because then it would actually serve as a shield for white's king. The white king could then move in front of the black king, allowing the pawn to queen on the next move because the black king blocks the black rook from checking the white king.

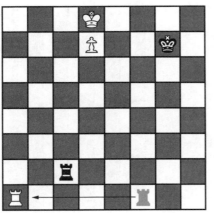
Figure 7-17

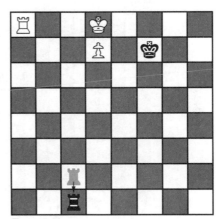
Figure 7-18

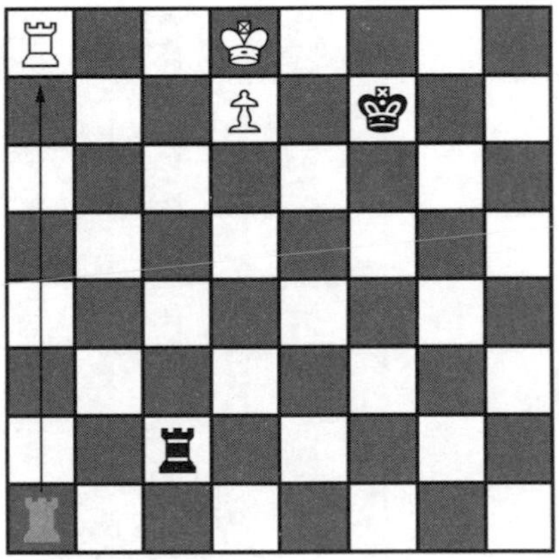

Figure 7-19

Figure 7-20

White attacks the black rook (see Figure 7-21) and forces it to move off the file. The black rook, therefore, has nothing better to do than attack the white pawn (see Figure 7-22). This strategy creates an escape route for the white king because white will now be in control of this file.

The white king moves to the square cleared for it by the rook and in turn clears the way for the advance of the pawn to the last rank, as shown in Figure 7-23. Black must now check the king to prevent the pawn from queening (see Figure 7-24). If, instead, the black king approached the pawn again, white could win by checking the king with the rook, supported by the pawn. This would force the king to retreat, allow the pawn to queen, and force black to give up the rook for the pawn. The mate with king and rook versus king is demonstrated in Chapter 6.

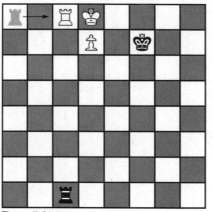

Figure 7-21

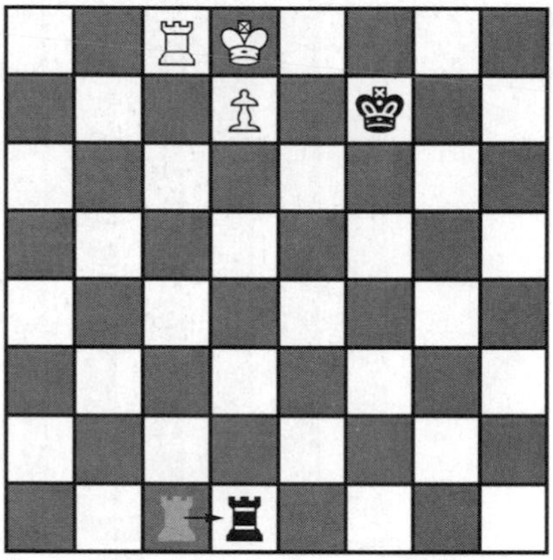

Figure 7-22

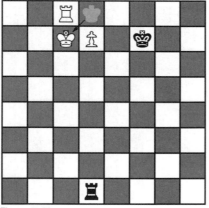

Figure 7-23

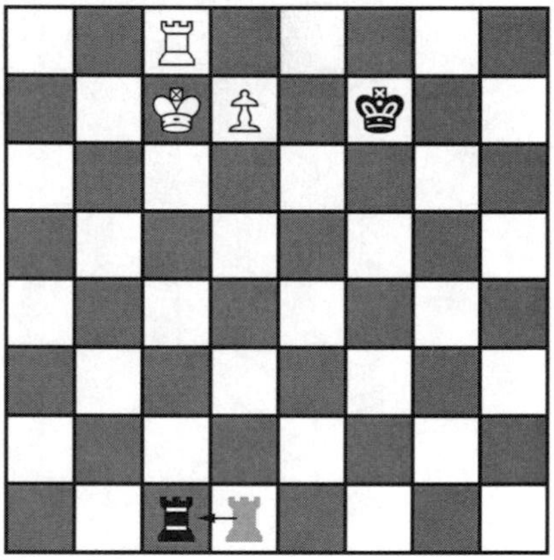

Figure 7-24

The white king approaches the black rook, moving out of check (see Figure 7-25). Black can continue checking the king with the rook — but only until the king advances far enough to attack the rook. At that point, black must surrender the rook for the pawn and eventually get checkmated.

Figure 7-25

Bridge building

The other winning method using Lucena's position is often called *building a bridge*. White uses the rook to shield the king from checks. Your starting position is the same as that shown in Figure 7-16. The first step, then, is for white to move the rook to the fourth rank, as shown in Figure 7-26. (The reason for this move becomes clear later on.) The black rook can only mark time in one of several ways, which do not affect the ultimate outcome (see Figure 7-27).

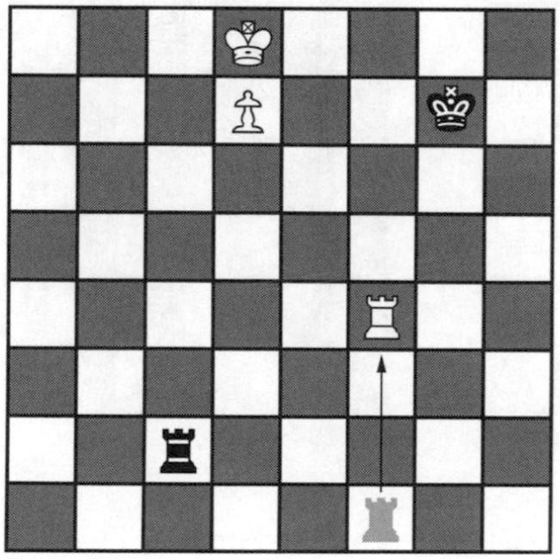

Figure 7-26

Figure 7-27

White's king now comes out from under the cover of the pawn (see Figure 7-28). The best defense available to black is to constantly harass the white king, so black then checks the white king with the rook (see Figure 7-29).

Figure 7-28

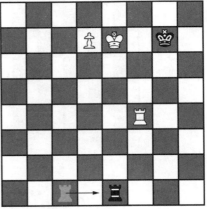

Figure 7-29

The king moves onto the same file as the pawn, as shown in Figure 7-30. Black checks the king again (see Figure 7-31).

Figure 7-30

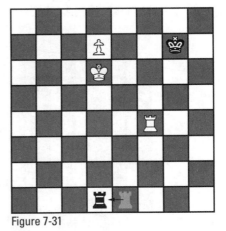

Figure 7-31

White moves the king away and still protects the pawn (see Figure 7-32). Black checks the king again (see Figure 7-33).

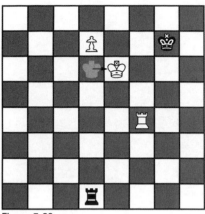
Figure 7-32

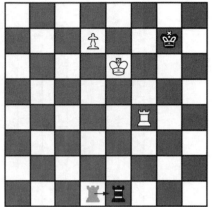
Figure 7-33

White advances the king toward the black rook, again moving out of check (see Figure 7-34). Black gives check one last time (see Figure 7-35).

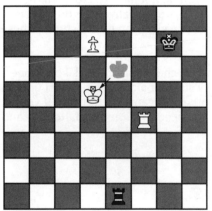
Figure 7-34

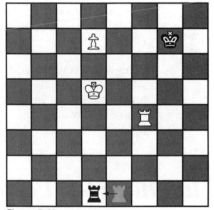
Figure 7-35

White then completes the covered bridge by covering the king with the rook. (see Figure 7-36). Now the reason why white moved the rook to the fourth rank back in Figure 7-26 is finally clear.

Lucena's position, with its two methods of play, is only one of many such endgame patterns you can use to strengthen your game. Building your chess vocabulary with this and other endgame patterns, however, requires a great deal of study. And as is true of study in any other field, mastering the subject matter takes work. Remember, too, that Lucena's pattern was first documented way back in 1497. Many more such patterns have been added to chess literature in the intervening years.

Figure 7-36

An outstanding introduction to endgame patterns such as the one I just discussed is *Chess Endings: Essential Knowledge* by Yuri Averbakh.

The good news, however, is that you do not have to study all the various endgame patterns that are available — especially if all you want is to enjoy playing chess. Just play with someone else who hasn't studied these patterns either!

If, however, your goal is to become a chess master, well, I can't offer you any shortcuts. I think that I can safely say that all masters know Lucena's position, for example — as well as many other endgame patterns! So if you have any desire to play in those leagues, you need to learn this pattern — and others like it, too.

Summing Up Patterns

Chess is all about pattern recognition. As you become familiar with such tactics as the pin or the fork, you are actually learning to recognize a pattern. As you study mating patterns, you build up a store of knowledge that can help you during play. You suddenly "see" possible moves much farther ahead in the game, and you play that much better. If you can learn the ins and outs of a few patterns of pawn structures, your play in the opening and early middle games becomes much more coherent and pointed. Finally, by developing your technique in the endgame, you add the last piece to the puzzle of playing a well-rounded game of chess.

Chapter 8
Strategy: The Principles of Play

● ●

In This Chapter

▶ Centralizing your game

▶ Attacking even when outnumbered

▶ Controlling key squares

▶ Blockading pesky pawns

▶ Exchanging pieces

● ●

Sometime after I first started playing tournament chess, a friend of mine occasionally walked up to me during his own tournament game and lamented, "I've got the position I wanted, but I just can't do anything!"

Everyone who has ever played chess has felt this way at one time or another during a game.

The question is what to do if you can't pin and win, use a fork, or find a mating pattern (as explained in Chapters 4, 5, and 6)? The answer becomes clearer as you develop your knowledge of positional play. Even if no specific tactics are currently available to you, you can always develop a strategy.

In fact, tactics don't simply materialize out of thin air, especially if you're engaged at higher levels of play. Tactics spring from a well-developed plan — a *strategy*. The great attacking master Rudolf Spielmann (1883-1942) was said to have claimed that he could make sacrifices just as well as Alekhine (who was world champion at the time) could — but just couldn't reach the same positions!

Entire volumes have been written about planning in chess. This chapter, therefore, can serve only as an introduction to the topic. But I hope that the chapter, brief as it must be, impresses one thing onto the chess-playing nodes of your brain: Employing even a little bit of strategy is better than having no strategy at all up your sleeve — or, as we chess enthusiasts often say, even a bad plan is better than no plan at all.

The Center and Centralization

Not all squares on the chessboard were created equal. The four central squares on the board are the most important in chess (see Figure 8-1). The squares next to them are the next-most important and so on. Logically, therefore, the player who controls the center of the board controls the game.

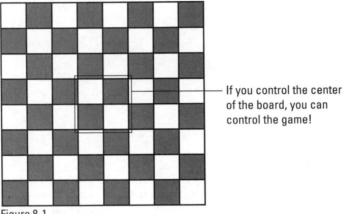

If you control the center of the board, you can control the game!

Figure 8-1

Pieces generally increase in power as they come into contact with the center. Rooks, queens, and bishops can control squares from a distance, but pawns and knights must move closer to the action in order to be effective. Bringing pieces to bear on the center is called *centralization*.

The struggle for the center is the primary theme behind most games' openings. I could use just about any opening sequence to demonstrate this concept, but in this case, I draw your attention to an opening known as the *Queen's Gambit* (see Chapter 5 for more about gambits). In the Queen's Gambit, both sides open by advancing the pawns in front of their queens (see Figure 8-2 and Figure 8-3).

White advances the queen's bishop pawn to attack the black center pawn (see Figure 8-4). Black can accept the Queen's Gambit and capture the pawn, but doing so means abandoning the center.

If black captures the pawn, we call the opening the *Queen's Gambit Accepted.* This results in perfectly playable positions, but the *Queen's Gambit Declined,* when black does not capture the pawn, is the more usual choice. In the Queen's Gambit Declined, black uses another pawn to support the queen's pawn and maintain black's share of the center (see Figure 8-5).

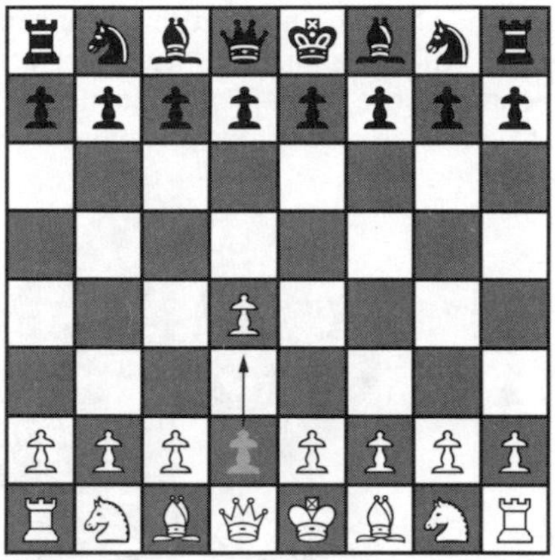

Figure 8-2

Figure 8-3

Figure 8-4

Figure 8-5

White chooses to develop a knight toward the center (see Figure 8-6). Notice how the knight is also now attacking the black center pawn. Black, in turn, also develops a knight toward the center, in defense of the attacked pawn (see Figure 8-7).

White develops another piece, this time moving the queen bishop out to attack black's knight (see Figure 8-8). The bishop now pins (see Chapter 4 for info on pinning) the black knight to its current position, otherwise the black queen would be exposed to attack by the foraging bishop. This move by white attacks the center pawn's defender (the black knight), so it indirectly influences the center. In Figure 8-9, black breaks the pin by developing the king bishop, which now defends the queen. This move enables the knight to again concentrate solely on defending the queen's pawn, although a slight difference in position is already evident: The white bishop is still attacking, and the black bishop is now defending. These positionings mean that the white bishop is more aggressively posted and can still influence the center by capturing the knight — but the black bishop has no such option.

Figure 8-6

Figure 8-7

Figure 8-8

Figure 8-9

In the next series of figures, the two sides move with an eye toward controlling the center. White advances a pawn and paves the way to centralize the king's bishop (see Figure 8-10). Black develops the remaining knight in support of the one under attack (see Figure 8-11). If white now chooses to capture the black knight with the queen's bishop, the other black knight can, in turn, capture the bishop and still defend the queen's pawn — so white would've accomplished nothing by the exchange of pieces.

Figure 8-10

Figure 8-11

White develops the remaining knight toward the center (see Figure 8-12). Black responds by castling (as shown in Figure 8-13). Castling safeguards the black king and prepares the way for the rook to move toward the center. (In case you need some details on castling, jump ahead to Chapter 9 where I explain some special chess moves.)

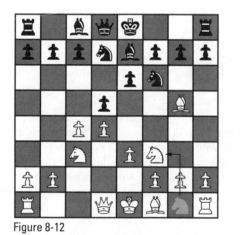

Figure 8-12

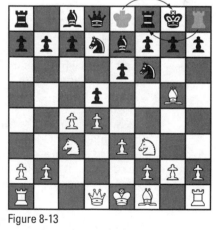

Figure 8-13

White develops the king's bishop and prepares to castle the king with the king's rook (see Figure 8-14). Black advances the queen's bishop pawn to support the center pawn once more (see Figure 8-15).

Figure 8-14

Figure 8-15

The placement of pieces on the board now reflect a classic position in the Queen's Gambit Declined. Black has staked out a foothold in the center and has developed several pieces with the aim of maintaining this hold on the center. White has developed pieces more aggressively by attacking the black center. This *initiative* (white attacking, black defending against white's attack) comes from having the first move and from making each move an aggressive one.

White enjoys a greater control of the center than does black because of the better arrangement of the white pieces. (In chess terms, these pieces are *more centralized* than black's.) This centralization has already left its mark on the position. Notice how white's white-squared bishop has much more freedom than black's white-squared bishop has. This additional freedom of movement is a positional advantage.

A positional advantage is not the same as a material advantage or an advantage in pawn structure. (See Chapter 3 for a discussion of chess elements). This type of advantage provides a player with a more subtle edge than other advantages and could evaporate quickly as a result of inexact play. White cannot force the win of material or ruin black's pawn structure and must now think in terms of forming a strategic plan that can maintain and even increase the positional advantage.

White normally continues by castling and then by centralizing the queen and rooks. Black wants to centralize these pieces, too, but is going to have a more difficult time doing so because of the cramped position of the black pieces. White would then try to create a weakness in the black position and exploit that weakness.

The Minority Attack (Doing More with Less)

One particular strategy that players often use in the Queen's Gambit Declined is so common and so effective as to deserve a name all to itself — the minority attack.

The minority attack derives its name from a pawn advance on one side of the board. Two pawns advance to attack three pawns. The idea is to exchange two for two and leave the opponent's remaining pawn unsupported and weak. Then pieces are used to attack the pawn and force the other side to use pieces in its defense. In this way, one side is constantly aggressive and the other passive. In theory, the attacker must eventually be able to outmaneuver the defender.

The minority attack may result from a position such as the one shown in Figure 8-16.

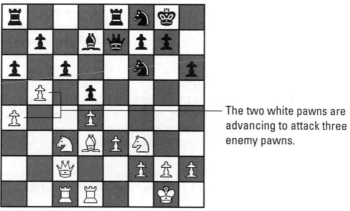

The two white pawns are advancing to attack three enemy pawns.

Figure 8-16

The advance of the white pawns has created a dilemma for black. If black captures the white pawns, the remaining black queenside pawn is isolated and weak. If black lets white's pawn capture one of black's pawns, black is left with a backward pawn that white can then attack (see Figure 8-17). See Chapter 3 for more on backward pawns!

The minority attack is an example of a strategy or plan in action. White does not try to immediately attack the well-defended black king but rather sets sight on the intermediate goal of provoking a pawn weakness.

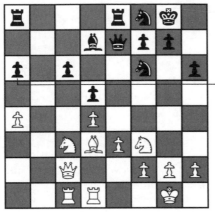

After an exchange of pawns, black is left with a backwards pawn guarded by a rook — who would rather be doing more important things.

Figure 8-17

You may think that creating a pawn weakness is a rather wimpy goal, but because black does not want to lose the pawn (which would cause a deficit in material, explained in Chapter 3), black may become passive in defense of it. At that time, tactical opportunities may appear for the aggressor, as if by magic. The successful implementation of a strategy almost always results in favorable tactics.

This idea is a lesson in life as well as in chess: to postpone immediate gratification. The beginner may attempt a brutal attack against his opponent's pieces to attempt an early checkmate. A master, however, postpones this immediate gratification (because experience shows that such a course rarely works) and puts in the necessary time and effort to set checkmate up for later.

One of the best guides to planning in chess was written by former world champion Max Euwe and is called *Judgment and Planning in Chess*.

Key Squares (That Lock Up an Advantage)

Sometimes the positional struggle in chess revolves around what chess players call a *key square* (generally an outpost for further invasion). The attacker desires control of this square and the defender disputes that control. The control and eventual occupation of the square by the attacking side generally leads to a superior placement of the attacking pieces. The defender drifts into passivity by merely guarding against the opponent's threats. Eventually the defender may not be able to successfully counter the attacker's maneuvers.

One important point to remember is that you should almost always use pieces rather than pawns to occupy key squares. Generally, the pawn is not mobile enough to exploit its advantageous position. The following figures illustrate this concept.

This pawn structure depicted in the following example may arise out of the Sicilian defense (see Chapter 20) and is characterized by a fight for the key square, which is marked in Figure 8-18. Black has a backward pawn and wants to advance and exchange the pawn for a white pawn. White wants to place a piece on that square and block black's potential pawn advance.

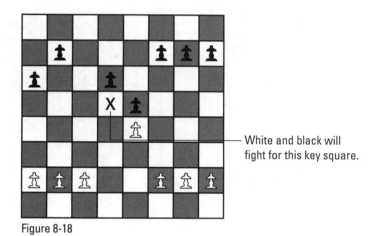

White and black will fight for this key square.

Figure 8-18

Now I add a knight for white (see Figure 8-19) in order to show how a piece may be used to occupy and secure a key square. Notice how the knight adds to white's control of the key square. If black can't dispute the point with a piece of equal value to the knight, white moves the knight to the key square, and that piece becomes a bone in black's throat for the rest of the game.

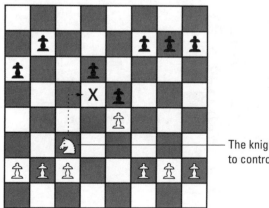

The knight allows white to control the key square.

Figure 8-19

In Figure 8-20, black now has a bishop in play, but the bishop is on the wrong-colored square. Black's bishop, therefore, can never contest the key square and can't support the advance of black's backward pawn. If black had a white-squared bishop, however, black could move that bishop into position to fight for the key square. This move is demonstrated in Figure 8-21.

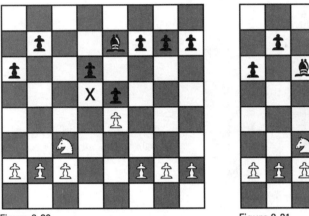

Figure 8-20

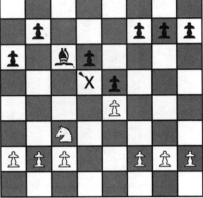

Figure 8-21

Now, if white occupies the key square with the knight, black can simply capture the knight with the bishop. White then captures the bishop with a pawn — and the key square loses its importance because of the pawn's restricted mobility (see Figure 8-22).

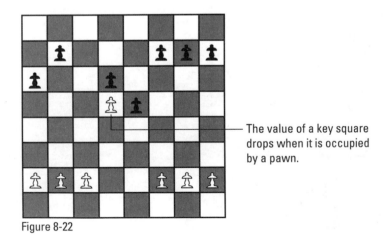

Figure 8-22

The value of a key square drops when it is occupied by a pawn.

If you add both sides' queens to the equation, however, you can see that this setup, too, may change matters (see Figure 8-23). As long as white can keep a piece on the key square, the backwards black pawn will be a weakness. Now white can move the knight to the key square and, should black capture the knight, white can recapture with the queen instead of the pawn. By keeping control of the key square, white thus preserves a slight advantage in position.

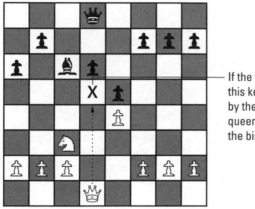

If the white knight moves to this key square but is captured by the black bishop, the white queen will advance to capture the bishop and occupy the square.

Figure 8-23

Chess players often refer to the key square in the preceding figures as a *strategic outpost.* Knights love to occupy these outposts. Many games have been won by creating an outpost in enemy territory and then sinking a knight onto that square!

The Blockade (No Trespassing!)

Aaron Nimzovitch was one of the first to systematically explain the fight for key squares in his 1925 book *Blockade.* In this book, he wrote of the pawn's desire to advance as "its tremendous lust to expand." He taught us to restrain pawn advances by blocking them with pieces. These pieces are not wasting time keeping a lowly pawn in check because such blockading pieces often find themselves well-posted for future attacks and unassailable from enemy counter-attacks.

As Nimzovitch was fond of saying, a passed pawn is "a dangerous criminal and must be kept under lock and key." He gives the following example (see Figure 8-24).

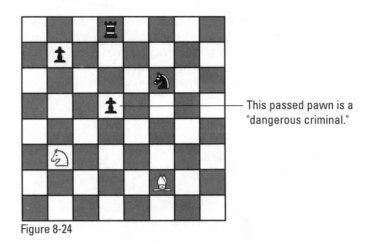

Figure 8-24

This passed pawn is a "dangerous criminal."

According to Nimzovitch's teaching, simply controlling the square in front of the pawn is not enough; rather you must occupy that square. This is the difference between merely restraining a pawn's advance (by controlling the square with pieces) and blockading the pawn (physically preventing it from moving). The correct move — in which white moves the knight to occupy the square in front of the black pawn — is now easy to understand (see Figure 8-25).

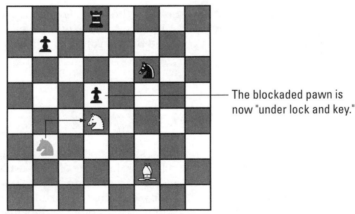

Figure 8-25

The blockaded pawn is now "under lock and key."

Now the pawn can't advance — or as Nimzovitch would say, the pawn is in jail and not merely under police watch! The knight is the ideal blockader because that piece retains its powers even while doing guard duty and can't easily be driven off.

As described in Chapter 3, an isolated pawn may be weak because that pawn lacks the support of its peers. You now know that the strategically correct way of combating an isolated pawn is to blockade it.

Exchanging Pieces

If one player captures a piece and the other player then captures the piece that first attacked, the pieces are said to have been *exchanged*. Knowing exactly when to exchange and when not to exchange pieces is often difficult, even for seasoned veterans. Positional understanding (the strategic knowledge in chess as opposed to the tactical knowledge) gives you the ability to determine whether an exchange is advantageous to you.

As your positional sense develops, you come to understand better that bishops should not be routinely exchanged for knights — unless you have a good reason to do so (such as winning material, time, or a key square). Two bishops together can cover the entire board, but one alone can cover only half the board. Bishops may also become more powerful as the endgame approaches because they can cover more of a relatively clear board than a knight can.

Yet, in many master games, one player does, in fact, trade a bishop for a knight. Why this seeming contradiction? Although exchanging a bishop for a knight for no reason is a mistake, many valid reasons actually may exist for making the exchange:

- ✔ Exchanging the bishop for the knight may be advantageous if making the exchange cripples the pawn structure at the same time.

- ✔ If the knight is occupying an important outpost, as described in the preceding section, removing the piece may be necessary, even at the cost of a bishop. Thus if the knight occupies or controls a key square, exchanging your bishop for the knight may indeed prove worthwhile.

- ✔ Less frequently, but often enough, you may decide to exchange a bishop for a knight to gain time. If the exchange results in a lead in development in your favor, trading these pieces may be to your advantage.

Generally, the cramped side seeks exchanges and the freer side seeks to avoid them. Exchanges ease the burden of defense, because such exchanges leave fewer attacking pieces on the board and decrease the likelihood of defending pieces tripping over one another.

Don't exchange pieces just because you can. Exchange only if you have a good reason. The aimless trading of pieces may leave you with the bad bishop versus the good knight! (See the sidebar "The Exchange" for more information.)

CHESS TALK

The Exchange

An odd custom in chess refers to a certain trade of pieces as *The Exchange*. (Notice that we old hands at the game always capitalize "The" when referring to this maneuver.) The Exchange occurs whenever one side trades a knight or a bishop for a rook. This exchange is considered odd, in case you're wondering, because chess players usually speak of exchanging pieces of equal value. You hear people say things such as, "I'll be okay if I can force the exchange of queens." The rook, however, is worth far more than either the bishop or knight and represents a material gain or loss for one side or the other

side, depending on who captures the other player's rook.

Nevertheless, this seeming uneven exchange occurs so often in chess that players routinely call this trade *The Exchange,* whether the term makes sense or not. You may hear players say, "I lost (or won) The Exchange." All experienced chess players know what this statement means. If you intentionally give up a rook for a bishop or knight, for whatever reason, you are justified in saying, "I sacrificed The Exchange," or as experienced players more typically phrase it, "I sac'd The Exchange."

Summarizing Strategy

CHESS MASTER

Chess is a game of strategy. On the surface, it may appear that short tactical skirmishes decide most games, but in reality it is the long-range planning efforts that set up these tactical skirmishes so that one side has more opportunity for success than the other. Strategy games can teach us many things: to plan for the future, to set realistic goals, and much more. As you continue to progress, you learn that there are even deeper subtleties to chess than you'd ever imagined. This endless process of discovery is at the heart of the game's appeal.

CHESS MASTER

Good knight versus bad bishop

A well-executed strategy may result in only a very subtle advantage. One way of exploiting a positional advantage, for example, may be to enter an ending with the better (more aggressive) minor piece or with the superior (more aggressive) king position. The classic example of a superior piece ending is that of the "good knight" versus the "bad bishop." (I like this ending because it's counterintuitive.)

Bishops and knights are generally considered essentially equal in value through most of the game, but bishops are quite often more powerful than knights in the endgame. This advantage comes because bishops may effortlessly roam the board from side to side, while knights must furiously hop around here and there to accomplish the same thing.

Chess masters can often sense if one or the other piece is better suited to a particular endgame. Although masters may prefer the bishop, all things being even (which, of course, they never are), cases may exist where the same players would opt for the knight if given the

choice. If, for example, the bishop is constrained from moving freely by pawns on the same colored squares, that piece may have less mobility than the knight. The knight, able to hop from white squares to black and back again with ease, taunts the poor bishop who remains in chains.

The "good" knight in such a case can almost always outplay the "bad" bishop and force the win of material. Often the player with the bad bishop runs out of good moves and is forced to play a bad one (as chess doesn't allow a player to pass but requires a move every turn). If compelled to make a move when all moves are bad, the player faces what chess players call *Zugzwang.* (There we go showing off our worldliness again. This is a German word which means that a player is forced to make a weakening move by the mere fact that the player is compelled to make any move.) Experienced chess players derive a peculiar joy in putting their opponents in Zugzwang. The situation is one of the few times you can be happy that this isn't your turn to move!

Chapter 9

Special Moves (The Ones That Start All the Arguments)

In This Chapter

▶ Capturing a passing pawn

▶ Promoting a pawn to a higher rank

▶ Castling to move your king quicker

*I*f you play enough chess, you eventually run into someone who plays by a different set of rules than the official ones. Such players may have learned chess from someone who knew "most" of the rules and fudged on a few others. Unfortunately, unless you lug a rule book around with you, convincing these people that you do know the correct rules may be difficult. In this chapter, I deal with the moves that are most often confused in one way or another. Knowing these special moves may not help you avoid the occasional disagreement, but you can at least argue with an air of authority — and for some chess buffs, that's almost as good as winning.

En Passant

CHESS TALK

Here we go again with our use of foreign phrases to pump ourselves up. *En passant* is French for "in passing" and simply means that a pawn can capture another pawn if the latter attempts to pass the first one on an adjacent square. Only at the end of a pawn's first move, however, can you capture it en passant and only then if the pawn uses its capability to move two squares on its initial move.

The en passant capture

The following example illustrates an en passant capture (see Figure 9-1).

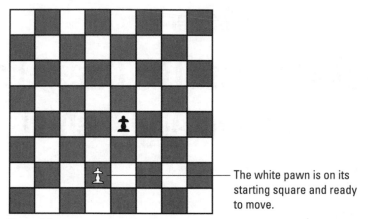

The white pawn is on its starting square and ready to move.

Figure 9-1

White moves the pawn forward two squares (see Figure 9-2). Black can, for one move — and one move only — legally capture white's pawn, just as though the pawn had moved forward only one square; in making the en passant capture, black's pawn takes the position the white pawn would have occupied by moving a single square (see Figure 9-3).

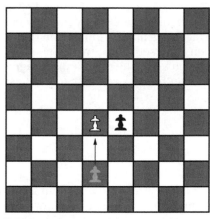

Figure 9-2

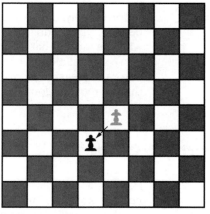

Figure 9-3

Of course, if your opponent doesn't know this rule, this ploy comes as quite a shock. Even worse, if you explain that you simply captured en passant, you may be accused of playing by French rules. Calmly explain that chess is an international game and that the en passant rule was adopted in the 15th century. You may also add that the rule was universally accepted by the late 19th century. If you're playing a casual game just for fun, however, the sporting thing to do is to allow your opponent to take the move back. But if the match is a tournament game, you must insist on your rights. That you know this rule and your opponent doesn't is not your fault!

The en passant details to keep in mind

Remember that the captured pawn must move two squares for en passant to be valid. And if you don't capture right away, you lose the right to do so. You are not required to capture en passant, however, and sometimes this capture isn't the best move on the board. Still, knowing all the options available to you in the game always pays off . . . sooner or later.

Pawn Promotion: Moving Up in the Ranks

After a pawn reaches the end of the board, that pawn can be *promoted* to any piece, except the king (there can be only one king). In essence, after its promotion, the pawn actually becomes that other piece, with all its powers. Not bad for a lowly pawn. Almost always, players make the pawn into a queen because the queen is the most powerful piece on the board (Theoretically, you can have nine queens at one time. The eight promoted pawns and the original queen. Quite a harem for the king!) Only in odd, problem positions do players promote a pawn to anything other than a queen — a condition known as *underpromotion*.

Promote your pawn according to your needs

White is about to move in this next situation. White is a pawn ahead but cannot checkmate the black king with only the pawn and king. White moves the pawn to the last rank in order to promote it (see Figure 9-4). In this case, promoting the pawn to a queen makes sense, especially because the newly promoted queen immediately delivers checkmate (see Figure 9-5). Promoting the pawn to a rook would also deliver checkmate in this particular example, however, so either choice is equally powerful here. Underpromoting to a knight or bishop would be folly because these pieces can't checkmate the king by themselves.

Protect the queening square

Players often call the square on which a player can promote a pawn the *queening square* because, in all likelihood, the pawn becomes a queen after reaching that square. Control of the queening square is important so that, should your opponent's pawn reach that square, you can capture the pawn right away — before promotion creates a bigger threat.

Three-king circus

The famous chess teacher George Koltanowski is fond of telling the following story: He was teaching the rules of the game to a brand new student, and the student was eager to play a game right away. George easily set up a *mating net* (a situation where checkmate is eventually unavoidable), in which the student's king could not escape checkmate. While George was setting up the checkmate, the student was busy pushing a pawn forward toward the queening square (the last rank). George saw that the pawn could queen, but didn't mind because he was going to deliver checkmate the very next move.

George was stunned after the student pushed the pawn to the queening square and promoted it to — a king! Seems that George had told the student that the pawn could be promoted into any other piece and forgot to mention the restriction involving kings. The student made him stick to his own rule! This may be the only case involving more than two kings on a chessboard. With a sly wink, George always ends the story by saying he played a move that checkmated both kings simultaneously!

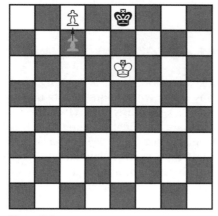

Figure 9-4

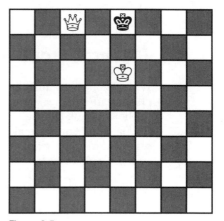

Figure 9-5

Castling

Castling is also the only time in chess when you can move two pieces at once. You may castle on the kingside or on the queenside, but the rule is the same: The king moves two squares to the right or left, and the rook slides around the king and occupies the adjacent square, ending up on the opposite side of the king from where the piece started. Take a look at a couple of examples of what the king can do in a certain position, starting with the setup shown in Figure 9-6.

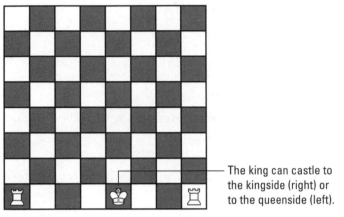

The king can castle to the kingside (right) or to the queenside (left).

Figure 9-6

White can castle kingside (see Figure 9-7) or queenside (see Figure 9-8).

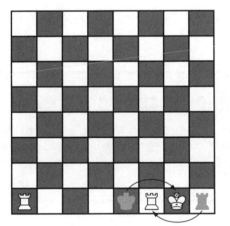

Figure 9-7

Figure 9-8

In both cases, the king moves two squares to the side and the rook slides around to the other side of the king. The correct method of castling involves touching the king first. Technically, if you touch the rook first, you must move that piece and *only* it. Avoid fights and always castle by moving the king first!

Some complaints among players focus on when you can legally castle and when castling is illegal.

When you can't castle

You can't castle in any of these situations.

- ✔ If another piece is between the king and rook.
- ✔ If the king has already moved.
- ✔ With a rook that has already moved (but you may be able to castle by using the other rook).
- ✔ When in check.
- ✔ If the king must pass through a square controlled by the opponent.

When you can castle

You can castle, on the other hand, even if any of the following is true.

- ✔ The rook is under attack.
- ✔ The rook (but *not* the king) must pass though a square controlled by the opponent.

Even champions can forget

Even the best players get confused sometimes. Viktor Korchnoi (1931–) has been a leading contender for the world championship title for nearly two decades. But during one tournament game he moved his king, later on moved the king back to its original square, and still later castled! Neither he nor his opponent noticed!

Part III
Let the Play Begin

In this part . . .

A game of chess is often divided into three distinct phases. In this part, I give general recommendations about how to play the opening, middle, and ending phases of the game. I even have a section on chess etiquette so that you can be prepared to play politely, too.

Chapter 10

The Opening: First Things First

In This Chapter

▶ Developing your attack

▶ Getting off to a good start

▶ Using traditional opening moves

*I*n chess, quicker is not necessarily better. If you are trying to checkmate your opponent as fast as possible, you are almost certain to make inferior moves in the opening phase of the game. If, instead, you use your opening moves to rapidly deploy your pieces to good squares, your ultimate goal of checkmate eventually comes within your grasp. If you reach for the brass ring too early in the game, however, you're bound to fall off your knight . . . er, horse.

At the highest levels of chess, knowing tons of opening variations is extremely important. Entire volumes are available describing even some of the most obscure chess openings. Rest assured, however, that, for the vast majority of chess players, such intense knowledge is not at all necessary to compete — and to compete well.

Instead of simply memorizing the opening moves or suggestions of masters (which are referred to as *opening theory*), you need to understand some general principles of opening play. After you grasp these principles, you can play reasonably well in this phase of the game. Certainly, on occasion, you are still going to make mistakes or get caught in inferior positions, which chess players call *traps*, but making errors is how you gain experience in the game. No one attains master status in chess without getting a few bloodied noses. You make far more progress in chess by learning *why* you got the worst of a particular opening than in spending hours of study time beforehand hoping to avoid that fate.

Develop!

The first lesson you must learn on the road to improving your game is to get your priorities straight. Not only should you *not* be trying to checkmate your opponent in the opening, but you shouldn't even be trying to win material. Save both objectives for later in the game. The primary objective of the opening is the rapid deployment of your pieces to their optimal posts. You can't put a piece on a good square however, if that piece can easily be driven away by your opponent's pieces, so getting your pieces not only on good squares, but also on *safe* squares, is critical to your opening game. (For details on controlling key squares, see Chapter 8.)

The rapid mobilization of pieces is called *development*. Development is not considered complete until the knights, bishops, queens, and rooks are moved off their original squares. Normally, getting the knights, bishops, and queen off the back rank also is important. Rooks may be effective fighting from their starting rank, but the other pieces usually increase in power only as they move toward the center.

Control the center

As described in earlier chapters, control of the center and centralization of your pieces are critical objectives in a chess game. The pieces generally increase in power as they are centralized. In the opening phase, you want to try to maximize the power of the pieces in a minimum amount of time. Moving one piece three times to position it on the best square doesn't help much if, in the meantime, your other pieces languish back on their original squares.

Watch your opponent

Just as important as developing quickly is preventing your opponent's development. Some otherwise strange-looking moves can be explained only in this way. If you waste two moves to force your opponent to waste three, well, those moves weren't wasted after all!

This idea brings us to yet another chess maxim: Don't get so caught up in your plans that you forget about your opponent's moves. Just as you are, your opponent is trying to interfere with your development while developing his or her own pieces — at your expense.

Follow basic principles

As you become familiar with the game, you begin to pick up on a few basic principles of opening play, not only from your own experiences, but also from other players. (Remember, however, that many such principles are just guidelines — don't think you're bound by them. If, for example, your opponent slips up and gives you the opportunity to deliver checkmate, do so! Don't worry that such a move develops your queen too early!)

Grandmaster Ludek Pachman, in his outstanding book *Modern Chess Strategy,* offers the following four principles of opening play:

- ✔ Place the pieces without loss of time where they can develop their greatest power.

- ✔ Do not move a piece that is already developed unless you have a strong reason for doing so.

- ✔ Avoid putting pieces on squares where they can be driven off by moves that also contribute to the development of enemy pieces and pawns.

- ✔ Pawn moves in the opening game serve only as an aid to development of your pieces and as a means of fighting for the center; keep such moves, therefore, to a minimum.

Pachman goes on to caution against applying these principles dogmatically. He teaches that the real meaning of development is not how many pieces you bring out but whether you develop your pieces to maximize their power.

Attack!

The question that naturally occurs next is — so what's the big deal about a lead in development? How can you translate a lead in development into a more permanent advantage, such as a material edge or a superior pawn structure?

The simple answer is — Attack! If you have a lead in development and fail to attack, you are almost certainly going to see your advantage slip through your fingers. If you enjoy a lead in development, open up the game. You want open files and diagonals leading to your opponent's vulnerable points. You want to use these open lines to move your pieces to increasingly more aggressive locations. Ideally, you want to combine your development with strong threats to your opponent. If you can develop a piece and simultaneously threaten an enemy piece (or pieces!), your opponent may lose additional time scurrying to defend against your attack. Your pieces become increasingly threatening and the defender's increasingly passive. Then comes the time to try to win material or play for checkmate.

The player who's ahead in development seeks to open up lines of attack; the player who's behind in development seeks to keep those lines closed. If you can combine a superior development with open lines of attack, you quickly find that whatever tactics you employ seem always to work out in your favor. On the other hand, if those lines remain closed, you soon find that your advantage in development is not nearly so great an asset and that your work is really cut out for you in winning the game.

Opening Moves: Getting Ahead

At this point, I want you to examine some alternatives in white's first move; see whether you can understand why these moves are good or not-so-good from the twin perspectives of development and control of the center.

The good opening move

First, take a look at the most common first move in all of chessdom. By advancing the pawn in front of the white king two squares, white occupies one central square and attacks another. The attacked square is indicated by an *X* in Figure 10-1. (The pawn could, of course, attack the other square to its right, but I'm talking about central squares here.)

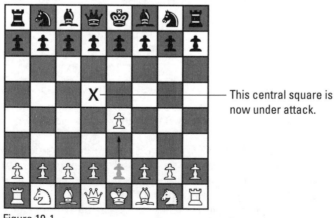

This central square is now under attack.

Figure 10-1

From the perspective of control of the center, this move is obviously a useful one. Is the move also useful, however, in aiding the development of your pieces? Yes — absolutely. Notice how the pawn's advance opens a line for the bishop's development. (The bishop's line of development is indicated by *X*s in Figure 10-2.) The bishop, however, is not the only piece that now enjoys an open line. What about the queen? The queen also has a line open for its development (see Figure 10-3). So white's opening move proves useful not only for controlling the center but also for developing pieces. No wonder this particular opening move is so popular.

Figure 10-2

Figure 10-3

The next example looks at the second-most popular opening move in chess: moving the queen's pawn two squares forward (see Figure 10-4). By moving this pawn, white accomplishes pretty much the same object as described in our first example. Notice how one central square is occupied by the pawn and another is attacked by it. In terms of controlling the center, the moves in these two examples are pretty interchangeable.

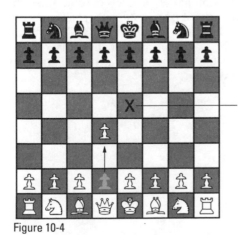

White can also attack a central square with this move.

Figure 10-4

In terms of development, these moves are also very similar. A diagonal path is now open for a bishop, just as in the first example (see Figure 10-5). But this time, the queen does not have an open diagonal — only a couple squares along the file (see Figure 10-6). The initial advance of the queen's pawn, therefore, does not do quite as much for development as does the initial advance of the king's pawn.

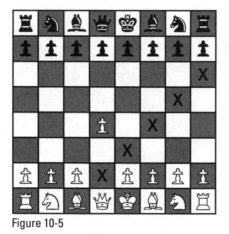

Figure 10-5

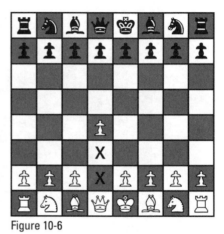

Figure 10-6

The not-as-good opening move

If you keep going with opening possibilities for white, you see that no other move accomplishes quite as much as our first two choices.

The move shown in the next example — advancing the queen's bishop pawn forward two squares — is fairly popular at all levels of tournament play. The pawn attacks a central square without occupying one (see Figure 10-7). This move opens up a diagonal for the queen (see Figure 10-8). This move, however, does not help the bishops in any way; experienced chess players, therefore, do not consider the move quite as strong an opening as our first two choices. And the following example is even weaker.

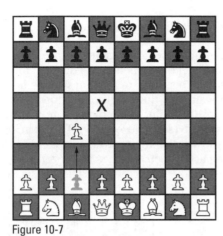

Figure 10-7

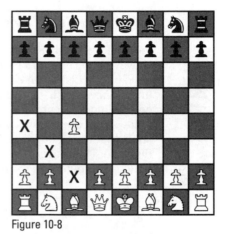

Figure 10-8

The not-so-good opening move

In the setup shown in Figure 10-9, the king's bishop pawn also attacks a central square, but no other piece is helped by this advance. In fact, the king's safety is called into question because a diagonal is now open that black may use as a path to attack the king.

— This pawn has jeopardized its king's safety!

Figure 10-9

Salvaging a weak opening move

Pawn moves farther from the center of the board generally are very weak. However, one exception is the *fianchetto*. The fianchetto occurs whenever you develop the bishop on either flank. This move may seem strange because, at first glance, the single-square advance by the knight pawn does little in terms of controlling the center (see Figure 10-10). But this move is almost invariably followed up by developing the bishop (see Figure 10-11). The *X*s in Figure 10-11 show that the bishop is now attacking the key central squares from a safe distance. This move can open a fairly effective attack but is generally not as difficult to counter as the first two moves first examined in this section.

Figure 10-10

Figure 10-11

Opening move philosophy

Advancing the king's pawn two squares on the first move generally leads to more open games, while advancing the queen's pawn tends to result in closed ones. Playing both pawns two squares forward is easier if you start with the king's pawn because the queen can support the advance of its pawn but the king can't provide similar support to its pawn. By advancing both pawns forward two squares, you can either open lines by forcing exchanges or end up controlling the center.

Opening Moves 101

Listing every chess opening ever used is impossible here, but I can at least draw your attention to some of the more common ones. If you hope to impress anyone with your lofty knowledge of the game, being able to identify the following openings by name is extremely important. In fact, sounding knowledgeable about chess openings is often much more important than actually being knowledgeable about chess openings when it comes to impressing your friends.

Please forgive me for not providing too much specific material in this chapter. It's impossible to give you enough guidance to play the opening even passably well in this amount of space and without the use of chess notation. The point of this chapter is to give you the basic principles of play in the opening. Specific variations are not to be recommended; this does more harm than good. If you retain the basic principles, you will do OK. If you try to remember too many specific sequences from this book, your learning may suffer.

The whole point of this section is to help you improve your chess vocabulary. If you do go to a chess club, you'll find it very useful in terms of speaking to others. For example, "I saw that you played a Sicilian in your last game. Can you show me how it went?" I'm not making this stuff up. Being able to speak about chess to others is important. Specific variations and illustrative examples belong in advanced texts.

Ruy Lopez (the game in Spain . . .)

If you simply follow the basic opening principles described in this chapter, you're likely to play a decent game. But if you don't know the French defense from the Spanish game, people may question your chess heritage. The hard part about many of the names of openings is that they're not always universally recognized. In the U.S., chess players call the following opening sequence the *Ruy Lopez,* after the player who popularized it. But in other parts of the world, the same opening is known more commonly as *the Spanish game,* after the country it became popular in.

There was no Internet 50 years ago, and local customs prevailed regarding naming conventions. Some became universally known based on a widely read publication or two, and some still are known by multiple names depending upon what part of the world you're in or from.

The Ruy Lopez begins with the mutual advance of the kings' pawns (see Figure 10-12). This sequence belongs to the general category of *double king pawn openings*. The next moves bring out the king's knight for white and the queen's knight for black (see Figure 10-13).

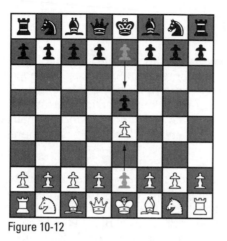

Figure 10-12

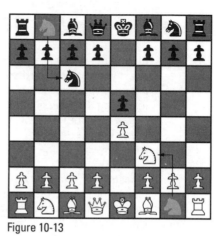

Figure 10-13

White's next move of the king's bishop defines the game as a Ruy Lopez (see Figure 10-14). I've always liked the logic of this opening. After the pawns move, the white knight comes out to attack the black pawn. The black knight comes out to defend it. The white bishop comes out to attack the knight that defends the pawn. Further play is characterized by the struggle around the control over the pawn (or more precisely, the *square* the pawn occupies): Black wants to maintain it, and white wishes to wrestle it away.

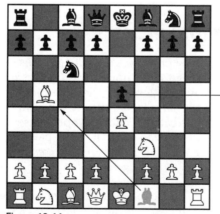

With the Ruy Lopez opening, this square is contested.

Figure 10-14

The Scotch

If, after the same opening sequence described in Figures 10-12 and 10-13, white advances the queen's pawn two squares instead of moving the bishop, the opening is now called *the Scotch* (see Figure 10-15). The name dates back to a correspondence match between the London and Edinburgh chess clubs begun in 1824. Curiously, the London team used the opening first, but the Scots liked it so much they began using it, too. The Scots won the match, and to the victors go the spoils — and the opening name.

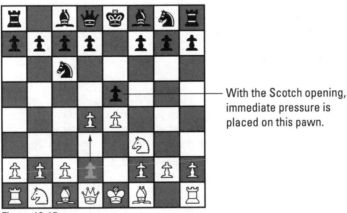

With the Scotch opening, immediate pressure is placed on this pawn.

Figure 10-15

The idea behind the Scotch is similar to that of the Ruy Lopez, to put pressure on the advanced black center pawn. This is a more direct method but generally leads to more early exchanges of pieces and pawns, which ends up reducing white's attacking chances. Most players today prefer the Ruy Lopez.

Petroff's defense

If, as shown in Figure 10-16, black moves out the king's knight on the second turn (instead of the queen's knight, as in Figure 10-13), the opening becomes *Petroff's defense,* named after a great Russian player of the 19th century.

The idea of this defense is different from the first two just presented. Instead of defending the attacked pawn, black produces a counter attack against white's advanced center pawn.

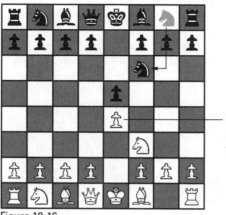

With Petroff's defense, the black knight has placed this pawn under attack.

Figure 10-16

The Petroff problem

There is a well known trap in this defense. It comes about very logically so falling into it is very easy. The starting position was shown in Figure 10-16. The next logical move by white is to capture the exposed black pawn (see Figure 10-17). Logically, one would expect black to carry out the same idea — that is, to capture the exposed white pawn (see Figure 10-18).

Figure 10-17

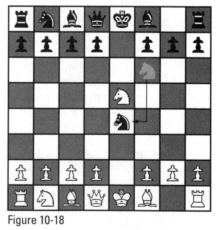

Figure 10-18

The problem is that the black king's file has been opened. This opening allows white to make a threat that black can't simply copy. In Figure 10-19, white attacks the black knight with the queen. Black may choose to move the knight away (see Figure 10-20).

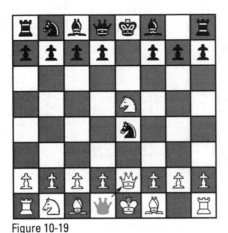

Figure 10-19

Figure 10-20

But if black does move the knight away, white wins the black queen with a discovered check as shown in Figure 10-21: The movement of the white knight has let the white queen check the black king — and the black queen is the victim of the white knight because black can't escape check and protect its queen on one move! (see Chapter 6 for details on the discovered check). Also, black can't maintain equality by copying the white queen move that was made in Figure 10-19 (see Figure 10-22).

Figure 10-21

Figure 10-22

Petroff's solution

Why can't black just copy what white does? Because if black simply copies the white queen move, white simply captures the black knight (see Figure 10-23) simultaneously protecting the white knight. No matter how hard black squirms from that point on, white will have an advantage. Starting back from the position in Figure 10-17, black can carry out the basic idea in another way by attacking the white knight with the queen's pawn (see Figure 10-24).

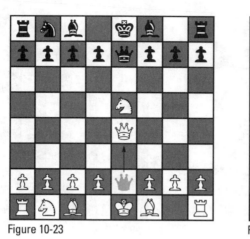

Figure 10-23

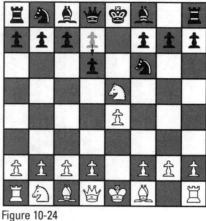

Figure 10-24

Black can force the white knight to retreat (see Figure 10-25) and then capture the white pawn (see Figure 10-26).

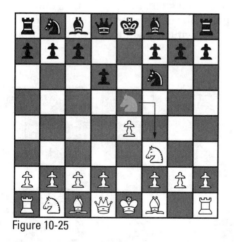

Figure 10-25

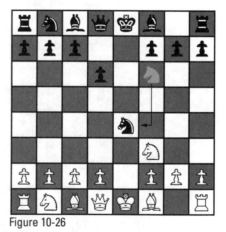

Figure 10-26

If white tries the same pin as before (see Figure 10-27), black simply answers by bringing the queen out (see Figure 10-28), breaking the pin. The game is then very even. Just remember to attack the knight before capturing the pawn, and you should do fine with this defense.

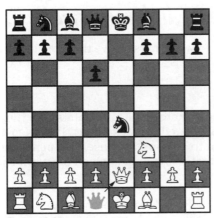

Figure 10-27

Figure 10-28

Philidor's defense

If black defends the attacked king's pawn with the queen's pawn on the second turn instead of using the queen's knight, as shown in Figure 10-29, this opening variation is known as *Philidor's defense* (for more about Philidor, see Chapter 19). (You can now see that chess opening names usually derive from either a player or place name.) In this opening, choosing to defend the attacked pawn with a pawn is a solid defensive strategy — but a passive one. Note one of the primary drawbacks is that black has locked in the black dark-squared bishop behind the pawn chain (see Chapter 7 for more on pawn chains). Today, most players prefer an active defense to a passive one and therefore Phildor's defense is rarely employed.

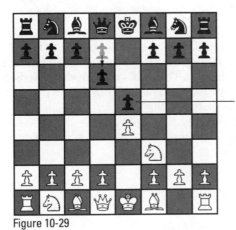

With Philidor's defense, black protects this pawn with another pawn — but locks in its own dark-squared bishop behind the resulting pawn chain.

Figure 10-29

Other black replies (different strokes . . .)

Now look at some other replies to white's first move that are not double king pawn openings.

The French

The French defense is described in more detail in Chapters 7 and 20, but the basic idea is to fight for the light-colored center squares. The defense is very solid but has a drawback similar to Philidor's defense, only in this instance it is the black light-squared bishop that gets trapped behind the pawn chain (see Figure 10-30).

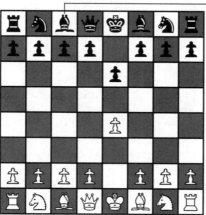

With the French defense, this bishop is trapped.

Figure 10-30

The Sicilian

This defense is very popular at all levels. In the Sicilian, a white center pawn is eventually traded for a black wing (side) pawn, shown in Figure 10-31, which leads to an imbalance (black would have two center pawns to white's one — but white would have compensating advantages in space and time (see Chapter 3 for space and time details). The imbalance produces tension because it is harder to judge whether one side's advantage outweighs the other or vice-versa. See Chapter 20 for more on the Sicilian.

Figure 10-31

With the Sicilian defense, white and black lose these pawns — which gives black two center pawns to white's one.

The Caro-Kann

This defense is also very popular but is considered less exciting than the Sicilian because, in the Caro-Kann, a white center pawn is usually traded for a black one early on in the game. (Figure 10-32 shows the development of the Caro-Kann.) This trade leads to a roughly balanced game, solid — but relatively lacking in tension. See Chapter 20 for more on the Caro-Kann.

Figure 10-32

With the Caro-Kann defense, black moves this pawn first in order to support an advance of its pawn on the d-file.

Alekhine's defense

Alekhine's defense is named after the former world champion Alexander Alekhine (see Chapter 19). It is a risky and provocative defense, which is not recommended for beginners. It is risky because it allows white the opportunity to establish a big advantage in space (as discussed in Chapter 3). Alekhine's defense is provocative because it dares white to advance the attacked pawn another square (see Figure 10-33). From there, the pawn will attack the black knight and force it to move once again. Black figures that the white center pawn will turn out to be over-extended and subject to later attack. If black's strategy is successful, white's center pawn formation (whichever one white chooses to set up) will crumble. If it is unsuccessful, black will end up cramped and passive.

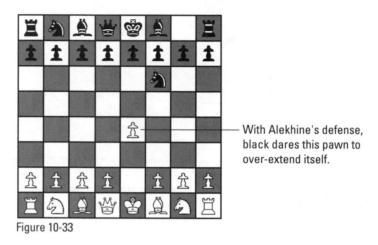

With Alekhine's defense, black dares this pawn to over-extend itself.

Figure 10-33

The Double Queen Pawn game (Ladies first)

The other most-common first move for white is to advance the queen's pawn two squares. If black responds the same way, as shown in Figure 10-34, you have a *Double Queen Pawn game.* For right now, I just want you to concentrate on learning to identify an opening by its name. Don't worry about the advanced strategy behind them.

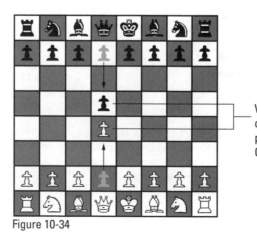

When both white and black develop first the queen's pawn, the result is a Double Queen Pawn game.

Figure 10-34

The Queen's Gambit

The most usual opening that begins with the Double Queen Pawn is the *Queen's Gambit* (see Figure 10-35). The Queen's Gambit can be accepted or declined, and both alternatives are covered in Chapter 5.

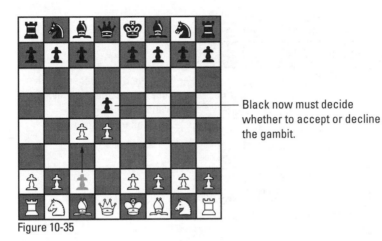

Black now must decide whether to accept or decline the gambit.

Figure 10-35

The Queen's Gambit accepted is shown in Figure 10-36. Figure 10-37 illustrates the Queen's Gambit declined (black refuses to take the white pawn on the c-file and instead develops the king's pawn).

Figure 10-36

Figure 10-37

The Slav

The *Slav* was popularized by the Slavic grandmaster Chigorin in the late 19th century. It is still a prime weapon today, even in the highest levels of competition (see Figure 10-38). See Chapter 20 for more on the Slav.

With the Slav defense, black supports its attacked pawn without blocking its light-squared bishop.

Figure 10-38

The Indian defenses

The other most-common reply to white's first move of the queen's pawn is to move the king's knight out (see Figure 10-39). This move leads to what is usually referred to as *the Indian defenses*. This naming convention comes to us from the precursor to chess, chaturanga, which originated in India in or before the 7th century A.D. It was very common to open a game of chaturanga by developing a bishop on the wing (in chess this is called a *fianchetto*). In chess, the knight move is made first by black in order to prevent white from establishing a center pawn-duo (see Chapter 3) by advancing the king's pawn two squares. This move is followed by a fianchetto on either wing. (See Chapter 20 for additional information on the Indian defenses.)

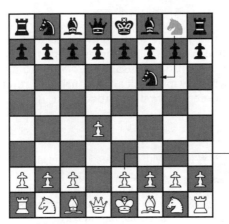

By moving its knight first, black prevents this pawn from advancing two squares.

Figure 10-39

The King's Indian

In the *King's Indian,* the bishop is fianchettoed on the kingside (see Figure 10-40). Black usually castles quickly and only then starts to attack white's center pawns with his own. This is an extremely popular way to combat the queen's pawn opening, but it is also a very complicated one. It is a better idea to play openings that are a bit easier, such as the double queen pawn game, when you are starting out. You can then graduate to the Indian defenses after you've become more experienced.

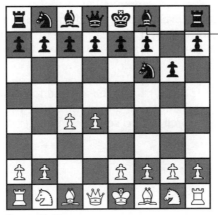

With the King's Indian, black develops this bishop and prepares to castle. Only then will black attack the center.

Figure 10-40

The Queen's Indian

In the *Queen's Indian,* the bishop is fianchettoed on the queenside (see Figure 10-41). The strategy is fairly similar to the King's Indian. Black tries to attack the white center only after castling. The bishops attack the center from the safety of their fianchettoed positions, which helps black accomplish this counterattack. Both Indian defenses are considered very reliable today.

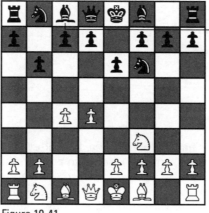

With the Queen's Indian, black develops this bishop first to prepare for an eventual castling to the queenside — all before attacking the center.

Figure 10-41

If you start out in one opening but then find yourself in another, you have *transposed* into the second opening. Many opening systems offer transpositional possibilities, and transposing from one opening to another is a subtle nuance you often find at the higher levels of play. Good chess players may try to fool you into playing an inferior variation of one opening by transposing into it from another. Transposing isn't all that important, however, for recreational players.

What *is* important for all players is to stick to the basics and to know some of the more common opening names. With this ammunition under your belt, you can play your opening games quite well — and sound even better.

CHESS TALK

Weird opening names

Most of the names given to chess openings make a good deal of sense. These openings are usually named after the player who popularized the opening or after the place where the opening was first introduced. Some opening names, however, have far less mundane origins. Be forewarned that these names are far from universally recognized, but most players know what you mean if you refer to any of the following openings:

✔ The Dragon

✔ The Orangutan

✔ The Hedgehog

Less familiar but still generally understood are these openings:

✔ The Vulture

✔ The Rat

✔ The Kangaroo

One chess opening is even called *the Woozle*, but don't ask me why. In the U.S., chess players call another opening the *Fried Liver attack* — so you can see that just about anything goes! To get credit for a new opening system, you must play that opening in a major tournament or publish your analysis to back up your claim. Don't try too hard, however, because coming up with something no one has tried before is very, very hard these days — believe me.

A good source of weird opening names may be found in *Unorthodox Openings*, by Joel Benjamin and Eric Schiller.

Chapter 11

The Middlegame: What Do I Do Now?

· ·

In This Chapter

▶ Formulating a plan

▶ The art of attack

▶ Rules of thumb

· ·

"The core of a chess game is a creative battle of plans, a struggle of chess ideas, which reaches its highest form in the middlegame."
— Grandmaster David Bronstein

The opening phase of a chess game is the place for researchers with glasses and pocket protectors (no offense), but the middlegame is the province of swashbucklers, mad dogs, and Englishmen. Openings and endings may involve some tactics, but middlegames are replete with tactics galore. Don't forget, however, as I always remind my students, that good tactics come from good plans. (See the following section "Formulating a Plan," for details on tactical planning.)

Muddling Through a Middlegame

The *middlegame* commences after the pieces are developed. This part of the game begins after the opening phase of the chess game ends. You don't have an arsenal of theory for use in the middlegame, as you do in the openings and endings. The absence of any vast repository of standardized middlegame theory means that you are usually on your own during this phase of play — but it also means that this part of the game is where your own personal creativity can shine through the most.

The middlegame is extremely difficult to play correctly. Quite often, players who are otherwise quite good at the game find themselves unable to navigate these murky waters adequately. They may know the opening principles and understand where to put their pieces initially, but after those moves, these players are at a loss as to what to do next.

But be of good cheer — especially if you find yourself among the ranks of the middlegame-challenged — for the middlegame, too, has its own governing principles. If you bone up on your tactics and stick to these principles, you can play this phase of the game quite well indeed.

The elements of piece mobility and king safety take priority in the middlegame. The rapid mobilization of your forces enables you to attack your opponent, and if you can induce a weakness in the enemy king's position, you may be able to win material or play directly for checkmate. Even if your opponent safeguards the king, you still may be able to force some other sort of concession, which is usually enough to pave the road to victory.

Formulating a Plan

Chess is not a game that you can easily reduce to the simple sum of its parts. You may understand each element in isolation but still struggle to put the total package together or come to the correct understanding of any given position. Nevertheless, you must be able to judge a position correctly (or at least adequately) before you can hope to formulate the correct plan. If you can't plan well in chess, you end up aimlessly shuffling pieces about, hoping for a glaring error from your opponent. Players who fall into this non-planner category are referred to in chess circles as *woodpushers*. Don't be a woodpusher.

Former world champion José Raúl Capablanca (1888-1942) once wrote in his *A Primer of Chess* that ". . . you may be behind in all three of the other elements, Material, Space, and Time, and yet have a winning *position*. This does not mean that you should neglect any of the other three elements, but that you should give preeminence to the element of *position*."

Today we conceptualize this idea a bit differently and rarely refer to position as an element of chess, but the point remains the same. Every position must be judged on its own merits. The rules of chess have so many exceptions that a blind adherence to any formula is doomed to failure. Checkmate can contradict any rule of thumb. Some players wail that no justice is to be found in chess because they can be doing everything right according to the principles and still lose. The more mature among us refer to "the equalizing injustice of chess," by which we mean that the exception that spoils your plan today may be the exception that spoils your opponent's plan tomorrow.

Ludek Pachman, in *Modern Chess Strategy,* writes: "To judge a position correctly and recognize its peculiarities is an essential prerequisite for finding a suitable plan." In other words, one must evaluate the position correctly *before* embarking on a plan, and to be successful, the plan must correspond to the demands of the position.

Pachman gives us the following factors to consider in evaluating any certain position:

- ✔ The material relationship — that is, the material equality or the material superiority of either side
- ✔ The power of the individual pieces
- ✔ The quality of the individual pawns
- ✔ The position of the pawns — that is, the pawn structure
- ✔ The position of the king
- ✔ Cooperation among the pieces and pawns

A superiority in material tends to be a lasting advantage, as does a superiority in pawn structure, while an edge in piece placement may be a more fleeting advantage. Pieces can move around quite quickly and change the nature of the game. Plans may need to be adopted or dropped if this type of change occurs. You can't stick to a plan that your opponent has thwarted but must readjust yourself to the new position instead. This sort of thing may occur many times in a single game.

Essential pawn structure

The pawns are less mobile than the pieces, and so you can more readily fix the placement of pawns than pieces. The conclusion, therefore, is that the essential characteristic (mobile, locked, and so on) of the pawn structure at this point in the game is your most trustworthy guide to the feasibility — and your adoption — of any particular plan.

I can think of no better illustration of the idea of the preeminence of pawn structure than the example shown in the following series of figures. This example comes from a composition written by W.E. Rudolph in 1912 and published in the French chess journal *La Stratégie.* (Positions that are constructed by an individual are called compositions in order to distinguish them from positions that occur in actual play. See Chapter 14 for more information on compositions, studies, and problems.) I first encountered the composition in the classic work *Pawn Power in Chess,* by Hans Kmoch (1894-1973).

In Figure 11-1, black is way ahead in material — but the position is a draw! Compositions begin with a declaration of who is to move and what the desired outcome is. In this case, it is white to move and force a draw.

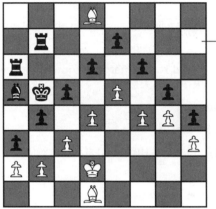

In this chess composition, it's white's turn to move. White's task is to force a draw despite black's advantage in material.

Figure 11-1

White first moves his white-squared bishop up from the first rank to check black's king, as shown in Figure 11-2. Black has no choice except to capture the checking bishop with the king (see Figure 11-3). Otherwise white has a perpetual check (see Chapter 6) on the black king (the bishop checks from the fourth rank, then from the third, then from the fourth, and so on).

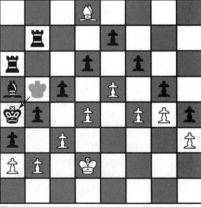

Figure 11-2   Figure 11-3

What follows next is as amusing as it is instructive. On each turn, white advances a pawn to check the king. Black has no choice but to go along for the ride. White delivers check with the pawn in (see Figure 11-4), and black has only one square to move to that is free from check (see Figure 11-5).

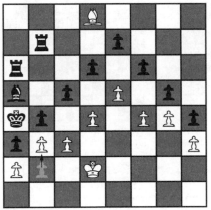

Figure 11-4

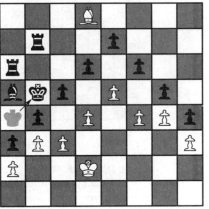

Figure 11-5

White uses the exact same idea in Figure 11-6. A pawn again checks the harassed black king, which has only one safe square to move to (see Figure 11-7).

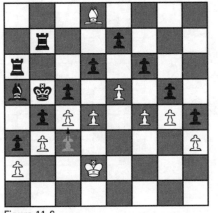

Figure 11-6

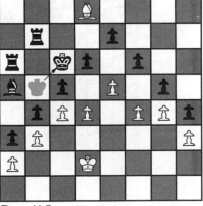

Figure 11-7

Yet again, white uses a pawn to check the black king (see Figure 11-8), and the black king moves to the only square available to it (see Figure 11-9).

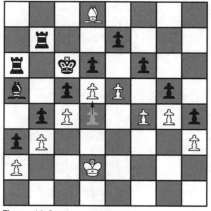

Figure 11-8

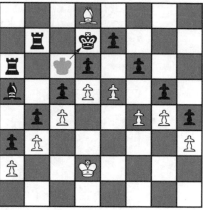

Figure 11-9

One last time, white gives check with a pawn (see Figure 11-10). Now, black finally has some choice as to where to move, but this new freedom doesn't matter anymore. Black can take the bishop, as shown in Figure 11-11, or not — but black can never break through the fortress of pawns covering the board, despite being two rooks and a bishop to the good!

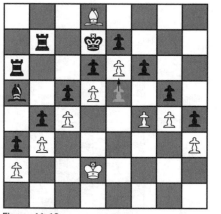

Figure 11-10

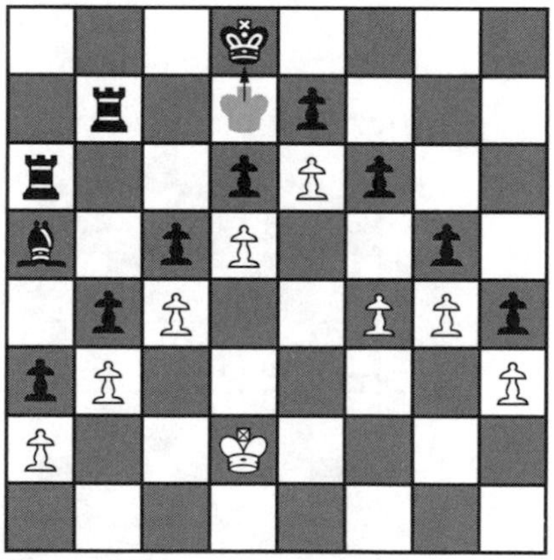

Figure 11-11

White seals the position with a final pawn move (see Figure 11-12). Neither side can cross the neutral zone staked out by the reverse pawn wedges. The game ends in a draw! As you can now see, sometimes material advantage just doesn't matter.

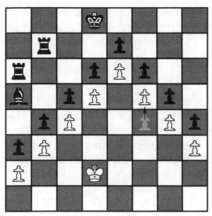

Figure 11-12

The minority attack in practice (and practice makes perfect)

Usually the pawns are not quite that dominant in a real game of chess, but they do influence the placement of the pieces and the selection of plans. In the chapter on strategy (Chapter 8), I examine the plan called the minority attack. The following example shows this plan in practice, with comments based on those by David Bronstein on the planning aspect, excerpted from his immortal *The Chess Struggle in Practice*.

The position shown in Figure 11-13 occurred in a game between Vasily Smyslov (1921-), who played white, and Yuri Averbakh (1922-), in the great Zurich tournament of 1953. In the game, Smyslov wants to use the minority attack by advancing his queenside pawns and exchanging them for black's, but Averbakh doesn't allow it (see Figure 11-14).

Figure 11-13

Figure 11-14

His move prevents Smyslov's original plan (by grabbing more space on the queenside for black before white can do so himself), and forces him to come up with a different one. Averbakh must then respond to the new plan and to the next one, and the next one, if need be.

The ability to correctly adjust and re-adjust your plan is a rare one, however, and you can achieve many fine victories if you simply evaluate a position and attempt to come up with the appropriate plan for that position. Think to yourself something like the following: "I'm going to advance my pawns and weaken my opponent's pawns and then attack them with my pieces." After you decide on the plan, you're no longer faced with a bewildering array of possible moves but have narrowed your choices down considerably.

Any time you don't know what to do in a chess game, just tell yourself to make a plan. Decide which move helps you best carry out that plan — and make that move. After every move (your own and those of your opponent), reevaluate the plan in light of the changed situation. Perhaps the original plan's still appropriate, but maybe a new idea occurs to you that's even better. Try not to switch aimlessly back and forth between plans, but have a real reason to either stick with the plan or change to a new one. If the new idea seems about the same as the old one, stick with the old one.

The Art of Attack

Old hands at the game have a saying in chess: If you have a temporary advantage, you must attack. Otherwise, the advantage usually slips through your fingers. Attacking is a fundamental part of the game, but you must not attack too soon. You first must build up your position to the point that launching an attack is warranted.

You have no hard and fast rules for deciding when to launch an attack. This ambiguity raises the level of decision-making involved in attacks into an art form. The great geniuses of the game seem to have an intuitive sense of when to commence an attack and how to punish one launched by their opponents, if the attack is in any way premature.

Attack types (the type you don't want to meet)

Vladimir Vukovic (1898-1975) wrote a tremendous book on this subject called, quite naturally, *The Art of Attack in Chess*. In the book, he adopted the following classification system for attacks:

- ✔ The main action is not in fact an attack on the king, but the possibility of such an attack is possible in the position.

- ✔ A player's action really does contain a direct threat to the opponent's king, but his opponent can stave off this threat at a certain price — for example, by giving up material or spoiling his position.

- ✔ The attacker carries out an uncompromising mating attack; a considerable amount of material may be invested in the attack as long as mate is certain in the end.

Attack, however, involves risk, and some players hate to take risks. Yet one of the great joys of chess is to conduct well a difficult attack. The point is not to attack for attack's sake, but to attack after you've made the appropriate preparations (secured your position and weakened your opponents).

A lengthy course in attack is beyond the scope of this book, but you still can make considerable progress in your attacking ability by reading the chapters on strategy (Chapter 8) and tactics (Chapter 4). By successfully implementing strategic concepts, you soon find that you can build a sound foundation for an attack against your opponent's king and can then employ the specific tactics necessary to deliver checkmate.

Rules for middlegame attacking

A few generalizations can be made about the middlegame, as long as you understand that every position is unique and that exceptions are lurking out there like fleas just waiting to bite you in the ankle. The following are a few of the generalizations.

Attack if you control the center

If you attack without controlling the center, you are exposed to a counter-attack in the center and your forces may be split.

Meet a flank attack with action in the center

If your opponent attacks on either side of the board, your attack in the center divides your opponent's forces and conquers them.

Be prepared to develop quickly to any area

Your rapid deployment of pieces to one area of the board may be decisive if your opponent can't respond as rapidly.

Place queens in front of bishops and behind rooks during an attack

The bishop is not powerful enough to lead an attack, and the queen is too powerful to risk, if the rook can do the dirty work in her place.

Don't place your knights on the sides of the board

Knights control too few squares from the side of the board, and their attacking power is severely reduced.

Attack in the case of opposite-colored bishops

Because opposite-colored bishops can't be exchanged for one another or control the same squares, the attacker has what sometimes amounts to an extra piece.

Exchange pieces to help your defense

You have fewer pieces to trip over one another if you exchange pieces, and the attacker has fewer pieces to threaten you with.

Put the rooks on open files (and the same file)

Putting the rooks on an open file and then on the same file (which is called *doubling*) whenever possible is helpful. Other pieces can zigzag their way into enemy territory. The rook requires an open file in order to successfully invade. Two rooks acting together can control more territory than one alone.

Put rooks on the seventh rank

Rooks on the seventh rank can usually attack opponent's pawns that have remained on their original squares; sometimes the rooks can trap the opponent's king to the back rank.

Advance pawns to open lines

The opening is the time to develop your pieces not to waste time with excessive pawn moves. Conversely, in the middlegame the pieces are already developed; it may then be appropriate to make additional pawn moves in order to open lines or create weaknesses in your opponents position.

Always guard against a counter-attack

Never leave your king exposed! Chess players very often spoil promising positions in their zeal to attack because they forget to first take a few small precautions. Sometimes it's proper to take a move or two to safeguard your own king's position and only then resume your more aggressive pursuits.

Use knights in closed positions and bishops in open ones

Bishops need open lines in order to profit from their long-range attacking abilities. Knights are more effective in skirmishes at close quarters, and closed positions are more apt to produce that sort of skirmish.

RULE OF THUMB

Middlegame considerations

✔ Attack only if you control the center.

✔ You can best meet a flank attack (on either side of the board) with action in the center.

✔ A rapid deployment of pieces to one area of the board may be decisive if the defender cannot respond just as rapidly.

✔ Queens belong in front of bishops and behind rooks during an attack.

✔ Knights positioned on the rim (the side of the board) are grim (that is, *not* good).

✔ Opposite-colored bishops help the attacker.

✔ Exchanging pieces eases the burden of defense.

✔ Put the rooks on an open file and put them on the same file (which is called *doubling*) whenever possible.

✔ Rooks on the seventh rank are especially powerful.

✔ Unlike in the opening, in which extra pawn moves are frowned on, you may advance pawns in the middlegame to open lines or to create weaknesses.

✔ Guard against a counter-attack: Do not leave your king fatally exposed while you're off hunting your opponent's king!

✔ Knights are excellent attackers in closed positions, while bishops are better in open ones.

✔ Attack in the area where you control more space.

Attack where you control more space

If you attack wherever you control more space, you have more room to maneuver your pieces, and your opponent has less. You then have more squares to choose from when posting your pieces and you may be able to swiftly shift your pieces from one point of attack to another while the defender struggles to meet your threats.

I could say many more things about the middlegame. The best teacher, however, is experience. You can gain a great deal of experience by playing over the games of the masters, but you find no better way to learn how to navigate a successful middlegame than simply to play several yourself. Over time, you figure out when attacks work and when they don't — and why. Remember that everyone fears a strong attacker. No one wants to end up on the wrong side of a brilliant win!

Chapter 12

The Endgame: Can I Go Home Now?

"**W**hy should I worry about the endgame?" a friend once asked me. "I never get to one." He meant that he either won or lost a game well before the endgame entered into the picture. I told him that the reason he never got to an endgame was because he didn't know anything about endgames. I think the subtlety of the remark escaped him.

I'll try to spell out the idea a little more clearly here: You can't understand any phase of the game well unless you understand each phase of the game pretty well.

Players divide the chess game into its three phases — opening, middlegame, and endgame — to better understand the different demands of each one, but you really need to understand a game as a whole and not just in terms of its separate parts. Otherwise, playing the game can be a bit like eating Chinese food with one chopstick.

What Is an Endgame?

Just as middlegame planning flows logically from the opening, the *endgame* logically develops from the middlegame. In many cases, you can even anticipate the endgame as early as in the opening, where one side plays for an advantage in pawn structure that the player can truly exploit only in the endgame. In the words of the great champion Capablanca, ". . .whereas the endings can be studied and mastered by themselves, the middlegame and the opening must be studied in relation to the endgame."

The endgame arrives after the players lose a majority of pieces and, more or less, clear much of the board. Attacks become more difficult to execute with this reduction in material, and the emphasis of play shifts away from tactics to strategy. The importance of individual pieces may undergo a marked change in value, and the roles of the pawns and the kings become more prominent.

You can find a massive amount of documentation on the endgame in chess. Experienced players know of many positions — or types of positions — that lead to wins, losses, or draws. Unfortunately, no shortcuts are available to help you master such positions. You must study these positions if you intend to become a chess master. If you'd rather just play than study, however, you quickly find that learning just a few basic positions and a few common themes usually is sufficient. In this way, you come to understand a good deal about many endgame positions and can figure out others as you play.

Pawn Endings: The Little Ones Turn Up Big

The most basic type of ending is the king and pawn versus king ending. Sometimes it just comes down to a race for the queening square between the pawn and the enemy king. In that case, if the lone king cannot prevent the pawn from attaining its promotion to a queen, the game is lost. If the king can prevent the pawn's promotion, the game ends up a draw.

You have two easy ways to determine whether the king can prevent a pawn from promoting (or, as chess players usually say, queening — which I explain in Chapter 9). First, you can simply count the squares in your head. If you have a lot of squares to count, you may find the second method, called the *pawn square* (described later on), easier to use in determining the king's chances. (You may also see this method referred to as the *rule of the square,* or the *pawn quadrant,* but these different terms all refer to the same principle.) Let's take the counting method first.

With white to move in Figure 12-1 (don't worry about a missing white king, just concentrate on the race of the pawn and the black king to the queening square), can the black king prevent the white pawn from reaching the queening square?

If you simply count the squares, you can see that the white pawn can queen before the black king can stop its advance to the last rank. The white pawn needs four moves to queen, which means that the black king has only three moves in which to stop the pawn. Black needs four. You can also determine black's inability to stop the pawn in time by applying the principle of the pawn square.

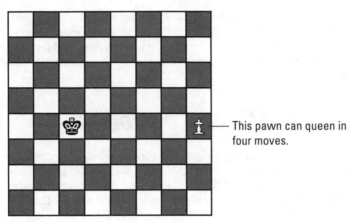

This pawn can queen in four moves.

Figure 12-1

The idea behind the pawn square is to create an imaginary square shape. The first side of the square is determined by extending from the pawn to the queening square. Because all sides of a square are of equal length, you can then create a mental picture of the other sides of the square, as shown in Figure 12-2 where the *X*s mark the boundaries of the pawn square. If the king is outside the pawn square, the pawn can queen.

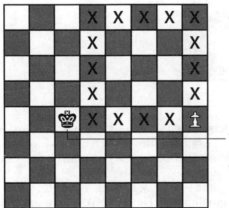

The king is outside the pawn square and thus can't prevent the pawn from queening.

Figure 12-2

In this case, the black king is outside the square, the king can't prevent the pawn from queening. If the king were on or inside the square, however, it would be able to stop the pawn from queening.

Sometimes, simply stopping the straightforward march of the pawn is not enough for the black king. In some positions, the pawn can queen with the assistance of its own king. Knowing exactly when a king and pawn can defeat a lone king and when they can't is crucial to the understanding of endgames.

The Opposition (Friend or Foe?)

The *opposition* is not your opponent! The term is what chess players use to refer to a fundamental and frequently occurring situation in king and pawn endings. Opposition occurs if the two kings face one another, as shown in Figure 12-3, and must make way for the other. The king that moved last is said to "have the opposition" because the other king must give ground.

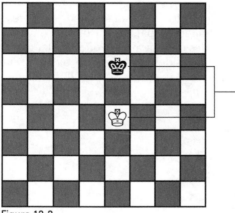

When two kings oppose one another, one of the kings will have to give ground.

Figure 12-3

Quite often, the opposition determines whether a game is won, lost, or ends in a draw. Often, however, as in the example shown in Figure 12-4, you must know which side moves next to correctly evaluate the position.

If white moves this turn, the game is a draw. If black moves this turn, white wins the game (as shown later, beginning with Figure 12-8). This setup reflects the essence of the opposition. If the kings face one another separated by an odd number of squares, the player who moved last has the opposition. (This situation is one of the few times in chess when you'd like to say, "I pass!")

Suppose that it is white to move next in Figure 12-4. King moves by white are useless (the king can't advance, only retreat) so there is no better option than to advance the pawn, as shown in Figure 12-5. Now black moves the king to occupy the queening square (see Figure 12-6).

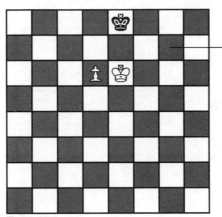

Whichever side moves next determines the outcome of this game.

Figure 12-4

Figure 12-5

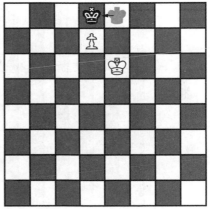

Figure 12-6

White must now either abandon the pawn to capture by black's king or give stalemate by moving into a protective position behind the pawn, as shown in Figure 12-7. Remember that stalemate is a draw.

If, on the other hand, black moves next in the original position shown back in Figure 12-4, white can eventually queen the pawn and win the game. Black must move the king, and the best chance black has now is to cover the queening square (see Figure 12-8), otherwise the advance of the pawn would cut black off from this key square, and white would then queen the pawn on the next turn.

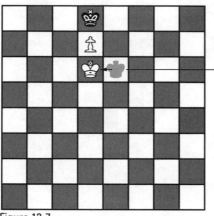

To achieve a stalemate, the white king must protect the pawn.

Figure 12-7

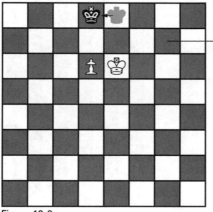

Imagine the same situation as in Figure 12-4, but now let it be black's move.

Figure 12-8

White can now advance the pawn in safety, protected by the white king, as shown in Figure 12-9. Black must move away to the only square in which the king is not in check (see Figure 12-10).

This move enables white to advance the king and control the queening square (see Figure 12-11). Black's only available moves are away from the queening square — which only prolongs black's agony. The white pawn can then advance to the last rank and get promoted to a queen; checkmate soon follows.

Many nuances to the opposition are beyond the scope of this chapter, but this endgame tactic is described in more detail in many works on the endgame. If you need to study and become completely familiar with one single concept in the endgame, learn the opposition.

Figure 12-9

Figure 12-10

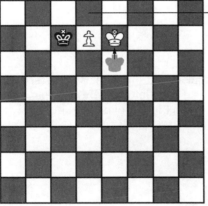

Figure 12-11

———— On the next move, white can advance the pawn to the queening square.

Endings with king and rook's pawn versus king always end in draws if the weaker side can get to the queening square. This outcome is inevitable, because the stronger side can't approach the queening square with its king and can't advance its pawn without giving stalemate (the black king has no escape route off to the side in the case of the rook's pawn).

Multiple Pawn Endings

Endings with king and pawns versus king and pawns can be deceptively complicated. You do have a few rules to follow, however.

Use one pawn to restrain two

Consider, for example, the position shown in Figure 12-12.

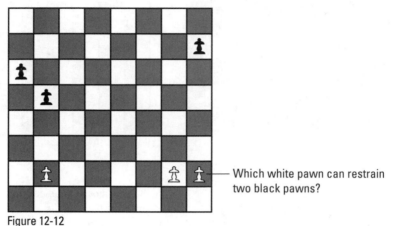

Which white pawn can restrain two black pawns?

Figure 12-12

Trying to count the number of pawn moves necessary to determine whether this situation is a win or a draw can get confusing. By applying our first rule of thumb, however, hitting on the correct first move for white — advancing the queen's knight pawn two squares — is a simple matter (see Figure 12-13).

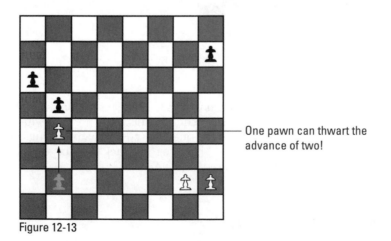

One pawn can thwart the advance of two!

Figure 12-13

Now, the single white pawn restrains the two black pawns. This position may also be used to highlight our second rule.

Advance an unopposed pawn

If faced with a choice of which pawn to advance, advance the pawn that is facing no opponent. White moves the unopposed king's knight pawn two squares forward (see Figure 12-14).

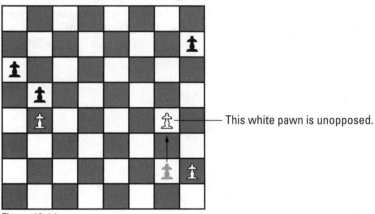

This white pawn is unopposed.

Figure 12-14

The consequence of ignoring rule number 2 is seen in Figure 12-15. If white had advanced the king's rook pawn instead of the king's knight pawn, black's response is to employ rule number 1 by moving the king's rook pawn up two squares to block both white pawns!

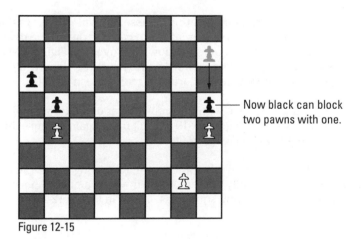

Now black can block two pawns with one.

Figure 12-15

Get a passed pawn

The next position is one that I show to all my students. This position vividly demonstrates that the power of a passed pawn is often worth all the knights in Columbus. (Chapter 3 provides details on passed pawns.)

A superficial glance at the position would tell us that the two sides are even in material but that the white king is too far away from the action (see Figure 12-16). A deeper look, however, suggests that the important point is not the position of the white king but the advanced position of the white pawns. How can white turn this setup into an advantage?

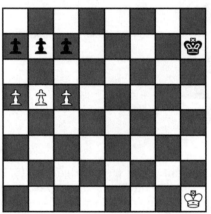

Figure 12-16

White can gain the advantage by creating a passed pawn! With its first move, advancing the middle pawn, white threatens to capture one of the defending black pawns and then to queen on the following move (see Figure 12-17). This threat forces black to capture the forward white pawn (see Figure 12-18). Which pawn black uses to capture white's marauder really doesn't matter.

White advances another pawn, with the same threat of capturing and queening on the next two moves (see Figure 12-19). Black must again capture the attacking white pawn, as shown in Figure 12-20.

But now, with white's next move, advancing the remaining pawn, the nature of the overall position is radically altered. White now has a passed pawn, which has a clear path to the queening square, as shown in Figure 12-21.

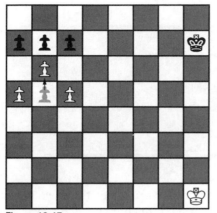

Figure 12-17

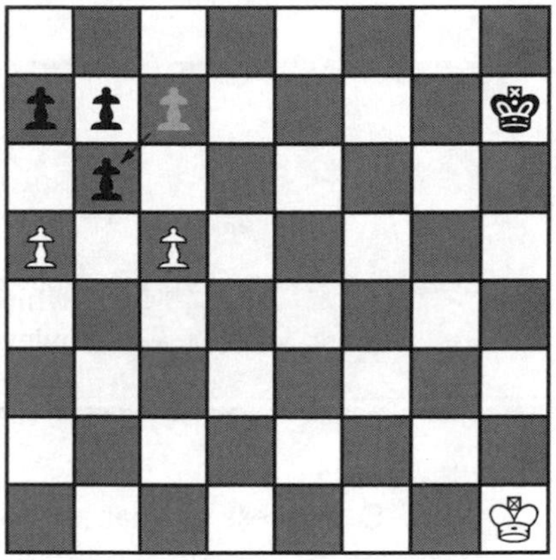

Figure 12-18

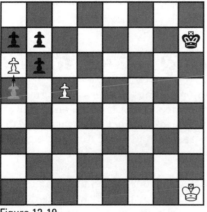

Figure 12-19

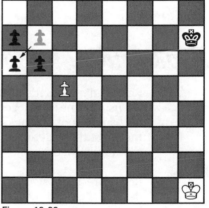

Figure 12-20

Figure 12-21

White has gained a passed pawn that can queen in two moves.

Pawn endings

- ✔ Always use one pawn to restrain two if possible.
- ✔ If faced with a choice of which pawn to advance, advance the pawn that is facing no opponent.
- ✔ Obtain a passed pawn.

Regardless of what black does now, white can queen the pawn in two moves. After white queens the pawn, the win is straightforward. Always be on the lookout for an opportunity to create a passed pawn that can continue marching unimpeded toward the queening square. The two pawns who gave their lives so that the third could achieve promotion deserve burial with full military honors!

Rook Endings (Towering Above the Rest)

Rook endings are the most common endings in chess — mainly because rooks are usually the last pieces you develop and the last you and your opponent exchange. Rook endings are awfully tricky. In fact, one wag suggested a rule to the effect that "All rook endings are draws." Not all rook endings, however, lead inevitably to a draw.

Rooks are aggressive pieces and become despondent if relegated to passive defense. Keep this characteristic in mind, especially if you're defending an inferior position. Following are several rules for rook endings.

Activate your rook

Give up a pawn to turn a passive rook into an aggressive one. This sacrifice may well be worth it.

Put your rooks behind passed pawns

You can best position rooks behind passed pawns. The next best rook position is to the side of passed pawns, and the least desirable position is in front of passed pawns.

Advance connected passed pawns against rooks

Connected passed pawns are most effective against rooks so advance these pawns together.

Put your king on the queening square

If you're defending your king with one rook against a rook and a pawn, occupy the queening square with your king, if possible.

Harass your opponent's king with your rook

If defending, you may want to harass the enemy king with repeated checks by your rook. Harass from a safe distance, however, and keep your rook as far away from the enemy king as possible to avoid losing it.

Look (out) for the draw in rook endings

Rook endings, when both sides have pawns all on one side of the board, are often drawn: The defender can usually set up a blockade.

RULE OF THUMB

Rook endings

- Activate your rook. Giving up a pawn to turn a passive rook into an aggressive one is often worth the sacrifice.

- You can best position rooks behind passed pawns. The next best rook position is to the side of passed pawns, and the least desirable position is in front of passed pawns.

- Connected passed pawns are most effective against rooks. Advance these pawns together.

- If you're defending your king with a lone rook against a rook and a pawn, try to occupy the queening square with your king.

- If defending, you may find useful the tactic of harassing the enemy king with repeated checks by your rook. Perform this maneuver only from a safe distance, however, and keep your rook as far away from the enemy king as possible, so as not to expose it to capture.

- Rook endings, when both sides have pawns all on one side of the board, are generally drawn, because the defender can usually set up a blockade.

Bishop and Knight Endings

The endings that involve minor pieces are a little bit easier to understand than rook endings. Knights are better than bishops if the endgame commences with pawns in locked positions, but bishops become stronger than knights in open positions with pawns on both sides of the board. A knight can restrict a bishop's movement only with great difficulty, while a bishop can far more readily restrict a knight's movement — especially if the knight is positioned at the side of the board.

Consider the position shown in Figure 12-22. Here the bishop covers all the squares into which the knight can potentially move. This example serves to illustrate one of the advantages of having a bishop instead of a knight in an ending. The bishop can often trade itself for the knight and potentially turn the game into a favorable king and pawn ending. The knight rarely has this option.

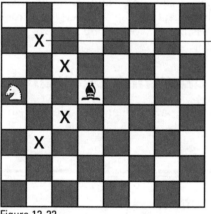

The bishop controls all the squares where the knight can move.

Figure 12-22

In some cases, however, you'd rather have a knight than a bishop. Such a situation is demonstrated in Figure 12-23. In this example, the white bishop can't attack any of the black pawns and must passively defend the white pawns. Only black has winning chances in this case, thanks to the knight's ability to move from one color square to the other and back. The knight can theoretically occupy any of the squares, but the bishop cannot. By improving the position of the knight and king, black may be able to force white into further concessions and even win the game.

This situation leads to the primary rule involving bishops in the endings, which is to put your pawns on squares of the opposite color from the bishop. Other-wise, the bishop will be hemmed in by its own pawns.

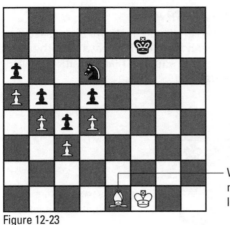

White's dark-squared bishop can never attack an opponent on a light square.

Figure 12-23

In all minor piece endings, you need to remember that neither bishop and king, nor knight and king, can deliver checkmate by themselves. This inability on the part of the knight and bishop to force checkmate in endings means that the weaker side needs to try to exchange as many pawns as possible. If the weaker side can eliminate all the pawns, even by sacrificing a piece to do so, the game would be drawn. The following sections list some rules of thumb for the various combination of minor piece endings.

Knight versus knight (jousting was never like this!)

When knights square off against knights, the action is defined by the piece's lack of long-range attacking ability. Hand-to-hand fighting is much more common, so keep these rules in mind.

Use your knight to blockade

Anchor your knight to the square in front of a passed pawn. This strategy prevents the pawn from moving without diminishing the knight's attacking power. Knights are good soldiers, and do not take offense at performing guard duty, as rooks and queens do.

Beware of outside passed pawns

Outside passed pawns (see Chapter 3) are especially effective against the knights. Knights are good at short range but weak at long range, because the knights can influence only one side of the board at a time.

Sacrifice the knight to get a passed pawn

Consider sacrificing the knight to create an unstoppable passed pawn. In Figure 12-24, black has succeeded in blocking the white pawns on the kingside (they cannot force their way to a queening square). Black's outside passed pawn is threatening to advance towards its queening square.

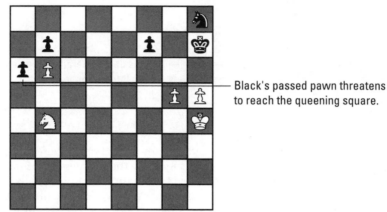

Black's passed pawn threatens to reach the queening square.

Figure 12-24

White can prevent this potential queening by sacrificing the knight, as shown in Figure 12-25.

If black captures the knight (see Figure 12-26) . . .

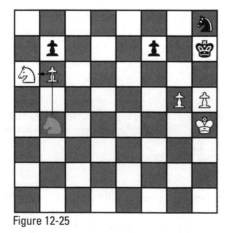

Figure 12-25

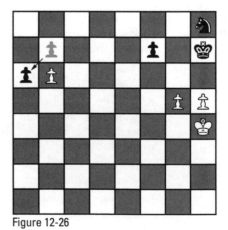

Figure 12-26

. . . white would have an unstoppable passed pawn (see Figure 12-27) and would win.

Knight versus knight

- The knight is the ultimate blockader. Anchor your knight to the square in front of a passed pawn.
- Outside passed pawns are especially effective against the knights.
- Be alert to the possibility of sacrificing the knight to create an unstoppable passed pawn.

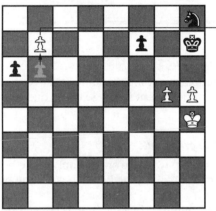

White's passed pawn can't be stopped.

Figure 12-27

Knight versus bishop

Here are some things to keep in mind for endings involving knights and bishops.

Use bishops in open positions

Knights like closed positions and bishops like open ones. Endings are usually open, so bishops tend to be superior in the endgame.

Reduce the mobility of bishops with pawns

By placing your pawns on the same color squares as the opponent's bishop, it is possible to restrict its mobility. Ideally you want your opponent to restrict his or her own bishop. Be careful that the bishop cannot attack and win your pawns. Follow this rule only if it restricts the bishops mobility and the pawns are safe from capture.

Knight versus bishop

✔ Knights like closed positions and bishops like open ones. Endings tend to be open, so bishops tend to be superior.

✔ Use pawns to restrict the scope of the bishop.

✔ Look to trade into winning king and pawn endings.

✔ The bishop's advantage increases if pawns are on both sides of the board. The less symmetrical the position, the better it is for the bishop.

Look for one-king-and-pawn endings

It is easier to win a one-king-and-pawn ending than any other type of ending. If you can trade your piece for your opponent's and go into a one-king-and-pawn ending, do it!

Use bishops if the pawns are spread out

The bishop's advantage increases if pawns are spread out on the board. The less symmetrical the position of the pawns, the better it is for the bishop.

The bishop's superiority to the knight lies in its ability to attack both sides of the board at once. The knight cannot defend on one side and attack on the other simultaneously, but the bishop can.

Bishop versus bishop

There are two completely different types of bishop versus bishop endings: when the bishops are of the same color, and when the bishops are of opposite colors.

Look (out) for a draw with opposite-color bishops

Bishops of opposite color increase the chances of a draw: They can never capture one another! In addition, opposite-colored bishops can't get past each other's blockade.

Use a long-range bishop to control a passed pawn

The bishop can prevent the advance of a passed pawn by controlling the square in front of the pawn. Remember that the bishop can control a square from a long distance.

RULE OF THUMB

Bishop versus bishop

✔ Bishops of opposite color increase the chances of a draw because they can't capture one another or overcome each other's blockade.

✔ The bishop can prevent the advance of a passed pawn, even from a distance, by controlling the square in front of it.

✔ In same-colored bishop endings, you can often force the weaker side to give ground by offering an exchange of bishops.

The farther apart passed pawns are, the better the stronger side's chances are of winning. If the pawns are close together, the enemy king can be used to help establish a blockade. If they are further apart, this is not possible. The king can be used on one side or the other, but not both.

Trade same-colored bishops if you're stronger

In same-colored bishop endings, you can force the weaker side to give ground by offering to exchange. Put your bishop on the same diagonal as the one your opponent's bishop is on. Support your bishop with the king. If you have more pawns, your opponent will not wish to trade and will be forced to cede the diagonal to you.

The General Winning Endgame Strategy

All endings are different, but the following methodology can serve you well as a guide devising to the correct endgame plan, if you find yourself uncertain about what to do next.

First, *advance your king.* The king comes out of hiding in the endgame and becomes a critical factor. Advance the king toward passed pawns or toward pawns that are weak and vulnerable to attack. Otherwise, generally advance the king toward the center.

Next, *push your passed pawns.* As Nimzovitch once said, passed pawns have a lust to expand. Don't go overboard, however. Advance the passed pawn only if doing so is safe. Advancing a pawn into the enemy's teeth, where its capture is certain, is essentially pointless.

Always be on the lookout to *trade* into a simpler ending by offering to exchange pieces. Generally speaking, the more material that's still on the board, the more complicated is the ending. Don't trade from a winning ending into a drawn ending, of course, but stay alert to the possibility of trading down into a simpler — yet still winning — end.

Know your pieces. If your pawns are still sitting on the same colored-squares as your bishop, try not to go into the ending in the first place! You probably have better chances in the middlegame. Steer the game into the type of ending where your pieces are more suitable to winning than are your opponent's.

Know the basics. If you can only study a little bit of chess, study the endgame. Learn the basic winning and drawing techniques for the various endings, and you should find yourself playing the openings and middlegames much better, too!

Endgames are deceptively complex. Because there are so few pieces remaining, the natural tendency is to conclude that endgames are easier than middlegames or openings. In fact, endgames are equally complicated. The difference is that they are easier to study. The openings and middlegames have too many possible variations to make heads or tails of them. The endings, however, are clearer in that an idea may be proven or disproved to win. By studying the pieces in isolation in various endgame positions, you can then begin to understand them in combination with others. This strategy helps you to understand middlegame positions and even openings. The road to chess mastery should begin with the endgame.

Rules for the endgame

- Activate your king.
- If you have more pawns than your opponent, exchange pieces not pawns.
- If you have fewer pawns than your opponent, exchange pawns not pieces.
- Try to create a passed pawn.
- Protected passed pawns are very strong.
- Outside passed pawns are also very strong.
- Outside, protected passed pawns are usually decisive.
- Try to promote a passed pawn.
- If your opponent has a passed pawn, try to blockade that pawn.
- Bishops are generally stronger than knights.
- Bishops of opposite color increase the chances of a draw.
- Be aggressive with your rooks; if your choice is between defense and counter-attack, always counter-attack.
- Rooks belong behind passed pawns.

Chapter 13

Chess Etiquette (Why Was He So Mad at Me?)

• •

In This Chapter
▶ Knowing when and how to resign
▶ Offering a draw
▶ Respecting the touch move rule
▶ Hovering your hand
▶ Adjusting a pawn or a piece

• •

C hess is supposed to be fun, but quite often people take it very seriously. When you play someone like that, you should know the do's and don'ts of chess etiquette. Chess etiquette is especially important in tournament chess.

In a serious encounter, both players are staring at the board for hours at a time. A raised eyebrow will be noticed by your hypersensitive opponent, and a sneeze may cause someone to go into shock. Heaven forbid that you would have a nervous tic or a habit of drumming your fingers or humming (mostly) to yourself. Chess players have complained about all of these things and more.

You may properly address your opponent during the game only to offer a draw or to say check or checkmate. If you have a complaint, the safest course of action is to bring it up to the tournament director. If the game is only for fun, use common sense — but above all, avoid distracting an opponent who is thinking about a move.

There is a famous story about one grandmaster complaining about another who kept an unlit cigar next to the chessboard. "It's a no-smoking tournament," the former complained to the tournament director. The director, quite rightly, pointed out that the cigar was unlit. The grandmaster insisted, however, claiming that his opponent was threatening to smoke! There is at least some basis in the chess world for this absurdity, because we have a saying that the threat is stronger than the execution!

Chess at these levels is an incredibly tense activity, and there is no physical release. Even otherwise placid individuals have been known to lose their cool over a real or imagined infraction. The best thing to do is just play for the fun of it, but even then it's important to know the basics.

Resigning

Beginners are coached never to give up and to always play the game out to checkmate. "No one ever won by resigning," they are often told. Although this may be true, a few other considerations are important to bear in mind.

When to resign

If you are hopelessly behind in material, you may as well start another game (see Chapter 3 for a discussion of material). Over the course of your lifetime you may spend hours hoping to save one or two completely lost positions when instead you can be spending that time starting over from scratch. Moreover, you rarely — if ever — learn anything from these types of positions. It is much better to spend your time figuring out where you went wrong and then trying not to get into that mess again.

It's possible that your opponents enjoy seeing you squirm and that you are merely playing into their hands by continuing on. More likely, they will get annoyed that you don't know when to resign and they may refuse to play with you anymore.

I quit going to one club in particular because the players there kept playing on in hopeless positions. I would find myself driving home well after midnight week after week. If the members knew when to resign, I might still be playing there.

The bottom line, however, is that *resignation is a personal decision.* You never resign just because your opponent wants you to, but you should resign when you objectively decide that there is no way to save the game. After the conclusion is inevitable, you may as well shake your opponent's hand.

How to resign

Just as important as when to resign is how to resign. The formal method is to tip your king over on its side. This is a universally recognized surrender. It is then important to extend your hand to congratulate your opponent. This show of sportsmanship is a valued ritual in chess. It demonstrates that you have at least a touch of class.

Many players will shake hands after the game but then undo the goodwill gesture by complaining that they should've, by all rights, won the game themselves. "If I'd just done this, instead of that, it was curtains for you," they might say. This talk is just childishness. Far more effective is to ask, "What would you have done if I'd played this instead of that?"

This approach accomplishes a couple of things. First, it acknowledges that your opponent's opinion, by virtue of the victory, might have some validity. Secondly, it allows you to listen to your opponent's ideas. It's much better to pick your opponent's brain in this manner than to try to explain away why you lost the game.

Sometimes both you and your opponent will spend considerable time discussing the game. Chess players call these *post mortem* sessions. Try to be respectful during these sessions and concentrate on learning — not proving a point. You will make many chess friends if you follow this advice.

Offering a Draw

If you have determined that you can't checkmate your opponent, you may wish to offer a draw (see Chapter 6 for details on a draw). Under tournament conditions, you may make a draw offer only after you have made a move and before you have started your opponent's clock. Never offer a draw to your opponents on their time. That behavior is a breach of etiquette, and repeated offenses may cause you to lose the game by forfeit.

Offering a draw under any other circumstances may be considered annoying, and your opponent may report you to the tournament director. What's worse is that the draw offer may be accepted or rejected and you may still get scolded. In other words, if you make an improper draw offer, your opponent has the right to accept it *and* complain about it.

If you make a draw offer without making a move, your opponent has the right to ask to see your move and then decide whether to accept or reject your offer. Repeated draw offers may be considered annoying, so wait until the position has changed substantially before making another offer.

If the position is about to be repeated for the third time, a draw may be claimed. You must do so before making the move that would repeat the position for the third time.

Food and drink . . . and chess

Generally it is considered improper to eat or drink anything at the chessboard except for water or coffee. Of course, if you're playing in your own living room, all bets are off. The ground rules are determined by the home team in that case.

My worst experience with food at the chessboard came in my very first big tournament in New York. It was the last-round game and whoever won the game would clinch a sizable prize. My opponent came to the board with a sloppy meatball sandwich and proceeded to get the sauce all over his hands. He then decided to adjust all of my pieces covering them with the sauce.

I was too inexperienced to complain and too young to shrug it off. Instead, I let it affect my play, which is what my opponent had hoped would happen, and managed to lose rather badly. Needless to say, this was a severe breach of chess etiquette, and I should have complained to an official at once.

Touch Move

One of the most touchy subjects in chess is the *touch move rule.* This rule simply means that, if you touch a piece, you must move it — if it is legal to do so. If you touch a piece that has no legal move, you are free to move any other piece. The move is considered complete when your hand is removed from the piece.

Sometimes one player claims that the other touched a piece and the second player denies doing so. If there are witnesses, the director may be able to make an informed decision. In the absence of witnesses, the claim is generally not upheld on the first complaint.

Did Kasparov cheat?

During one tournament game against Judit Polgar, Kasparov made his move and seemed to take his hand away from the piece for a split second. He then moved the piece to another square. The shocked Polgar did not make a claim, but later indicated that she thought the champion had indeed taken his hand off of the piece. Kasparov denied doing so.

However, the game was being videotaped, and a careful review of the tape showed that Kasparov did in fact let go of the piece. Unfortunately, there is no instant replay in chess, and no protest was possible after the game was concluded. If even world champions break the rules, what hope do the rest of us have?

The Hand Hover

A frequent cause of complaints involving the touch move rule is the *hand hover*. The hand hover occurs when a player positions his or her hand over a piece and leaves it there. The hand hover is a distraction and should not be practiced. Don't reach for a piece until you've decided to move it.

No less a player than Capablanca (see Chapter 19) warned against the danger of using the hand hover. He claimed that it interfered with your thought processes and that it was to be discouraged.

J'adoube and Such

Sometimes a pawn or a piece may not be resting completely on one square or another. It's permissible to adjust that pawn or piece or even a whole bunch of them — if it is on your time and if you warn your opponent first. The French phrase *J'adoube* is considered to be the proper warning. This means "I adjust" in English, but it is also proper to use the English translation.

As long as you have issued the warning, the touch move rule is temporarily waved. Keep in mind that you cannot say "J'adoube" or "I adjust" *after* you have touched a piece!

The worst losers in chess history

Mike Fox and Richard James, in their delightful *The Even More Complete Chess Addict*, nominate the following three candidates for the title of worst loser in chess history. In their own words:

In third place, former World Champion Alexander Alekhine, a notorious temperamental loser. At Vienna in 1922, Alekhine resigned spectacularly against Grünfeld by hurling his king across the room.

In the silver medal position, another famous loser, Aaron Nimzovich. At a lightning chess tournament in Berlin, he said out loud what all of us have at one time felt. Instead of quietly turning over his king, Nimzo leapt onto his chair and bellowed across the tournament hall: "Why must I lose to this idiot?" Not nice, but one knows the feeling.

But the gold medal, plus the John McEnroe Award for bad behavior at a tournament, goes to the lesser-known Danish player (reported in the *Chess Scene*) who lost as a result of a fingerslip involving his queen. Unable to contain his despair, he snuck back into the tournament hall at dead of night, and cut the heads off all the queens.

Part IV
Who to Play, When, Where, and How

The 5th Wave   By Rich Tennant

In this part . . .

1f you want to play chess, you have to have someone (or something) to play with you. In this part, I write about the various types of competition — from clubs to computers. In addition, I have a section on chess notation so that you can play a game of chess by e-mail or regular mail with people from all over the world. Knowing some chess notation also lets you read about chess as well as write about your own experiences.

Chapter 14

Competitive Chess
(Is There Any Other Kind?)

● ●

In This Chapter

▶ Finding national tournament chess

▶ Finding international tournament chess

▶ Determining the ratings

▶ Playing correspondence chess

● ●

*I*f you're like me, you'll be nervous the first time you enter a tournament. Don't let that stop you! World champions had to play in their first tournament, too. Most of us remember what it feels like not to know the ropes. Just ask questions to the first quasi-official person you lay eyes on, and chances are you may make a new friend in the process.

National Tournament Chess

Tournament chess in the United States is certified and rated by the United States Chess Federation (USCF). It can be reached by calling 800-388-5464 or by writing to:

USCF
3054 NYS Route 9W
New Windsor, NY 12553

In order to play a tournament game, you should know all the rules and be familiar with chess etiquette (see Chapter 13). Normally, the tournaments are run by a tournament director, require membership in the USCF ($40), and require an entry fee. You should also bring your own equipment: a chess board, set, and clock (see Chapter 21 to find out some good sources for this equipment).

Generally speaking, there are three kinds of tournament competition: the Swiss System, round robin, and match.

Swiss System

Most tournaments in the United States are run according to the rules of the Swiss System. The *Swiss System* ranks all players by rating (and ranks unrated players alphabetically) and splits the list in half. The top player of the top half is paired against the top player of the bottom half and so on until the bottom player of the top half is paired against the bottom player of the bottom half. In case of an uneven number of players, the bottom-most player is usually given a one-half point bye (which means they are paired as if they'd made a draw, even though they didn't play the game).

Winners get one point, draws score one-half point, and losers get zero points. In the next round, winners play winners, losers play losers, and so forth, following the same procedure of dividing the lists in half and pairing the two lists accordingly.

Gradually you begin to play players of your approximate strength, because — in theory anyway — you should be scoring roughly the same amount of points against the same kind of competition. The strongest players, or the players having the best tournament, are increasingly likely to play one another as the tournament goes on. The winner is the player scoring the most number of points.

The Swiss Gambit

Usually the first rounds of a tournament run under the Swiss System involve mismatches. Strong players play weaker players, especially early on in the tournament. Some players use a dubious strategy, called the Swiss Gambit, designed to avoid the toughest competition. This strategy involves allowing a draw with a weaker player, which gets the Gambitor easier pairings (the winners play other winners, but the Gambitor plays someone else who only drew) in the next few rounds. The hope is that, in the later rounds, the strongest players will be playing each other — and the Gambitor will sneak into the prize money by playing inferior competition.

This strategy, like any other designed to manipulate results, is just as likely to backfire as succeed. Who knows whether you really will get weaker pairings? In all cases, you should play your best.

Round robin

A *round-robin* tournament is one where every one plays everyone else. These tournaments are regarded as a more accurate judge of a player's performance because there is no "lucky" pairing. Round-robin tournaments are used to determine most national championships and international tournaments. A drawback to a round-robin tournament is that it normally takes a longer period of time to complete and is therefore more expensive to produce.

A sub-set of the round robin is the Quad, where four players of roughly equal strength play one another. This type of system is popular in the U.S. because it is inexpensive and avoids mismatches.

Match competition

Match competition is not tournament competition, but it is another popular form. In a match, one player plays another for a pre-determined number of games. This head-to-head competition is the purest method for determining the stronger player and is usually adopted in order to determine the world champion — or the world champion's challenger.

Tournaments are advertised in *Chess Life,* the monthly publication of the USCF (the United States Chess Federation), which is included with your membership dues. *Chess Life* has a section that includes the upcoming events and the name and phone numbers of the tournament directors. This listing will look like Greek to you the first time you see one. Call the director and tell him or her that you are an unrated player and ask any questions you may have. Everyone was a beginner at some point, and these directors will take the time to show you the ropes.

State Organizations

I usually advise my students to get involved in a club prior to playing in a tournament. A club is usually a friendlier environment and the best place to get your feet wet. You'll probably meet some tournament veterans who may be willing to take you under their wing. That's how most of us got started in tournament chess.

In order to find a club near you, contact the state chapter. The following list changes fairly often, but the people listed here will usually know what's going on. If you reach a disconnected number or can't make progress at the state level, you can try calling the USCF directly; the USCF may have a more current contact.

Alabama
Alabama Chess Federation
11050 Oak Bluff Dr.
Northport, AL 35476
contact: Walter Schaetzle
205-339-9587
dues: $10, $4 jrs.

Arizona
Arizona Chess Association
1444 W. Sixth St.
Tempe, AZ 85281
contact: Myron Lieberman
602-967-4054
dues: none

Arkansas
Arkansas Chess Association
Apt. 3B Hiland Pl.
Benton, AR 72015
contact: Bill Beck
501-778-4632
dues: $6, $4 jrs.

California (North)
CalChess
2047 Monticito Avenue
Mountain View, CA 94043
contact: Richard Koepke
415-964-2640

California Chess Journal (quarterly)
James Eade
521 Fanita Way
Menlo Park, CA 94025

California (South)
Southern California
Chess Federation ("SCCF")
1815 N. Broadway, #49
Escondido, CA 92026
contact: Alina Markowski
619-743-3044
dues: $12, $7 jrs.

Rank and File (bimonthly)
Paul Cornelison
same address

Colorado
Colorado State Chess Association
308 Ruxton Ave.
Manitou Springs, CO 80829
contact: Richard Buchanan
719-685-1984
dues: $12, $6 jrs. and srs.

Colorado Chess Informant (quarterly)
Matt DeElena
1473 S. Dudley St.
Lakewood, CO 80232

Connecticut
Connecticut State Chess Assn.
P.O. Box 4726
Waterbury, CT 06704
contact: Rob Roy
203-755-9749
dues: $12, $6 jrs.

Connecticut Chess Magazine (quarterly)
Rob Roy
same address

Delaware
Delaware Chess Association
210 N. Railroad Avenue
Camden/Wyoming, DE 19934
contact: Lyle Milton Baltrusch
302-697-1720
dues: $10

District of Columbia
D.C. Chess League
c/o U.S. Chess Center
1501 M. Street NW
Washington, DC 20005
contact: Ralph Mikell
202-408-1950
dues: $5

King's File (quarterly)
Sam Bisbey
same address

Florida
Florida Chess Association
P.O. Box 5772
Pompano Beach, FL 33074
contact: Bob Smith
305-429-3497
dues: $10, $5 jrs.

Florida Chess News (quarterly)
Donald Schultz
same address

Georgia
Georgia Chess Association
5611 Place Apt. 5
Atlanta, GA 30308
contact: Gary R. Southerland

Hawaii
Hawaii Chess Federation
1253 Mokulua Drive
Kailua, HI 96734
contact: Lawrence Reifurth
808-262-5475
dues: $5

Idaho
Idaho Chess Association
5869 Cobbler Lane
Boise, ID 83703
contact: Dennis Hevener
208-853-2652
dues: $7

Illinois
Illinois Chess Association
P.O. Box 157
Morton Grove, IL 60053
708-466-4886
dues: $14, $8 jrs.

Illinois Chess Bulletin (bimonthly)
Tim Williams
16 W 472 Honeysuckle Rose, #114
Hinsdale, IL 60521
708-887-3706

Indiana
Indiana State Chess Association
1002 Summitview Pl.
Bloomington, IN 47401
contact: Michael Turner
812-331-8331
dues: $10, $6 jrs.

Chess in Indiana (5 times a year)
Jay A. Carr
105 Diplomat Ct. No. 2
Beech Grove, IN 46107

Iowa
Iowa State Chess Association
3208 50th St.
Des Moines, IA 50310
contact: Randy Bauer
515-253-9069
dues: $10, $6 jrs.

Iowa Chess En Passant (quarterly)
John J. Nash
214 SW Arlon Dr.
Ankeny, IA 50021

Kansas
Kansas Chess Association
3500 W. 24th St.
Lawrence, KS 66047
contact: Rich Hodges
913-865-2411
dues: $7, $5 jrs.

Plains Chess (quarterly)
Alan Piper
2720 Epworth Village #4
Hays, KS 67601

Kentucky
Kentucky Chess Association
P. O. Box 35383
Louisville, KY 40232
contact: Stephen Dillard
502-895-1779
dues: $8, $4 jrs. and srs.

Kentucky Chess News (quarterly)
6101 Upland Rd.
Louisville, KY 40206

Louisiana
Louisiana Chess Association
2551 Whippletree Dr.
Harvey, LA 70058
contact: Robert Ballard
504-340-3447 (evenings)
dues: $10

Maine
Maine Chess Association
68 Prospect St.
Portland, ME 04103
contact: Stuart Laughlin
207-772-4103
dues: $12, $6 jrs.

Chess Horizons (bimonthly)
Joe Sparks
40 Boston St.
Somerville, MA 02143
617-623-5619

Maryland
Maryland Chess Association, Inc.
14919 Belle Ami Dr.
Laurel, MD 20707
contact: Allen Beadle
301-776-0488
dues: $5, $3 jrs.

Maryland Chess Newsletter (quarterly)
Kurt Eschbach
410-360-6341
mdchess@aol.com

Massachusetts
Massachusetts Chess Association
19 Glen Street #2
Malden, MA 02148
contact: Gus Gosselin
617-397-0919
dues: $10, $5 jrs.

Chess Horizons (bimonthly)
Joe Sparks
40 Boston St.
Somerville, MA 02143
617-623-5619

Michigan
Michigan Chess Association
27519 E. River Rd.
Grosse Ile, MI 48138
contact: Peter C. Nixon
313-676-2985
dues: $12, $6 jrs. and srs.

Michigan Chess (bimonthly)
David Moody
7500 Anthony
Dearborn, MI 48126

Minnesota
Minnesota State Chess Association
401 E. Burnsville Pkwy #236
Burnsville, MN 55337
contact: Phillip R. Smith
612-890-2644
dues: $7, $4 jrs.

Minnesota Chess Journal (quarterly)
Northern Chess News (bimonthly)
Phillip R. Smith
same address

Mississippi
Mississippi Chess Association
125 Ferry Drive
Brandon, MS 39042
contact: George Brooks
601-825-4848

Missouri
Missouri Chess Association
4255 Louisiana Ave.
St. Louis, MO 63111
contact: Tim Blaco
314-842-2407
dues: $9

Montana
Montana Chess Association
453 Minnesota
Missoula, MT 59802
contact: Sherwood Moore
406-728-1695
dues: $6, $3 jrs., $50 patrons

Montana Chess News (bimonthly)
P.O. Box 3984
Missoula, MT 59806

Nebraska
Nebraska State Chess Association
14002 Frederick Circle
Omaha, NE 68138
contact: Bruce Draney
402-896-2003
dues: $6, $3 jrs.

The Gambit (bimonthly)
Kent Nelson
same address

Nevada
Nevada Chess Inc.
1905 Oakleaf Lane
Las Vegas, NV 89102
contact: Allen P. Magruder
702-871-7088
dues: $5

Nevada Chess Newsletter
4971 San Rafael Ave.
Las Vegas, NV 89120

New Hampshire

New Hampshire Chess Association
252 E. High St. No. 3
Manchester, NH 03104
contact: Ray Dubois
603-627-3541
dues: $10, $6 jrs.

Chess Horizons (bimonthly)
Joe Sparks
40 Boston St.
Somerville, MA 02143
617-623-5619

New Jersey

New Jersey State Chess Federation
25 Beacon St.
Haworth, NJ 07641
contact: Harrison Coleman
dues: $10, $15 out of state, $6 jrs., $8 srs.

Atlantic Chess News (bimonthly)
David Burris
31 Dogwood Rd.
Morris Plains, NJ 07960
201-644-4662

New Mexico

New Mexico Chess Association
P.O. Box 9285
Albuquerque, NM 87119
contact: Wm. C. Moffatt
505-844-7062
dues: $7, $4 jrs.

Desert Knight (3 issues a year)
Victor L. Winter, Tim D. Pointon
same address

New York

New York State Chess Assn.
P.O. Box 340511
Brooklyn, NY 11234
contact: Alan Benjamin
718-336-3988
dues: $8, $6 jrs.

Empire Chess (quarterly)
Carrie Goldstein
7 Briarcliff Lane
Glen Cove, NY 11542

North Carolina

North Carolina Chess Assn.
6705 Terry Lane
Charlotte, NC 28215
contact: Nolan Tomboulian
704-383-7271
tomboulian@aol.com
dues: $10, $8 jrs.

Carolina Gambit (bimonthly)
Karl Ehrsam
4 Craggy Circle
Asheville, NC 28803
704-254-4099

North Dakota

North Dakota Chess Assn.
1438 Fernwood Dr.
Grafton, ND 58237
contact: John K. Allensworth
701-352-0352
dues: $5, $3 jrs.

North Dakota Chess Assn. Newsletter
(quarterly)
Dale Sailer
3207 E. Elmwood Dr.,
Grand Forks, ND 58201
701-775-6692

Ohio
Ohio Chess Association
7722 Lucerne Blvd. # N35
Middlebury Hts., OH 44130
contact: James Pechac
jpechac@aol.com
216-826-3054
dues: $12, $8 jrs.

Ohio Chess Bulletin (bimonthly)
same address

Oklahoma
Oklahoma Chess Association
4842 Clearview Circle
Bartlesville, OK 74006
contact: Steve Wharry
918-335-1072
dues: $6

OK Chess Bulletin (quarterly)
Andy Olsen
2404 Old Farm Lane
Edmond, OK 73013

Oregon
Oregon Chess Federation
P.O. Box 77
Dorena, OR 97434
contact: Mike Vaughn
503-946-1373

Northwest Chess (monthly)
Matthew Goshen
6085 Bethel Hts. Rd. NW
Salem, OR 97304
503-361-1247

Pennsylvania
Pennsylvania State Chess Federation
400 Newtown Rd.
Warminster, PA 18974
contact: Ira Lee Riddle
215-674-9049, 674-8892
dues: $5, $3 jrs.

The Penns Wood Pusher (quarterly)
same address

Rhode Island
Rhode Island Chess Association
20 Reservoir Rd.
Cumberland, RI 02864
contact: Howard W. Cook
401-333-6942
dues: $10, $5 jrs.

Chess Horizons (bimonthly)
Joe Sparks
40 Boston St.
Somerville, MA 02143
617-623-5619

South Carolina
South Carolina Chess Association
564 Rainbow Circle
West Columbia, SC 29170
contact: Robert J. McCrary
803-935-6394

Palmetto Chess (quarterly)
Dr. M. Lee Hyder
33 Longwood Rd.
Aiken, SC 29801

South Dakota
South Dakota Chess Association
P.O. Box 1053
Rapid City, SD 57709
contact: Terry Dean Likens
605-348-1015
dues: $10, $3 jrs.

Tennessee
Tennessee Chess Association
P.O. Box 381
Crossville, TN 38557
contact: Harry Sabine
615-484-9593
dues: $6, $4 jrs.

Texas
Texas Chess Association
P.O. Box 1427
Austin, TX 78767
contact: Michael Simpson
512-472-6453
dues: $10, $7.50 jrs., $12.50 srs./foreign,
$15 family, $25 patron

Texas Knights
Selby Anderson
P.O. Box 501
Helotes, TX 78923

Utah
Utah Chess Association
574 K Street
Salt Lake City, UT 84103
contact: Kent Lindquist
801-595-8432
dues: none

En Passant (quarterly)
Paul LaCourse
4445 S 1950 W, No. 23
Roy, UT 84067
801-731-3672

Vermont
Vermont Chess Association
22 Whitewater Circle
Williston, VT 05495
contact: Alan M. Byington
802-879-0198
dues: $12, $6 jrs.

Thursday Knights
Taylor Kingston
1 Wild Ginger Lane
Shelburne, VT 05482
802-660-2150

Virginia
Virginia Chess Federation
3430 Musket Drive
Midlothian, VA 23113
contact: Helen Hinshaw
804-272-3000
dues: $10, $5 jrs.

Virginia Chess Newsletter (bimonthly)
Macon Shibut
2101 N. Harrison St.
Arlington, VA 22205

Washington
Washington Chess Federation
P.O. Box 84746
Seattle, WA 98124
contact: Ollie LaFreniere
206-634-2318
fax: 206-547-7001
dues: $20, $13 jrs.

Northwest Chess (monthly)
Matthew Goshen
6085 Bethel Hts. Rd. NW.
Salem, OR 97304
503-361-1247

West Virginia
West Virginia Chess Association
4375 Bowman Hill Rd.
Huntington, WV 25701
contact: Thomas O. Bergquist
Buckhannon, WV 26201
304-529-1986
dues: $7, $4 jrs.

West Virginia Bulletin (quarterly)
Thomas LaBue
Rte. 3, Box 372
Huntington, WV 25701

Wisconsin
Wisconsin Chess Association
201 Liberty St. #3
Mauston, WI 53948
contact: Mike Nietman
608-847-7333
dues: $1

Wyoming
Wyoming Chess Association
1736-A Private Dr.
FW AFB
Cheyenne, WY 82005
contact: Brian L. Walker
307-634-0163
dues: $5, $2.50 jrs.

International Tournament Chess

The international governing body in chess is called the *Fédération Internationale des Échecs* (FIDE, pronounced fee-day). FIDE is comprised of the member nations of the world who pay dues and elect FIDE officials. FIDE supervises the world championship and Chess Olympiads, where countries send teams to compete. FIDE also awards titles to individual players. These titles are:

✔ **Grandmaster:** The grandmaster (GM) title is the highest title awarded by FIDE and is earned by turning in sufficient performances (called norms) in competition with players who already own the title.

The FIDE/PCA Split

In 1993, the FIDE world championship match was supposed to be between champion Gary Kasparov and England's Nigel Short, Kasparov's rightful challenger. However, Kasparov was not happy with the prize fund and helped to found the Professional Chess Association (PCA).

The Kasparov-Short match was held under the auspices of the PCA, and FIDE was left with a sham match between two players whom Short had defeated already. Kasparov won the match convincingly and defended his title against Anand of India in 1995. The primary sponsor of the PCA was Intel — but Intel withdrew its support recently, and the future of the PCA is in doubt.

Negotiations for a reunification match, between Kasparov and the FIDE champion Karpov, are currently underway, but it is not clear what the eventual outcome will be. Kasparov had tried getting around FIDE once before with the Grandmaster Association (GMA, established in 1987) but ended up abandoning that organization when it no longer served his interests.

These goings-on call into question a fundamental historical division in chess: Does the title of world champion belong to the title holder or to the organization that grants it?

- ✔ **International Master:** The international master (IM) title is the next highest and is also achieved by making norms in events that include a sufficient number of grandmasters or international masters.

- ✔ **FIDE Master:** The FIDE master (FM) title is the third and last awarded by FIDE, and is awarded to players who maintain a rating of 2,300 or above in FIDE sanctioned events.

Ratings

Ratings in chess are a measure of expected performance versus known opposition. FIDE ratings are sometimes referred to as *ELO ratings* after one of its prime developers, Arpad Elo.

The USCF uses a similar rating system, which is generally fifty to seventy points higher than the FIDE one. The USCF system divides the rating population into classes as shown in Table 14-1.

Sandbaggers

When high-fee, high-class prize tournaments became popular, some chess players tried to manipulate their own ratings. These players would intentionally lose rating points in low-cost events in order to play in a class below their true strength in the big-money tournaments — with the hope of defeating weaker competition and collecting relatively large cash prizes. This un-ethical practice is referred to as *sandbagging*. Calling a player a sandbagger is one of the worst insults in chess!

Table 14-1	USCF Rating System
Points	*Class*
2,400 and up	Senior Master
2,200-2,399	Master
2,000-2,199	Expert
1,800-1,999	Class A
1,600-1,799	Class B
1,400-1,599	Class C
1,200-1,399	Class D
1,199 and below	Class E

The average tournament player has a rating in the Class C range. This is actually a fairly high rating because tournament players tend to be quite serious about their chess. Casual players might be very strong, of course, but usually active tournament players tend to be the strongest in the country.

The USCF class system has led to the development of class prizes. This means that a typical Swiss System tournament will offer cash prizes in each of the rating divisions, which allows the organizer to demand high entry fees. This setup can lead to a sort of ruthless competition, which is another reason to start out in clubs or smaller events, where the competition is still fierce — but more friendly.

Correspondence Chess

Correspondence chess (or as it is sometimes called, *postal chess*) is generally played by sending postcards through the mail. Clearly, you have to know chess notation in order to participate (and I explain it in Chapter 17). Correspondence chess is an excellent way to find opponents from outside your geographical area. But beware: The games can take quite a long time to complete!

In order to find opponents, you usually need to belong to a postal organization. The USCF has a number of correspondence events, and *Chess Life* often has a column dedicated to postal chess. Magazines are even dedicated to this type of chess competition.

APCT News Bulletin
Helen Warren
P.O. Box 70
Western Springs, IL 60558
American Postal Chess Tournaments

Chess Correspondent
Jerry Honn
Box 3481
Barrington, IL 60011
Correspondence Chess League of America

NOSTalgia
Ronleigh Dale
700 South Shafter Avenue 101
Shafter, CA 93263
kNights of the Square Table

International correspondence organizations also exist. Further information may be obtained by writing to:

Chess Director Joan Dubois
U.S. Chess
3054 NYS Route 9W
New Windsor, NY 12553

Chapter 15

Computer Chess

· ·

· ·

C omputer chess is a topic that ranges from computers as the adversaries of human chess players to computers as our tutors helping us to play a better game. Computers can even provide the sort of background support that allows us to keep track of everything that chess players need to keep track of! Just what can't they do?

Computers versus Humans

Computer chess used to fascinate me, but now I'm not so keen on it. Certainly computers are playing a stronger game, but the point is that they are not really playing chess. They're simply performing calculations.

I can hear the peanut gallery now, "Duh, computers are supposed to calculate!" Nevertheless, this is an important distinction. In the old days, chess was used as the ideal application for artificial intelligence (AI). The reasoning was that, if an artificial intelligence could be created to play chess like a human did, we would have made a huge advance in understanding how the human mind worked. At that point other simulations would be possible, or at least so the thinking went.

The triumph of the number crunchers

However, the emphasis in computer chess has shifted from playing a chess game like a human would to simply playing as well as possible. This is far less interesting to me. The early AI approach was to use what were called *heuristics* in order to try to map out the game the way a human would. Other approaches were simply crunching numbers. Early on, both approaches seemed equally valid because both led to equally bad play.

Soon, however, the speed of the modern computers increased many times over, and the number crunchers triumphed. Nowadays, little effort is made to have a computer play like a human would play. Instead, programmers simply try to calculate as many positions (or *ply* in computerspeak) as possible.

This to me is the crucial difference. I can play stupidly. A computer can only play mindlessly. If a computer could play stupidly, that would be something to write home about. It would be playing like a human.

The other thing that bugs me about computer chess is that people keep thinking of it in terms of man versus machine. This is just silly. Humans are doing something completely different from computers when they try to play a chess game. It doesn't matter who plays better any more than it matters that an automobile can go faster than the best human sprinter in the world.

Besides, the computer programmers are humans too, aren't they? I mean, sure they may not be the life of the company party, but they are people, after all. This isn't so much human versus machine, as unarmored human versus armored human. What's the big deal about that?

Of course, the public is intrigued by this man-machine confrontation, just as people have always been interested in the plight of organic life versus inorganic technology. Who among us would've rooted for the tractor over the horse? But this is stating the problem incorrectly, as dramatic as it may be to do so. Machines do not tire. They do not worry. They do not truly compete. The essence of the drama of human competition is missing when a machine is involved — and that is why human chess matches will always fascinate me far more than those involving the computers.

Kasparov takes on Deep Blue

For those who are interested in the progress made by the computer in challenging for the world championship, you can have a look at the last game from the 1995 match between champion Kasparov and Deep Blue. In order to follow the game, you need to be familiar with chess notation, which I explain in Chapter 17.

If you want to jump ahead to the chapter on chess notation, set up your chessboard, and follow along with the moves, you'll see that Kasparov shows how to play positionally — and completely outplays the machine.

G. Kasparov versus Deep Blue

1. Nf3	d5		23. Qd3	g6
2. d4	c6		24. Re2	Nf5
3. c4	e6		25. Bc3	h5
4. Nbd2	Nf6		26. b5	Nce7
5. e3	c5		27. Bd2	Kg7
6. b3	Nc6		28. a4	Ra8
7. Bb2	cxd4		29. a5	a6
8. exd4	Be7		30. b6	Bb8
9. Rc1	0-0		31. Bc2	Nc6
10. Bd3	Bd7		32. Ba4	Re7
11. 0-0	Nh5		33. Bc3	Ne5
12. Re1	Nf4		34. dxe5	Qxa4
13. Bb1	Bd6		35. Nd4	Nxd4
14. g3	Ng6		36. Qxd4	Qd7
15. Ne5	Rc8		37. Bd2	Re8
16. Nxd7	Qxd7		38. Bg5	Rc8
17. Nf3	Bb4		39. Bf6+	Kh7
18. Re3	Rfd8		40. c6	bxc6
19. h4	Nge7		41. Qc5	Kh6
20. a3	Ba5		42. Rb1	Qb7
21. b4	Bc7		43. Rb4	1-0
22. c5	Re8			

I'm no Luddite though. Computers certainly have their place. In fact, computers are essential for a chess player who wants to compete well in the highest levels of chess. Players are more likely to lug a laptop computer to a tournament these days than a set and board. There are several different categories of computer chess, each with their distinct uses and admirers.

The Harvard Cup and Aegon

For those who really enjoy the human versus machine contest, two annual events should fit the bill. The Harvard Cup pits some of the best programs versus grandmasters. The grandmasters are winning by about a two to one margin. In 1995 the top scoring programs were Virtual Chess and Chessmaster 4000. The top humans were Joel Benjamin and Michael Rhode.

The 11th annual Aegon tournament took place April 10–17, 1996, and matched fifty computer programs with fifty humans of varying strength. The computers won the six-round event by a score of 162.5–137.5. However, Grandmaster Yasser Seirawan, of Seattle, won all six of his games. The top computer programs, finishing with 4.5 out of 6, were Capture, Nimzo, Now, Quest, and Rebel 7.

Chess Playing PC Programs

Many commercially available chess playing programs are available, and the best one isn't necessarily the strongest one. Almost all the programs can defeat 99 percent of the tournament players in rapid chess. Most of them can beat masters even at slower time controls. The best program for you will depend upon what you want most from it.

The chess world is mostly DOS- or Windows-based. These programs will be noticeably stronger than the ones for other platforms, but Mac users can have their fun, too.

Chessmaster 5000

Chessmaster 5000 from Mindscape, Inc., as seen in Figure 15-1, has the best combination of affordability and features (including instruction and playing strength). You can't go wrong with this one. (Call Mindscape, Inc., at 800-866-5967 if you want more information.) Programmer: Johan de Konig. A new Mac version of Chessmaster was scheduled for release in 1996.

M-Chess Pro 5.0

This program won the title of Absolute Microcomputer Chess Champion in the 1995 competition held in Paderborn, Germany. M-Chess Pro 5.0 also is compatible with other computer-based chess training programs such as Book-up and Chess Assistant (see the section on "Chess Databases"). Programmer: Marty Hirsch.

Figure 15-1   (Chessmaster and Mindscape are registered trademarks of Mindscape, Inc.)

Chess Genius 4.0

Chess Genius has been considered to be the strongest playing program over the last few years but has recently been nosed out by M-Chess Pro 5.0. This program has extensive online help facilities and is Windows-based. Programmer: Richard Lang.

Rebel 7.0

This very strong program supports many database formats and includes many other useful features. It's recommended that, in order to get the maximum playing strength out of the program, a computer with Windows 95 should be started in DOS mode. Programmer: Ed Schroder.

Chess Playing Mac Programs

The Mac platform has some contenders as well. Overall, however, the PC environment has more variety and stronger playing programs.

HIARCS 1.0 MAC

This is the first professional playing program to be ported to the Mac. HIARCS is full featured and very strong. Power PC users will want to install Speed Doubler to maximize its playing strength. Programmer: Mark Iniacke.

Sargon V

My first chess-playing program was a version of Sargon running on an Apple IIe. Needless to say, things have gotten much better since then. Much cheaper than HIARCS, Sargon still plays pretty darn well. Programmers: Dan and Kathe Spracklen.

MacChess 2.0

The best thing about this program is that it is freeware. It's strong and comes with many features. How can you go wrong? Programmers: W.A. Beusekom.

Chess Playing Stand-Alones

If you don't own a computer, you can still get a strong and tireless playmate. There are many stand-alone models to choose from. The penthouse crowd will opt for TASC R-30 Version 2.5, with its autosensory board and $2,500 price tag. The rest of us will have to settle for portable or desktop models from Novag, Saitek, or Excalibur.

Chess Databases

A chess database is just like a regular database that sorts information. In this case, the information relates to chess — chess games, chess players, and so on. If you would like to see all the games Kasparov played in 1990, for example, you can sort the database to list only those games. The sort combinations are quite extensive and allow you to zero in on your areas of special interest. Of course, you are generally charged for the data (the games, for example) and for the program that performs the sort operations.

Serious chess players care about this data; they want as many games as possible in a format that makes them easy to both sort and play over. The two main databases that I've worked with are *ChessBase* and *Chess Assistant*. Both have fanatical followings and both think that they're the best. If you want a few hundred thousand games for a few hundred dollars, you can't go wrong with either. ChessBase also has a version for the Mac.

Another system available for both platforms is *Book-UP*. This program uses a different approach than the others and concentrates on chess openings. If you have a computer and you want the best resource for drilling yourself on your favorite openings, Book-UP is the program to buy.

Computer-Assisted Chess Instruction

Most of the chess software that is available is designed for the serious player. Although manufacturers often try to build in instruction for the less advanced player, it is usually as an afterthought. Two programs that I am aware of, and have reviewed, were specifically designed to make use of the computer's abilities to assist in instruction. This field has a great deal of promise but as yet seems relatively underdeveloped.

The Chess Starter

A simple Windows-based help file has been developed by Good Morning Teacher publishing. A help file is easy to use, runs on any Windows based platform, and is an effective way to teach the absolute beginner the basics. The number is 415-342-6700, and e-mail inquires may be directed to lorem@aol.com.

Chess Mentor

The absolute best use of computer-assisted instruction (CAI) that I've ever seen has to be the Chess Mentor program from Aficionado, Inc. This program really will improve your chess because it is a learning-tool first and a CAI program second. Reach Aficionado, Inc., at 800-465-9301 (or e-mail to info@chess.com).

For the most complete computer chess product review, subscribe to *Web Computer Chess Reports* on the World Wide Web. A subscription costs only $25 per year (unlimited access) and can be ordered by calling 800-645-4710. *Web Computer Chess Reports* includes reviews and articles. Find this information online at http://www.ICDchess.com.

Chapter 16
Chess Online

*T*he thing to remember about the Internet is that it is always changing. New sites pop up and old ones go away, especially in the chess world. Search engines can help you find new sites, and most sites point to others, which point to others, and so on. But once you get connected to a particular site, it's time to start surfing.

I assume that you know enough about the Internet to reach the sites listed in this chapter. If you don't know the ins and outs of the Internet, there's a great book in a popular series that you might want to check out (*The Internet For Dummies,* 4th Edition, by John R. Levine, Carol Baroudi, and Margaret Levine Young, from IDG Books Worldwide, Inc.).

World Wide Web Chess Sites

The fastest growing segment of the Internet is the Web, and chess on the Web is no exception. Just about any chess player can create a personal Web page, but a few sites stand head and shoulders above the rest.

Frequently Asked Questions

http://www.clark.net/pub/pribut/chess.html

Everyone has to start someplace — and it might as well be here because this place is a handy guide to what every beginner needs to know about chess on the Internet. This site is organized in a frequently-asked-questions (FAQ) way and is based on vast experience in addressing the needs of the Internet chess newcomer. Pointers lead to other reference information, as well.

This Week in Chess

http://www.tcc.net/twic/twic.html

This outstanding service is usually referred to as TWIC. It contains the most current information about what's going on in the chess world and is an outstanding source for finding games played in national or international events. The index provided will point you directly to your specific area of interest.

U.S. Chess Online

http://www.uschess.org

The United States Chess Federation has its own Web site. This is a good place to start Web surfing. It contains most of the information you need to get involved in organized chess in the United States as well as pointers to other sites of interest. (See Figure 16-1.)

Figure 16-1

Inside Chess

http://www.tcc.net/chess/chess.html

This site is the electronic version of a truly terrific magazine for the advanced player. Publisher Yasser Seirawan is also a grandmaster. Inside Chess contains both high-level analysis and purchasing information for books and equipment. (See Figure 16-2.)

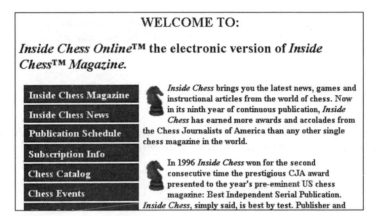

Figure 16-2

Hundreds of chess-related Web sites exist — and after you get into the system, it will be hard to get out. (I recommend that your Internet provider give you unlimited access for a flat fee!)

Chess Forums

If you're interested in debate and opinion, these forums are the places to be. There are five newsgroups (forums for information and opinion) related to chess.

rec.games.chess.play-by-e-mail

This newsgroup is devoted to the electronic version of correspondence chess.

rec.games.chess.computer

This newsgroup covers both the computers that play chess and the programmers behind the curtains.

`rec.games.chess.politics`

This newsgroup is especially interesting to those involved with chess governance on a national or international level.

`rec.games.chess.analysis`

Here is the newsgroup to go to in order to find descriptions of games and positions.

`rec.games.chess.misc`

This newsgroup is for everything not specifically covered in the others. The opinions are wide ranging, and just about any chess topic goes.

Chess and FTP

Some excellent sites are available through File Transfer Protocol (FTP). Usually sites have a `read.me` document that helps you understand what the home ground rules are.

One excellent site is the host `caissa.onenet.net`. Here are some of the directories contained on that site:

`pub/chess`	General chess directory
`pub/chess/PGN`	Portable Game Notation (PGN) directory
`pub/chess/PGN/Standard`	ASCII version of the PGN Standard
`pub/chess/PGN/Standard.TOC`	Table of Contents for the preceding
`pub/chess/PGN/Events`	Directory of directories of events by year
`pub/chess/PGN/Players`	Directory with many PGN games by player
`pub/chess/Tests`	Directory with many chess program test positions
`pub/chess/Tests/Manifest`	Description of EPD test files
`pub/chess/PGN/Tools`	PGN tools and utilities directory
`pub/chess/Unix/SAN.tar.gz`	Standard Algebraic Notation source kit

A personal favorite of mine is the University of Pittsburgh site. The address is: `ftp.pitt.edu`

Bulletin Board Systems (BBSs)

Chess Bulletin Board systems were the predecessors to the Web sites. They still provide a useful vehicle for access to chess files and information but are generally more primitive in nature. They are also closed systems, which means that you can only get information the BBS operator (called a sysop) arranges for you to see.

Canada

- Alberta: Chess Hackers (403-456-5808)

USA

- CompuServe (800-848-8990)
- HoloNet: 800-NET-HOLO (800-638-4656)
- Prodigy (800-284-5933)
- ImagiNation Network (800-IMAGIN-1)
- CA: Charles Rostedt's chess BBS (data: 310-634-8549, voice: 634-8477)
- CA: Chess Hotline BBS (310-634-8549)
- CA: Strategies and Tactics (714-458-0818)
- Berkeley, CA: Berkeley BBS (510-486-0795)
- Modesto, CA: Flightline of dBASE (209-551-2227)
- Waterbury, CT: Chess Horizons BBS (203-596-1443, voice: 755-9749)
- Plant City, FL: The ChessBoard (813-754-6043)
- Chicago, IL: ChessBoard (312-784-3019)
- IL: Free! Board (312-275-0848)
- Louisville, KY: The Chess Board (502-271-5233)
- Metairie, LA: High Tech BBS (504-837-7941)
- New Orleans, LA: Woodpusher BBS (504-271-5233)
- Chevy Chase, MD: The Mystery Board BBS (301-588-9465, 588-8142)
- Fort Meade, MD: Interstate Express (301-674-6835)
- Durham, NC: The Isolated Pawn (919-471-1440)
- Brooklyn, NY: The Round Table BBS (718-951-6652)

- ✔ Columbus, OH: The Endgame BBS (614-476-3351)

- ✔ Mansfield, OH: DK Jet-Works (419-524-3959)

- ✔ Mansfield, OH: Procyon (419-524-7825)

- ✔ Portland, OR: PDX Chess BBS (503-232-2282)

- ✔ Erie, PA: The Basement (814-838-7344, 838-8237)

- ✔ Austin, TX: Austin Chess Studio (512-448-4861)

Playing Chess on the Net with Telnet

The Internet Chess Servers (ICS) was originally developed by Michael Moore (mmoore@dsd.es.com). Two primary servers are in the United States, ICC and FICS. ICC and FICS allow interactive chess games for those with Internet telnet capability. Use telnet to connect (for example, telnet chess.lm.com 5000 or telnet ics.onenet.net 5000).

Note that this is not e-mail chess, this is *real time*. Players are from all over the world, and somebody is always ready for a game.

ICC (Internet Chess Club)

To play on the ICC (USA), all you need to do is type the following:

telnet chess.lm.com 5000

You will be asked for a name. Type in any name you want.

You will then be logged in as an "unregistered" player.

If you want a "registered" account, type help registration and follow the directions. The fee is $49, with half price for students. Unregistered users can play for free, but there are some good reasons to register:

- ✔ A new program called *timestamp* became available in the Spring of 1995, and it limits or eliminates delays. Timestamp is available only to registered members of the ICC.

- ✔ Special events sometimes require you to be registered, and if you are registered, your games can be saved.

- ✔ You can have access to most of the games played on this system, which is well worth the price of admission.

- ✔ You must be registered in order to get a rating.

One grandmaster told me that playing on the Internet was more fun than watching a comedy show on television because people can comment on the games in progress and argue with one another.

FICS (Free Internet Chess Server)

A new location for FICS appeared at `ics.onenet.net 5000` in 1995. This chess server was begun in response to the institution of charges at ICC.

The old net is alive and well here, where people not only play for free but also sometimes provide free programming code to improve the software. The competition for features rages alive and well between the two servers.

ICS (Internet Chess Server) addresses

Euro Server	`anemone.daimi.aau.dk 5000`	(130.225.18.58 5000)
US Server	`chess.lm.com 5000`	(164.58.253.10 5000)
U.S. FICS	`ics.onenet.net 5000`	
Dutch Server	`dds.hacktic.nl 5000`	(193.78.33.69 5000)
Aussie Server	`lux.latrobe.edu.au 5000`	(131.172.4.3 5000)

ICS (Internet Chess Server) backup servers: unsaved games

```
telnet iris4.metiu.ucsb.edu 5000
telnet coot.lcs.mit.edu 5000
```

E-Mail Chess on the Net

Chess through e-mail is a bit more leisurely than interactive play. All you need is for one person to act as the tournament director and to provide you with the address of another person who is also looking to play (one or more) games in this fashion.

International E-mail Chess Group (IECG)

The International E-mail Chess Group has a Web site full of information on playing chess by e-mail. Visit the site at `http://www.ub.uit.no/chess/ iecg/iecginfo.html`

International E-mail Chess Club (IECC)

This group was founded and is run by Lisa Powell (`drpowell@uoguelph.ca`). To join, e-mail her and include the following information:

> *First name and last name*
>
> *Country*
>
> *Current or past rating, and from what chess organization (or your best guesstimate)*
>
> *Activities you elect to participate in.*

The last word on this section has yet to be written. The Internet technology is ever changing, as are the site managers and information providers. A vast amount of material is available on the net — but be advised that the way to find information today may be out of date tomorrow.

Chapter 17

Chess Notation
(What the Heck Does Nf4 Mean?)

In This Chapter

▶ Using notation for the chessboard and pieces

▶ Keeping track of the moves

▶ Eliminating ambiguity in notation

▶ Writing chess shorthand

▶ Following chess in a newspaper column

Chess history is preserved for us through the use of *notation*. There are many kinds of notation, from forsythe (a notation that computers understand), to different ones for different languages; but one kind of notation is universally understood. The universally accepted form of chess notation is called *algebraic*. This notation system replaced the older English *descriptive* notation, because chess is for people, not just the English speaking people. Algebraic notation is the one to learn.

Algebraic notation assigns a letter to each piece and a letter and number to each square on the chessboard. Sure, algebraic notation looks goofy and is hard to make sense of at first — but believe me, it just takes a bit of practice.

Chessboard Notation at a Glance

In chess, rows are called *ranks* and columns are called *files*. I introduce this concept in Chapter 1, but I'll give you a quick refresher lesson here. In any case, you may want to check out my diagrams in Chapter 1.

The bottom rank is called the first rank, the next rank is called the second rank, and so on. The first rank is indicated in Figure 17-1. The second rank is indicated in Figure 17-2. This numbering is the same all the way through the eighth rank.

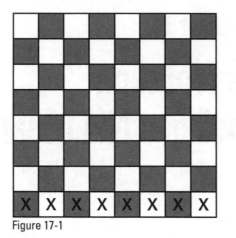

Figure 17-1

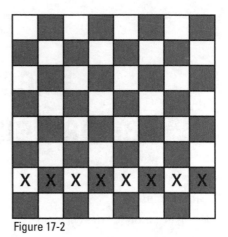

Figure 17-2

The files are indicated by letters starting with the a-file, as shown in Figure 17-3. The b-file is shown in Figure 17-4. This lettering is the same all the way across the board, ending with the h-file.

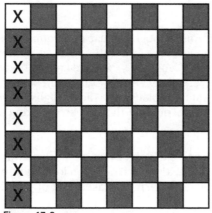

Figure 17-3

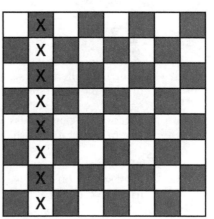

Figure 17-4

The chessboard can be thought of as being made up of individual squares, each with its own name, ranging from a1 to h8. Now you can refer to each square by a *letter-number* combination indicating a file-rank (see Figure 17-5). Most of us have played Bingo, where every square has a letter and a number, or Battleship, where every spot in the ocean is kept track of in the same manner. Of course, in Battleship you get to see only your pieces and have to guess where your opponent's are. In chess, you know where the pieces are already — you just have to guess where they're going to move to!

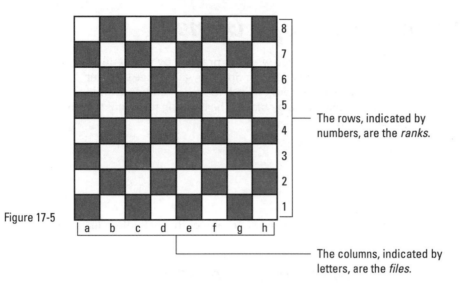

Figure 17-5

The rows, indicated by numbers, are the *ranks*.

The columns, indicated by letters, are the *files*.

Keeping Track of the Pieces

As with each square for a chessboard, each chess piece also needs to be referred to by some notation. The king is indicated by K, the knight by N (since K was taken!) and so on. The pawn, poor thing, is not given any identification. Table 17-1 shows the notation for the pieces.

Table 17-1	Chess Notation
Piece	*Notation*
King	K
Queen	Q
Bishop	B
Knight	N
Rook	R

The letters must be capitalized to indicate a piece, otherwise they indicate a square. Don't forget that the pawn is not really a piece, and as a further insult the pawn doesn't even get a notation! If no piece is indicated by the notation, it's assumed that the move in question involves a pawn.

Writing the Moves of a Game

Take a look at how this notation works in practice by examining one of the most common openings, the Ruy Lopez, or Spanish, game (see Chapter 20 for information on this opening move). Each move is numbered and includes one move by white and one move by black. The opening moves of the Ruy Lopez are written like this:

1. e4   e5

2. Nf3   Nc6

3. Bb5

In the following sections, I explain what each of these notation lines means.

A typical opening in notation

1. e4   e5

Remember, the absence of a piece designation means that it is a pawn move. White moves first, followed by black. Only one pawn can move to e4 for white and only one to e5 for black. Figure 17-6 shows where white and then black have moved the pawns.

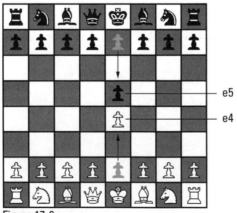

Figure 17-6

2. Nf3   Nc6

Because the king has taken the letter K for his notation, the knight uses N (which follows along with the pronunciation, anyway!). Now, the white knight moves to f3 and the black knight moves to c6, as seen in Figure 17-7.

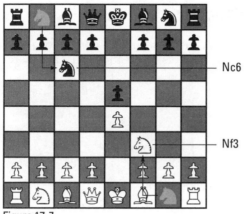

— Nc6

— Nf3

Figure 17-7

3. *Bb5*

Now, white moves the bishop out to attack the knight. Remember that a capital B means bishop, and a lowercase b means b-file. Figure 17-8 shows the white bishop moving out to the b5 square. And notice that I haven't given the corresponding black move here. Because I give just the white move, I can also give the black move alone (but still next to a "3." because it is part of the third set of moves). However, if I give the black move alone, I need to precede it with an ellipsis (...). You can see an example of this convention in the next section.

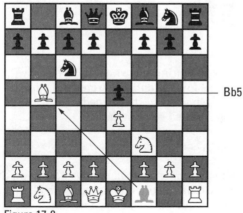

— Bb5

Figure 17-8

Indicating captures

To indicate a capture with chess notation, you use an "x" along with the name of the square the capture is made on. This convention will make more sense in the following example that I use.

Imagine that the game begins like this:

1. e4 e5

2. d4

These first moves are shown in Figure 17-9.

The second move that white makes is the pawn to d4.

Figure 17-9

Black would have the option of capturing the white pawn on d4 with its pawn. This capture would be written as follows and illustrated in Figure 17-10. (Remember that a black move written without the preceding white move is indicated by the use of the ellipsis, as I've done here.)

2. ...exd (or 2. ...exd4, which is more precise)

Either notation is OK, because the black pawn can only capture on that one square on the d-file. You may also have noticed that only the file (e), not the file-rank (e5), of the attacking pawn is given. That's because black has just one pawn on this e-file.

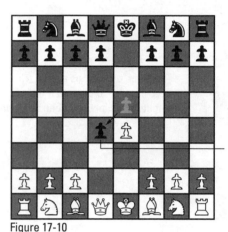

On black's second move, the black pawn moves from the e-file to the d-file to capture the white pawn on d4.

Figure 17-10

Sometimes in place of the notation *2. ...exd* you will see simply *2. ...ed*. People who do notation this way don't think it is necessary to indicate captures, but most of us think that using the x to indicate a capture makes following the game easier. In any case, you may see either convention used in other chess books.

More notation practice

To go back to the Ruy Lopez for a moment, one common variation is called the *exchange variation*. This is when white captures the black knight with the bishop (or exchanges the bishop for the knight). See whether you can follow some of this following notation on your own chessboard.

1. e4   e5

2. Nf3   Nc6

3. Bb5   a6

4. Bxc6

If you were able to follow those preceding moves, you can tell that white, on its fourth move, captures the black knight that occupied c6. Figure 17-11 shows the result of this capture (and also shows you how your own chessboard should look!).

Now, black can capture the bishop with one of two pawns.

The white bishop has moved from b5 to c6 in order to capture the black knight (which black placed there on its second move).

Figure 17-11

4. ...dxc6

Black has decided to capture the white bishop with its pawn from d7. I must remind you that the ellipsis (...) is used to show a black move without the preceding white move. Take a peek at Figure 17-12 to see the result of all this action. Are your chessmen in the same places on your board as the ones in the figure?

The black pawn moves from d7 to c6 in order to capture the foolhardy white bishop.

Figure 17-12

If you don't need a chessboard to follow this notation, you may be ready for blindfold chess and maybe to take on George Koltanowski's world blindfold record (see the glossary) where you play a game without sight of the board — just by calling out the notation!

Or what if black decides to take the bishop with his pawn from the b7 square instead? I'm going to try this variation now. (I didn't really take my hand off that other pawn!)

4. ...bxc

Remember, I'm showing a variation here; I'm not letting black move twice in a row! If black captures the bishop with the pawn from the b7 square, this is how the notation would read now (4. ...bxc). Figure 17-13 illustrates this setback for the white bishop.

Black may decide to take the white bishop by moving a pawn from b7 to c6.

Figure 17-13

5. 0-0

White's next move may be to castle (see Chapter 9 for castling details). This action would be written as 0-0 and is shown in Figure 17-14. While the notation for castling on the kingside is 0-0, the notation for castling on the queenside is 0-0-0.

Even though algebraic notation tries to keep things as simple as possible, some situations that arise may still be confusing. Some people use the fewest characters possible while still avoiding ambiguity, and others spell things out in more detail.

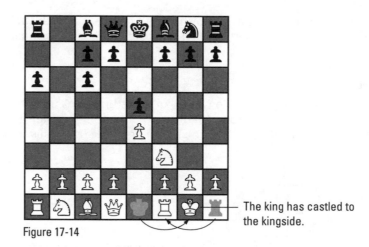

The king has castled to the kingside.

Figure 17-14

Ambiguities (Which Knight, for Pete's Sake?)

For example, what if two pieces can capture on, or move to, the same square? In Figure 17-15, you can see that two knights can move to the same square. Chess players solve that potential dilemma by adding the file to the piece designation, as in N/bd2. This notation means that the knight standing on the b-file is the one that moves to d2.

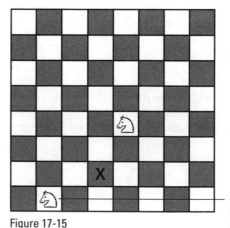

Figure 17-15

Both knights can move to d2, but N/bd2 informs you that the knight on the b-file moves.

But, what if two knights on the b-file can move to d2 (as in Figure 17-16)? To indicate which knight moves in that case, write the entire designation of the originating square, such as: N/b3d2. Or for clarity's sake, write: N/b3-d2. This means that the knight on b3 moves to d2. Don't worry, this doesn't happen all that often! (But when it does, the pesky knights are usually the culprits.)

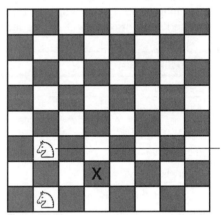

The knight on b3 is the one that moves to d2, as indicated by N/b3d2.

Figure 17-16

CHESS MASTER

Special chess events (no cover charge needed)

You may play lots of games without ever capturing en passant or promoting a pawn (see Chapter 9 for these special moves), but if you do end up doing one or the other (or both), you'll need to be able to write them down correctly.

When capturing en passant, you may have two pawns that could make the same capture. This is not ambiguous, however, because you always indicate the originating file that the capturing pawn is on (*exd,* for example). Very, very rarely, however, it is possible to have two pawns on a file, one which can capture en passant, and one

that can capture normally. This case is handled by adding the abbreviation *e.p.* to the notation as in *exd e.p.,* for example. The lack of the trailing e.p. would indicate that it was the other pawn on that file that made the capture.

Notation accounts for the promotion of a pawn by adding the piece designation to the move. For example, if on your 40th move you played your pawn to the eighth rank on the b-file and promoted it to a queen, you would write: *40. b8Q.* If you promoted to a bishop, for some reason, you would write: *40. b8B.*

Chess Shorthand

Some notation marks aren't needed when writing down your moves during a game, but you can use them to *annotate* a game (that's to say, to comment about a game that has been played previously). These annotations, which usually include symbols, are made to enhance the reader's ability to understand a game and are used in chess books, magazines, and newspaper columns. See Table 17-2 for the most commonly used annotations and their definitions.

Table 17-2	Chess Annotation
Annotation	*Definition*
!	A good move
!!	A very good move
?	A bad move
??	A very bad move
1-0	White won the game
0-1	Black won the game
1/2	The game was a draw
=	The position is considered to be equal
+/-	White is considered to have the advantage
-/+	Black is considered to have the advantage
+	Check
#	Checkmate

Chess in the Newspaper

Many newspapers carry a chess column. Sometimes it is daily, but more frequently it is weekly. Newspapers usually have space constraints and typically give one game and one diagram of a position of special interest. The conventions for newspapers are that white is positioned at the bottom of the diagram and moving up, while black is positioned at the top and moving down. Typically, if a move isn't indicated, white is assumed to be on the move (see Figure 17-17 for a sample of chess in the newspaper).

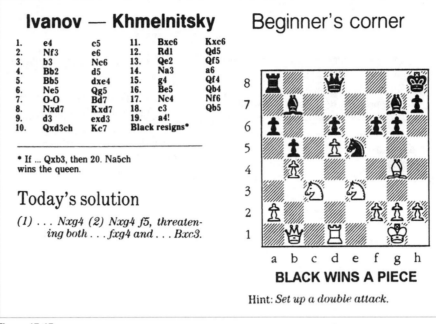

Ivanov — Khmelnitsky

1.	e4	c5	11.	Bxc6	Kxc6
2.	Nf3	e6	12.	Rd1	Qd5
3.	b3	Nc6	13.	Qe2	Qf5
4.	Bb2	d5	14.	Na3	a6
5.	Bb5	dxe4	15.	g4	Qf4
6.	Ne5	Qg5	16.	Be5	Qb4
7.	O-O	Bd7	17.	Nc4	Nf6
8.	Nxd7	Kxd7	18.	c3	Qb5
9.	d3	exd3	19.	a4!	
10.	Qxd3ch	Kc7		Black resigns*	

* If ... Qxb3, then 20. Na5ch
wins the queen.

Today's solution

(1) ... Nxg4 (2) Nxg4 f5, threatening both ... fxg4 and ... Bxc3.

Beginner's corner

BLACK WINS A PIECE

Hint: *Set up a double attack.*

Figure 17-17

Often a diagram is used in a newspaper column to indicate the starting position of a neat combination or problem. This practice is normal when space constraints are a consideration.

Chess notation has an important role in the world of chess. It allows us to record games for posterity and gives us the chance to review the history of the game's development to date. It is required for official competitions — but fortunately, not for games played for fun! See Appendix B for more on the international symbols used in chess.

Keeping score

In a tournament game, both players are required to write down all the moves (called keeping a gamescore). This scorekeeping helps the director settle potential disputes. For example, if one player claims a draw because the same position has occurred three times (a draw according to the rules), the director would use the scoresheet to decide whether this is actually the case. This written record is also used to determine whether players have made the minimum number of moves in a given time period.

Some grandmasters are notorious for their poor handwriting, and it's impossible to make heads or tails of their scoresheets. Tournament officials usually rely on their opponent's scoresheet in order to reconstruct the game. It can be a problem when two players with awful handwriting play one another!

Part V
The Part of Tens

The 5th Wave   By Rich Tennant

"I'm pretty sure that chess program has a lower skill level you can access."

In this part . . .

*I*n this part, I take a look at the best players of all time, the most famous chess games ever played, and the most common chess openings. I also have a section on the ten best chess resources. No one book can do justice to the richness of the game, and I hope you use these resources to continue to learn and improve!

As an added bonus, you can find a handy glossary of chess here, too, along with examples of international chess notation.

Chapter 18

The Ten Most Famous Chess Games

*S*ome games are part of our common chess heritage. Every game here will be familiar to some extent to just about every tournament player, and being able to speak intelligently about them is important. This knowledge establishes your reputation as a good talker — if not a good player!

Most of these games are from a long time ago. There are several reasons why older games appear so often in lists such as these. First, older games have all been included in many more references than the newer ones, and more people are likely to have studied them. Second, everyone today can understand these games — while some of the best games of recent years are more difficult to follow. Lastly, players of long ago did not understand defense as well as we do today, and their lack of defense led to amazing games that are simply not likely to occur in modern competition.

And some of these chess games are so well known that they've even been given names! Of course, many people will have a different list of the top ten most famous games. Maybe even David Letterman!

In order to enjoy these games, you must understand chess notation. See Chapter 17 for my explanation of this notation (and get out your board so that you can follow along better).

When chess players write about chess games, we tend to follow a few simple conventions. The player who played white is listed first, for example. We also generally try to include the place and year of the game, if known, and then we try to give the name of the chess opening. Interestingly enough, for a class of people who claim to be logical, the names of the chess openings are often a subject of debate. This is sort of similar to scientists who want credit for inventing or discovering something when a different scientist also wants to have credit. Quite often, it just comes down to a matter of personal preference. In this book, I use the names that are commonly accepted by chess players in the United States.

Conventions such as these make it easier to know which game in particular is being written about. After all, Gary Kasparov and Anatoly Karpov have played over 160 games of chess against each other. We have to have some way of differentiating among them!

Annotating a famous game is always dangerous. Not only can you be wrong, but you may break the spell these games cast over people the first time they see them. However, I've found it worth taking the risk in most cases, because, for many people, some explanation is better than none.

Adolf Anderssen vs. Lionel Kieseritzky: The Immortal Game

London, 1851 (King's Gambit)

Nowhere is it more evident than in this game that the players of the mid-1800s loved attack first and material last!

1. e4	e5
2. f4	exf4
3. Bc4	Qh4+

Anderssen wishes to develop rapidly, even if it means losing the right to castle.

4. Kf1	b5

Kieseritzky shows an equal disdain for anything other than rapid development.

5. Bxb5	Nf6
6. Nf3	Qh6

Most analysts have roundly criticized this move by Kieseritzky, but the German grandmaster Robert Hübner has demonstrated that it is better than the suggested *6 ....Qh5*.

7. d3

Hübner suggests that *7. Nc3* is better.

7. ...Nh5

7. ...Bc5 has been suggested as superior. These suggestions are not to be taken as evidence that these players were not very good, however. Anderssen and Kieseritzky were simply playing by the principles that were understood at the time. Rapid development and attack were all that really mattered to them.

8. Nh4

This move is sometimes praised as an example of Anderssen's great feel for the attack, but other analysts have decided that *8. Rg1* was even better.

8. ...Qg5

9. Nf5   c6

This last move attacks the bishop and unpins the queen pawn, but perhaps *9. ...g6* — immediately attacking the overly aggressive knight — was better.

10. g4

Hübner suggests that *10. Ba4* was more circumspect.

10. ...Nf6

Again, Kieseritzky should play *g6* attacking the knight.

11. Rg1

11. ...cxb5

Violating the principle of development over material! This is an interesting error by Kieseritzky and, according to Hübner, the decisive mistake. He suggests *11. ...h5*.

12. h4	Qg6
13. h5	Qg5
14. Qf3	Ng8

15. Bxf4   Qf6

16. Nc3   Bc5

17. Nd5

17. d4 would gain a tempo, but then we wouldn't have this brilliant finish.

17. ... Qxb2 (See Figure 18-1.)

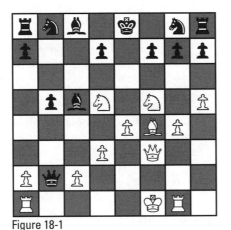

Figure 18-1

18. Bd6

Almost every text gives this move two exclamation points in honor of its brilliance. Hübner, however, gives no fewer than three better moves and gives the move a question mark. Nevertheless, it leads to the following immortal conclusion.

18. ...Bxg1

19. e5   Qxa1+

20. Ke2   Na6

21. Nxg7+   Kd8

22. Qf6+   Nxf6

23. Be7

Checkmate! It is most remarkable to have the few remaining white pieces combine in such a way as to overcome the huge remaining black army. Even if Anderssen and Kieseritzky didn't play the absolute best moves, they certainly played the most entertaining ones!

Adolf Anderssen vs. J. Dufresne: The Evergreen Game

Berlin, 1852 (Evans Gambit)

1. e4	e5
2. Nf3	Nc6
3. Bc4	Bc5
4. b4	Bxb4
5. c3	Ba5
6. d4	exd4
7. 0-0	

The Evans Gambit was an old favorite of the Romantic age players and is still dangerous today. White sacrifices material for an advantage in development and open lines for the pieces.

7. ...d3

This is a weak response. Either *7. ...dxc* or *7. ...d6* would've been better.

8. Qb3	Qf6
9. e5	Qg6

The pawn is immune to capture. If *9. ...Nxe5, 10. Re1 d6, 11.Qb5+* picks up a piece.

10. Re1	Nge7
11. Ba3	b5

In those days, development was considered to be more important than puny amounts of material.

12. Bxb5	Rb8
13. Qa4	Bb6
14. Nbd2	Bb7
15. Ne4	Qf5

This is a difficult position to play correctly, but this last move is simply a waste of time.

    16. Bxd3   **Qh5**

Now Anderssen begins one of the most famous combinations in all of chess history.

    17. Nf6+!   **gxf6**

    18. exf6   **Rg8**

    19. Rad1!

Obviously, Anderssen has already conceived of the brilliant finish.

    19. ...Qxf3 (See Figure 18-2.)

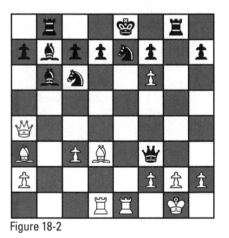

Figure 18-2

One can only speculate whether Dufresne ever saw it coming!

    20. Rxe7+   **Nxe7**

    21. Qxd7+!   **Kxd7**

    22. Bf5+!   **Ke8**

    23. Bd7+   **Kf8**

    24. Bxe7

Checkmate!

Paul Morphy vs. Duke Karl of Braunschweig & Count Isouard

Paris (at the Opera), 1858 (Philidor Defense)

This offhand game is one of the most instructive examples of how to develop rapidly and attack. Legend has it that the Duke was roundly criticized in the next day's papers for playing a game of chess at the Opera!

1. e4	e5
2. Nf3	d6
3. d4	

BAD MOVE

| 3. ... Bg4 |

A weak move, but one with a certain logic to it. The white knight and pawn are attacking black's pawn at e5. Black's pawn is only defended by the d6 pawn. Rather than bringing up another defender (say, with *3. ...Nd7*), black chooses to pin the knight. The drawback to this idea is that there is a tactic at white's disposal that forces black to trade the bishop for the knight.

| 4. dxe5 | Bxf3 |

Not *4. ...dxe5, 5. Qxd8+ Kxd8, 6. Nxe5* winning a pawn.

| 5. Qxf3 | dxe5 |

Material balance has been restored, but Morphy has one piece (the queen) developed already and can now develop another. Morphy has a lead in development and the two bishops.

| 6. Bc4 | Nf6 |

Black must guard against the threatened capture on f7.

| 7. Qb3 | Qe7 |

Morphy, with his move, renews the threat to capture on f7, and his opponents are forced to guard against it (by moving the queen) on their turn. This move guards f7 but blocks the king's bishop. Morphy's edge in development continues to grow.

| 8. Nc3 | c6 |

Morphy could've won a pawn by *8. Qxb7,* but after *8. ...Qb4+* he would've been forced to trade queens. Morphy correctly decides that continuing his development (because that is where his advantage lies) is more important than winning a pawn. Black takes a moment to guard the b7 square with *8. ...c6,* which is a necessary precaution, but this move does not help his development.

9. Bg5   b5?

Another pawn move! This time Morphy decides that the time is ripe for sacrifice.

10. Nxb5!   cxb5

11. Bxb5+   Nbd7

12. 0-0-0   Rd8

Both knights are pinned, and black can barely move, but how is white to capitalize?

13. Rxd7!   Rxd7

Now Morphy has sacrificed a rook for two pawns, but his lead in development is so overwhelming that the material deficit is immaterial! Notice that the black king's rook and bishop have yet to move.

14. Rd1   Qe6

Duke Karl and Count Isouard reason that, if they can trade queens, they will survive the attack and win with their extra material. Morphy never gives them the chance.

15. Bxd7+   Nxd7 (See Figure 18-3.)

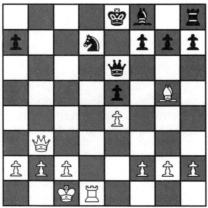

Figure 18-3

16. Qb8+   Nxb8

The final sacrifice is of the queen, but even she is willingly parted with for checkmate!

17. Rd8+

Checkmate.

Wilhelm Steinitz vs. Kurt Von Bardeleben

Hastings (England), 1895 (Italian Game)

This game is famous for the concluding combination and for the report that Von Bardeleben did not bother to resign but simply got up and walked away without a word.

1. e4	e5
2. Nf3	Nc6
3. Bc4	Bc5
4. c3	Nf6
5. d4	exd
6. cxd	Bb4+
7. Nc3	d5

Steinitz (white) was willing to sacrifice a pawn (or more!) in return for a lead in development. Von Bardeleben declines the offer to win material (by *7. ...Nxe4*) and strikes back immediately in the center. The struggle then shifts to a fight for control of the d5 square.

8. exd	Nxd5
9. 0-0	Be6

Steinitz was again willing to sacrifice a pawn (*9. ...Nxc3, 10. bxc3 Bxc3*) in return for speedy development, and again Von Bardeleben prefers to concentrate on reinforcing his control over what he perceives to be the key d5 square.

10. Bg5	Be7

Steinitz develops with a threat (by attacking the black queen), which is usually very strong. Von Bardeleben must take a moment to defend against the threat. Now both white and black have four pieces developed, but white has also castled and is on the move.

11. Bxd5	Bxd5
12. Nxd5	Qxd5
13. Bxe7	Nxe7
14. Re1	f6

Steinitz initiated the preceding series of exchanges for a very subtle reason. Now Von Bardeleben can't castle because the king is needed to guard the knight. He now hopes to escape his predicament by playing his king to f7 and then a rook to e8, but does he have time to do so?

15. Qe2	Qd7
16. Rac1	c6

If *16. ...Kf7* at once, *17. Qc4+* followed by *18. Qxc7* would win a pawn for white.

17. d5!	cxd

Steinitz has sacrificed the d-pawn in order to clear the d4 square for his knight. The time gained to bring the knight into the attack is worth more than the pawn. Notice how Von Bardeleben's rooks still stand on their original squares.

18. Nd4	Kf7
19. Ne6	Rhc8

Steinitz was threatening to invade with *20. Rc7.*

20. Qg4	g6

Von Bardeleben must guard against *21. Qxg7+ Ke8, 22. Qf8#*

21. Ng5+	Ke8 (See Figure 18-4.)

22. Rxe7+	Kf8

An extraordinary situation. Black can't capture the white rook, but white can't capture the black queen! If *22. ...Qxe7, 23. Rxc8+* (or *22. ...Kxe7, 23. Re1+ Kd8, 24. Ne6+*) is winning for white, but *23. Rxd7* (or *Qxd7*) *Rxc1#* wins for black! Now a comical series of moves takes place where Steinitz's impudent rook essentially thumbs its nose at Von Bardeleben's king.

23. Rf7+	Kg8

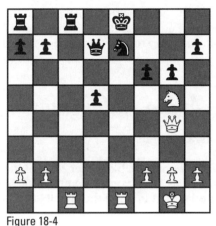

Figure 18-4

Not *23. ...Kd8, 24. Qxd7#*

24. Rg7+	Kh8
25. Rxh7+	Kg8
26. Rg7+	Kh8

Steinitz's checks have not been without purpose. Now that Von Bardeleben's h-pawn has been eliminated, Steinitz can bring the queen into the attack with check. White must not allow black to play Rxc1+, so it is critical to keep the black king in check. By replacing the harassing rook with a marauding queen, white increases his attacking force by a decisive amount.

27. Qh4+	Kxg7
28. Qh7+	Kf8
29. Qh8+	Ke7
30. Qg7+	Ke8

If *30. ...Kd6, 31. Ne4+ dxe4, 32. Rd1+* removes the mate threat and wins the black queen.

31. Qg8+	Ke7
32. Qf7+	Kd8
33. Qf8+	Qe8
34. Nf7+	Kd7
35. Qd6#	

Von Bardeleben walked away from the board without playing out the final sequence, which is bad manners, but understandable in this case. He must've been completely frustrated by his inability to move anything other than his king for so long.

Georg Rotlewi vs. Akiba Rubinstein

Lodz (Poland), Russia, 1907 (Tarrasch Defense)

This is another game where the few remaining black pieces combine to overwhelm the vastly superior white pieces. Rubinstein's combination is remarkable in that he continues to offer material right up until the end. It is known as Rubinstein's Immortal Game.

1.	d4	d5
2.	Nf3	e6
3.	e3	c5
4.	c4	Nc6
5.	Nc3	Nf6
6.	dxc	Bxc5
7.	a3	a6
8.	b4	Bd6
9.	Bb2	0-0
10.	Qd2	Qe7
11.	Bd3	dxc

Rotlewi (white) and Rubinstein have adopted very similar set ups. There are two subtle differences, however, both of which favor black. The first is that black waited to play *11. ...dxc* until after white's king bishop moved. This gained a tempo for black. The second difference is that the black queen is better placed on e7 than white's queen on d2. Black's queen is safe while the white queen is exposed on the open d-file. Are these small advantages enough to allow black to win? Maybe, and maybe only if your name is Rubinstein.

12.	Bxc4	b5
13.	Bd3	Rd8
14.	Qe2	Bb7

As you can see, the positions are almost mirror images of one another. The difference is that Rubinstein has already castled and played his rook to d8. Clearly black has gotten an advantage in development out of the opening.

15. 0-0   Ne5

16. Nxe5   Bxe5

17. f4   Bc7

Is Rotlewi gaining an edge in the center, or is Rubinstein provoking weaknesses in the white king's position?

18. e4   Rac8

19. e5   Bb6+

20. Kh1   Ng4

It is now clear that the safety of white's king is the most critical element at the moment. *21. Qxg4 Rxd3* is clearly better for black.

21. Be4   Qh4

22. g3 (See Figure 18-5.)

Figure 18-5

22. ...Rxc3!

A remarkable sacrifice of a queen which cannot be refused. *If 24. Bxc3 Bxe4+, 25. Qxe4 Qxh2#.*

23. gxh	Rd2!

It was not enough for Rubinstein to sacrifice his queen. He now throws a rook into the mixture.

24. Qxd2	Bxe4+
25. Qg2	Rh3!

And checkmate by *26. ...Rxh2* cannot be avoided. Rubinstein wins!

Stepan Levitsky vs. Frank Marshall

Breslau (Poland), 1912 (French Defense)

After Marshall's *23. ...Qg3!!* move, the spectators were said to have showered the board with gold pieces! Although legends are more fun to believe in, it should be noted that the chess journalist and international master I. A. Horowitz reports that Marshall's wife, Caroline, "disclaims even a shower of pennies."

1. d4	e6
2. e4	d5
3. Nc3	c5
4. Nf3	Nc6
5. exd	exd
6. Be2	Nf6
7. 0-0	Be7
8. Bg5	0-0
9. dxc	Be6
10. Nd4	Bxc5
11. Nxe6	fxe
12. Bg4	Qd6
13. Bh3	Rae8
14. Qd2	Bb4

Marshall now threatens *15. ...Ne4,* which prompts Levitsky to exchange his bishop for black's knight. As a result, Marshall's pieces are more aggressively posted and he is ahead in development. How can he translate this into victory?

15. Bxf6	Rxf6
16. Rad1	Qc5
17. Qe2	Bxc3
18. bxc	Qxc3
19. Rxd5	Nd4

By exploiting the pin on the e-file, Levitsky has retained material balance, but Marshall again gains time by centralizing the knight along with an attack on white's queen.

20. Qh5	Ref8
21. Re5	Rh6

Marshall again repositions a piece with gain of time by the attack on the queen. The black pieces are now optimally posted for tactics.

22. Qg5	Rxh3

Levitsky cannot play *23. gxh3* because of *23. ...Nf3*. Instead, Levitsky wants to play *23. Rc5* and *24. Rc7* with an attack of his own.

23. Rc5 (See Figure 18-6.)

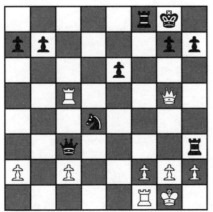

Figure 18-6

23. ...Qg3!!

Levitsky resigns! Levitsky has no fewer than three ways (shown with asterisks) to capture Marshall's queen — but all of them lose:

*24. hxg	Ne2 checkmate.	
*24. fxg	Ne2+	
25. Kh1	Rxf1 checkmate	
*24. Qxg3	Ne2+	
25. Kh1	Nxg3+	

And Levitsky cannot recapture with *26. fxg* because of *26. ...Rxf1 checkmate.*

Emanuel Lasker vs. José Raúl Capablanca

St. Petersburg (Russia), 1914 (Ruy Lopez, Exchange Variation)

This historical encounter pitted the world champion Lasker versus the sensational young Capablanca. Lasker proves that he wasn't yet ready to roll over and die before the next generation. Besides the historical significance of the game, this match is noteworthy for Lasker's simple winning strategy, seemingly flowing right from the opening. Simple for him, that is! What this game lacks in brilliant combinations is made up for by the sheer elegance of Lasker's play.

1. e4	e5
2. Nf3	Nc6
3. Bb5	a6
4. Bxc6	dxc
5. d4	exd
6. Qxd4	Qxd4
7. Nxd4	Bd6
8. Nc3	Ne7
9. 0-0	0-0

Both sides have developed pieces and castled. Lasker has an edge in the center and consequently an advantage in space. Lasker exploits this advantage by seizing even more space on the kingside. He is not opening himself up to attack, as white did in the previous game, because so much material has already been exchanged.

10. f4	Re8
11. Nb3	f6

The threat was *12. e5,* trapping the black bishop.

12. f5	b6
13. Bf4	Bb7
14. Bxd6	cd

Lasker does not mind repairing Capablanca's damaged pawn structure because he has his sights set on the e6 square for his knight.

15. Nd4	Rad8
16. Ne6	Rd7
17. Rad1	Nc8

Notice how Capablanca's pieces are struggling to defend the d6 pawn without getting in each other's way. This is often the consequence of having a spatial disadvantage.

18. Rf2	b5
19. Rfd2	Rde7
20. b4	Kf7
21. a3	Ba8

Lasker has control over the center and has slowed Capablanca's advance on the queenside. Lasker now improves the position of his king and seizes more space on the kingside.

22. Kf2	Ra7
23. g4	h6
24. Rd3	a5
25. h4	axb
26. axb	Rae7
27. Kf3	Rg8
28. Kf4	g6
29. Rg3	g5+
30. Kf3	Nb6
31. hxg	hxg

Lasker has now opened the h-file and takes control of it with a rook.

32. Rh3	Rd7
33. Kg3	Ke8
34. Rdh1	Bb7

Capablanca hopes that his position is defensible and merely marks time, but Lasker now takes the opportunity to bring his queenside knight into the game, even at the cost of a pawn.

35. e5!	
35. ...de	
36. Ne4	Nd5
37. N6c5	Bc8

Capablanca can't guard everything and decides to give up a rook for one of the pesky knights. Lasker retains his trumps — the h-file and the spatial advantage — and now adds a slight material edge to the equation.

38. Nxd7	Bxd7
39. Rh7	Rf8
40. Ra1	Kd8
41. Ra8+	Bc8
42. Nc5	

Capablanca resigns because *43. Ne6+* is devastating.

Donald Byrne vs. Robert J. Fischer

New York , 1956 (Grünfeld Defense)

Here the young Bobby Fischer plays one of the greatest games of all time. It was quickly dubbed the game of the century, but it was certainly played in the spirit of the last century.

1. Nf3	Nf6
2. c4	g6
3. Nc3	Bg7

4. d4	0-0
5. Bf4	d5
6. Qb3	dxc
7. Qxc4	c6
8. e4	Nbd7
9. Rd1	Nb6
10. Qc5	Bg4

This is an interesting position. Byrne seems to have complete control over the center, which normally leads to an advantage, but notice that Fischer has completed the development of his minor pieces and castled. Byrne's king's bishop and rook are still on their original squares. Byrne should attend to his development and not bother with his next move, which meets with a tactical response.

11. Bg5?

11. ...Na4!

If Byrne now plays *12. Nxa4 Nxe4, 13. Qc1 Qa5+* wins a pawn.

12. Qa3	Nxc3
13. bxc	Nxe4
14. Bxe7	Qb6

Fischer is willing to sacrifice his rook for white's bishop in return for an attack against white's king. Byrne decides to forego the win of material in order to try to castle, but Fischer keeps the pressure on and gives him no time to bring his king to safety.

15. Bc4

15. ...Nxc3!

16. Bc5   Rfe8+

17. Kf1 (See Figure 18-7.)

17. ...Be6

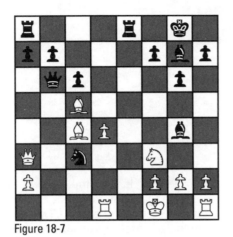

Figure 18-7

An amazing queen sacrifice that is justified by the white king's precarious position and black's lead in development! *18. Bxe6* would be met by *18. ...Qb5+*.

18. Bxb6	Bxc4+
19. Kg1	Ne2+
20. Kf1	Nxd4+
21. Kg1	Ne2+
22. Kf1	Nc3+
23. Kg1	axb

White takes time out to capture the piece because it doesn't lose any time. The capture includes a threat to capture the white queen on black's next move.

24. Qb4	Ra4
25. Qxb6	Nxd1
26. h3	Rxa2

Fischer continues to gobble up material while improving the position of his pieces.

27. Kh2	Nxf2
28. Re1	Rxe1
29. Qd8+	Bf8
30. Nxe1	Bd5

31. Nf3	Ne4
32. Qb8	b5
33. h4	h5
34. Ne5	Kg7

By breaking the pin, Fischer allows the king's bishop to join in on the final assault.

35. Kg1	Bc5+
36. Kf1	Ng3+
37. Ke1	Bb4+
38. Kd1	Bb3+
39. Kc1	Ne2+
40. Kb1	Nc3+
41. Kc1	Rc2#

Gary Kasparov vs. Viswanathan Anand

New York, 1995 (Ruy Lopez)

Although it is dangerous to include such a modern game because we haven't had a chance to digest it yet, I'm convinced that this one will be remembered for a long time. Anand had just taken the lead with a win in game nine, which broke a record streak of draws to open a world championship match. This game was Kasparov's quick answer and features an amazing rook sacrifice in a well-known opening. The annotations are by Grandmaster Larry Christiansen, and first appeared in *On Top of the Chess World,* 1995, Hypermodern Press (reprinted here with permission from the publisher). The game was complicated enough to bring in a guest annotator!

1. e4	e5
2. Nf3	Nc6
3. Bb5	a6
4. Ba4	Nf6
5. 0-0	Nxe4
6. d4	b5
7. Bb3	d5

8. dxe5	Be6
9. c3	Nc5
10. Nbd2	d4
11. Ng5!?	

Another battle of preparation!

11. ...dxc3

For the record, *11. ...Qxg5, 12. Qf3 0-0-0 (12. ...Kd7 13. Bd5, 12. ...Bd7 13. cxd4 and so on.), 13. Bxe6 fxe6, 14. Qxc6 Qxe5, 15. b4* is good for white.

12. Nxe6	fxe6
13. bxc3	Qd3
14. Bc2!	

Game Six continued *14. Nf3 0-0-0* and so on; the last move is Kasparov's improvement.

14. ...Qxc3

15. Nb3!! (See Figure 18-8.)

Figure 18-8

Gary and Team found this stunner the preceding weekend according to Kasparov in his postgame news conference. (Subsequently, we learned that this was originally an idea of Tal's.) Offering the Ra1 as bait, white aims to mobilize an irresistible onslaught against the exposed enemy king. Kasparov made the move *15. Nb3* with a showman's touch — a flip of the wrist and a fierce grin, making little effort to hide his excited joy. A visibly nervous Anand sank into deep thought here, recognizing the fact that the real Gary Kasparov had finally made his appearance.

15. ...Nxb3

Played after 45 minutes thought. The critical alternative is *15. ...Rd8!?, 16. Bd2 (16. Qh5+? g6, 17. Bxg6+ hxg6, 18. Qxh8 Nxb3 is good for Black) Qxe5, 17. Re1 Qd5 18. Rc1! (Fritz3) and now:*
1) 18. ...Be7, 19. Nxc5 Bxc5, 20. Be4 Bxf2+, 21. Kxf2 0-0+ (21. ...Qxd2+, 22. Qxd2 Rxd2+, 23. Ke3 Rxa2, 24. Rxc6 is hopeless; 21. ...Qd4+, 22. Kg3 0-0, 23. Kh3!+-:), 22. Kg1 Qd4+, 23. Kh1 Ne5, 24. Bc3 Qxd1, 25. Rexd1 Rxd1, 26. Rxd1 Ng4, 27. Kg1 and White is technically winning;
2) 18. ...Nxb3, 19. Be4! Qxd2, 20. Bxc6+ Ke7, 21. Qxb3 Rd6, 22. Bf3! and Black has slim prospects for survival (22. ...Kd8, 23. Rcd1, 22. ...c5, 23. Bg4).

16. Bxb3   Nd4

Or *16. ...Qxa1, 17. Bxe6! Rd8 (17. ...Nd4 transposes into the game and 17. ...Qd4, 18. Qf3 is crushing) 18. Bf7+! Kxf7, 19. Qf3+ Ke8, 20. Qxc6+ Kf7, 21. Qf3+! Ke8 (21. ...Kg8, 22. Qb3+; 21. ...Kg6, 22. Qg4+ Kf7, 23. Qf5+ Ke8, 24.,Qe6+ Be7, 25. Bg5+-) 22. e6 Qf6, 23. Qc6+ Ke7, 24. Ba3+ Rd6, 25. Qd7 mate.* Kasparov said afterward that he and his analysts had prepared the more extravagant winning method *17. Qh5+ g6, 18. Qf3 Nd8!, 19. Qf6! Rg8, 20. Bg5 Qc3, 21. Rd1, and so on.*

17. Qg4!

Kasparov was still playing at near-blitz tempo.

17. ...Qxa1

What else? Otherwise White can boast a withering attack for "chump change." (See Figure 18-9.)

Figure 18-9

18. Bxe6   Rd8

Or *18. ...Qc3, 19 Bd7+ Kf7 (19. ...Kd8, 20. Bg5+ Be7, 21. Bxe7+ Kxe7, 22. Qxg7+ Kd8, 23. Bg4 and so on). 20. Be3* and the multiple threats are too much.

19. Bh6!

Pow! Kasparov gave this shot a little extra twist for emphasis. He was still in blitz mode and still in his home preparation.

19. ...Qc3

19. ...Qxf1+, 20. Kxf1 is utterly hopeless — *20. ...gxh6, 21. Qh5+ Ke7, 22. Qf7mate.*

20. Bxg7   Qd3(!)

Anand finds a way to extend the battle.

21. Bxh8   Qg6

21. ...Ne2+, 22. Kh1 Ng3+, 23. hxg3 Qxf1+, 24. Kh2 Rd1, 25. Qh5+ Kd8, 26. Bf6+ Be7, 27. Bxe7+ Kxe7, 28. Qf7+, and mate next.

22. Bf6   Be7

23. Bxe7   Qxg4

Sadly forced. Unfortunately, *23. ...Kxe7, 24. Qh4+ Ke8, 25. Bg4* wins at once.

24. Bxg4   Kxe7

25. Rc1

Making sure Anand doesn't develop counterplay by means of *...c7-c5-c4.*

25. ...c6

26. f4   a5

27. Kf2   a4

28. Ke3   b4

29. Bd1

Not falling for *29. Rc4? a3!* and black has survival chances.

29. ...a3

30. g4   Rd5

31. Rc4   c5

31. ...b3, 32. axb3 Ra5, 33. Rc1 a2, 34. Ra1 Nb5, 35. Be2 (among others) is easily winning.

32. Ke4	Rd8
33. Rxc5	Ne6
34. Rd5!	Rc8

Of course *34. ...Rxd5, 35. Kxd5 Nxf4+, 36. Kc4* is hopeless.

35. f5	Rc4+
36. Ke3	Nc5
37. g5	Rc1
38. Rd6!	

Black resigns. After *38. ...b3,* simplest is *39. f6 Kf8, 40. e6 Nxe6, 41. Bxb3,* and so on.

Deep Blue vs. Gary Kasparov

Philadelphia, 1996

There's no danger in picking this game for the list of the ten best chess games, however. Never has there been as much publicity over a chess game as there was for this match. In this, the first of their six-game match, the computer causes a sensation by defeating the world champion. This is the first time a world champion has been beaten by a computer at regular tournament time controls, and the media all over the world picked up this story.

1. e4	c5
2. c3	d5
3. exd5	Qxd5
4. d4	Nf6
5. Nf3	Bg4
6. Be2	e6
7. h3	Bh5
8. 0-0	Nc6
9. Be3	cxd4
10. cxd4	Bb4?

This gets the world champion into trouble. The normal course of action is to develop the bishop to e7. Kasparov is undoubtedly trying to get the computer into unknown territory because the computer's memory contains all these moves up to this point from previous games. It isn't "thinking" yet, just "remembering." Now it starts its own calculations.

11. a3	Ba5
12. Nc3	Qd6
13. Nb5	Qe7
14. Ne5	Bxe2
15. Qxe2	0-0

The computer's advantage is a subtle one. The knights have been allowed to make two moves each for black knight's one.

16. Rac1	Rac8
17. Bg5	Bb6
18. Bxf6	gxf6

Forced because *18. ...Qxf6, 19. Nd7* would win material for white.

19. Nc4	Rfd8

Not *19. ...Nxd4, 20. Nxd4 Bxd4* because of *21. Qg4+* and *22. Qxd4*. The computer will never miss this kind of tactical trick. Now the computer ruins Kasparov's queenside pawn structure — a thing it "knows" is good to do.

20. Nxb6	axb6
21. Rfd1	f5
22. Qe3	Qf6

Kasparov is pressuring the pawn at d4. The computer now makes an excellent decision. Instead of becoming passive by defending the pawn, it chooses to advance it and attack. Well done!

23. d5	Rxd5
24. Rxd5	exd5
25. b3	Kh8

Kasparov will try to swing his rook to the g-file and attack. The computer correctly assesses that this attack is not dangerous and simply begins to "eat" material on the queenside.

26. Qxb6	Rg8
27. Qc5	d4
28. Nd6	f4
29. Nxb7	Ne5

The computer will not fall for *30. Qxd4 Nf3+* winning the white queen.

30. Qd5	f3
31. g3	Nd3
32. Rc7	Re8

Kasparov's attack looks very dangerous, but the computer is not rattled by appearances.

33. Nd6	Re1+
34. Kh2	Nxf2
35. Nxf7+	Kg7
36. Ng5+	Kh6
37. Rxh7+	

Kasparov resigns in the face of *37. ...Kg6, 38. Qg8+ Kf5, 39. Nxf3* where he has no threats and Deep Blue has too many. Score: Silicon 1, Carbon 0. Of course, this setback just made Kasparov mad, and he proceeded to soundly defeat the computer in the rest of the match.

Chapter 19

The Ten Best Players of All Time

● ●

In This Chapter

▶ Capablanca

▶ Fischer

▶ Kasparov

▶ Morphy

▶ Lasker

▶ Steinitz

▶ Alekhine

▶ Botvinnik

▶ Tal

▶ Honorable mentions

▶ Could-have-beens

● ●

*I*f you want to start an argument, picking the ten best players is a good way to do it. Many people feel very strongly about this particular issue. Books have even been written about it. Elaborate cases have been made to try to "prove" who was the best ever by estimating peak ratings.

I will do no such thing, of course. That would be too much work. The way I've decided to judge the best players is a simple one. How much did they stand above their contemporaries? I think it is the only valid way to compare players from different generations. Here they are, in the order in which I think they most dominated their respective eras.

Capablanca, José Raúl (1888-1942), Cuba

Capablanca was world champion from 1921 to 1927. Many people considered him the strongest player in the world prior to 1921, but he was unable to arrange a match with the then champion, Emanuel Lasker (see Lasker, later in this chapter).

When public sentiment became overwhelming in demand of a match, Lasker simply tried to resign his title to Capablanca. This behavior seems to add credence to the view that Capablanca was the better player years before the match finally took place. In fact, beginning in 1914 Capablanca lost only a single game over the next ten years.

Capablanca's dominance was so great that he was nicknamed "the chess machine." Even great players felt that he was unbeatable. Capablanca eventually became somewhat bored with chess because it was too easy. For him, it may have been.

Fischer, Robert James, (1943-), United States

In 1971 Fischer shocked the chess world by winning 19 consecutive games against an extremely high level of competition. This feat has been compared to throwing back to back no-hitters in baseball. During his peak playing period, players spoke of "Fischer Fever," where they would feel ill just having to play against him. Just as with Capablanca, Fischer had an aura of invincibility — which was not far from the truth. Fischer was head and shoulders above the best players of his day.

His abrupt withdrawal from chess was tragic. Rumors of Fischer sightings were rampant, and the public was often tantalized by stories of his impending re-emergence. Unfortunately, Fischer waited more than twenty years before playing in public again. His behavior, always intense, had become increasingly odd over the years, and it is doubtful that he will ever again subject himself to the rigors of tournament or match chess.

Kasparov, Gary (1963-), Armenia

Kasparov won the world championship in 1985 in the first of several titanic struggles with Anatoly Karpov (see Karpov, next). He has never been defeated in a match since that time. Kasparov's tournament results during his peak were just as impressive.

Kasparov entered only the very strongest tournaments and routinely won them. Only Karpov could challenge him — and because Karpov is also one of the ten best players of all time, this restriction only adds to Kasparov's résumé. The two of them were fierce combatants in what must be considered the greatest chess rivalry of all time.

Karpov, Anatoly (1951-), Russia

Although Kasparov eventually eclipsed Karpov, no one would dream of leaving Karpov off of this list. Karpov won the championship by default when Fischer refused to defend his title. Many people considered this a black mark on Karpov's record because Karpov never actually won the title by playing a championship match, but I think that's silly. Perhaps it was this event that spurred him on to incredible achievements in tournament chess.

Only the great Viktor Korchnoi was able to test him in match play, but even he could not best Karpov, and Karpov dominated the tournament scene. From 1978 to 1981, Karpov played in ten major tournaments and finished clear first, or in a tie for first, in nine of them. Karpov was clearly the dominant player after Fischer and before Kasparov.

Morphy, Paul (1837-84), United States

Morphy's career was meteoric. He burned brightly for a short period of time and then never played again. It is quite sensible to move him up or down this list depending upon how much or how little you value longevity.

Morphy defeated all the best players of his day with the exception of Howard Staunton — who managed to avoid playing Morphy. Most historians give Staunton no real chance of ever being able to defeat Morphy in a match. It was not so much that Morphy won but how he won that set him so far above his contemporaries. Morphy played scintillating chess. His games still serve as classic examples of how powerful rapid development can be.

After defeating the best and the brightest, Morphy retired from chess to set up his law practice in New Orleans. Unfortunately, what many believe to have been serious mental health problems surfaced and haunted him for the remainder of his days.

Lasker, Emanuel (1868-1941), Germany

Lasker is an interesting case. Some people put him first and others put him towards the bottom. The major criticism is that he played infrequently. The major argument in his favor was that he was world champion from 1894 until 1921 — longer than any other player in history. Many people believe that Lasker ducked the toughest opposition, but it is clear from his results that he was the world's best player for a considerable period of time.

Lasker established his credentials by winning four consecutive major tournaments (these tournaments were infrequent in those days): St. Petersburg 1895-96, Nuremberg 1896, London 1899, and Paris 1900. From 1895 to 1924, Lasker played in ten major tournaments, finished first eight times, second once, and third once. This achievement was clearly the best record of anyone during that time.

Steinitz, Wilhelm (1836-1900), Austria

The first world champion, Steinitz was considered the best player in the world for a period of about 20 years. By virtue of his match and tournament record, Steinitz was probably the best player in the world during the late 1860s and certainly was by the early 1870s. From 1862 to 1894, Steinitz had an unbroken string of 24 match victories.

It wasn't until 1886, in a match versus Zukertort, that a winner was officially given the title of world champion. Steinitz won with a score of ten wins, five losses, and five draws. Steinitz then successfully defended his title several times before losing, at the age of 58, to the young Lasker.

Alekhine, Alexander (1892-1946), Russia

Alekhine was single-minded in his pursuit of the world championship and his drive eventually overcame Capablanca's skill. Alekhine's results were never as dominating as those higher on this list, but he still managed an impressive string of results. From 1921 through 1927, he competed in 15 major tournaments and won 8 of them. From 1930 to 1934, he won 5 strong tournaments but let his weakness for drink get the best of him. He lost the title to Max Euwe in 1935, primarily because of his poor physical condition.

Alekhine cleaned up his act and won the return match to regain the title, which he kept until his death. However, his last years were sad ones. His play was unrecognizable, and his physical condition continued to deteriorate. Nevertheless, Alekhine belongs on this list by virtue of his many tournament and match victories.

Botvinnik, Mikhail (1911-1994), Russia

Botvinnik won seven consecutive major tournaments from 1941 to 1948, including the tournament held to determine the champion upon Alekhine's death. There is little doubt that he would've defeated Alekhine, and it seems certain that he was the best player of the 1940s.

Remarkably, Botvinnik was an engineer by profession and did not dedicate himself to chess the way most of the champions had. He lost his title to Smyslov in 1957 but won it back in the return match the next year. He then lost to Tal in 1960 but again recaptured the title in the return match. The return match clause was stricken in 1963 when he lost to Petrosian, and no one will ever know whether he would've managed to score the hat trick.

Despite a fairly tarnished record in championship match play, Botvinnik was clearly the best player in the world for many years. None of his challengers could make that claim.

Tal, Mikhail (1936-1991), Latvia

Tal barely makes the top ten because health troubles kept him from performing at peak efficiency. Otherwise, he may have been much higher on the list. Botvinnik once said, "If Tal would learn to program himself properly, he would be impossible to play."

Tal won the world championship title from Botvinnik in 1960 but lost the return match. Before this return match, Tal became unwell with kidney trouble but refused to postpone play. Tal eventually lost one of his kidneys and was never really well afterwards.

Nevertheless, from 1949 to 1990, Tal played in 55 strong tournaments, winning or sharing 19 first and 7 second prizes. He won 6 Soviet championships, which were some of the strongest tournaments of that time. He also compiled a record of 59 wins, 31 draws, and only 2 losses in 7 Olympiads. Famous for his intimidating stare, Tal joins Capablanca and Fischer as the most feared opponents in history. When playing Tal, players were always afraid of winding up on the losing side of a soon-to-be famous game.

The best of the 18th century?

André-François Philidor (1726-95) of France was reported to be the best player of his time, and the surviving games show a striking superiority to that of most of his contemporaries in his knowledge of the game. Unfortunately, we do not have enough information on this time period to truly document his dominance, and this lack of data keeps him from making the top ten.

We do know, however, that he authored the most influential chess book of his age, *L'analyse des échecs*, published in London in 1749. Philidor entered an important choir at the age of six and must be considered something of a musical prodigy. He learned chess when the court musicians had spells of inactivity and passed the time playing chess. When his voice broke around the age of fourteen, he began playing chess in earnest. Even so, his musical compositions were numerous and some of them are even performed today.

Honorable mentions

Other world champions must be included in any such list, because all of them were dominant to some extent. Although these players may not appear on every best-ever list, they all deserve consideration. They are:

- ✔ **Spassky, Boris** (1937-) Russia.
- ✔ **Petrosian, Tigran** (1929-84), Armenia.
- ✔ **Smyslov, Vasily** (1921-), Russia.
- ✔ **Euwe, Max** (1901-81), Netherlands.
- ✔ **Anderssen, Adolf** (1818-79), Germany.

  Arguably the best player of his time, before the title of world champion was established, Anderssen also deserves consideration as an honorable mention.

The strongest players never to be world champion

If you don't get enough controversy from trying to establish the best players of all time, ask who the strongest player was to never win the title of world champion. That question usually does the trick. The prime candidates, in chronological order, are:

Chigorin, Mikhail (1850-1908), Russia

Chigorin played two championship matches with Steinitz and lost both of them, but these matches were considered to be closely contested, and the second match in particular could've gone either way. In 1893, Chigorin drew a tremendous fighting match with Tarrasch, who also makes this list.

Tarrasch, Siegbert (1862-1934), Germany

From 1888 to 1892, Tarrasch won five consecutive major tournaments. He never challenged Steinitz for the title — although he was certainly qualified to — reportedly due to his obligations as a medical doctor. When he finally got his chance against Lasker in 1908, he was past his prime and soundly beaten.

Pillsbury, Harry Nelson (1872-1906), United States

Pillsbury's first international tournament was Hastings 1895, one of the strongest and most famous tournaments in history. Unbelievably, he won the event ahead of Steinitz, Lasker, Chigorin, and Tarrasch. No one had ever done anything like it before. His career tournament record against Lasker was four wins, four losses, and four draws — the best result of any of his contemporaries. His untimely death, due to a terminal illness, may have been the only thing between him and the title.

Rubinstein, Akiba (1882-1961), Poland

In 1912, Rubinstein won four major tournaments and was clearly at the top of his game. He then began negotiations with Lasker for a title match. Sadly, he fared badly in the great tournament in St. Petersburg, 1914, and lost his potential backing. Then World War I broke out; his best opportunity was gone.

Reshevsky, Samuel (1911-92), Poland

During the years 1935 to 1950, Reshevsky played in 14 major tournaments and won half of them. He finished lower than third only once. This record is all the more remarkable because he was only a part-time player and held a full-time, non-chess job. He was perhaps the greatest child prodigy in chess history. He also continued to play at an extremely high level well into his seventies and once drew a match with Fischer in 1961.

Keres, Paul (1916-75), Estonia

Keres won some of the strongest tournaments in the late 1930s, but the advent of World War II dashed his title hopes. After the war, he was a candidate for the title no less than seven times but never made it to the finals. His near misses took on almost tragic proportions.

Korchnoi, Viktor (1931-), Russia

Korchnoi won four Soviet championships and competed as a candidate many times over the course of his career. He came within a hair's breadth of winning the title from Karpov in 1978. Korchnoi was a defector from the Soviet Union, and all of that country's resources were used against him. Of all the players on this list, Korchnoi may have the strongest claim.

Chapter 20

The Ten Most Common Chess Openings

*T*hese opening systems occur frequently at all levels of chess play. It's important to be able to recognize them and label them correctly, or people will sniff out the fact that you're a beginner. It also helps to be able to talk about your games with newfound friends. You can say, "I tried the French Defense for the first time, but I got a bad game." Or, "I like the Sicilian, how about you?"

Being able to talk chess is almost as much fun as playing chess. It also helps fill up the minutes before a round starts at the club. Remember, you have at least one thing in common with everyone there.

You need to know chess notation (explained in Chapter 17) in order to completely understand this chapter. If you don't know chess notation, it is possible just to associate the positions with the opening names — and you'll still sound as if you know what you're talking about!

The Ruy Lopez (or Spanish Game)

The Ruy Lopez is also called the Spanish game, because, well, Ruy Lopez came from Spain. The position in Figure 20-1 is reached after the following moves:

1. e4   e5
2. Nf3   Nc6
3. Bb5

With the Ruy Lopez opening, the white bishop attacks the defender.

Figure 20-1

The Ruy Lopez is one of the most logical openings in chess, which probably explains its popularity. The kings' pawns advance, a white knight attacks, a black knight defends, and then a white bishop attacks the defender. All very understandable. Of course, it has been played and studied so often that entire books have been written about some of the variations.

If you are just playing at the club level, it will be okay to follow the general opening principles. If you wish to play tournament chess, you'll have to hit the books!

The Sicilian Defense

The Sicilian Defense got its name from the homeland of Carrera, who first published the opening system in 1617. It took another couple of centuries before it really caught on, however.

The Sicilian Defense is nowadays an extremely popular choice because it leads to unbalanced positions that create more chances to win or lose the game. White usually uses the e-file to advantage, and black uses the c-file. Because each is using a different file, the pieces don't get exchanged as easily, and the more pieces there are, the more chances each side has.

The Sicilian (see Figure 20-2) is reached after the following moves:

1. e4   c5

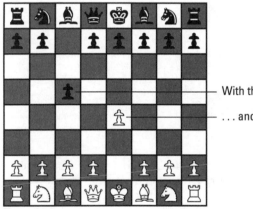

With the Sicilian, black uses the c-file . . .

. . . and white uses the e-file.

Figure 20-2

Bobby Fischer played the Sicilian, so many American players do, too. There are many variations, and almost as much analysis has been done on the Sicilian as has been done on the Ruy Lopez. Even so, it remains extremely popular at all levels.

The French Defense

The French Defense is my personal favorite and has been a featured weapon of many a grandmaster. It was given its name when a team from Paris defeated a team from London in a correspondence match in 1834, primarily by using this defense.

Unlike the Ruy Lopez (which is an open game) or the Sicilian (which is a semi-open game), the French is a *closed system,* which keeps the pieces on the board for a long time. It is difficult to open lines for an attack, and the game takes on a more strategic character.

The French (see Figure 20-3) is arrived at by the following moves:

1. e4   e6

With French defense, black has trouble developing its light-squared bishop.

Figure 20-3

The chief drawback of the French Defense is that white can usually establish and maintain a spatial superiority. It is also difficult to develop black's light-squared bishop to an effective post. Nevertheless, even Bobby Fischer found the French Defense a tough nut to crack.

The Caro-Kann

The Caro-Kann takes its name from the British player Horatio Caro (1862-1920) and the Viennese player Marcus Kann (1820-1886) who published their analysis of this opening. The Caro-Kann (see Figure 20-4) is reached after the following moves:

1. e4   c6

The Caro-Kann has many similarities to the French — but two distinct differences. In the Caro-Kann, black usually has a weaker center than the French does, but the problem bishop of the French Defense is free to move. Infrequently played before the mid-20th century, it is now considered the primary defense of many top players.

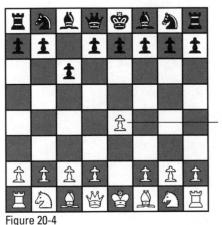

With the Caro-Kann, white can develop a stronger control of the center than can black.

Figure 20-4

The Pirc/Modern

This setup was named after the Yugoslav player Vasja Pirc (1907-1980). It is properly pronounced "peerts." The Pirc (see Figure 20-5) is characterized by these moves:

1. e4   d6

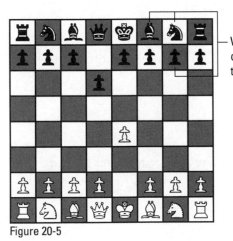

With the Pirc, black will now concentrate on moving these three chessman.

Figure 20-5

The Pirc (or modern) defenses usually involve the moves Nf6, g6, and Bg7 by black in almost any order. This flexibility is much in favor with the modern player.

The Indians

This complex is made up of the King's Indian, Nimzo-Indian, and Queen's Indian defenses. It usually involves the development of a bishop on the wing, which was common in the Indian game considered the forerunner to chess. The King's Indian (see Figure 20-6) is normally reached by these moves:

1. d4	Nf6
2. c4	g6
3. Nc3	Bg7

Figure 20-6

The Nimzo-Indian (see Figure 20-7) occurs after these moves:

1. d4	Nf6
2. c4	e6
3. Nc3	Bb4

And the Queen's Indian (see Figure 20-8) occurs after these moves:

1. d4	Nf6
2. c4	e6
3. Nf3	b6

All the Indian defenses defer the occupation of the center by pawns and try to strike out at the center with pieces and well-timed pawn thrusts. They tend to be very complicated and appeal to the modern player because of this complexity.

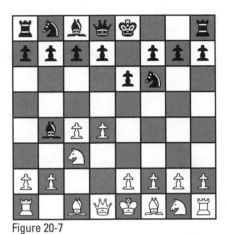

Figure 20-7

Figure 20-8

The Queen's Gambit Accepted

Unlike some of the other openings presented so far, the Queen's Gambit does not refer to a person or place but to the strategy of offering a pawn for rapid development. The Queen's Gambit Accepted (see Figure 20-9) arises after these moves:

| 1. d4 | d5 |
| 2. c4 | dxc4 |

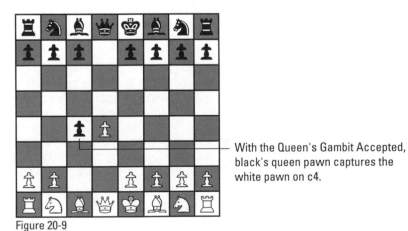

With the Queen's Gambit Accepted, black's queen pawn captures the white pawn on c4.

Figure 20-9

It will prove difficult to hold onto the black pawn; today's players routinely allow white to win it back and just go about the development of their other pieces.

The Queen's Gambit Declined

The Queen's Gambit Declined (see Figure 20-10) occurs when black supports the attacked pawn, as in this continuation:

1. d4   d5
2. c4   e6

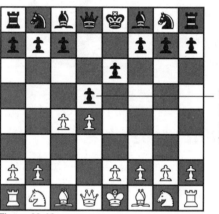

With the Queen's Gambit Declined, black's queen pawn refuses to capture and is then supported by the king's pawn.

Figure 20-10

The Queen's Gambit Declined gives white a slight edge because the black queen's bishop will have trouble developing to an active post.

The Slav Defense

The Slav Defense (see Figure 20-11) was popularized by Chigorin in the late 19th century. The Slav supports the attacked pawn in a way that does not block in the black bishop, and has become more popular than the Queen's Gambit Declined.

The Slav can become very complicated and some of the lines have been worked out many moves deep. Some player's simply play *3. cxd5* and transpose into the exchange variation of the Queen's Gambit Declined. This is one way to frustrate a Slav player looking for a fight.

With the Slav Defense, black supports its attacked pawn with the queen's bishop pawn — thus allowing its light-squared bishop more mobility.

Figure 20-11

The English Opening

The English Opening is the favorite choice of those players who do not wish to play the most common moves: either *1. e4* or *1. d4*. It is begun with *1. c4* instead (see Figure 20-12).

The idea behind the English is to control the d5 square. Often, white's first few moves are made with that goal in mind. Figure 20-13 shows the main idea behind the English. The d5 square is marked with an *X*.

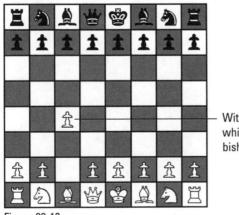

With the English Opening, white advances the queen's bishop pawn.

Figure 20-12

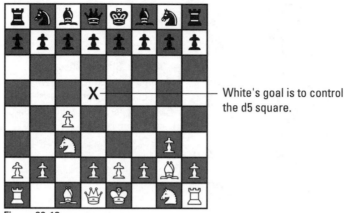

White's goal is to control the d5 square.

Figure 20-13

Depending on what black does in the meantime, white will choose to develop while maintaining a lock on the d5 square.

These openings are some of the most common in chess — but there are many, many more. Some range from reasonable to bizarre, and almost every combination of opening moves has been tried. The important point is to be able to understand the ideas behind the openings and play according to the general principles of opening play (see Chapter 10 for opening play info).

Chapter 21

The Ten Best Chess Resources

The world of chess includes a lively market in the buying and selling of chess-related materials. It's impossible to list all of the resources available, so I've decided to limit the scope of this chapter to just those resources that I have had completely positive experiences with — in the hopes that you will, too!

Chess books to begin with

Chess players like to brag about their chess libraries. More books are sold about chess than any other game. Hundreds of books are worth recommending, but it's best to start out modestly and purchase (or borrow) only what you need.

Official Rules of Chess, 4th Edition

The United States Chess Federation's book is edited by Goichberg, Jarecki, and Riddle. Published by David McKay, this is an indispensable guide that allows you to win all the arguments about rules you are bound to have. It also includes a complete set of international rules.

The Oxford Companion to Chess, 2nd Edition

This book is by Hooper and Whyld, published by Oxford University Press. It includes everything from A to Z about chess — and is the handiest single-source reference book around.

The Even More Complete Chess Addict

Written by Fox and James, published by Faber and Faber. This is the trivia book to get. The authors are witty and thorough in digging up gems — such as the man who was British Ladies Champion. A *must have*.

If you have access to the World Wide Web (see Chapter 16 for details), look up the reference for more information about which books to get your hands on.

Purchasing chess equipment

Serious chess players tend to buy lots of books, but everybody needs a chess set and board. If you wish to play in tournaments, you also should buy a clock. The following resources have large inventories and reliable service.

The United States Chess Federation

The United States Chess Federation has plenty of books and all the equipment you need, from the least expensive tournament regulation sets, clocks, and boards to some collector's items.

USCF
3054 NYS Route 9W
New Windsor, NY 12553
(800-388-5464)

Chessco

Proprietor Bob Long is famous for his gruff manner — and his outstanding selection and service. You can contact him for his catalog at this address:

Chessco
P.O. Box 8
Davenport, IA 52803
(800-397-7117)

Your Move Chess & Games

Your Move Chess & Games is touted as America's Largest Chess Store and the country's premier chess mail-order company. Contact this company at the following address:

Your Move Chess & Games
21 Walt Whitman Road
Huntington Station, NY 11746
(800-645-4710) or
(516-424-3300)
Web site: http://www.ICDchess.com

Chess resources on the Internet

I'll give one Web site and one Usenet forum the nod for best resources on the net. However, the Web especially is designed to be surfed, so don't limit yourself to what you see here. Also, because the Web changes on a daily basis, I recommend that you develop your own list of sites you enjoy and keep exploring every now and then to see what else is new.

This Week in Chess (TWIC)

The most current and complete information is TWIC.
The URL is http://www.brad.ac.uk/~mdcrowth/TWIC.html

Your Move Chess & Games

The largest chess Web site in the world is at http://www.ICDchess.com

Rec.games.chess.misc

Subscribe to the rec.games.chess.misc newsgroup to get the most gossip, opinions, and — on the odd chance — facts.

Places to visit, people to see, games to play

You can visit a number of places of special interest, if you get the chance.

Manhattan & Marshall Chess Clubs

Both located in New York, they each have a rich tradition and plenty of action.

The Manhattan Chess Club	The Marshall Chess Club
353 West 46th Street	23 West 10th Street
New York, NY 10036	New York, NY 10011
(212-757-0613)	(212-477-3716)

John G. White Collection

Located on the third floor of the Main Library at 125 Superior Avenue, Cleveland, OH, this is the chess world's largest research and reference library. It includes some of the rarest books and materials available in this country. The collection also includes a tremendous collection of chess sets and pieces.

U.S. Chess Center

The U.S. Chess Center is the home of the United States Chess Hall of Fame, located at this address:

U.S. Chess Center
1501 M Street NW
Washington, DC 20005-1700
Web site: http://www.chessctr.org

The Hall of Fame is dedicated to telling the stories of the greatest players in U.S. history. It also has some wonderfully rare material — my favorite one being the 1st edition of the tournament book of the first true International in 1851!

Appendix A
A Glossary of Chess

· ·

*N*ote: If you encounter chess notation (1. e3 Nc7, and so on), you may want to turn to Chapter 17 for a quick lesson on how to read it. Chess notation is an important — and essential — way to communicate the game of chess.

action chess   See *rapid chess*.

active   (i) Description of a move that increases your mobility; (ii) Description of a piece that is mobile. See also *passive*.

adjournment   The postponement of play in an unfinished game. At the adjournment, the player on the move writes down the move on paper and places it in an envelope that is taken by the tournament director or arbiter. Hours, sometimes even days, may pass before an adjourned game is resumed and both players (their friends and their computers too!) are free to analyze the position.

adjudication   The selection of a winner of an unfinished chess game, made by a qualified, impartial expert. Adjudication is most common in club games and team matches.

adjust   To touch a piece or pawn (generally to move it to the center of its square), but without the intention of making an official move. A player should announce "I adjust" or "J'adoube" *before* touching the piece. See Chapter 13 for information on chess etiquette. See also *J'adoube, touch move* in this glossary.

algebraic notation   A system of recording the moves of a chess game (first devised in the 19th century) in which each square on the board has a unique identifier. From white's side of the board, the files are letters from a to h moving from left to right, and the ranks are numbered 1 to 8, moving from bottom to top. Piece moves are designated by a one-letter abbreviation for the piece followed by its destination square. Pawn moves are designated by the destination square alone. Chapter 17 has the details on understanding algebraic chess notation. See also *notation, long algebraic notation, descriptive notation* in this glossary.

annotation   Commentary on a chess game that attempts to explain the game in general terms or by examining alternatives to the moves played.

arbiter   A person who (i) ensures that the rules are observed; (ii) supervises the game(s); (iii) enforces the rules and his own decisions regarding them; and (iv) imposes penalties on players infringing on the rules. See also *International Arbiter*.

attacking move   Move that is aggressive and that often elicits a defensive response.

B   Abbreviation for bishop.

back rank   A player's own first rank.

back rank mate   Checkmate delivered by playing a queen or rook to an opponent's back rank when the king is kept from moving out of check by his own pawns.

backward pawn   A pawn that has pawns of its own color on adjacent files only in front of it, so it has no pawn protection of its own.

bad bishop   A bishop whose effectiveness is hampered by its own pawns.

BCA   See *British Chess Association*.

BCF   See *British Chess Federation*.

BCF grading system   The chess rating system used in Britain by the British Chess Federation (BCF). BCF grades and Elo ratings are related by the formulas: Elo = 8 (BCF) + 600 and BCF = $^1/_8$ (Elo) − 75. See also *Elo Scale*.

BCM   See *British Chess Magazine*.

bishop   The chess piece that moves diagonally over any number of unoccupied squares. The bishops that begin the game on f1 and c8 move only on the light-colored squares and the bishops that begin the game on c1 and f8 move only on the dark-colored squares.

bishops of opposite colors   Situation where one player has a bishop on the light squares and the other player has a bishop on the dark squares. Endings with bishops of opposite colors are often drawn.

bishop pair   Two bishops, usually compared to an opponent's two knights or a bishop and knight. In many positions, the bishop pair has a slight advantage over these other two configurations of minor pieces due to greater mobility.

blindfold chess   Chess played without seeing the board or pieces. Originally a player was in fact blindfolded; now in blindfold chess a player usually sits with his back to the board. Famous players who have played simultaneous blindfold chess include Philidor, Morphy, Alekhine, and Koltanowski.

blitz   Chess played very quickly. Each player is given a small amount of time, commonly five minutes, in which to play the entire game.

blockade   Situation where one side is prevented from advancing. Originally, Nimzovich used the term to describe the blocking of a pawn by a piece.

blunder   A bad move that results in mate, the loss of material, or a seriously weakened position.

book move   The term for a standard move, one generally recommended in books cataloging openings or books concerned with the opening in question.

brilliancy   A game containing original, innovative, sometimes surprising moves.

brilliancy prize   An award given for the best brilliancy at a tournament. The first brilliancy prize was awarded to Bird in 1886 for his win over Mason.

British Chess Association   Organization founded in the mid-19th century, which suffered from Staunton's active opposition. Officials of the Association included Lord Tennyson, Lord Randolph Churchill, Robert Peel, and John Ruskin. The organization collapsed in the mid-1890s.

British Chess Federation   Founded in 1904, and commonly called simply the BCF, this organization governs chess in Great Britain. The BCF organizes the annual national championship tournaments and participates in FIDE events such as Olympiads.

British Chess Magazine   Monthy chess magazine begun in October 1872 (then under the title Huddersfield College Magazine; the current name was adopted in 1881). It is currently the oldest chess magazine with a continuous run of publication.

Caissa   The goddess (or muse) of chess. Caissa is first mentioned in the 1763 poem "Caissa" by Sir William Jones, based on the medieval poem by Vida, "Schacchia Ludus" (The Game of Chess) in which the character that Jones called Caissa is actually named Scacchis.

candidates matches   Matches held by FIDE in order to select a challenger to the World Champion. The participants in candidates matches are: the loser of the previous World Championship match, the losing finalist in the previous candidates matches, and the six players chosen through Interzonal Tournaments. Candidates matches began in 1965. See also *Interzonal Tournament, FIDE*.

candidates tournaments   Before the advent of candidate matches, this was the final stage in the selection by FIDE of a challenger to the World Champion. The participants were essentially the same as in today's candidates matches, but the challenger was selected in tournament, rather than match play.

castling   A single move involving both the king and a rook. Castling kingside moves the king from e1 (e8 for black) to g1 (g8 for black) and the rook from h1 (h8 for black) to f1 (f8 for black). Castling queenside moves the king from e1 (e8 for black) to c1 (c8 for black) and the rook from a1 (a8 for black) to d1 (d8 for black). Castling is only permitted if: (i) the king is not in check; (ii) neither the king nor the relevant rook has previously moved in the game; (iii) there are no pieces between the king and the rook; and (iv) none of the squares the king must move across are attacked by an enemy piece or pawn. See Chapter 9 for an illustrated explanation of castling.

center   The squares e4, e5, d4, and d5. Sometimes the term is used to encompass also the squares adjacent to these four.

centralization   The act of bringing pieces to the center where they can control the largest amount of the board.

chatrang   The name given by Persians to an early version of chess.

chaturanga   The name of the first game from which modern chess is derived. Chaturanga is the Sanskirt word for "four-membered," and when this game was developed in India in the sixth century, armies had four components: infantry, cavalry, chariots, and elephants.

cheapo   Slang expression for a swindle or a cheap trick that does not withstand serious scrutiny. See also *swindle*.

check   An attack on the opponent's king by either a piece or a pawn. When in check, a player must do one of the following: (i) move the king out of check; (ii) interpose a piece or pawn; or (iii) capture the checking piece. Although once common to utter the word "check" when making such a move, this practice is not only unnecessary but often frowned upon. Chapter 6 covers check possibilities. See also *checkmate*.

checkmate   When a king is in check and cannot make any move to get out of check. The king is said to be checkmated (or simply mated) and the game is over. See Chapter 6 for checkmate information.

chess clock   A device made up of two clocks that records the amount of time each player uses while on the move. Only the clock of the player to move is running; after making his move, the player pushes a button that stops his clock and starts the clock of his opponent. See also *flag, Fischer clock*.

Chess Life & Review When the U.S. Chess Federation acquired the rights to *Chess Review* from Horowitz in 1969, it merged that publication with *Chess Life* under a single title. Later, the title was again shortened to *Chess Life.*

Chess Monthly (UK) British chess magazine from 1879 to 1896. It was one of the first chess magazines to make good use of annotated games.

chess problem A composed chess position that identifies that checkmate (or another conclusion, such as helpmate where the solver is required to checkmate himself) is to be given in a specified number of moves.

Chess Review American monthly chess magazine founded in 1933. It was eventually sold to the U.S. Chess Federation. See also *Chess Life and Review.*

chessic Relating to chess.

chessist Term to describe someone interested in chess.

chessman Term that refers to both pieces and pawns. Sometimes the term is shortened to *man.* The term *unit* is sometimes used interchangeably with chessman. See also *piece, pawn.*

classical Style of chess play that developed in the late 19th century emphasizing rapid development and control of the center with pawns. See also *center, development.*

clock See *chess clock.*

closed file A file that has at least one pawn of each color on it. See also *file, open file.*

closed game A game where piece movement is restricted by interlocked pawn chains and play centers on positioning pieces outside of the center, in anticipation of the opening of the position. Most of the pieces are usually still on the board and are behind the pawns, which may impede their movement. See also *open game.*

combination A series of forced moves (usually involving a sacrifice) that leads to an advantage for the intiating player.

compensation An advantage that compensates for a disadvantage elsewhere. For example, a gain of tempo may compensate for the loss of a pawn.

connect To move rooks of the same color onto the same rank, unseparated by pieces or pawns.

consolidate   To maintain an established advantage.

consultation chess   A game in which at least one side consists of two or more players who consult with each other in the play of the game. One of Morphy's most spectacular games was against the Duke of Brunswick and Count Isouard. This pair played Morphy in consultation and suffered a stunning loss.

cook   A defect in a chess problem. See also *chess problem*.

correspondence chess   Chess played by mail. The earliest correspondence game whose moves have been preserved was played in 1804. Chess played via electronic (computer) mail has recently become popular. Unlike over-the-board play, the consultation of books is permitted in correspondence chess. Also known as *postal chess*.

cramped position   Position in which the pieces have little room to move. See also *closed game*.

crippled majority   A group of pawns on one side of the board that outnumber the opponent's pawns on this side, which because of structural weaknesses (for example, doubled pawns) can't result in the creation of a passed pawn. See also *majority*.

critical position   The point in a game where the decisive series of moves begin.

cross-check   A reply to a check that is itself a check. See also *check*.

crosstable   A chart in grid form that lists the complete results of a tournament.

decoy sacrifice   A sacrifice that entices the movement of an opponent's piece. The move may place the hostile piece on a disadvantageous square or simply remove it from a part of the board where it was more effective.

descriptive notation   System of recording the moves of a chess game based on the names of the pieces and places they occupy before the game begins. A move is given by the name of the man moving, followed by the square to which it moves. This notation is now almost completely replaced by algebraic notation. See also *notation, long algebraic notation, algebraic notation*.

desperado   A piece that is trapped or must inevitably be captured and that is moved in order to inflict the greatest possible damage to the opposing side.

Deutsche Schachzeitung   The oldest chess magazine still in existence. It was founded in 1846 (then under the title *Schachzeitung*) by L.E. Bledow and took its current name in 1872. There was a five-year hiatus in publication at the end of World War II.

development   The movement of pieces from their initial squares.

diagonal   Any contiguous line of squares along which a bishop may move. If a bishop is not on one of the four corner squares of the board, it is on a square that represents the intersection of two diagonals, which are referred to as the *short diagonal* and the *long diagonal*.

diagram   A drawing of a chess position where white is at the bottom of the picture and black is at the top.

discovered attack   The movement of a piece or pawn that results in an attack by a piece not moved. The stationary piece is now able to attack because the piece that was moved previously blocked the attack. See also *discovered check*.

discovered check   The movement of a piece or pawn that results in a check by a piece not moved. See also *discovered attack*.

double attack   A simultaneous attack by a single piece or pawn on two pieces of the opponent. Any pawn or piece can theoretically make a double attack, except pawns on the a- or h-files.

double bishop sacrifice   The sacrifice of both bishops to open up the enemy king. The Lasker-Bauer game of 1889 at Amsterdam is the first documented example of this maneuver. See also *sacrifice*.

double check   Discovered check in which the moved piece also gives check. Only the movement of the king can meet a double check. See also *discovered check*.

double round robin   Tournament where each contestant plays two games (one as white and one as black) with every other contestant. See also *match tournament, round robin*.

doubled pawns   Two pawns of the same color on the same file, which are nearly always a positional weakness.

draw   A completed chess game in which there is no winner. There are several ways for a draw to result: (i) by agreement of both players; (ii) by stalemate; (iii) by the declaration and proof of one player that the same position has appeared three times (with the same player to move); (iv) by the declaration and proof of one player that there have been 50 moves during which no piece has been taken and there have been no pawns moved, although there are some exceptions to the 50 move rule; (v) by adjudication; (iv) by the falling of one player's flag (on the chess clock) when his opponent has insufficient material to perform checkmate. See also *stalemate, fifty-move rule, adjudication*.

duffer   Disparaging term to describe a very poor player.

dynamism   Type of play where positional weaknesses are permitted in favor of agressive counterplay. Dynamism developed out of the hypermodern school of chess play. See also *hypermodern*.

ECO   See *Encyclopedia of Chess Openings*.

edge   The outside squares of the chess board, namely the first and eighth ranks and the a- and h-files.

Elo Scale   System for ranking chess players in order of relative strength based upon results in rated games. The important factor in comparing two players is the difference in their Elo ratings, not the absolute level of either rating. The Elo system was adopted by the USCF in 1960 and by FIDE in 1970. The system was devised by physicist Arpad Elo.

en passant   French for "in passing." The capture of a pawn that has moved two squares forward by an opponent's pawn on the fifth rank. This move can only be made immediately following the move of the pawn two squares forward. The capturing pawn moves diagonally forward one square and captures the pawn as if it had moved only one square forward. An en passant capture is sometimes recorded with "e.p.," for example: exd5 e.p. See Chapter 9 for illustrated information on en passant.

en prise   French for "in a position to be taken." A chessman is en prise if it is left or moved to a square where it can be captured without loss to the capturing player.

Encyclopedia of Chess Openings   Five volume collection of opening analysis edited by Matanovic. Originally published in the 1970s, it continues to be issued in revised form.

endgame   Also called the ending, this is the final state of the game, characterized by the relatively few chessmen on the board. The king is typically used more agressively in the ending than in the opening or middlegame. One of the most common concerns in the endgame is promotion of pawns. Check out Chapter 13 for endgame information. See also *opening, middlegame, promotion* in this glossary.

endgame study   A composed chess position in which white must locate the unique win (sometimes a draw) according to the requirements set out by the composer. Studies tend to be more realistic than problems. Enthusiasts of studies value those of great originality and beauty. See also *problem, endgame.*

ending   Another term for the endgame. See also *endgame.*

equalize   To achieve a position where the opponent's initiative is negated. For example, white usually has the initiative in the opening and black works to equalize, or overcome this initiative.

escape square   A square to which a king in check can move. Also called *flight square*.

exchange   The capture of a piece or a pawn while giving up material of equal strength. When capturing a rook while giving up only a bishop or a knight, one is said to "win the exchange." See also *minor exchange*.

fers   The medieval name for the piece we now call the queen, derived from the Persian word *vizier*.

fianchetto   The placement of a bishop on b2 or g2 for white, b7 or g7 for black. The term is derived from the Italian *fiancata*, meaning *moves played on the flank*.

FIDE   Fédération Internationale des Échecs, the international chess federation founded on July 20, 1924 in Paris. FIDE has more than 120 member countries and concerns itself with all aspects of the game of chess.

FIDE Master   Title below that of International Master. A player with a FIDE Master title usually has an Elo rating of at least 2,350. See also *Elo Scale*.

fifty-move rule   Chess rule that declares a game drawn when a player demonstrates that 50 moves have been played without the move of a pawn or without any captures. There are a small number of positions (for example, king and two knights versus king and pawn) where the number of moves is extended past 50 moves before a draw can be declared.

file   Any of the eight columns on a chessboard, denoted by its algebraic notation letter, for example *the a-file*. See also *algebraic notation*.

Fingerfehler   German for finger-slip, a description of an obvious, but bad, move made without thinking.

first board   Also called top board, a term to describe the board in a team match that usually has each team's strongest player.

Fischer clock   A clock that, in addition to serving the usual functions of a chess clock, adds a certain amount of time to each player's clock after each move, in order to avoid desperate time scrambles at the end of a game, which often result in poor moves.

fish   Derogatory term for a chess player of little skill or experience.

five-minute chess   See *blitz*.

flag   Part of an analog chess clock. As the minute hand on the clock nears the 12, the flag is pushed upward. When the minute hand reaches 12, it no longer holds up the flag and it falls. The falling of the flag indicates that the player's time has expired, and if the requisite number of moves have not been played the player is said to "lose the game on time" (that's to say, the game is lost because time ran out, not because of the position on the board, although many games are lost on time when the position is poor and the losing player uses large amounts of time in an effort to try to find a way to save the game).

flank   Sometimes called *wing*, it is one side of the chessboard, such as the a-, b-, and c-files or the f-, g-, and h-files.

flank development   Developing pieces on either flank, for example to fianchetto a bishop. See also *development, flank, fianchetto*.

flank openings   Openings where white does not makes early advances of the d- or e-pawns, but develops on the a-, b-, and c-files or f-, g-, and h-files. The fianchetto is a common motif in flank openings. See also *flank, fianchetto*.

flight square   A square to which a king in check can move. Also called *escape square*.

fluid pawn center   Any position where the center pawns can be advanced or exchanged.

FM   See *FIDE Master*.

fool's mate   The shortest possible chess game ending in checkmate: 1.g4 e5 (or e6) 2.f4 (or f3) Qh4 mate. See also *scholar's mate*.

forced move   A move for which there is only one reply (or if more than one reply, all but one are undesirable).

fork   An attack on two enemy chessmen at the same time. See also *skewer*.

Forsyth notation   Compact and simple means of recording a chess position, devised by Scottish player David Forsyth. Beginning at the top, left-hand corner of the board (a8) the position of the chessmen as well as the unoccupied squares are recorded, rank by rank. White's men are recorded with capital letters, and black's with lowercase letters.

French bishop   Black's light-squared bishop in the French Defense, which tends to be very weak because of the black pawn on e6.

frontier line   Nimzovich's term for an imaginary line running between the fourth and fifth ranks.

gambit   Any opening that contains a planned sacrifice of material, usually to promote rapid development or control of the center.

Game of the Century   Widely-used, descriptive term for the Fischer-Byrne game (a Grünfeld Defense) in the 1956 Rosenwald tournament. Fischer, 13 years old at the time, mated International Master Byrne using a queen and rook sacrifice. Kmoch used the term *Game of the Century* in his *Chess Life* article to refer narrowly to chess played by youngsters.

Gens una sumus   Latin for "we are one family." The official motto of FIDE. See also *FIDE*.

GM   Abbreviation for International Grandmaster. See also *International Grandmaster*.

good bishop   A bishop unhindered by its own pawns and thus very mobile. See also *bad bishop*.

grading   A numerical representation of the strength of a chess player based on his results in games against other graded players. In the U.S., the term rating is used in place of grading.

grandmaster   Shortened form of International Grandmaster. See also *International Grandmaster*.

grandmaster draw   Deprecating term for a short, drawn game between grandmasters where it is obvious that neither player has made any attempt at playing for a win.

Grandmaster of Chess   Title bestowed by Czar Nicholas II upon the finalists of the 1914 St. Petersburg tournament: Alekhine, Capablanca, Lasker, Marshall, and Tarrasch.

half-open file   A file on which only one of the players has a pawn or pawns.

half-pin   A pin in which the chessman subject to the pin may move along the same line (file, rank, or diagonal) that it shares with the attacker.

handicap   A means of trying to equalize chances in a game played between opponents of greatly different strengths. There are numerous methods of implementing a handicap. The stronger player might (among other things) treat a draw as a loss; play several opponents at the same time; give his opponent more time on the clock; give his opponent two moves in a row at the opening of the game; or remove one or more of his pieces from the board before play begins.

hanging   Slang term to describe a piece left en prise. See also *en prise.*

hanging pawns   Steinitz's term for two adjacent pawns that are on the fourth rank, can't be supported by other pawns, are not passed pawns, and that are on half-open files.

hole   Steinitz's term for the square directly in front of a backward pawn where an opponent's piece cannot be attacked by a pawn.

Hypermodern   A school of thought developed after World War I in reaction to the views of Steinitz and Tarrasch. The most important idea of the hypermodern school is that occupation of the center isn't vital — one can put pressure on the center or even just carefully monitor it and still win. The leaders of the hypermodern movement — Nimzovich, Réti, Breyer, Grünfeld, and Tartakower — were strong players and often witty writers. Many hypermodern ideas are still considered valid today, but so are many of the ideas of Steinitz and Tarrasch.

ICS   See *Internet Chess Server.*

illegal move   A move that is in violation of the laws of chess. If an illegal move is discovered during the course of a game, the game will be returned to the point it was before the illegal move was made. The player who made the illegal move must move the piece he had previously moved illegally, if he can make a legal move with that piece. Otherwise, he is permitted to make any legal move. See also *illegal position.*

illegal position   A position that is not the result of a series of legal moves. Thus, an illegal move necessarily leads to an illegal position. Other sources of illegal positions include incorrect positioning of the chess board and incorrect arrangment of the chessmen either at the beginning of the game or at the time an adjourned game is resumed. If it is possible, the position must be corrected, otherwise a new game must be played.

IM   Abbreviation for International Master.

Immortal Game   Name given to the Anderssen-Kieseritsky game of 1851, a spectacular example of the King's Bishop Gambit. The game was played in one of London's great chess salons, Simpson's-in-the-Strand.

Indian Defenses   Hypermodern defenses to 1. d4 beginning with 1. ...Nf6. Indian defenses commonly employ a bishop fianchetto and slow development. Its name comes from this slow development, common in India, which only permitted pawn moves of a single square, long after Europe had adopted the option of a two-square advance on the first move of a pawn. See Chapter 20 for more details on these and other common openings.

initiative   Term to describe the advantage held by the player who has the ability to control the action and flow of the game, thus forcing the opponent to play defensively.

Inside Chess   Chess magazine founded in 1988, with Yasser Seirawan as editor. It is published in Seattle, Washington.

International Arbiter   A title first awarded by FIDE in 1951. A candidate is nominated by his federation and may be selected by the qualification committee if he: has a complete knowledge of the rules of chess and FIDE regulations; is objective; has knowledge of at least two FIDE languages (English, French, German, Spanish, and Russian); has experience in controlling four important tournaments, two of which must be international.

International Computer Chess Association (ICCA)   The association that organizes the World Computer Chess Championship held every three years, and the World Microcomputer Chess Championship held every year.

International Grandmaster   Title established in 1950 and awarded by FIDE. FIDE has detailed requirements for the title, which is awarded to only the best players in the world. A player with a FIDE Grandmaster title, often abbreviated GM, usually has an Elo rating of at least 2,500. See also *FIDE, Elo Scale.*

International Master   Title established and awarded by FIDE, often abbreviated IM. An IM is a stronger player than a FIDE Master, but not as strong as an International Grandmaster, and usually has an Elo rating of at least 2,400. See also *FIDE, Elo Scale.*

International Rating List   A list of the world's strongest players, compiled by FIDE using the Elo rating scale. It was first published in July, 1971. See also *FIDE, Elo Scale.*

International Woman Grandmaster   Title established in 1976 and awarded by FIDE to the world's strongest women players. See also *FIDE.*

Internet Chess Server   Any of several computers on the Internet (an international computer network) that permit computer users to play real-time chess games with other players on the Internet. People connected to the ICS can also observe other games in progress and communicate with each other.

interposition   The movement of a piece in between a piece that is attacked and its attacker.

Interzonal Tournament   One tournament in a series of competitions held by FIDE to select a challenger to the World Champion. Winners of the 14 Zonal championships compete in the Interzonal tournaments, which were first held in 1948. The top players from the Interzonals play in the Candidate matches that conclude when a challenger emerges. See also *FIDE.*

isolated pawn   A pawn whose adjacent files contain no pawns of the same color. An isolated pawn is weak because it, and the square in front of it, can't be defended by other pawns.

J'adoube   French for *I adjust*. Expression used by a player on the move before touching a chessman, generally to move it to the center of its square. A piece or pawn so adjusted does not have to be the man that will be the subject of the player's official move. See also *adjust, touch move*.

K   Abbreviation for king.

key   The unique, first move in the solution to a chess problem. See also *problem*.

kibitz   To comment during a game, or during analysis following a game, within the hearing of the players. The term is often used in a pejorative sense, and is in many occasions applied to the comments of a spectator for whom the players have little respect. See also *kibitzer*.

kibitzer   One who kibitzes.

king   The most important of the chessman, and consequently usually the largest. The king may move one square in any direction, and a game is over when the king is checkmated. See also *castling*.

king hunt   A prolonged attack on the opponent's king that usually dislodges it from a shielded, defensive position with a series of checks and sacrifices. A successful king hunt ends in checkmate.

king pawn opening   Any opening beginning with 1. e4.

knight   A chess piece that moves either two squares vertically and one square horizontally or two squares horizontally and one square vertically. In the first step of this move, the knight may pass *through* squares already occupied. The knight's move has not changed since chess was devised.

knight fork   Any double attack by a knight. See *double attack*.

knight's tour   A chess puzzle whereby the knight is moved 64 times, landing on each square only once. A solution is called "re-entrant" if the knight finishes on a square that is a knight's move away from the square where it began.

ladder   A fluid method of ranking chess players within a club or other group. The ladder is usually established by listing players according to their chess rating. Any player may challenge someone one step above them on the ladder (sometimes two or more places). If the challenger wins, he moves up the ladder and his opponent moves down.

Laws of Chess   The rules that govern the play of the game. During the 1850s, Staunton was one of many players who first sought to establish a unified set of chess laws. FIDE established its own laws of chess in 1929. See also *FIDE*.

legal move   Move permitted by the laws of chess.

Légal's Mate   A mating sequence appearing in the game between M. de Kermar Légal and Saint Brie in about 1750: 1. e4 e5, 2. Bc4 d6, 3. Nf3 Bg4, 4. Nc3 g6, 5. Nxe5 Bxd1, 6. Bxf7+ Ke7, 7. Nd5 mate.

lever   Kmoch's term for a white and a black pawn that are diagonally adjacent so that either can capture the other.

Lewis chessmen   Chess pieces made of walrus tusk discovered on the Isle of Lewis (outer Hebrides) in 1831. They were probably made in the 11th or 12th century and now are on display in the British Musuem.

libraries   Libraries distinguished by their volumes on chess include the Cleveland Public Library (containing the J.G. White Collection) and the Royal Library in The Hague (containing the Van der Linde-Niemeijer Collection).

light bishop   A bishop that moves on light-colored squares.

light piece   Another expression for minor piece: a bishop or a knight.

lightning chess   Another term for speed or blitz chess. See *blitz*.

liquidation   The exchange of chessmen to stunt an opponent's attack or to solidify one's own advantages or improve one's own position.

living chess   The performance of a chess game where the pawns and pieces are represented by real people. The performance may be a re-enactment of a famous game or a new game.

long algebraic notation   A form of algebraic notation. A move is designated by a letter indicating the piece moved, plus the square the piece moves from as well as the square the piece moves to (for example, Bc1-g5). Pawn moves are designated by the starting square and the destination square (for example, e2-e4). See also *algebraic notation*.

long castling   Expression sometimes used to describe castling queenside. See also *castling*.

Long Whip, The   Line in the King's Gambit: 1. e4 e5, 2. f4 exf4, 3. Nf3 g5, 4. h4 g4, 5. Ne5 h5.

Longest Game   The longest game played by top players was played in Belgrade in 1989. Nikolic and Arsovic drew in 269 moves.

losing the exchange   To exchange a rook for either a bishop or knight.

Lucena position   A well-known and well-analyzed rook and pawn ending first analyzed in a book by Lucena, published in 1497.

Luff   Kmoch's expression for the part of a rank divided by a pawn having the greater number of squares.

Luft   German for *air*, a flight-square for the king.

major piece   A queen or a rook. See also *minor piece*.

majority   A player's numerical superiority of pawns on one flank. Such a majority is important because it may lead to the creation of a passed pawn. See also *passed pawn*.

Manhattan Chess Club   Oldest chess club in the U.S., founded in 1877. Club members organized important New York tournaments in 1924 and 1927.

Marshall Chess Club   New York City chess club founded by Frank Marshall in 1915 (originally named the Chess Divan); rival of the Manhattan Chess Club.

Marshall swindle   Another expression for swindle, so named because Marshall was well-known for finding ways to play on in what seemed like lost positions. He named a collection of his games "Chess Swindles." See also *swindle*.

Master   Title offered by many national chess federations to strong players. See also *National Master.*

Master tournament   A tournament held simultaneously with another tournament of greater strength, the latter usually containing many grandmasters as participants. The winner of the master tournament is often granted an invitation to the following year's higher level tournament.

match   (i) A contest between two players only, as distinguished from a tournament. The term often refers to a contest of many games, but is sometimes used to describe a single game. The first major chess match was between La Bourdonnais and McDonnel in 1834. (ii) A contest between two teams, played on several boards.

Match of the Century   The 1970 match between the USSR and the Rest of the World that was played in Belgrade. The match consisted of four games on each of 10 boards. The USSR team won by 20¹/₂ to 19¹/₂. The individual scores were as follows (Soviet players listed first): Spassky and Stein 1¹/₂, Larsen 2¹/₂; Petrosian 1, Fischer 3; Korchnoi 1¹/₂, Portisch 2¹/₂; Polugayevsky 1¹/₂, Hort 2¹/₂; Geller 2¹/₂, Gligoric 1¹/₂; Smyslov 2¹/₂, Reshevsky and Olafsson 1¹/₂; Taimanov 2¹/₂, Uhlmann 1¹/₂; Botvinnik 2¹/₂, Matulovic 1¹/₂; Tal 2, Najdorf 2; Keres 3, Ivkov 1.

match tournament   A tournament where contestants play matches with all other participants in the tournament. Such matches are generally four games or more. See also *double round robin*.

mate   Short for checkmate. See also *checkmate*.

mating attack   An attack that aims at checkmate.

mating net   A position where one player has mating threats.

mating sacrifice   A material sacrifice made to achieve checkmate.

MCO   Abbreviation for *Modern Chess Openings*.

mechanical move   A move made with little thought because it seems to be obvious.

Mephisto   Constructed by Charles Godfrey Gumpel and first demonstrated in London in 1878, Mephisto was described as a chess-playing automaton. It was in fact a device that contained a person who played chess.

middlegame   The part of a chess game that follows the opening and comes before the endgame. Consult Chapter 11 for details on the middlegame. See also *opening, endgame*.

miniature   (i) Also called *brevity*, a short game — usually about 20 moves or less. Many writers use the term only for entertaining games and therefore do not generally include draws in this category. (ii) Any chess problem featuring seven or fewer pieces. See also *problem*.

minor exchange   Tarrasch's term for the exchange of a knight for a bishop. Because he preferred bishops, he described the player who gave up the knight as winning the minor exchange. See also *exchange*.

minor piece   A bishop or a knight. See also *major piece*.

minority attack   The advance of one or more pawns on a flank where the opponent has a pawn majority.

mobility   The ability to move one's pieces to important parts of the board quickly and easily.

Modern Chess Openings   An influential encyclopedia of chess openings first published during the 1930s and regularly updated. Its editors have included R.C. Griffith, J.H. White, Ruben Fine, and Larry Evans.

Muse of Chess   Another term for Caissa. See also *Caissa*.

My System   Aaron Nimzovich's immensely influential work describing his theory of chess, first published in English in 1929.

mysterious rook move   The movement of a rook to a closed file to discourage the opponent from making a freeing move because such a move would bring the rook into play, a strategy advocated by Nimzovich.

N   Abbreviation for knight.

National Chess Day   October 9th, 1976. U.S. President Gerald Ford set the day aside "to give special recognition to a game that generates challenge, intellectual stimulation, and enjoyment for citizens of all ages."

National Master   Title granted by national federations to strong players, usually those with a sustained Elo rating of 2,200 or above. See also *Elo scale*.

neo-romantic   A style of play developed in the 20th century. This style incorporates the romantic tradition of aggressive attack and couples this aspect of play with a strong defense.

New in Chess   Monthly chess magazine edited by Jan Timman and quarterly volumes edited by Gennadi Sosonko published in Holland since 1984.

norm   The number of points a player in an international tournament must score to gain one qualification for a FIDE title. The weaker the tournament, the more points a player must score for any given norm. See also *FIDE*.

notation   Any means of recording a chess game. See also *algebraic notation, long algebraic notation, descriptive notation*.

novice   A beginning chess player.

obstructive sacrifice   A material sacrifice to hinder an opponent's development. See also *sacrifice*.

odds   See *handicap*.

Official Rules of Chess   Official FIDE publication setting forth the laws of chess. See also *FIDE*.

Olympiad   Tournaments organized by FIDE, now held every two years in which teams from FIDE member countries compete. The first Chess Olympiad was held in London in 1927. The first Olympiad for women chess players was held in 1957.

open file   A file that has no pawns. Sometimes called an open line. See also *file*.

open game   A term usually used to denote games beginning 1. e4 e5, and which are characterized by piece mobility.

open tournament   A tournament that is open to any player.

opening   The beginning part of a chess game, during which the players develop all or most of their pieces. The opening is followed by the middlegame. Chapter 10 covers the opening. See also *middlegame, endgame*.

opposite-colored bishops   See *bishops of opposite colors*.

opposition   A position where the two kings are on the same rank, file, or diagonal. When only one square separates the kings, they are said to be in direct opposition. When there are three to five squares separating them, they are said to be in distant opposition. A player is said to "have the opposition" if the kings are in direct opposition and his opponent must move, thus allowing the player with the opposition to advance his king.

Orangutan   1. b4. Also known as Sokolsky's Opening, Polish Opening, and Polish Attack.

organic weakness   Any permanent imperfection in a pawn structure.

OTB   See *Over the Board*.

outpost   Term coined by Nimzovich; a piece placed on a square (on an open or semi-open file) on the opponent's side of the board, protected by a pawn, which cannot be attacked by an enemy pawn. The power of the piece on the outpost can be so strong the opponent may be forced to exchange it, even at the cost of material or positional loss.

outside passed pawn   A passed pawn away from most of the other pawns on the board.

Over the Board   A description of games played face to face, as opposed to correspondence chess.

over-protection   Nimzovich's concept of concentrating many pieces and/or pawns — even more than might seem necessary — on an important square. This creates a strong square that interacts beneficially with the over-protecting pieces.

overload   A situation where a pawn or piece must perform too many defensive functions so that a weakness will be created.

P   Abbreviation for pawn in descriptive notion. It is also sometimes employed by analysts who use algebraic notation, not in the recording of the game, but in annotations to make clear that the writer is describing a particular pawn (for example, Pe5) and not a particular square.

pairings   A listing of who plays whom at a tournament.

parry a check   To place a chessman between a king in check and the checking piece. This is one of three ways to meet a check, the other two being to move the king or to capture the checking piece. If a player in check cannot employ one of these three ways to meet the check, the king is checkmated and the game is over. See also *check, checkmate*.

partie   French for *game*.

passed pawn   A pawn that has no enemy pawn opposing it on its own file or on any immediately adjacent file.

passive   (i) Description of a move that contains no threats; (ii) Description of a piece with limited mobility; that's to say, a piece that is not active. See also *active*.

Patzer   A weak player (taken from German). Sometimes used more specifically to describe a weak player who either does not recognize his deficiencies or who may boast of his ability.

pawn   Physically, the smallest unit on the chessboard. A pawn moves straight ahead but captures diagonally. Originally, a pawn could only move a single square forward. During the Renaissance, a player was given the option of moving a pawn forward two squares on its first move. If a pawn reaches the eighth rank, it must be promoted to another piece. See also *promotion, underpromotion*.

pawn chain   A diagonal set of pawns that protect each other.

pawn grabbing   Deprecating term to describe the act of winning pawns at the expense of development or countering an opponent's attack. Also known as *pawn snatching*.

pawn promotion   See *promotion*.

pawn push   Another term for pawn storm. See *pawn storm.*

pawn roller   Another term for pawn storm. See *pawn storm.*

pawn snatching   See *pawn grabbing.*

pawn storm   The general advance of two or more connected pawns. A pawn storm may be employed to attack the king, to promote one of the pawns, or to keep some of the opponents' pieces away from another part of the board, among other things.

pawn structure   Description of the overall position of one player's pawns on the board. Consult Chapter 3 for information on pawn structure. See also *passed pawn, pawn chain, doubled pawns, backward pawn, phalanx.*

PCA   See *Professional Chess Association.*

PCA Candidate's Matches   Matches organized by the PCA to select a challenger for Kasparov, who won the first PCA World Championship in 1993. See also *Professional Chess Association.*

perfect score   Term to describe the score of a player who wins all his games in a tournament or match.

perpetual check   A position where one player can continue to place his opponent's king in check without threatening checkmate. Such a game is drawn because either the player with perpetual check will eventually be able to make a threefold repetition of the position or both players will agree to a draw.

phalanx   Pawn structure where two or more pawns of the same color are side-by-side; that's to say, on the same rank and on adjacent files. See also *pawn structure.*

piece   A king, queen, rook, bishop, or knight.

pin   A piece or pawn that is immobilized because it stands between its king (or other piece) and an opponent's piece that would otherwise be attacking the king (or the other piece).

play-off   A method of breaking a tie where the tied players play one or more games against each other.

pocket chess set   A small, portable chess set. Such a set usually folds, and most have either (i) flat pieces that are magnetic or that fit into slots or (ii) pieces that have pegs on them to insert into holes into the accompanying chessboard.

poisoned pawn   A pawn (often white's pawn on b2) that is undefended during the opening but that, if taken, often permits the player who gave up the pawn to engage in a strong attack, or to later win the piece taking the pawn.

positional sacrifice   A sacrifice of material that improves the position of the sacrificing player.

post mortem   The discussion of a game after it has been completed. A post mortem may be made by the two players (alone or with others), may be made by one of the players with other interested parties, or may be made by people who were not involved in the game.

postal chess   See *correspondence chess.*

postalite   Informal term for a player of postal or correspondence chess. See also *correspondence chess.*

Praxis   German for *practice* and commonly used in chess literature because of the great influence of Nimzovich's book *Chess Praxis.*

prepared variation   An opening line that a player discovered in study before a tournament and that the player only makes public when played over the board.

preventive sacrifice   Sacrifice made to prevent the opponent from castling. Also known as *Anti-castling sacrifice.* See also *castling, sacrifice.*

problem   A composed chess position that identifies that checkmate (or another conclusion, such as helpmate, where you checkmate yourself) is to be given in a specified number of moves.

promotion   When a pawn reaches the eighth rank, it must immediately become a piece of its own color (except a king) at the player's choice — regardless of what pieces he may still have on the board. Generally, a player will promote a pawn to a queen. See also *underpromotion.*

Prophylaxis   Nimzovich's expression for positional play strategy where the opponent's position is kept constricted.

Professional Chess Association   Organization founded by Gary Kasparov and Nigel Short in 1993 when they decided not to play for the world championship under the auspices of FIDE. See also *FIDE.*

protected passed pawn   A passed pawn that is protected by another pawn. See *passed pawn.*

Q   Abbreviation for queen.

queen   The strongest piece on the board (but second in size to the king), which combines the moves of the bishop and the rook — namely is able to move along diagonals, ranks, or files as far as such lines are unobstructed.

queen pawn opening   1. d4.

queening square   The eighth rank square to which a pawn is moved and then must be promoted. This promotion square is called the queening square because the promotion choice is nearly always a queen. See also *promotion*.

queenside   The a-, b-, c-, and d-files.

queenside castling   See *castling*.

quick play   See *rapid chess*.

quiet move   A move that contains no immediate threat, that does not make a capture, and that is not a check.

R   Abbreviation for rook.

rank   Any horizontal row on a chessboard.

rapid chess   A chess game where each player has 30 minutes in which to complete the game; previously called *active chess* by FIDE. In the U.S., the preferred term is *active chess*, and in the UK the expression *quick play* is employed.

Rat   Another name for the Modern Defense.

rating   A numerical representation of the strength of a chess player based upon his results in games against other graded players. In the UK, the term *grading* is used in place of rating.

re-entrant   See *knight's tour*.

recording a game   The process of writing down all the moves of a game, generally done at or near the time each move is played.

rec.games.chess   A chess discussion group on the Internet (an international computer network) where subjects discussed include tournament results (recent and old, local and international), openings, player biographies, computers, the Internet Chess Server, magazines, and chess controversies.

refute   To prove that a previously accepted move, line, or opening is deficient when best play is pursued by both sides.

Remus German for *draw*.

repetition of position A player may claim a draw if he can demonstrate that a three-fold repetition of the position has occurred, with the same player having the move each time.

resign To admit defeat of a game before being checkmated. The resigning player commonly tips over his king to signal resignation or says "I resign" to the opponent. Resignation immediately ends the game.

retrograde analysis To analyze a position to deduce previous moves or to explain how the position was reached.

round robin Tournament where each contestant plays one game with every other contestant. See also *match tournament, double round robin*.

royal game Commonly used description for the game of chess.

Ruy Lopez 1. e4 e5, 2. Nf3 Nc6, 3. Bb5. One of the oldest chess openings, it was analyzed by Ruy Lopez in his 1561 book *Libro del Ajedrez*. Also known as the *Spanish Game*.

sacrifice To deliberately give up material to achieve an advantage. The advantage gained might be an attack, gain in tempo, greater board control, creating an outpost, and so on.

sandglass Early form of chess clock, also known as an hourglass. Each player was given his own sandglass, which was set upright on the player's move and sand would fall. After the move was made, the sandglass was set on its side so no more sand would fall and the opponent's sandglass was set on its end.

scholar's mate 1. e4 e5, 2. Bc4 Bc5, 3. Qh5 Nf6, 4. Qxf7mate. See also *fool's mate*.

score (i) a written record of a game containing all the moves; (ii) a player's result in a game, match, or tournament.

score sheet The paper on which a chess score is recorded. See also *score*.

sealed move The last move made before a game is adjourned. The move is not played on the board, but recorded on the player's score sheet. Both players' score sheets are then placed in an envelope that is sealed and presented to the arbiter. See also *adjournment*.

second Term for someone who assists a chessplayer, generally providing advice on openings and assisting with analysis. The assistance may be in preparation for a match or tournament, or may take place during a match or tournament (before an adjourned game is resumed, for example) or both.

see-saw   Term to describe a series of alternating direct and discovered checks.

seventh rank   The rank on which an opponent's pawns are placed at the beginning of the game. The seventh rank is an important location for rook placement.

sham sacrifice   A move that on the face of it appears to be a sacrifice, but if accepted will yield the player offering the piece a gain in material or a strong positional advantage.

sharp   Descriptive term applied to a move or a series of moves that could be considered risky.

short castling   Castling on the kingside. See also *castling*.

shot   Colloquial term for a very strong and unexpected move.

simultaneous display   Event where a single player (commonly a strong player) plays several people all at the same time. Numerous boards are set up, in a circle or rectangle, and the single player stands inside this area, moving from board to board, usually playing a single move at a time. Also known as *simultaneous exhibition* or *simul*.

simplify   To exchange material in order to reduce the possibility of an opponent's attack. The player with the better position is more likely to simplify than the player with the worse position.

simul   Another term for *simultaneous display*.

skewer   An attack on a piece that results in the win of another, less valuable piece that is on the same rank, file, or diagonal after the attacked piece is moved.

skittles   Informal or casual chess games, often played quickly.

smothered mate   A form of checkmate where the king is unable to move because all the squares around him are occupied by chessmen.

Soul of Chess   Philidor's description of pawns in *Analyse du jeu des échecs* (Analysis of Chess).

Spanish Game   See *Ruy Lopez*.

speculative   Description of a move or series of moves when the outcome cannot be known.

spite check   A check by a player facing a mating attack that does not prevent the mating attack but only delays it.

stalemate   Situation where a player on the move is not in check but cannot make a legal move. For over 100 years this has been deemed a draw. Before that, stalemate was treated differently in different places. For example it has been held to be a win, a loss, and illegal, among others. See Chapter 6 for information on stalemate.

Staunton chessmen   Chessmen designed in 1835 by Nathaniel Cook who convinced Howard Staunton in 1852 that they should be designated Staunton chessmen. They are the chessmen required by FIDE. See also *FIDE*.

steamroller   Another term for pawn storm. See *pawn storm*.

strategy   The overall, long-range plan for a chess game. Chapter 8 provides more information on chess strategy. See also *tactics*.

swindle   A combination employed by a player with a losing position that converts his position into a win or draw. Such a combination is generally considered to be either avoidable by the opponent or the result of luck.

Swiss system   A method of pairing players at a tournament, developed in Switzerland in the 19th century by Dr. Julius Muller and first employed in 1895. The three fundamental rules of the Swiss System are: (i) No player meets the same opponent twice; (ii) Pairings should match players with scores that are as similar as possible; (iii) The number of games as white and as black for each player should be kept as close as possible to equal throughout the tournament.

symmetrical pawn structure   Position where the pawns of one side mirrors the position of the pawns of the other side.

symmetry   Position where the chessmen of one side mirrors the position of the chessmen of the other side.

tactics   A move or moves that are expected to yield benefits in the short-term. Chapter 4 covers chess tactics. See also *strategy*.

TD   Abbreviation for "Tournament Director."

tempo   Latin for time. Generally, to lose a tempo is disadvantageous, and a general rule of thumb is that the loss of three tempi is equivalent to the loss of a pawn.

text move   In annotations, a reference to the move actually played or the main line being analyzed.

thematic move   A move that is consistent with the overall strategy pursued by the player. See also *strategy*.

theory   Term to refer to the general body of accepted chess knowledge.

threat   A move that contains an implied or expressed attack on a piece or pawn, or the position of the opponent.

tiebreaking system   A method used to determine a single winner when tournament play produces a tie. One tiebreaker is the play-off, but due to the time it takes to play additional games, this is often not feasible. Ties are sometimes resolved in favor of the player who won the most games, the player who won the individual game between the tied players, or the player who had black if the individual game between the players was drawn.

time limit   The amount of time allocated to each player in which a prescribed number of moves must be made. Failure to make all the moves within the time allotted results in a loss (or a draw in a small number of situations).

time trouble   Situation where a player has a small amount of time to make a large number of moves.

TN   Abbreviation for "Theoretical Novelty" — a new move in an established opening.

top board   In a team match, the player who competes against the strongest opponents. Sometimes referred to as *first board*.

touch move   Chess rule that requires a player who touches a piece to actually move that piece (if it is his own) or take that piece (if it belongs to his opponent). If the piece touched cannot be legally moved or captured, the player may make any move. A player may touch a piece and not be compelled to move or capture it if he first announces "J'adoube" or "I adjust." See also *J'adoube*.

tournament   A contest among more than two chess players.

tournament book   A collection of all the games of a tournament (or selected games if the tournament is very large). Generally a tournament book will also include some or all of the following: crosstables, complete or partial results, annotations of interesting or important games, background information on players or the tournament, and photographs.

trap   A move whose natural reply results in a disadvantage to the replying player.

triangulation A process whereby a king is moved twice to reach a square that could be attained in a single move. The beginning square and the two squares to which it is moved form a triangle. Triangulation is generally employed only in endings.

tripled pawns Three pawns of the same color on a single file.

underpromotion Promoting a pawn that has reached the eighth rank to a piece other than a queen. See also *promotion*.

undoubling To move one of a set of doubled pawns onto an adjacent file that contains no pawns of its own color, via a capture. See *doubled pawns*.

unit A term that refers to both pieces and pawns. See also *piece, pawn, chessman*.

United States Chess Federation Official governing body for chess in the United States. Often referred to by its abbreviation, USCF.

vacating sacrifice A sacrifice intended to clear a square for another piece.

weak square An important square that cannot be easily defended.

wing See *flank*.

winning move A move that creates a position in which the player can or does win.

winning the exchange Giving up a knight or a bishop for a rook. See also *exchange*.

woodpusher Derogatory term for a player who shows no understanding for chess but rather appears to simply push his pieces around the board.

World Chess Federation See *FIDE*.

x A symbol used in both algebraic and descriptive notation to indicate a capture. See *algebraic notation, descriptive notation*.

X-Ray Another term for skewer. See *skewer*.

Zugzwang Situation where a player's position is weakened by the mere fact that he is compelled to make a move.

Zwischenzug German for *intermediate move*. A move that is made in between an apparently forced sequence of moves, improving the position of the player making the intermediate move.

Appendix B

International Chess Notation

● ●

*T*his section is not for the faint of heart — but it should be mastered if you're interested in reading chess books that are not in English. Because chess is played all over the world, chess players need to communicate with one another in a language that they can all understand. A system has been devised, not only to write down the moves, but also to convey common ideas.

In the game that follows, the actual moves of the game are in bold, the symbols (which are the German Grandmaster Robert Hübner's notes to the game) are in italics, and my own translations that follow Hübner's notes are mainly in normal text. Quotation marks will indicate where words are substituted for symbols.

You may notice the variation between Hübner's notation and mine, such as the spacing and the number of periods in an ellipsis. Although chess notation is fairly standardized, you will often encounter small differences. You should still be able to read the notation if you know the basics, however.

Browne–Hübner

Round 1, San Francisco, 1995

[E15/4]

Look at the preceding header information. The game was contested between American Grandmaster Walter Browne (who was white and listed first) and Robert Hübner (who had black). It was from the first round of a tournament game played in San Francisco in 1995.

Every chess opening is classified so that chess players can organize games into coherent categories. The first character is a letter, in this case the letter "E," which indicates a class of opening that begins with either

1. d4	Nf6
2. c4	e6

or with

1. d4	Nf6
2. c4	g6

. . . and all continuations except those with the third move *3. ...d5*

The next two characters are numerical and represent a specific opening in that general classification. In this case the "15" refers to the Queen's Indian Defense. Finally, the separator "/" and another numerical character refer to a particular variation in that opening.

Tournament players tend to learn the codes associated with the openings they play and generally ignore the rest.

1. d4	Nf6
2. c4	e6
3. Nf3	b6
4. g3	Ba6
5. Nbd2	d5
6. cxd5	exd5
7. Bg2	Be7
8. Ne5	0-0
9. 0-0	Bb7?!

△9...c5=

Hübner assigns the symbol **?!** to his ninth move, which means he considers it a dubious move. He says "better is" 9...c5 which is "equal."

10. b3	c5
11. Bb2	Nc6
12. Nxc6	Bxc6
13. Rc1	

△14.dxc5 bxc5 (14. ...Bxc5 15.b4) 15.Bxf6

"With the idea" of *14. dxc5 bxc5* "or alternatively *(14. ...Bxc5 15.b4) 15. Bf6.*

13. ...Bb7

13...Rc8 14.dc5 Bc5 15.Nf3 Ne4 16.Nd4 Bd7 (16...Bb7 17.Bh3) 17.e3±

Hübner gives another possible variation, which he assesses as "white stands slightly better."

14. dxc5   Bxc5

14...bxc5? 15.Bxf6±

14. ...bxc5 would be "a mistake" because of *15. Bxf6* where "white has the upper hand."

15. Nf3   Ne4

16. Ne5

16.Nd4 Qf6=△ 17.e3 Ba6

We've already learned these two. Hübner is telling us that if white had instead played *16 .Nd4*, the reply *16. ...Qf6* would be "equal," "with the idea" of answering *17. e3* with *17. ...Ba6*.

16. ...Qe7

17. Nd3   Rac8

17...Ba3? 18.Bxa3 Qxa3 19.Rc7±, 17...Rfe8 18.Nxc5 bxc5 19.e3 Rac8 20.Qg4±

All of these codes have been previously covered. Hübner evaluates one move and two positions. See for yourself which move is a "mistake" and which position is evaluated as "white stands slightly better" and which is "white has the upper hand."

18. Nxc5   bxc5

19. e3   Qe6

19...Rfd8!?

The alternative *19. ...Rfd8* is considered "a move deserving attention."

20. Rc2

△21.Qa1 f6 22.Rfc1; 21.Qc2!?

20. Rc2 was played "with the idea" of following up with *21. Qa1*, although *21. Qc2* would also be "a move deserving attention."

20. ...Ba6

21. Re1   **Rfd8**

22. f3

22.Qa1 Bd3 23.Rc1 f6 (23...Qf5 24.Bxg7 Qxf2 25.Kh1 ∞) 24.Rcd1 Bc2 25.Rc1 Bd3=.

The variation offered instead of *23. ...f6* ends in the evaluation "unclear," while the main note ends in the evaluation "equal."

22. ...Nd6!?

22...Nf6 23.Qc1 Nd7 ±

Hübner considers the text "a move deserving attention" and gives an alternative that he rates "white stands slightly better."

23. Rxc5

23.Qc1 c4 △ 24.Bd4 Nb5=.

Hübner tells us what he would've replied, if Browne had played *23. Qc1* instead of the text, and demonstrates that he thinks it would've lead to an equal position.

23. ...Rxc5

24. Qd4   **Qf6**

25. Qxc5   **Qxb2**

26. Qa5   **Re8**

27. Qxa6   **Qc3 □**

27...Nf5? 28.Qd3 Nxe3 29.Rxe3 Qc1 30.Kf2 +-

Black's 27th is "the only move," while the evaluation at the end of the variation is that "white has a decisive advantage." Notice how Hübner communicates degrees of superiority through symbols.

28. Re2

28.Kf2 d4 29.Qxd6 (29.e4 Re6↑) 29...dxe3 30.Kf1 Qc2 31.Re2 (31.Rxe3? Qc1 -+) 31...Qc1-+) 32.Re1 Qc2=.

Here's a new symbol after *29. ...Re6*. Hübner is saying that black can play this move "with the initiative." In the note after *31. ...Qc1*, "black has a decisive advantage." Notice how the evaluation remains the same for white or black but the symbols are reversed. +- is decisive for white, while -+ is decisive for black.

28. ...Nf5

29. Qb5   Rd8

29...Kf8?! 30.Qxd5 Qc1 (30...Nxe3 31.Qd2±) 31.Kf2 Nxe3 32.Qd2 Nd1 33.Ke1 (33.Kg1? Nc3) 33...Rxe2 34.Kxe2 Nc3 35.Kd3 Qxd2 36.Kxd2 Nxa2 37.Kd3 Ke7 38.Kc4 Kd6 39.f4±

Nothing new in this note, but see whether you can follow along in your head.

30. Kf2   ...d4

31. Qxf5

31.exd4? Qxd4 32.Ke1 (32.Kf1 Ne3 33.Kg1 Ng4 -+) 32...Qg1 33.Bf1 Ne3 34.Rd2 Rc8.

These symbols have already been covered. Hübner is showing us that the game could swing either way at any point, but the combatants are finding the correct moves to keep the game in balance.

31. ...d3

32. Re1   g6

33. Qe4   Qd2+

34. Kf1   Rc8

35. Bh3

35.f4 Rc1 36.Qe8 Kg7 37.Qe5 Kg8 38.Rxc1 Qxc1 39.Kf2 Qc2 (39...Qd2 40.Kf3 Qe2 41.Ke4 ± d2 42.Bf3) 40.Kg1 (40.Kf3 d2) 40...Qc1=(41.Bf1 d2).

Another detailed note that reaches a balanced conclusion.

35. ...Rc2

35...Rc1=

36. Qe8+   Kg7

37. Qe5+   Kg8

37...f6? 38.Qe7 Kh6 (38...Kg8 39.Be6) 39.Qf8 Kg5 40.f4 Kh5 41.g4 Kh4 42.Qh6#; 37...Kf8 38.Qh8 Ke7 39.Qe5 Kf8 (39...Kd8 40.Qd6 Ke8 41.Bd7 +-) 40.Qh8=

Now here's a new symbol following *42. Qh6.* It means *42. Qh6 checkmate!* Obviously, black wouldn't play into this line, but it is included to instruct the reader why that road was not followed.

38. Qe8+ Kg7

39. Qe5+ ¹/₂-¹/₂

The final symbol in this game is the symbol for "draw agreed."

It should be clear now that chess symbols not only bridge the language gap but also convey a great deal of meaning in an extremely precise and concise way. In the hands of a Hübner, chess symbols can be pure poetry. If you find it difficult to follow a game annotated in this fashion, don't despair! With a little practice (and a cheat sheet) you can be fluent in no time.

Index

● ●

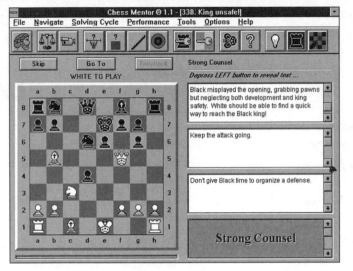
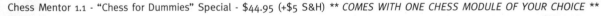

Join U.S. ♔ Chess and get a video ... FREE!

U.S. Chess Federation membership offers many benefits:
- An official membership card
- The right to earn a national rating!
- A national magazine packed with information
- The right to play in local, regional, and national tournaments
- The right to play officially rated chess by mail
- Big discounts on chess merchandise

Plus: **Play Chess I** — teaches new players what they need to know to be good players. Covers the basics, plus winning strategic tips.

Or: **Play Chess II** — Picks up where the first tape leaves off, includes how and what to study. Takes beginners who know the moves all the way to their first tournament!

Yes! Enroll me as follows:
- ☐ Adult, $40 (1 year), $75 (2 years)
- ☐ Senior (age 65 or older), $30/yr.
- ☐ Youth (age 19 or under), $15/yr.
- ☐ Scholastic (age 19 or under; includes bimonthly *School Mates* instead of monthly *Chess Life*), $10/yr.

- ☐ Also, I want my FREE *Play Chess* video (a $19.95 value). I include $4.50 to cover shipping and handling costs.
- ☐ Send me *Play Chess I* or
- ☐ *Play Chess II*

Check or money order enclosed, in the amount of $_____ or charge it.

[MasterCard] [DISCOVER] [VISA] [AMERICAN EXPRESS]

Credit card number_____
Expiration date_____
Authorized signature_____
Daytime telephone _____

Name_____
Address _____
City _____ State _____ ZIP _____
Birthdate _____ Sex _____

Call toll free: 1-800-388-KING (5464) mention Dept. 83 when responding.
FAX: 1-914-561-CHES (2437)

Mail: U.S. Chess Federation
Dept. 83
3054 NWS Route 9W
New Windsor, NY 12553

Note: Membership dues are not refundable.
Canada: Add $6/yr. for magazine postage and handling.
Other foreign: Add $15/yr.

ORDER FORM

IDG BOOKS WORLDWIDE

Order Center: **(800) 762-2974** *(8 a.m.–6 p.m., EST, weekdays)*

Quantity	ISBN	Title	Price	Total

Shipping & Handling Charges

	Description	First book	Each additional book	Total
Domestic	Normal	$4.50	$1.50	$
	Two Day Air	$8.50	$2.50	$
	Overnight	$18.00	$3.00	$
International	Surface	$8.00	$8.00	$
	Airmail	$16.00	$16.00	$
	DHL Air	$17.00	$17.00	$

*For large quantities call for shipping & handling charges.
**Prices are subject to change without notice.

Ship to:

Name _____

Company _____

Address _____

City/State/Zip _____

Daytime Phone _____

Payment: ☐ Check to IDG Books Worldwide (US Funds Only)

☐ VISA   ☐ MasterCard   ☐ American Express

Card # _____ Expires _____

Signature _____

Subtotal _____

CA residents add
applicable sales tax _____

IN, MA, and MD
residents add
5% sales tax _____

IL residents add
6.25% sales tax_____

RI residents add
7% sales tax_____

TX residents add
8.25% sales tax_____

Shipping_____

Total _____

Please send this order form to:

IDG Books Worldwide, Inc.
Attn: Order Entry Dept.
7260 Shadeland Station, Suite 100
Indianapolis, IN 46256

Allow up to 3 weeks for delivery.
Thank you!

IDG BOOKS WORLDWIDE REGISTRATION CARD

RETURN THIS REGISTRATION CARD FOR FREE CATALOG

Title of this book: **Chess For Dummies**™

My overall rating of this book: ❏ Very good [1] ❏ Good [2] ❏ Satisfactory [3] ❏ Fair [4] ❏ Poor [5]

How I first heard about this book:

❏ Found in bookstore; name: [6]   ❏ Book review: [7]

❏ Advertisement: [8]   ❏ Catalog: [9]

❏ Word of mouth; heard about book from friend, co-worker, etc.: [10]   ❏ Other: [11]

What I liked most about this book:

_____

_____

What I would change, add, delete, etc., in future editions of this book:

_____

_____

Other comments:

_____

Number of computer books I purchase in a year: ❏ 1 [12] ❏ 2-5 [13] ❏ 6-10 [14] ❏ More than 10 [15]

I would characterize my computer skills as: ❏ Beginner [16] ❏ Intermediate [17] ❏ Advanced [18] ❏ Professional [19]

I use ❏ DOS [20] ❏ Windows [21] ❏ OS/2 [22] ❏ Unix [23] ❏ Macintosh [24] ❏ Other: [25]_____
(please specify)

I would be interested in new books on the following subjects:
(please check all that apply, and use the spaces provided to identify specific software)

❏ Word processing: [26]   ❏ Spreadsheets: [27]

❏ Data bases: [28]   ❏ Desktop publishing: [29]

❏ File Utilities: [30]   ❏ Money management: [31]

❏ Networking: [32]   ❏ Programming languages: [33]

❏ Other: [34]

I use a PC at (please check all that apply): ❏ home [35] ❏ work [36] ❏ school [37] ❏ other: [38] _____

The disks I prefer to use are ❏ 5.25 [39] ❏ 3.5 [40] ❏ other: [41]_____

I have a CD ROM: ❏ yes [42] ❏ no [43]

I plan to buy or upgrade computer hardware this year: ❏ yes [44] ❏ no [45]

I plan to buy or upgrade computer software this year: ❏ yes [46] ❏ no [47]

Name: _____ Business title: [48] _____ Type of Business: [49] _____

Address (❏ home [50] ❏ work [51]/Company name: _____)

Street/Suite#

City [52]/State [53]/Zipcode [54]: _____ Country [55]

❏ **I liked this book!** You may quote me by name in future
IDG Books Worldwide promotional materials.

My daytime phone number is _____

IDG BOOKS®

THE WORLD OF
COMPUTER
KNOWLEDGE

❏ YES!

Please keep me informed about IDG's World of Computer Knowledge.
Send me the latest IDG Books catalog.

COMPUTER
BOOK SERIES
FROM IDG